Ranade IBM Series

K. Bosler: *CLIST PROGRAMMING* 0-07-006551-9

H. Murphy: *ASSEMBLER FOR COBOL PROGRAMMERS: MVS, VM* 0-07-044129-4

H. Bookman: *COBOL II* 0-07-006533-0

P. McGrew, W. McDaniel: *IN-HOUSE PUBLISHING IN A MAINFRAME ENVIRONMENT*, Second Edition 0-07-046271-2

J. Ranade: *DB2: CONCEPTS, PROGRAMMING, AND DESIGN* 0-07-051265-5

J. Sanchez: *IBM MICROCOMPUTERS HANDBOOK* 0-07-054594-4

M. Aronson: *SAS: A PROGRAMMER'S GUIDE* 0-07-002467-7

J. Azevedo: *ISPF: THE STRATEGIC DIALOG MANAGER* 0-07-002673-4

K. Brathwaite: *SYSTEM DESIGN IN A DATABASE ENVIRONMENT* 0-07-007250-7

M. Carathanassis: *EXPERT MVS/XA JCL: A COMPLETE GUIDE TO ADVANCED TECHNIQUES* 0-07-009816-6

M. D'Alleyrand: *IMAGE STORAGE AND RETRIEVAL SYSTEMS* 0-07-015231-4

R. Dayton: *INTEGRATING DIGITAL SERVICES* 0-07-016188-7

P. Donofrio: *CICS: DEBUGGING, DUMP READING AND PROBLEM DETERMINATION* 0-07-017606-X

T. Eddolls: *VM PERFORMANCE MANAGEMENT* 0-07-018966-8

P. Kavanagh: *VS COBOL II FOR COBOL PROGRAMMERS* 0-07-033571-0

T. Martyn: *DB2/SQL: A PROFESSIONAL PROGRAMMER'S GUIDE* 0-07-040666-9

S. Piggott: *CICS: A PRACTICAL GUIDE TO SYSTEM FINE TUNING* 0-07-050054-1

N. Prasad: *IBM MAINFRAMES: ARCHITECTURE AND DESIGN* 0-07-050686-8

J. Ranade: *INTRODUCTION TO SNA NETWORKING: A GUIDE TO VTAM/NCP* 0-07-051144-6

J. Ranade: *ADVANCED SNA NETWORKING: A PROFESSIONAL'S GUIDE FOR USING VTAM/NCP* 0-07-051143-8

J. Towner: *CASE* 0-07-065086-1

S. Samson: *MVS: PERFORMANCE MANAGEMENT* 0-07-054528-6

B. Johnson: *MVS: CONCEPTS AND FACILITIES* 0-07-032673-8

P. McGrew: *ON-LINE TEXT MANAGEMENT: HYPERTEXT* 0-07-046263-1

L. Towner: *IDMS/R* 0-07-065087-X

A. Wipfler: *DISTRIBUTED PROCESSING IN THE CICS ENVIRONMENT* 0-07-071136-4

A. Wipfler: *CICS APPLICATION DEVELOPMENT PROGRAMMING* 0-07-071139-9

J. Ranade: *VSAM: CONCEPTS, PROGRAMMING, AND DESIGN*, Second Edition 0-07-051244-2

J. Ranade: *VSAM: PERFORMANCE, DESIGN, AND FINE TUNING*, Second Edition 0-07-051245-0

DB2

Concepts, Programming, and Design

Jay Ranade

Mukesh Sehgal

Phyllis Elkind

Joseph Grossman

McGraw-Hill, Inc.

New York St. Louis San Francisco Auckland Bogotá
Caracas Hamburg Lisbon London Madrid
Mexico Milan Montreal New Delhi Paris
San Juan São Paulo Singapore
Sydney Tokyo Toronto

Library of Congress Cataloging-in-Publication Data

Ranade, J.
  DB2—concepts, programming, and design/J. Ranade . . . [et
al.].

  1. IBM Database 2 (Computer system).   2. Relational Data
bases.   I. Ranade, Jay.
  QA76.9.D3D38547   1990   90-5908
005.75′65—dc20   CIP
ISBN 0-07-051265-5

9 0   DOC/DOC   9 8 7

ISBN   0-07-051265-5

*The sponsoring editor for this book was Theron Shreve, the editing supervisor
was Jim Halston, the designer was Naomi Auerbach, and the production
supervisor was Suzanne W. Babeuf. It was set in Century Schoolbook by
McGraw-Hill's Professional & Reference Division composition unit.*

Printed and bound by R. R. Donnelley and Sons Company

Subscription information to BYTE Magazine:
Call 1-800-257-9402 or write Circulation Dept.,
One Phoenix Mill Lane, Peterborough NH 03458.

Contents

Part 5. Design and Implementation of a Database

Chapter 13. Logical Database Design   291

Chapter 14. Data Definition and Data Control   309

Part 6. Miscellaneous Topics

Chapter 15. DB2 Performance   **329**

Chapter 16. Performance Considerations and EXPLAIN   **349**

Preface

DB2 is IBM's most widely used database management system (DBMS) for MVS/XA and MVS/ESA environments. It is based on the relational model, which was developed by Dr. E.F. Codd in 1969–70. With IBM's emphasis on Relational DBMSs, DB2 has already acquired a much larger user base than its predecessor, IMS/DB, which is based on the hierarchical model. Unlike hierarchical DBMSs, which have been implemented under MVS (called IMS/DB) and DOS/VSE (called DOS DL/I), relational DBMSs exist under all key IBM operating systems. DB2's equivalent under VM and DOS/VSE is called SQL/DS, under OS/400 it is called SQL/400, and under its flagship PC operating system, OS/2 Extended Edition, it is called Database Manager.

Why This Book?

The information on DB2 in IBM's publications is scattered over a multitude of manuals and publications, constituting approximately 20 pounds of reading material. Different sets of manuals provide varying amounts of information regarding various job functions such as application programmers, system designers, system programmers, operators, and database administrators (DBAs). Although it would be nice to read all of the literature and to know everything there is to know about DB2, it would be a very time consuming effort. IBM must give information about each and every feature of their products in order to provide a complete picture. However, in real life, you use only part of such information to effectively carry out your job function. This book is based upon the 80–20 rule. Twenty percent of the information provided by IBM will be used 80 percent of the time, so that's what this book presents. Once you are proficient in developing DB2 applications, you may want to read the IBM manuals to learn about less frequently used features.

Who This Book Is For

This book can be used by application programmers, database designers, database administrators, technical support personnel, and anybody else who deals with DB2. However, the primary audience for this book is the DB2 application developer. The contents are applicable to programmers developing applications for batch, TSO, or CICS environments. Although we have not specifically talked about the IMS/DC environment, all of the chapters except the one on CICS are useful for such environments as well. Since COBOL is the predominant language, all of the imbedded SQL examples are given using COBOL program examples only. PL/I, Fortran, or Assembler language examples are not included. However, Parts I, II, III, V, and VI are applicable to all of the environments and are independent of any language considerations.

Part II deals primarily with the use of the SQL language and should be useful to anybody who wants to learn this powerful fourth generation language. Since SQL is the same for other DBMSs like SQL/DS, SQL/400, and OS/2 EE Database Manager, there should be no problem in transporting your skills to such environments. Be aware that SQL is also used by non-IBM database management systems like Oracle, Sybase, Microsoft's SQL Server, and many others.

A Word on the Style Used

This book has been structured in such a way that it may be used as a *self-teaching guide* without additional guidance. It is the opinion of the authors that you may need 45–50 person-hours to read this book from cover to cover.

This book may also be used as a textbook for a 3–5 day in-house or public seminar on DB2. The basic style is similar to that of a textbook, but once you have finished it, the numerous diagrams, tables, and practical examples may be used for guidelines and reference purposes.

The style of this book has purposely been kept simple and conversational. The authors understand that the reader has a limited amount of time to spare to learn new things in a constantly changing environment. The authors, as well as many reviewers, have worked hard to enhance the readability of this book so that it remains a pleasant experience rather than a strenuous mental exercise. We would like to know if we have succeeded in our endeavor.

What Is the Prerequisite?

If you have been an applications programmer for a couple of years, you can understand this book. If your prior experience has been in a non-IBM or non-MVS environment, we would expect you to gain some familiarity with TSO/ISPF in order to understand and use SPUFI panels. If you have already had experience working with a database management system (e.g. IMS/DB), it will be a plus. However, in writing this book, we did not assume any database management system experience. Part I will give you sufficient background to understand the theoretical aspects of DBMSs.

In order to understand the COBOL programs in Part IV, you will need to know that language. However, other parts of this book are primarily non-COBOL oriented. In a nutshell, the prerequisite for this book is a knowledge of COBOL, familiarity with TSO/ISPF, and a strong drive to learn DB2.

Why This Book Is Complete

A typical DB2 applications programmer needs to know SQL, its use in a COBOL program, and have some knowledge of QMF. It's all in here. However, you will also find discussions on database design, performance aspects of application code, DB2 utilities, and other relevant subjects. Although a COBOL programmer may not need to know these things, it pays to understand them so that you can communicate effectively with your Database Administrator, Data Administrator, Systems Programmer, and Systems Designer.

We have a complete chapter on DB2 access in a distributed database environment. Basically, it encompasses the new features announced in Version 2.2 of the DB2 product. We anticipate that IBM will make major enhancements to the distributed DBMS environment in future releases of the product to include intercommunication between SQL/DS (VM), SQL/400 (OS/400), and Database Manager (OS/2 Extended Edition). We also intend to keep this book current and incorporate any changes as they occur.

What Environment This Book Is For

As mentioned previously, the primary audience for this book is the MVS/XA and MVS/ESA environments. However, from an application programmer's point of view, there should not be much difference if you work in an SQL/DS environment under VM or DOS/VSE operating systems. The SQL usage skills that you get from Part 2 should be applicable to any relational DBMS such as Oracle, Sybase, Informix, Microsoft's SQL Server, OS/2 EE Database Manager, and about a dozen other softwares.

And Finally

After reading this book, you will not only know SQL and its usage in COBOL programs, but also many other features that will help you to work more effectively in your job. Numerous coding examples and diagrams will help you understand the subject. You will be able to incorporate various techniques and styles to suit y~~our particul~~ar environment. It is the authors' intent that, after finishing this book, you will be able to develop DB2 applications with a high degree of confidence and competence.

Jay Ranade
Mukesh Sehgal
Phyllis Elkind
Joe Grossman

Acknowledgments

And now the pleasant job of acknowledging the help and assistance of friends, reviewers, spouses and editorial staff. First and foremost we are grateful to Carol Lehn for spending many hours in reading, reviewing and criticizing all the chapters. Her editorial suggestions as usual were without parallel. It is a pleasure to acknowledge this debt in public. Kyungjoo Suh, an acknowledged DB2 expert, was primarily responsible for ensuring that we focus upon the needs of application developers. Her criticism of the technical contents and style was invaluable and we have strived to incorporate her suggestions in the final draft.

Joe and Phyllis would like to thank their friends—Ellen Andors, Roberta Campos, Design Five, Christina Frank, Joan Franklin, Bruce Follmer, Lee Kirby, Kathy Kirk, Ralph Klein, Susan Laidler and Richard Piccioni—whose generosity and encouragement have contributed to this book. Mukesh would like to acknowledge the encouragement and assistance provided by Emily Paytons, Tom Espeland, Robert Brockbank and Terry Tanzer. Jay would like to thank Jonathan Vidler and Richard Breunich for their encouragement.

We especially want to thank our senior editor, Theron Shreve, for his constant encouragement, and Jim Halston, editing supervisor at McGraw-Hill, for taking care of so many minute details during production.

And finally Jay, Phyllis and Mukesh would like to thank their respective spouses—Ranjna, Dee and Radhika—for their understanding when numerous evenings and weekends were spent in isolation in writing this book.

Introduction to DB2

1

Database Concepts

If you can remember when businesses operated without the help of computers, you can appreciate the significance of data processing's accomplishment—the automation of repetitive manual procedures. This was the goal of first-generation data processing. The programs that were written at that time were tightly coupled to the data files developed to support them. This meant that any change in a data file required a change to the programs that accessed it. The emphasis was on standalone systems rather than on the complete application portfolio of an enterprise. This resulted in redundancy and inconsistency in the data and often a duplication of effort. The bottom line was higher maintenance costs.

Dissatisfaction with the direction things were moving gave birth to the notion of a new environment in which systems would be integrated and data would be shared—the database environment. This book is about a particular database product, DB2, which has increasingly become the database management system (DBMS) of choice for IBM's mainframe customers.

1.1 WHAT IS A DATABASE?

A database can be thought of as a collection of interrelated data capable of serving multiple applications. The data requirements for related applications are integrated, creating a data pool which can then be shared by current and future applications. Let's look at a very simple example (Fig. 1.1).

Company JNR, Inc., sells products to customers. The marketing department needs customer information to evaluate the current market and the products that are being sold. They need demographic information about the customers—name, geographic area, age, level of education, and number of children—and information about the company's

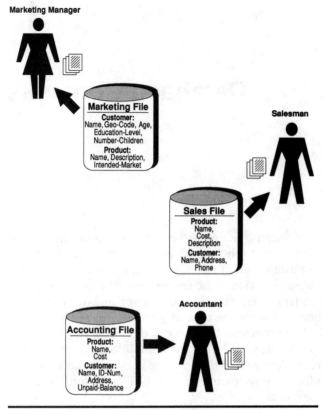

Figure 1.1 Information needs of JNR, Inc., in a file-based system.

products—name, description, and intended market. The sales department needs to know each product's name, cost, and description. They also need the names, addresses, and phone numbers of current customers so that they can try to sell them additional products. Accounting is responsible for producing bills. They need to know each product's name and cost; the customer name, identification ID, and address; and the customer's unpaid balance.

You can see that all three departments are looking at different aspects of customer and product information, some of which is overlapping. All of these requirements can be merged into one centralized database that will provide all three areas with the information they need (Fig. 1.2). New customers will be added in just one place reducing redundancy.

As you can see from our example, a database must be able to hold many types of data. This is no different from a collection of individual files. What makes a database unique is that besides being able to hold many types of data, it is also able to maintain the links between related data. In this way, redundancy within a file is reduced. Let's see how this works. Figure 1.3 compares a nondatabase system, in which each record contains information about a customer and associated products, and a database system, in which the information on each customer and product is held once, along with the linkages between the two.

You can see that holding the related data in a flat file requires repetition of information. Paul Green bought three products; therefore, in the file-based system, there are three records for each purchase, each containing Paul's age, geocode, and education level and the full information about each product. In the database system, on the other hand, there are two data stores, one for customers and one for products. The information about each customer and product exists only once. In Fig. 1.3 we have used arrows to link each customer to the products bought. Later in this chapter, you will see the various software means used by different database systems to physically implement these linkages.

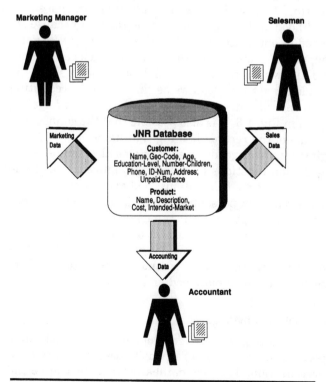

Figure 1.2 Information needs of JNR, Inc., in a database system.

```
File-Based System  C-    C-EDUC-                                P-INTENDED-
   C-NAME     C-AGE GEOCODE LEVEL  P-NAME  P-COST   P-DESCRIPTION  MARKET
|PAUL GREEN   |25|NY007|COLLEGE|RADIO|   42.99|AM-FM-ALARM |TEENS |

|AMANDA BURNS|14|CA012|HIGHSC |RADIO|   42.99|AM-FM-ALARM |TEENS |

|PAUL GREEN   |25|NY007|COLLEGE|TV   |  330.89|13IN-BLK-WT |FAMILY|

|PAUL GREEN   |25|NY007|COLLEGE|CLOCK|   17.50|LIGHTED DIAL|PRFSNL|

|AMANDA BURNS|14|CA012|HIGHSC |CLOCK|   17.50|LIGHTED DIAL|PRFSNL|


Database System   C-    C-EDUC-                                 P-INTENDED-
   C-NAME     C-AGE GEOCODE LEVEL         P-NAME  P-COST  P-DESCRIPTION  MARKET
|PAUL GREEN   |25|NY007|COLLEGE|       RADIO|   42.99|AM-FM-ALARM |TEENS |

|AMANDA BURNS|14|CA012|HIGHSC |        TV   |  330.89|13IN-BLK-WT |FAMILY|

                                       CLOCK|   17.50|LIGHTED DIAL|PRFSNL|
```

Figure 1.3 The database system can link nonredundant data.

We have said that a database system reduces redundancy. What is the significance of this? One obvious result is a savings in space. Additionally, the likelihood of data inconsistency is reduced because information is changed in one place only. Going back to our JNR example, what will happen if Amanda Burns marries and changes her name? In Fig. 1.1, in which there is redundancy among files, the change must be made three times. Can we be sure that the accounting department will tell the sales department about the name change? In the file-based system in Fig. 1.3, it is also possible that the change will be made on only some of the records holding that name.

Besides managing data storage, database systems also handle many of the data manipulation functions that used to require considerable programming effort, e.g., sorts, calculations, and even report generation. That means a savings in personnel, which is one of the reasons that database systems are popular with management.

A database system also supports concurrent data access and update by multiple programs and users and provides services for data integrity, security, and recovery. In this environment, the data itself becomes a corporate resource to be managed and understood.

1.1.1 Roles in the Database Environment

Database technology has required the development of new job functions and new specialties. Divisions of responsibilities will vary from organization to organization. The new database functions can be the responsibility of specialists or may be merged with other job functions. In a small installation particularly, functions may be less specialized. Let's take a brief look at the functions that must be supported.

Technical support is needed to manage the database software. This is provided by the database administration (DBA) function. It is their job to oversee the day-to-day processes of implementation, backup and recovery, performance, and tuning. The physical design of a database also belongs to the DBA function. Although aspects of this subject are touched on, it is not discussed in any detail in this book.

A database cannot be developed in bits and pieces; it requires planning. For data to be shared, a group is needed to oversee the data requirements from an overall perspective. This is the job of the data administration (DA) function (smaller organizations may merge this into the job of the DBA). Data administration is not concerned with physical details. Their job is to understand the enterprise's data requirements and use that understanding as the basis for logical database design.

Finally, the data must be put to use. Application teams are responsible for writing programs to access the data. All the major databases support access from application programs. DB2 goes beyond this by also offering interactive access to the database. This means you can retrieve or change information in the database without having to embed the statements in a program.

1.2 DATABASE SYSTEM COMPONENTS

The major components of a database system are hardware, data, database management software, and users. Let's look at each of them.

1.2.1 Hardware

The hardware is the configuration of CPU, direct access storage devices (DASD), and I/O devices, etc., that are required to run the database software. DB2 can run on any IBM 308x, 309x, or 43xx hardware. Some database products are associated with database machines where the hardware is specifically designed to support the database system which runs on it (e.g., Teradata's DBC-1012). Although we do not include it in our list of components, we assume the presence of system software, i.e., operating system, access methods, etc., which are required interfaces to the hardware environment.

Figure 1.4 shows the relationships between the other three components: data, users, and database management software. As you can see, the users make requests for data by interfacing with the database management software, which, in turn, performs the necessary data access.

1.2.2 Data

The collection of stored data is what "database" actually refers to. In practice the data is distributed among several distinct databases since

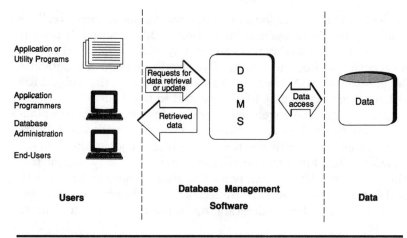

Figure 1.4 The DBMS stands between the user and the actual stored data.

a single database relating all of a company's informational requirements would be operationally impractical. The nature of the business generally directs what is grouped together. Frequently, you'll find that either all of the data that supports a particular business unit is grouped or, more commonly, all of the data that supports a particular business function is grouped (i.e., accounting, sales, marketing). The data within any given database is shared by multiple users, with each one interested in different and overlapping subsets of the whole.

1.2.3 Users

The users of databases include database support personnel, application programmers, end users, and application or utility programs. Users with varying levels of technical expertise may employ different means of accessing the DBMS. But, as Fig. 1.4 shows, all users are insulated from accessing the data directly. In between the user and the data there is always the database management software.

1.2.4 Database Management Software

The software component is comprised of many interrelated parts performing different functions within the system. The overall name for this software is the database management system, or DBMS. To be accurate, when we speak of a database product like DB2, we are speaking of a DBMS. While it is not within the scope of this book to describe the internals of a DBMS in any detail, in a few moments we'll look at some general concepts that are useful to users.

It is the DBMS which provides the facilities for security, recovery, concurrency, integrity, and other tasks. It also acts as a sophisticated access method for the more sophisticated requirements of a database. Just as file access methods (VSAM, BDAM, etc.) simplify the user's attempt to store and retrieve data, the DBMS stands between the user and the data, insulating the user from the actual physical storage medium. The user cannot interact with the stored data directly. It is interesting to note that DBMSs are built upon the foundation provided by existing file access methods. For example, DB2 uses the VSAM access method as the basis for its storage strategy.

The DBMS is responsible for storing the data and then making it available to the user for retrieval or update upon request. An analogy would be a closed stack library whose books are stored on the shelves in alphabetical order by author. The reader looks at a title listing and then makes a request to the librarian, who retrieves the book. How the book is stored and retrieved is invisible to the reader. Similarly, the user requests the DBMS to obtain a particular subset of data from the database. The file access services of the DBMS retrieve the requested data. Although the ease with which the user can make this request varies among database products, in every case the DBMS stands between the user and the actual data storage.

Continuing with our analogy, the librarian may have multiple lists of books for people with diffferent interests, such as a list of mysteries or sports books. Similarly, the DBMS must be able to support different views or subsets of data for users with different needs and privileges. For example, in a banking database, divisional marketing personnel might have access to data for their region only; head-office marketing would have access to all accounts.

Hardware, data, database software, and users are common to all DBMS products. The products will differ, however, in other respects.

1.3. CATEGORIES OF DBMSs

DBMSs are categorized by the manner in which they present the data to the user. For example, DB2 presents data to the user in the form of tables while IMS uses parent-child structures.

1.3.1 Data Models

The central issue in each representation is the framework used to describe "things of interest" and the relationships among them. These relationships are the links that were illustrated with arrows in Fig. 1.3. The things of interest are formally called "data entities" and the framework is called the "data model." DBMSs are categorized by the data models they support.

1.3.2 Four Types of DBMSs

There are four major categories of DBMS data models: hierarchical, network, inverted list, and relational. They are listed in Fig. 1.5 along with their data models and some of the products associated with each. Let's explore them a little.

The hierarchical data model uses a tree structure much like a family tree diagram (Fig. 1.6). The "segments" of the tree are department, employee, and pay history. Department is at the highest level, also called the "root." Any one department may have one or more employees. The relationship between department and employee forms a parent-child structure. The same is true for employee and pay history. Any one employee may have several instances of pay history. In a DBMS based on a hierarchical data model, to get from the highest level down to the lower levels, you must traverse through each suc-

DBMS	Data Model	Products
Hierarchical	Parent → Child, Child → Grand-Child, Grand-Child	IMS System 2000
Network	Parent1, Parent2 → Child1, Child2	IDMS TOTAL
Inverted List	Indexes for access Ordered files	ADABAS Model 204 Datacom
Relational	All data is presented to the user as a collection of tables.	DB2 SQL/DS INGRES Oracle

Figure 1.5 Different DBMSs are characterized by different data models.

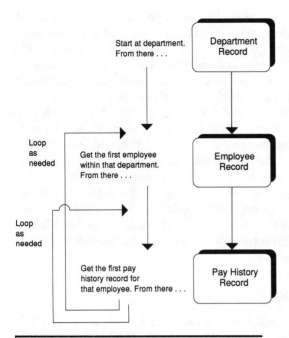

Figure 1.6 A hierarchical model requires navigation.

ceeding level. If you want to get information about an employee's pay history, you have to start at the highest level, the department segment, from there go to the employee segment, and from there go to the pay history segments. This is a simplification of what is called database navigation in a hierarchical database. The language associated with this navigation must include operators to describe the paths to be taken. The DBMS presets the paths that are possible by embedding pointers in the records along with the data, which is how a hierarchical database implements linkages among related entities.

All of the above is also true for the network model; however, it has an additional capability. While the hierarchical model cannot easily represent the many-to-many relationship in which one or more children are linked to two parents, the network data model is designed to show this relationship easily. In Fig. 1.5, you can see that Child2 is linked to both Parent1 and Parent2 in the network model.

The inverted list data model shows each data entity as a file with associated indexes used to access those files. For any given file any number of search keys can be defined. The indexes are built on those search keys and are used for access to the files.

In the relational data model, the DBMS presents the complete infor-

mation content of the database to the user as a collection of tables. A DBMS based on this model of data is called a relational database management system (RDBMS). DB2 is an RDBMS. The relational data model differs from the hierarchical and network models in several ways. For one, there are no special operators to describe navigation and, as far as the user is concerned, no pointers are embedded in the data. The user only requests the data, naming the tables which contain it. The links between associated tables are made by a relational DBMS by matching the values in one table with those in another. The user specifies only what is to be accessed, not how it is to be accessed. This increases the simplicity of the request tremendously.

The relational model also differs from the others in that it is a formal model with formal criteria which define it. Relational software, like DB2, adheres only incompletely to the theoretical model. We will first look at the relational model as theory and then compare that to DB2's implementation of it.

1.4   RELATIONAL MODEL

The Relational Model of Data was developed by Dr. E. F. Codd in 1969–70. Dr. Codd based his theory on the principles of relational mathematical theory, which has a terminology all its own. This terminology, along with the corresponding terminology used by RDBMS products and that used by traditional data processing systems, are listed in Fig. 1.7. We will use the more common RDBMS equivalents rather than the mathematical terminology in the following discussion.

While you don't need to know mathematical theory or relational data theory to use DB2, it is interesting to look at DB2 in the context of the theory from which it was developed. The three aspects of data that the relational model addresses are data structure, data manipulation, and data integrity.

1.4.1   Data Structure

In the relational model, all data is externally structured into tables. That is, the user sees only tables. A table represents an entity (or thing of in-

Relational	RDBMS	Conventional
Relation	Table	File
Tuple	Row	Record occurrence
Attribute	Column	Field
Primary key	Primary key	Key ID
Degree	Number of columns	Number of fields
Cardinality	Number of rows	Number of records

Figure 1.7 Terminology.

BRANCH:

BRANCH_ID	BRANCH_CITY	BRANCH_MGR	BRANCH_ADDR
12	NEW YORK	HIRO TANAKA	43 WEST 57 STREET
300	YONKERS	BRUCE HOFFMAN	7 MORANI STREET
450	ROCHESTER	ANGELA VALENTINO	351 TEAL PLAZA
670	NEW YORK	MATTHEW GREEN	900 WALL STREET
890	YONKERS	ZILYA KOLKER	610 OSIO LANE
13	CORNING	JOE GROSSMAN	ONE FEDERAL PLAZA

Figure 1.8 The BRANCH table.

terest) in the enterprise. A bank, for example, would want to maintain information about each of its branches. Figure 1.8 shows a branch table that contains the branch's ID, city, manager, and address.

As you can see, a table is made up of rows and columns. Each row of the table is one instance of the entity that the table represents, a branch in our example. Each column represents an attribute of that entity (ID, city, etc.). In the relational model, rows and columns are not stored in any particular order. Incidentally, in this discussion we are not talking about internal storage. When we talk about a data model we are always talking about external representation.

Within each row, only one value may exist for each column. For instance, each branch may have only one address in the BRANCH_ADDR column of the branch table. The total collection of all values that may occur within a given column is its domain. The domain for the city column would be all valid cities.

In the relational model, it is assumed that each instance of an entity is unique. Therefore, no duplicate rows may occur in a table. *Those columns which are required to ensure the row's uniqueness are the table's primary key.* A primary key might consist of one column or, in an extreme case, every column in a table. In the branch table, the branch's ID will always be unique and can therefore be used as the table's primary key.

We have said that in an RDBMS, *relationships between tables are made through the values in the tables. The columns which maintain this link are foreign keys.* Take a look at the customer table in Fig. 1.9. It contains a CUST_BRANCH column whose values are drawn from

CUSTOMER:

CUST_SOC_SEC	CUST_NAME	CUST_DATE_OF_BIRTH	CUST_BRANCH	CUST_RATING
111111111	PHYLLIS ELKIND	1962-03-29	12	4
222222222	JAY RANADE	1960-09-21	890	8
333333333	RICHARD GREEN	1947-08-15	12	7
444444444	------------------	1965-12-25	670	9
555555555	HEIDI SCHMIDT	1942-06-04	890	2
666666666	MUKESH SEHGAL	1957-10-24	300	5
777777777	LAI-HA NG	1970-01-01	450	7
888888888	GEORGE SCHMIDT	1950-07-04	12	2

Figure 1.9 CUST_BRANCH in the CUSTOMER table is the foreign key.

the same domain as those in BRANCH_ID in the branch table. The CUST_BRANCH column in the customer table is a foreign key because it provides the information that enables the RDBMS to establish the relationship with the branch table.

1.4.2 Data Manipulation

The ability to structure data into tables is one component of Codd's model. Another is the operators that allow you to manipulate the data. Each operator operates on either one or two tables and produces a new table as a result. An example is the select operation which enables you to create a subset of the customer table by "selecting," for example, only those rows, or customers, that belong to branch 12. This subset is itself a table (Fig. 1.10).

```
CUST_SOC_SEC   CUST_NAME          CUST_DATE_OF_BIRTH   CUST_BRANCH   CUST_RATING
---------+---------+---------+---------+---------+---------+---------+---------+
  111111111   PHYLLIS ELKIND     1962-03-29                  12             4
  333333333   RICHARD GREEN      1947-08-15                  12             7
  888888888   GEORGE SCHMIDT     1950-07-04                  12             2
```

Figure 1.10   A subset of the CUSTOMER table for customers in Branch 12.

1.4.3 Data Integrity

The third component of the relational model is data integrity, which controls the consistency of data in tables. *Data integrity rules require that every column that is part of the table's primary key must have a value in it.* This is entity integrity. Since it is the social security number which identifies a customer in our example, we may not add a customer (a row) to the table without a social security number for that customer.

The data integrity rules which maintain the consistency of relationships between tables are called referential integrity. Referential integrity requires that every foreign key value in one table must have a matching primary key value in a corresponding table or be labeled not applicable (the term used for this is null). That means that if one of the bank's branches closes and its row is deleted from the branch table, each customer belonging to that branch needs either a new branch ID or a not applicable (null) indicator in the CUST_BRANCH column.

1.5 IMPLEMENTATION OF THE RELATIONAL MODEL IN DB2

No database system supports the relational model in its entirety. However, several, including DB2, are considered relational because they do support the model's major criteria: data structure, manipulation, and integrity. Let's see how this is true for DB2.

1.5.1   Data Structure

In DB2, data is presented externally to the user in the form of tables, which is a central criteria of the relational model. DB2 tables can be further broken down into physical tables called base tables and logical tables called views.

DB2's data structure is consistent with the relational model in that there are no repeating groups. That is, there are never multiple values in any one column of any particular row. However, unlike a true "relation," DB2's columns are ordered left to right, according to the creator's definition of the table, and it is possible, as you will see, to influence the physical order of rows within a table. It is also possible to order the rows according to a particular sort sequence. These are deviations from the relational model.

Another deviation is that DB2 does not support the use of restricted domains. There is no mechanism to let you specify the pool of values from which a particular column's values may be drawn. This may permit invalid comparisons. For example, if columns BRANCH_ID and QUANTITY are both defined as numeric, DB2 will allow the user to compare the two columns even though the comparison does not make sense from a business perspective. While this may not seem unusual to you, since this is the case in all traditional file structures, it does violate the principle of domains as stated in relational theory.

The final distinction between the model and DB2 is that while relations, by definition, do not include duplicate rows, DB2's default is to allow duplicate rows, i.e., nonunique keys. This can be overridden, however, by explicitly declaring a UNIQUE INDEX on one or more columns in the table's definition.

1.5.2   Data Manipulation

DB2 users are able to formulate relational operations on the database through DB2's language interface, SQL. Although SQL does not explicitly contain the same operators as the relational model, it is, with its operators, able to support essentially the same functionality. Like the relational model, the result of any operation is a new table.

1.5.3   Data Integrity

From its first release, DB2 has included support for the entity integrity component of relational data integrity. DB2 allows you to specify that there must be values in the columns which make up the table's primary key. DB2 also provides support for referential integrity. It is possible to specify to DB2 a table's primary key and foreign key(s). DB2 will then automatically maintain the required relationship.

It is important to note that DB2 does not force users to comply with the two integrity rules (entity and referential) of the relational model. It only provides the facilities, which can be used at the user's discretion, to maintain data integrity. To that extent it deviates from the relational model.

Having introduced you to databases in general, and the principles behind an RDBMS and DB2 in particular, we can now move on, in the next chapter, to an overview of the DB2 product.

2

DB2 Overview

This chapter will give you a bird's-eye view of DB2. Many of the topics covered are discussed in more detail further on in the book, so don't worry if you don't absorb all of the information at this point. This chapter is intended to let you see the forest before we get down to discussing the trees.

2.1 ORIGIN AND HISTORY

DB2 is a relational database management system (RDBMS) for the MVS operating system environment. It was announced by IBM in 1983 and DB2 release 1 was delivered in 1984. Since then, IBM has announced new releases at an impressive pace. Figure 2.1 documents DB2's evolution.

As we discussed in Chap. 1, the main advantage of a relational database lies in its simplicity. Structured Query Language (SQL, pronounced "sequel"), the language interface to DB2, is a nonprocedural language; users only have to specify what they want, not how to get it. This makes DB2 an ideal product for ad hoc queries and end users.

When DB2 was first introduced, the big question about relational systems was not their suitability for ad hoc queries, but their ability to provide acceptable throughput rates for transaction processing. In fact, initially, IBM positioned DB2 as a tool for decision support only; IMS (IBM's hierarchical DBMS) was marketed for transaction processing. With subsequent releases of DB2, however, IBM made substantial performance and operational enhancements to the product. DB2 is now an appropriate choice not only for ad hoc applications but for most transaction processing applications as well.

Version.Release	Announcement date	Features
1.1	June 1983	First release
1.2	February 1986	Performance and availability enhancements
1.3	May 1987	SQL enhancements (date, time support, etc.); positioning for MVS/ESA and new 3090 hardware features
2.1	April 1988	Referential integrity; use of MVS/ESA, performance and operational enhancements
2.2	September 1989	Distributed relational DBMS

Figure 2.1   DB2's history.

2.1.1 DB2's Predecessors

Dr. Codd's theoretical work on the relational model in 1969–70 was followed by several research prototypes in various IBM labs. These included the Peterlee Relational Test Vehicle in the United Kingdom and the Extended Relational Memory in Cambridge, MA. At the same time, a parallel effort to define a language which would realize the features of Dr. Codd's relational model was underway at the Santa Teresa Research Labs in San Jose, CA. The product of this research, SEQUEL-XRM, was announced in 1974. This was followed by a revised version, SEQUEL/2, in 1976, which later became SQL. The advent of SEQUEL led to the development of a prototype relational DBMS for the VM/CMS environment. The prototype was called System R and it became operational in 1977.

System R paved the way for the introduction, in 1981, of SQL/DS, IBM's RDBMS for the small systems environment. SQL/DS runs under DOS/VSE and VM/CMS operating systems and is still marketed today. SQL/DS was followed by DB2 in 1984. The main difference between SQL/DS and DB2 is that SQL/DS has a small systems orientation while DB2 is designed for the large systems (MVS) environment.

2.1.2 Benefits of DB2

DB2's increasing popularity can be attributed to the real benefits it provides. Some of these benefits are those of any relational database system and some are directly due to DB2's particular design and implementation.

DB2's ease of use is one of its major advantages. If you are used to IMS or any of the other nonrelational DBMSs, you'll certainly find DB2 an easier product to use. Many of DB2's other advantages are also related to ease of use. With DB2, users only specify what they want, not how to get it. This is called automatic navigation. Associated with this is the feature called automatic access path selection. In nonrelational DBMSs, the programmer must specify which index to use and when to use it. With automatic access path selection, that choice is made by DB2 through the Optimizer.

DB2's language interface, SQL, processes sets of data rather than processing a record at a time. While this requires a mental adjustment from COBOL and other languages, you'll consider it an advantage when you see how easy it is to obtain information with a few lines of code rather than a few pages. Also, SQL uses only four basic operators for data manipulation, which makes it quite simple to learn.

Another advantage to DB2 is its interactive facilities which make testing, debugging, and application development easier for you, the programmer. Because you use the same language, with very minor adjustments, for both interactive database access and access from programs, it is possible to test a statement used in a program through one of DB2's interactive interfaces. DB2 also provides panels for program preparation and execution which simplify these tasks.

In addition to these benefits, DB2 provides the advantage of increased data independence. Data independence is the degree to which a program is unaffected by changes to the storage structures. While all DBMSs support data independence by standing between the users and the data, DB2 increases this data independence. For example, with DB2 it is possible to remove an index from the database without having to change or recompile the programs that have used that index. DB2 uses its catalog to determine that the index has been deleted and then automatically reconsiders its access path selection.

2.2 ENVIRONMENT

DB2 requires either MVS/XA (extended architecture) or MVS/ESA (enterprise systems architecture) as the operating system. Both MVS/XA and MVS/ESA have a much larger amount of virtual storage than the other MVS operating system (MVS/SP), which is no longer adequate for the newer releases of DB2. This is important because there is a strict correlation between the size of virtual storage and the number of users and transactions DB2 can support.

There are three MVS host environments through which applications can access DB2 resources. They are TSO, CICS/VS, and IMS/VS, which are illustrated in Fig. 2.2. A DB2 application running under IMS/VS or CICS/VS can access both DB2 data (via SQL statements) and IMS data (via DL/I calls). In addition, CICS/DB2 applications can also access VSAM, ISAM, and DAM datasets. TSO is the work environment for DB2's interactive facilities, e.g., program preparation and execution panels, interactive database access tools, etc. DB2 data can be accessed from application programs written in COBOL, PL/I, Fortran, Assembler, or C. Online programs can run under the control of either TSO, CICS, or IMS.

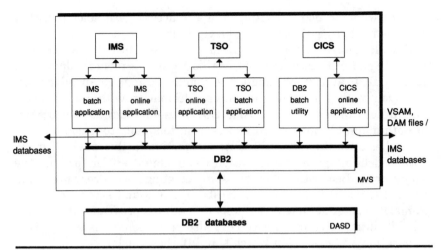

Figure 2.2   DB2 environment overview.

Batch programs can run under TSO or IMS. This book assumes the CICS environment and COBOL for online applications and the TSO environment and COBOL for batch applications.

2.2.1   DB2 Attachments, DSN, and Threads

DB2 requires its own address space. Therefore, for each of the three possible MVS host environments, DB2 must provide services to manage the interface between the host address space and the DB2 address space. These services are called attachment facilities. The connection between DB2 and the host environment is implemented by link-editing a copy of the appropriate attach code (i.e., TSO, CICS, or IMS) to the host language program. In the case of TSO, a program goes through a further layer, DSN. DSN is the TSO command processor provided by DB2 to act as an interface between TSO and DB2. To submit a DB2 batch program, you submit JCL, which executes program IKJEFT01, which is the TSO Terminal Monitor Program (TMP). TMP is, in effect, TSO itself. Control cards in the JCL then tell TSO to invoke DSN to run your DB2 program. Unlike the non-DB2 batch programs you are used to, you cannot submit your DB2 batch programs as MVS jobs; they must run under TSO TMP.

DB2 does, however, provide the Call Attach Facility (CAF) software, which makes it possible to access DB2 directly from MVS. CAF is used mostly by software vendors as the link to DB2 for their DB2-based products. You will not need to use CAF in your work. DB2 also provides an extensive collection of utility programs for database and system administrators and, to a lesser degree, applications programmers. These utilities execute as standard MVS batch jobs and use their own internal attach mechanisms to provide fast sequential access to data.

DB2's attachment facilities make the connection, or thread, from DB2 to other subsystems possible. A thread is started with the execution of the first SQL statement of an application. At any given moment, the number of active threads equals the number of users (programs, utilities, interactive users, etc.) accessing DB2. The maximum number of concurrent threads is set at installation time. If that number is exceeded, an application will wait until a thread becomes available.

2.2.2 Interactive Access to Data

Unlike nonrelational DBMSs, DB2 provides access to the data interactively as well as from user-written programs. As we said earlier in the chapter, you will find this a big help when you are developing and testing a program. Interactive access to the data is possible from TSO through SPUFI or QMF. SPUFI (pronounced "spoofy") stands for SQL Processor Using File Input. It is a subcomponent of DB2I (DB2 Interactive) and is provided with DB2. QMF (Query Management Facility) is a separate IBM product but is used in most DB2 installations.

Both SPUFI and QMF can be used interactively to process any type of SQL statement, although QMF is most often used for data retrieval only. While SPUFI does format its output, QMF offers sophisticated report formatting options and can be used as a report writer as well as a query tool. It is, in fact, increasingly being looked upon as a productivity tool to replace traditional report writing programs. Another difference between SPUFI and QMF is that SPUFI has been designed for technically proficient users (i.e., application programmers, database administrators, and system administrators) while QMF is intended for a broad spectrum of users, including end users. In our own work, we have found both to be very useful.

2.3 COMPONENTS AND FEATURES

DB2's architecture is a complex subject. In the following sections, we'll give you a high-level look at the components and features central to DB2's design.

2.3.1 IRLM, System Services, Data Base Services

The three major components of DB2 are the IMS Resource Lock Manager (IRLM), the System Services, and the Data Base Services. Each functions within its own address space. Figure 2.3 shows how these components interact with each other and the host environment.

Let's start with the IRLM, which handles locking services. DB2 treats data as a shared resource and, therefore, allows any number of transactions (users) to access the same data simultaneously. A concurrency control mechanism, called locking, is required to isolate different users from each other and to maintain data integrity. The IRLM provides this mechanism.

Look at Fig. 2.3 to find the System Services. They control the overall DB2 execution environment. This includes managing the log data sets, gathering statistics for performance monitoring, handling system startup and shutdown, and providing DB2 command support. At the center of the architecture is the Data Base Services, whose functions are most relevant to you as a programmer and user. They support the functions of the SQL language, i.e., definition, access control, retrieval, and update of user and system data. This component has several subcomponents, among them the Relational Data System (RDS), the Data Manager, and the Buffer Manager.

The RDS is the interface to your application program or your interactive query. It manages the execution of each SQL request by making calls to the Data Manager. It also includes the Optimizer and BIND functions, which we will look at in a moment. The Data Manager supervises access to the physical database. It can be thought of as a high-level access mechanism to the VSAM datasets where the data is actually stored. It interfaces with the RDS, which passes it your requests, the IRLM and System Services for locking and logging, respectively, and the Buffer Manager for I/O.

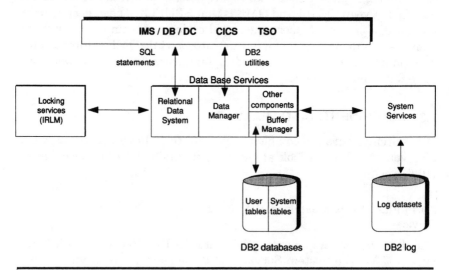

Figure 2.3   DB2 architecture.

The Buffer Manager controls the actual transfer of data from secondary storage (DASD) to virtual storage buffer pools. The buffering techniques employed are intended to maximize performance by minimizing the amount of physical I/O required.

2.3.2 DBRMs, BIND, PLANs, and the Optimizer

In DB2, the host language's procedural code is separated from the SQL code during a precompilation process. Each is compiled separately (the SQL compilation is called BIND) and then rejoined at execution time. In this section we will take a brief look at the components involved in this process.

As you can see in Fig. 2.4, the input to the Precompiler is the pro-

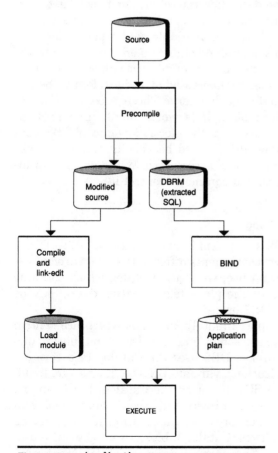

Figure 2.4 Application program preparation and execution.

gram source code. There are two outputs—a modified source module and a Data Base Request Module (DBRM). The modified source module contains host language calls to DB2 which the Precompiler inserts in place of SQL statements, which it comments out. The DBRM consists of the SQL statements from the program.

The modified source module is input to compile and link-edit steps to produce a load module, while the DBRM is input to a BIND step to produce a compiled set of run-time structures called an application plan. The application plan is stored in a system-controlled area called the Directory. The plan contains information about the DB2 resources and paths required to execute the SQL statements (data, indexes, etc.). The application plan and load module work together at execution time.

Although we will not describe the BIND process fully at this point, we will mention one part of it called optimization. We said that SQL statements specify only the data that you want, not how to get to it. The Optimizer performs automatic access path selection as part of the BIND process. It considers both the available access paths (indexes, sequential reads, etc.) and system-held statistics on the data to be accessed (the size of the table, the number of distinct values in a particular column, etc.). From this, it chooses what it considers to be the most efficient access path for each query. These access paths are "bound" into the application plan. It is worth mentioning that although we listed automatic access path selection as one of DB2's advantages, it is also a double-edged sword because at times you will wish you could control the choice of access path. While you can influence the Optimizer's choices, you can never control it.

2.3.3   DB2 Directory and Catalog

Information about the DB2 subsystem is maintained in DB2's Directory and Catalog. These two components differ in that the Directory is kept solely for DB2's internal use, while the Catalog which contains descriptive information about the plans (e.g., creation date), may be accessed by both DB2 and DB2 users.

DB2's Catalog contains approximately 30 tables which are central to DB2's functioning. These are sometimes called system tables to distinguish them from user tables. DB2 uses the Catalog to determine access paths, check authorizations, validate BIND requests, etc. In addition, DB2 users may use SQL to query the Catalog. For example, if you are a database administrator, you may look in SYSIBM.SYSINDEXES, which provides information for monitoring and tuning the system's indexes. Catalog tables can also be quite useful to programmers who can find, in SYSIBM.SYSCOLUMNS, for example, the length and data type of each column in an existing table. However, some installations do not grant the authority to read these tables to application programmers for fear of downgrading the system's overall performance. Figure 2.5 provides a list of the system tables; App. B provides a brief discussion of each table's use. More detailed information is available in IBM manuals.

The SQL statements used to get information from these system tables are the same as those used to get information from user tables. The difference is that you cannot update these tables directly with SQL, but you are able to update user tables. The only exception to this is the feature that allows you to update specific Catalog columns used for performance tuning. In general, system tables are modified as a result of definition statements which create the database, authorization statements which grant privileges to users of the database, the BIND process and DB2 utilities. For example, when you create a table, a row is inserted in the Catalog table that maintains a list of all DB2 tables (called SYSIBM.SYSTABLES). The columns of SYSIBM.SYSTABLES include the name of the table and the user ID of the table's creator. Likewise, removing a table from the database causes the deletion of the row that describes it in SYSIBM.SYSTABLES.

DB2 keeps track of privileges and levels of authorization for different users. When you instruct DB2 to BIND a DBRM into an applica-

```
SYSIBM.SYSCOLAUTH
SYSIBM.SYSCOLUMNS
SYSIBM.SYSCOPY
SYSIBM.SYSDATABASE
SYSIBM.SYSDBAUTH
SYSIBM.SYSDBRM
SYSIBM.SYSFIELDS
SYSIBM.SYSFOREIGNKEYS
SYSIBM.SYSINDEXES
SYSIBM.SYSINDEXPART
SYSIBM.SYSKEYS
SYSIBM.SYSLINKS
SYSIBM.SYSPLAN
SYSIBM.SYSPLANAUTH
SYSIBM.SYSPLANDEP
SYSIBM.SYSRELS
SYSIBM.SYSRESAUTH
SYSIBM.SYSSTMT
SYSIBM.SYSSTOGROUP
SYSIBM.SYSSYNONYMS
SYSIBM.SYSTABAUTH
SYSIBM.SYSTABLEPART
SYSIBM.SYSTABLES
SYSIBM.SYSTABLESPACE
SYSIBM.SYSUSERAUTH
SYSIBM.SYSVIEWDEP
SYSIBM.SYSVIEWS
SYSIBM.SYSVLTREE
SYSIBM.SYSVOLUMES
SYSIBM.SYSVTREE
```

Figure 2.5 DB2's system tables.

tion plan, a row is inserted into the SYSIBM.SYSPLANAUTH table. A column in that table specifies that you have the authority to execute the plan that you just created.

The execution of several DB2 utilities also updates the Catalog tables. The RUNSTATS utility gathers statistics about the database and updates tables in the Catalog accordingly. The Optimizer uses the Catalog to check these statistics when choosing an access path.

2.3.4 DB2 Governor

The Resource Limit Facility (RLF), or Governor, is provided to simplify the task of controlling DB2 resource usage. The DB2 Governor allows a site to limit, by user ID, plan, or both the amount of CPU time permitted for the execution of dynamic SQL statements. QMF's Governor, which already existed, is superceded by it, thereby making the QMF Governor somewhat redundant for the MVS/DB2 environment.

When you access DB2 through QMF or SPUFI, you are actually initiating a dynamic SQL program. It is called dynamic SQL because the SQL statement in the program is not known until you type it in at the terminal and press Enter. Interactive queries carry the risk that an end user may submit a complex SQL query and slow the whole MVS system down to a halt. The SQL statements which you embed in your programs do not have this exposure because the program can be tested for performance and CPU utilization first. By limiting CPU time for dynamic SQL statements, the DB2 Governor can have a major effect on maintaining your system's processing capabilities.

Incidentally, although you will often use dynamic SQL programs like SPUFI and QMF, you probably will not write dynamic SQL programs yourself very often. Its counterpart, static SQL, is far more common for application programming.

2.3.5 DB2 Subsystem

A DB2 subsystem is a copy of DB2 that runs on a CPU, complete with libraries, Catalog, and Directory. One CPU can have one or more DB2 subsystems running on it.

2.3.6 Distributed Data Facility

Distributed Data Facility (DDF) is available with version 2.2 of DB2. With DDF, a user connected to one DB2 subsystem can read and update data stored at another. The subsystem to which a user is connected is considered the local system; the other subsystems from which data may be accessed are considered remote subsystems. A local and remote subsystem may run on one computer or may run on two computers at different physical sites. The syntax and rules associated with distributed data access are described in Chap. 18.

2.4 OBJECTS

In previous sections we've mentioned tables and databases. These are examples of DB2 objects. (DB2 objects are databases, tables, tablespaces, indexes, indexspaces, views, and storage groups.) An object is anything you can create or manipulate with SQL. Information about DB2 objects is stored in the system tables of the DB2 Catalog. With the exception of indexspaces, the data definition language component of SQL is used to create or manipulate these objects. Indexspaces are automatically built any time an index is created. We will begin with the object most familiar to you, the table.

2.4.1 Table

In Chap. 1 we said that all data in DB2 is presented in the form of tables, called base tables, which are *collections of rows having the same attributes, or columns*. At the intersection of a column and a row is a value, which is the smallest unit of data that can be retrieved or changed. A row is the smallest unit of data that can be inserted or deleted.

2.4.2 Tablespace

Tables are assigned to tablespaces. A tablespace contains one or more VSAM ESDS datasets. In this way, the data from a table is assigned to physical storage on DASD.

Each tablespace is physically divided into equal units called pages. Each page, which may contain 4K or 32K bytes, holds one or more rows of a table and is the unit of I/O. You must use the larger page size if any row in the table is more than 4K bytes long. However, 32K pages are the exception, not the rule. The size of the tablespace's pages is based on the page size of the bufferpool specified in the tablespace's creation statement. Bufferpools are areas of virtual storage that DB2 uses to store data temporarily. They will be discussed later.

The rows of a table are physically stored as records on a page. A record is always fully contained within a page. Each record is made up of control information to identify the row and the table to which it belongs along with a field for each column of the table. Figure 2.6 illustrates how the table you see on your screen corresponds to the table in storage. Each field consists of the actual data plus a length prefix, for variable-length columns, and a null indicator prefix if nulls are per-

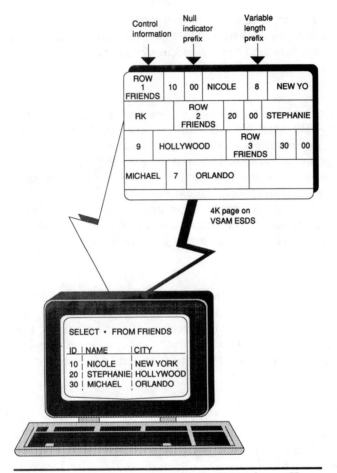

Figure 2.6   A table's rows are stored as records on 4K pages.

mitted. In our illustration, the column CITY is defined as a variable-length column; therefore there is a length prefix before each city. Similarly, NAME, which may be null, has a null indicator of binary 0s (low values) if NAME contains values, or binary 1s (high values) if it is null.

Tablespaces come in three flavors: partitioned, simple, and segmented. A partitioned tablespace is used for very large tables and may only contain one table. The table is divided among the tablespace's partitions, with each partition stored as a separate VSAM ESDS dataset. When you define the tablespace, you specify what key ranges will go into which partitions. Partitioning enables you to put different parts of a table on different device types. Thus, frequently accessed data can be put on faster devices. Also, partitioning may break up a very large table into more manageable pieces, which can be important for recovery.

A simple tablespace normally consists of only one VSAM ESDS and may contain one or more tables. However, DB2 has some major limitations in its support of multiple tables in a simple tablespace. For instance, you cannot perform a sequential read (called a tablespace scan) of one table without reading the entire tablespace; this increases I/O and decreases performance. As a result, database designers normally recommend only one table per simple tablespace. The only exception might be when several very small tables that are generally used together occupy the same tablespace.

To rectify these limitations, IBM introduced a new type of tablespace with version 2.1, a segmented tablespace. It was specifically designed to support multiple tables in a single tablespace. All the segments of a segmented tablespace are stored on one VSAM dataset. Each segment is a group of 4 to 64 pages. The segment size is defined when the tablespace is created. In a segmented tablespace, each segment contains rows for one table.

Segmented tablespaces provide improved performance, concurrency, and space management for multiple tables in a single tablespace. Enhancements include faster table scans and the ability to lock a single table within the tablespace. With segmented tablespaces, related tables can be efficiently placed together in one tablespace, resulting in fewer tablespaces. Fewer tablespaces can simplify database administration. Also, MVS places a limit of about 1600 on the datasets that any one job (such as the DB2 Data Manager) can have allocated at any one time. And, since each open dataset uses a certain amount of virtual storage, reducing the number of datasets can improve performance.

Segmented tablespaces can have performance advantages over single tablespaces even when, the tablespace contains only one table. In fact, IBM now recommends that all tables not requiring partitioning be placed in segmented tablespaces.

2.4.3 Index

An index is an ordered set of pointers to the data in a DB2 table. There is one physical order to the rows in a table and it is determined by DB2. You will see in a moment how you can specify a physical order with the CREATE INDEX statement, but you can never completely control or easily know the exact physical order chosen by the DBMS. Without an index, finding a particular row would require a scan of the entire table. Indexes provide an alternate means of access to the data, greatly decreasing the I/O and processing time required. Users create indexes on tables, but programs or users accessing DB2 data cannot explicitly specify that an index be used; this can only be specified by DB2's Optimizer, which makes that choice at BIND time.

An index is a separate physical entity. It is based on one or more columns of a table and can be created any time after the table is built. In practice, indexes are most often created at table creation time because this is more efficient operationally. A table may have zero to many indexes associated with it. A partitioned table, however, must have at least one index. This index is called the partitioning index and is used to define the scope of each partition and thereby assign the rows of the table to their respective partitions.

In addition to improving data retrieval performance, indexes can be created as UNIQUE. This means that DB2 will not allow two rows to be inserted into a table if the result would be duplicate index values. Earlier, we learned that in the relational model, every table has a primary key, consisting of one or more columns, which ensures that each row in a table is unique. When created, a unique index makes it possible to support the relational model's concept of a unique primary key.

An index may also be created as a CLUSTERing index. When DB2 sees that you have specified a clustering index, it physically stores the rows in order according to the values in the column(s) you have specified as the clustering index. You can specify ascending or descending order. If you create the customer table with a clustering index on the column CUST_SOC_SEC, when you insert your rows of data, DB2 will attempt to insert them in order based on the values in CUST_SOC_SEC. If it has stored the records for customers 111111111, 222222222, and 444444444 and then attempts to insert that of 333333333, it tries to find free space between 222222222 and 444444444. If no space is available, DB2 puts it elsewhere. DB2 has an elaborate algorithm which it uses to put a row as close as possible to where it belongs. When DB2 has been unable to put 5 percent of the rows in order, it flags the index as unclustered in the Catalog. This is useful information for the Optimizer because an unclustered index is a more expensive access path than a clustered index. When you do a REORG, DB2 can then put the rows into sequential order.

Since a clustering index defines the way data is actually stored in a table, there can be only one clustering index per table. If no clustering index is defined for a table, DB2 still attempts to load data in order according to the first index defined. In this case, however, it will not reorder the rows at REORG time, so it is always better to explicitly choose the CLUSTER option.

If a table is partitioned, it must have a clustering index on the columns that are used to specify the key ranges of the partitions. This index, the partitioning index, is used to divide the rows among the partitions.

2.4.4 Indexspace

Just as table data is physically stored in a tablespace, index data is physically stored in an indexspace. Each index resides within its own indexspace, which contains an ESDS. Additionally, if the index is partitioned, each partition of the index has its own indexspace. While a tablespace has to be explicitly defined, an indexspace is automatically created when an index is created.

The page size of an indexspace is always 4K bytes. You may specify that each page be broken into between 1 and 16 units of index locking, called subpages. The default is 4.

2.4.5 Database

A DB2 database consists of tables, their indexes, and the spaces (tablespaces and indexspaces) that contain them. DB2 maintains a structure called a DBD (database descriptor) for each database, as well as catalog entries associated with each database. But a DB2 database is not associated with specific datasets; this makes it different from previous DBMSs. In older systems, when you created a database, you defined what datasets were included in it. In DB2, databases are usually created for operational convenience only; the datasets (tablespaces and indexspaces) the database contains can be specified later, and the specification can be changed as needed. When you create a DB2 database, there are no associated datasets. It is only when you create a tablespace in that database that the database becomes associated with physical storage. In contrast, a table cannot be created unless a tablespace and its associated physical storage already exist.

You'll find that it is common practice to create different databases for each application's tables. This helps to minimize the effect of one application on another. For example, if you're creating or deleting an object in a database, no other user may create or delete an object in that database until you've finished. This is because DB2 locks the DBD for a database (there is one per database) when its objects are being created or deleted. If many applications were combined in a single database, the creation or deletion of an object for any one application would mean that the other application(s) would have to wait. Users within the same application can also interfere with each other, but it is likely that changes to an application's tables will be made by one person or at least be coordinated by those doing the changing. Also, by grouping related objects in the same database, you can also make all of them available or unavailable for access with the DB2 commands START and STOP, which operate at the database level.

2.4.6 Storage Group

We have talked about DB2 data being stored in VSAM ESDS datasets. Now let's look at the storage group that DB2 provides to simplify the job of defining those datasets. DBAs can use IDCAMS to explicitly define datasets and to specify the DASD volumes on which the datasets should be placed. Alternatively, the responsibility for defining the datasets may be left to DB2 itself through the use of storage groups. *A storage group is a set of one or more DASD volumes.* When a tablespace or indexspace is assigned to a given storage group, DB2 creates the necessary VSAM dataset and places it on one of the DASD volumes associated with that storage group. Clearly, if a DBA defines the datasets, he or she has control over which volumes to use. If you delegate the responsibility for the definition to DB2, you still have that control. The difference is that with storage groups, DB2 does the VSAM dataset creation for you on a volume in that storage group. In many installations the convention is to assign each volume to its own storage group so that the DBA indicates a specific volume by naming a storage group.

Until DB2 version 2.1, DBAs preferred to define their own VSAM ESDS datasets rather than use storage groups. While storage groups removed the burden of defining and deleting datasets, they were considered inflexible and were therefore seldom used. They were particularly troublesome when data had to be migrated to a different DASD. DB2 now has an Alter Storage facility which provides more flexibility and makes the use of storage groups a more attractive alternative.

2.4.7 View

The last object in our discussion is the view. A view is another way to present data, a different way to look at it. Views are derived from base tables, or from other views. Unlike base tables, which represent physically stored data, *views are virtual tables that have no associated physical storage.*

Figure 2.7 shows a table called CUSTOMER. Suppose you had a user who needed access to the table but you didn't want the user to look at the CUST_RATING (Fig. 2.8). Using SQL, this subset could be defined as a view with its own name, let's say BANK_CUSTOMER. The SQL statement which creates the subset is stored in one of

CUSTOMER:

CUST_SOC_SEC	CUST_NAME	CUST_DATE_OF_BIRTH	CUST_BRANCH	CUST_RATING
111111111	PHYLLIS ELKIND	1962-03-29	12	4
222222222	JAY RANADE	1960-09-21	890	8
333333333	RICHARD GREEN	1947-08-15	12	7
444444444	-----------------	1965-12-25	670	9
555555555	HEIDI SCHMIDT	1942-06-04	890	2
666666666	MUKESH SEHGAL	1957-10-24	300	5
777777777	LAI-HA NG	1970-01-01	450	7
888888888	GEORGE SCHMIDT	1950-07-04	12	2

Figure 2.7 CUSTOMER is a base table.

BANK_CUSTOMER:

CUST_SOC_SEC	CUST_NAME	CUST_DATE_OF_BIRTH	CUST_BRANCH
111111111	PHYLLIS ELKIND	1962-03-29	12
222222222	JAY RANADE	1960-09-21	890
333333333	RICHARD GREEN	1947-08-15	12
444444444	-----------------	1965-12-25	670
555555555	HEIDI SCHMIDT	1942-06-04	890
666666666	MUKESH SEHGAL	1957-10-24	300
777777777	LAI-HA NG	1970-01-01	450
888888888	GEORGE SCHMIDT	1950-07-04	12

Figure 2.8 BANK_CUSTOMER is a view of the CUSTOMER table which excludes the CUST_RATING column.

the DB2 Catalog tables (SYSIBM.SYSVIEWS) with the name BANK_CUSTOMER.

A view can also be derived from more than one base table or even from other views. Figure 2.9 shows a view, BRANCH_CUST, which is derived from the base tables, CUSTOMER and BRANCH. The branch number (BC_BRANCH) and manager (BC_MGR) are taken from the BRANCH table and combined with the associated customer name (BC_CUSTOMER) from the CUSTOMER table. In our BANK_CUSTOMER example, the view used the same column names as the base table. Here, we've used new names for the columns. Either is permitted.

You can access data from a view as you would from any base table. When DB2 receives your request, it finds the statement stored in SYSIBM.SYSVIEWS and retrieves the specified subset (that is, the

BRANCH_CUST:

BC_BRANCH	BC_MGR	BC_CUSTOMER
12	HIRO TANAKA	PHYLLIS ELKIND
12	HIRO TANAKA	RICHARD GREEN
12	HIRO TANAKA	GEORGE SCHMIDT

Figure 2.9 BRANCH_CUST is derived from two base tables.

view) of the base table(s). In the case of a view (let's call it View-A) of a view (View-B), DB2 first retrieves the subset specified by View-B, and then, from that subset, retrieves the subset specified by View-A. The process is transparent. You can deal with views as if they were any other base table.

Views provide several benefits. A view may be used as a security mechanism which allows the user to access only a portion of the table, as we did in our BANK_CUSTOMER view. Complicated queries can be stored as views so that to the end user, a request may appear to be very simple, although it actually performs a complex operation. The BRANCH_CUST view, which joins together information from two tables, could be used this way. Views can also minimize the program modifications that may be required when base tables change. If your program accesses only three columns from a table, you may use a view which includes only those columns. That way, you will not need to change your program when columns are added to the table. The view is still valid, as is your program.

2.4.8 Bufferpool

Bufferpools are not included in our list of DB2 objects but we include them here because they're an important part of our introduction to DB2. *Bufferpools are areas of virtual storage used by DB2 during the execution of an application program or an interactive SQL request to store pages of a table or an index temporarily.* When you need access to a row of a table, the page containing that row is read from the DASD and brought into a buffer. If data is changed, that buffer must be written back to the tablespace on DASD. If the data needed is already in a buffer, you have immediate access to it without waiting for it to be retrieved from DASD. The result is quicker performance.

DB2 has four different bufferpools to choose from: BP0, BP1, BP2, and BP32K. BP32K is only used with tablespaces containing 32K pages; the others are used for 4K pages. At installation time the number of pages in each bufferpool is specified. Three different bufferpools of 4K pages are provided. However, most shops do not use BP1 and BP2. IBM recommends that only BP0 be used because the efficiency gained by giving DB2 one large bufferpool to manage outweighs any advantage you might attempt to achieve by defining smaller bufferpools and assigning them, for instance, to heavily used tables or indexes. IBM says, in effect, that DB2 is better at managing buffers than are DBAs or systems programmers. However, you do have the option of assigning BP1 and BP2 to particular tables or indexes if you wish. If, for instance, you have some online data which must have fast response time, you might assign it to its own bufferpool so that it al-

ways stays in virtual storage. This might degrade DB2's overall performance, but the performance of this particular data, which would be
improved, might be worth it.

2.5 STRUCTURED QUERY LANGUAGE

Earlier we said that the three parts of the relational model are data
structure, data integrity, and data manipulation. SQL provides the
operators for data manipulation in DB2 as well as for defining and
controlling the database. SQL has evolved into a standard language
for relational DBMSs and has been adopted as such by both the American National Standards Organization (ANSI) and the International
Standards Organization (ISO). SQL also provides the database element of the common programming interface for IBM's Systems Application Architecture (SAA).

2.5.1 DML, DDL, and DCL

The Structured Query Language provides, as its name implies, rich
querying capabilities. It is also used to update the database. SQL has
three components which provide the facilities to create and manipulate a database. The Data Manipulation Language (DML) handles the
retrieval and updating of data. The Data Definition Language (DDL)
provides the language to define the objects which make up the database, and the Data Control Language (DCL) provides the language to
control authorization to access and use the database. These three components are three aspects of the same SQL language. Each, however,
has different SQL statements associated with it.

The SQL statements associated with DML are SELECT, UPDATE,
INSERT, and DELETE. SELECT allows you to retrieve a set of data
from one or more tables. It identifies the table from which the information is to be retrieved and the columns of the table to retrieve. Here
is a simple SELECT statement:

```
SELECT CUST_SOC_SEC, CUST_NAME, CUST_BRANCH
FROM CUSTOMER
```

Since you will probably not be interested in every instance of a col-
umn(s) all of the time, DB2 allows you to specify selection conditions.
We've added such a condition to the previous SELECT:

```
SELECT CUST_SOC_SEC, CUST_NAME, CUST_BRANCH
FROM CUSTOMER
WHERE CUST_BRANCH = 12
```

You can also use a single SELECT statement to retrieve a subset of
data from multiple tables based on multiple conditions.

DML's INSERT statement adds a single row to a table. It can also be used to copy a set of rows from one table to another. DELETE removes a row or rows from a table, while UPDATE modifies its columns. Update may affect one or more rows.

We've talked about DB2's objects—tables, tablespaces, indexes, indexspaces, databases, storage groups, and views. DDL statements provide you with the ability to create, change, and delete any of the DB2 objects. The SQL statements for this are CREATE, ALTER, and DROP. As with the DML statements, the function of each of these is self-explanatory.

The SQL statements associated with DCL are GRANT and REVOKE, which allow you to grant certain privileges to or revoke them from the users of the database. The privileges define exactly what the user may do with the database. An example is:

```
GRANT INSERT, DELETE
    ON CUSTOMER
    TO USER1
```

This says to give USER1 the ability to insert rows into and delete rows from a table named CUSTOMER.

2.5.2 Interactive and Embedded

We saw that a DB2 database can be accessed interactively (with SPUFI and QMF) or from an application program. Any of SQL's three components (DML, DDL, and DCL) can be used in either mode. However, the SQL format changes from one mode to the other. Interactive SQL is used with SPUFI or QMF and is simply referred to as SQL. Embedded SQL is used to code statements in the body of application programs. The term "embedded SQL" is sometimes also used to refer to other aspects of application programming required for access to DB2, like table declarations and the format for variables.

Embedded SQL statements can be used with programs written in COBOL, PL/I, Assembler, Fortran, or C. With only a few minor additions to the syntax, embedded SQL looks and performs exactly like interactive SQL. One difference is that delimiters are required to set SQL statements apart from host language statements. For example, in a COBOL application program, the embedded SQL will begin with EXEC SQL and end with END-EXEC.

The embedded format varies slightly with each host language. All of the examples in this book are based on COBOL.

The programming environment also requires some additional SQL statements. Since SQL is a set-oriented language, it processes multiple rows (records) at a time. Host languages, on the other hand, process only one record at a time. There are SQL statements that enable

SQL to work with the host languages by fetching a single record at a time from the set of rows returned by an SQL statement. A cursor points to the record to be fetched.

2.5.3 Data Types

DB2 offers four basic data types: character, graphic, numeric, and date/time (Fig. 2.10). Character and graphic data can be grouped into a category called string data. Some data types are used infrequently and are therefore excluded from the SQL examples in this book; they are LONG VARCHAR, GRAPHIC, VARGRAPHIC, LONG VARGRAPHIC, and FLOAT.

The basic rule of data type compatibility is that numbers and char-

STRING DATA

CHAR(n)	Fixed length character string of 'n' (1 to 254) bytes.
VARCHAR(n)	Variable length character string of up to 'n' (1 to 4056 for 4K pages and 1 to 32714 for 32K pages). It is considered LONG VARCHAR when greater than 254.
GRAPHIC(n)	Fixed length string of 'n' (1 to 127) 16-bit characters.
VARGRAPHIC(n)	Varying length string of up to 'n' 16-bit characters. It is considered LONG VARGRAPHIC when greater than 127.

NUMERIC DATA

SMALLINT	Halfword (2bytes) signed binary integer; the range of small integers is -32768 to 32767.
INTEGER	Fullword (4 bytes) signed binary integer; the range of large integers is -2147483648 to 2147483647.
DECIMAL(p,q)	Signed packed decimal number with 'p' (1 to 15) digits with an assumed decimal 'q' digits from the right. The value of 'q' must be 0 to 'p'. The maximum range is -999999999999999 to 99999999999999.
FLOAT(p)	Single-precision (fullword) and double-precision (doubleword) floating-point numbers. The range is -5.4E-79 to 7.2E+75.

DATE/TIME DATA

Note:	The external representation may be set to ISO, USA, EUR, or JIS. We use ISO.
DATE	Represented as yyyymmdd; external representation is a 10-byte character string (yyyy-mm-dd). Occupies 4-bytes in storage.
TIME	Represented as hhmmss; external representation is an 8-byte character string (hh:mm:ss). Occupies 3-bytes in storage.
TIMESTAMP	Represented as yyyymmddhhssmmssnnnnnn; external representation is a 26-byte character string (yyyy-mm-dd-hh.mm.ss. nnnnnn). You may exclude the microsecond portion from the external representation. Occupie 10-bytes in storage.

Figure 2.10 Data types.

acter strings are not compatible with each other, but all character data and all numeric data are compatible within their own class. For example, all numbers, integer and decimal, are compatible, as are all character strings (e.g., fixed length and variable). Although they are compatible, for processing, DB2 may have to do a temporary conversion to compare, for example, integer data to decimal data and this may cause performance degradation. Dates are compatible with one another and with character strings if the character string is a valid date string. The same is true for time and timestamps.

Since DB2 data may also be accessed by application programs, you should be aware of the data types in your programming language which correspond to those of DB2. The equivalent COBOL and DB2 data types are shown in Fig. 2.11. This will be a useful list to keep by your side as you program since DB2 considers it an error if data types do not correspond.

2.5.4 Constants

Constants, which are also called literals, are classified as string (character or graphic) or numeric. A string must be delimited with single quotes. Double quotation marks are less common but may be used if that character was chosen by your site as the delimiter at the time DB2 was installed. Alternatively, you may use a string of pairs of hexadecimal digits enclosed in quotes and preceded by the letter x (e.g., x'404040').

Numeric constants may be integer, decimal, or floating point. An integer constant is a signed or unsigned number of not more than 10 digits that does not contain a decimal point. A decimal constant is a

DB2		COBOL
FIELD_A	CHAR(n)	01 FIELD-A PIC X(n)
FIELD_A	VARCHAR(n)	01 FIELD-A 49 FIELD-A-LEN PIC S9(4) COMP 49 FIELD-A-TEXT PIC X(n)
FIELD-A	SMALLINT	01 FIELD-A PIC S9(4) COMP
FIELD_A	INTEGER	01 FIELD-A PIC S9(9) COMP
FIELD_A	DECIMAL(p,q)	01 FIELD-A PIC S9(a)V9(q) COMP-3 where a = p-q
FIELD_A	DATE	01 FIELD-A PIC X(10)
FIELD_A	TIME	01 FIELD-A PIC X(8)
FIELD_A	TIMESTAMP	01 FIELD-A PIC X(26)

Figure 2.11   DB2 data types and COBOL equivalents.

signed or unsigned number that may include a decimal point and has no more than 15 digits. A floating-point constant is written as two numbers separated by an E.

2.5.5 Nulls and Defaults

When a table is created, any of its columns may be defined to allow nulls. A null signifies that a value is not yet assigned, unknown, or not applicable. For example, in Fig. 2.12, the ACCT_CREDIT_BAL column of the account table refers to the balance on an account's credit line. What value should we use for Account JG20, which has no credit line balance because it has no credit line? ACCT_CREDIT_BAL is a numeric data type and we will be calculating sums and averages on the figures in the column. A zero for account JG20 would be misleading and would contribute to an inaccurate result when the average credit line balance is computed for the column. DB2 offers the concept of nulls to meet this need. By defining the column as null, we can omit a value for ACCT_CREDIT_BAL when we add the data for JG20, and DB2 will insert a null in its place. SQL's built-in AVERAGE function will ignore the rows containing nulls when it determines the average of the column's values.

DB2 implements nulls by adding a 1-byte prefix to each column that is defined as null. It puts HEX '00' in a field's prefix to indicate that a value is present and HEX 'FF' to indicate null. Look at Fig. 2.12 again and you will see that SPUFI represents the null with dashes. Nulls are necessary for the most accurate data representation, but they carry significant overhead in both memory space and processing time. In a large database, the amount of storage used can be significant. It is advisable that they be used only where absolutely necessary.

When creating a table, it is possible to specify NOT NULL WITH DEFAULT for any column. DB2 will fill a column with zeros for a numeric field or with spaces, for character data, if a value is not specified. The defaults for the DATE/TIME/TIMESTAMP columns are current date, time, or timestamp. In practice, using NOT NULL WITH DEFAULT is often the most useful approach.

```
ACCOUNT:

ACCT_NO   ACCT_BALANCE   ACCT_CREDIT_BAL   ACCT_CUST_ID   ACCT_START_DATE
--------+----------+----------+----------+----------+----------+----------+
AE11        12000.94          500.00      111111111      1987-03-17
AB21            .00           180.55      444444444      1989-02-12
JE21         700.50            0.00       333333333      1984-01-01
JG20        1010.00      ---------------  999999999      1978-04-01
```

Figure 2.12   ACCT_CREDIT_BAL may be null.

2.6 REFERENTIAL INTEGRITY

In Chap. 1, we presented the data integrity component of the relational model and a preliminary overview of DB2's implementation of it, which includes support for referential integrity (RI). *Referential integrity maintains the consistency of relationships between tables by requiring that every foreign key value in a table have a matching primary key value in a corresponding table or else be labeled null.* Now let's discuss the terminology associated with referential integrity in DB2 and its impact on performance.

A quick review of primary and foreign keys will help your understanding of what follows. A primary key consists of those columns that are required to ensure a row's uniqueness within a table. A foreign key consists of those columns in a table that are the same as the primary key in some other table and which function as a link to join associated data from the two tables.

DB2 tables can be classified as either parent, dependent, or independent tables. Parent tables contain the primary key, which may be referenced by one or more foreign keys. Dependent tables are those that contain a foreign key(s). A dependent table can also be a parent table in some other relationship. An independent table is neither a parent nor a dependent table (see Fig. 2.13). Table A is a parent table; its primary key is BRANCH. Table B is both a parent and a dependent table; it is a parent table with respect to table C, with primary key CUST_ID and is a dependent table with respect to table A; with foreign key BRANCH. Table C is a dependent table with a foreign key, CUSTOMER. Table D is an independent table with no links to other tables. You can see that tables D and C have primary keys which do not participate in a relationship to another table but are still needed to ensure each row's uniqueness.

We can now use this terminology to restate the referential integrity requirement—*every foreign key value in a dependent table must have a matching primary key value in a parent table or must be labeled null.*

DB2's implementation of referential integrity is accomplished through the definition of referential constraints, which are specified by including a foreign key clause in the DDL for a dependent table. This clause names the columns which make up the foreign key and the parent table to which it is associated. You may name the referential constraint in the foreign key clause or DB2 will automatically generate a name. Referential constraints are defined in the Catalog and enable DB2 to enforce referential integrity automatically. Note that DB2 does not require you to specify referential constraints; it is an option. DB2 will enforce no referential rules unless you tell it to. To the extent that it is not a requirement, DB2 deviates from the rela-

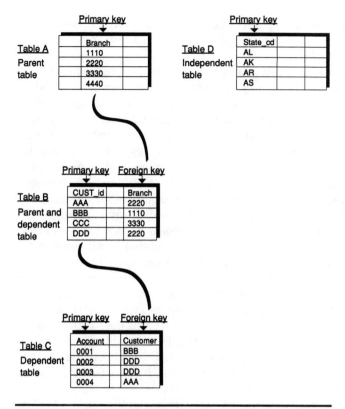

Figure 2.13 Foreign key values in dependent tables link to primary key values in parent tables.

tional model. Referential constraint violations can only occur when the columns which participate in the relationships are being modified, i.e., during the execution of the INSERT, UPDATE, and DELETE SQL statements.

Let's examine the impact of these operations on parent and dependent tables. Deleting a row from a dependent table does not affect referential integrity nor does inserting a new row in the parent table. This is because referential integrity does not require that there be a dependent table record for every parent table entry. In both of these cases, a parent table record will continue to exist. The existence of a dependent record is irrelevant.

Inserting a new row into a dependent table, however, requires the value in the foreign key to have a matching value in the parent table's primary key. This follows directly from the definition of RI and, therefore, does not need to be explicitly specified in the referential constraints. DB2 automatically enforces this. Updating the foreign key of a dependent table is basically the same as inserting a new row in the dependent table and also requires no specification in the referential constraints.

On the other hand, maintaining referential integrity when updating or deleting the primary key of a parent table is critical. It can be accomplished in one of three ways: restrict, cascade, and set to null.

The restrict option specifies that in a parent table, a row cannot be deleted or a column in the primary key may not be updated, if there are rows in the dependent table(s) with foreign key values equal to the primary key value that you would like to change in the parent table. Restrict is the default option. In Fig. 2.13, you would not be allowed to delete the row for branch 1110 in table A because the row for customer BBB in table B has a value of 1110 in its foreign key column.

The cascade option states that if a row of a parent table is either updated or deleted, the change will be propagated to all rows in the dependent table(s) having a foreign key value equal to the primary key value in the parent table's target row. Note that the change will also propagate to all other tables that are dependent on the dependent tables of the target parent table, if their referential constraints have also been defined as cascade. In Fig. 2.13, if you delete the row for branch 1110 from table A, a parent table, DB2 would also delete the row for customer BBB in table B if cascade had been specified. Be sure you know which option is in effect before you issue a DELETE statement.

The set to null option is similar to the cascade option except that all foreign key values in the affected rows of the dependent tables are set to null instead of being updated or deleted.

DB2's implementation of referential integrity does not support the cascade or set to null options for UPDATE, only restrict is supported. DB2 implicitly supports the INSERT and UPDATE rules for foreign keys in dependent tables. It supports all three options (restrict, cascade, and set to null) for the deletion of primary keys in parent tables.

The enforcement of referential integrity has an adverse impact on the performance of an application. More pages have to be read to examine the foreign key in the dependent tables and therefore both CPU cycles and I/Os increase. The establishment of referential integrity is optional. Since referential integrity is specified at the table level, the decision can be made on an individual basis as to whether or not it is advisable. In general, we recommend it unless business requirements make it impractical. For example, if a bank has a business rule that makes it possible for there to be customers (dependent table) who do not belong to a branch (parent table), you may not specify a referential constraint for that relationship unless you define the dependent table's foreign key as nullable. Otherwise DB2 will automatically restrict you from adding a row to the customer table without there being a corresponding row in the branch table.

This chapter has dipped into many different DB2 topics. Now we can begin to fill in the overview with the details you will need on your job. The next chapter tells you how to construct a sample database. It also introduces you to SPUFI.

3

Defining and Loading
a Sample Database

Now that we've surveyed databases in general and DB2 in particular, we can begin preparations for your hands-on introduction to DB2. We've designed the examples in this book around a sample database. The DML and QMF chapters make use of the tables in this database as do the three sample programs. In this chapter, we'll give you the tools to create this database at your installation. This will enable you to try each SQL example yourself, experiment with variations on the examples, and even run one of the sample programs.

Of course, not everyone will be in a position to install this database and play with SQL. Read this chapter anyway. Its description of the sample database will help you understand the book's SQL examples, and it provides a step by step introduction to DB2's interactive facility, SPUFI.

3.1 GAINING AUTHORIZATION
TO USE DB2

Before we begin, we need to take a brief look at DB2 security. DB2 protects its facilities and databases by controlling access and use through a system of authorities. The use of any DB2 resource must be granted to a user or set of users. The Catalog holds the information of authorities that have been granted. When you attempt to perform any action involving DB2, DB2 checks the Catalog to see if you have the proper authority. Once you have obtained permission from your management to use DB2 resources, you need to have your DBA grant you the DB2 authorization required to use them. The DBA does this

Section	Contents	Authority Required
PART I INTRODUCTION TO DB2	Use SPUFI to create four sample tables and their indices using DB's default database and storage group	EXECUTE on PLAN DSNESPCS and CREATETAB on default database DSNDB04
PART II DATA MANIPULA- TION LANGUAGE	Use SPUFI to retrieve and update information in the sample tables	EXECUTE on PLAN DSNESPCS and SELECT, UPDATE, INSERT, DELETE on the sample tables
PART III QUERY MANAGE- MENT FACILITY	Use QMF and the sample tables to create and save queries, procs, forms, and data	EXECUTE on PLAN QMF230 (for QMF Version 2.3), SELECT, UPDATE, INSERT, DELETE on the sample tables and USE on the default QMF tablespace which stores the QMF objects
PART IV APPLICATION PROGRAMMING	Use Program Preparation panels to prepare, BIND, and execute a COBOL/DB2 program	BINDADD
PART V DATA DEFINI- TION AND DATA CONTROL	Examples are not meant for execution and therefore require no authority	
PART VI MISCELLANEOUS TOPICS	Use SPUFI to create a PLAN_TABLE and runs EXPLAINS against the Catalog tables	EXECUTE on PLAN DSNESPCS and SELECT against the applicable Catalog tables.

Figure 3.1   DB2 authority you will need to execute examples.

through a component of the SQL language called Data Control Language (DCL).

Use Fig. 3.1 to let your DBA know the authorities you need for each part of this book. Sites differ in rules and methods for granting privileges to users. Your DBA may be able to grant you only a portion of the total list. He or she may also ask that you use some variation of the list which is in keeping with your site's standards. For instance, for simplicity, we have used DB2's system of defaults in creating the database's objects. We let DB2 associate the objects with default database DBNDB04 and default storage group SYSDEFLT. At your site, you may be required to associate your sample database with a particular database, tablespace, etc.

3.2   THE SAMPLE DATABASE

We have chosen a banking application for our sample database; it has four tables: BRANCH, CUSTOMER, ACCOUNT, and TRANSAC-TION. Figure 3.2 shows the data in these tables. The BRANCH table contains the ID, city, manager, and address for each of the bank's six branches. The CUSTOMER table holds information about eight customers including their social security number, name, date of birth, the branch to which they belong, and a rating number which the bank uses to separate the average customer from the better ones. In the ACCOUNT table, we find information about the nine customer accounts (customer 555555555 has two accounts). For each account, the bank maintains the account number, the account's balance and credit line balance, the account owner's social security number, and the date the account was opened. The last table, the TRANSACTION table, holds information about transactions made against the accounts—the type of transaction, the timestamp at the point of execution, the amount of the transaction, and the account associated with the trans-

```
BRANCH:

BRANCH_ID  BRANCH_CITY          BRANCH_MGR              BRANCH_ADDR
---------+---------+---------+---------+---------+---------+---------+
      12  NEW YORK             HIRO TANAKA             43 WEST 57 STREET
     300  YONKERS              BRUCE HOFFMAN           7 MORANI STREET
     450  ROCHESTER            ANGELA VALENTINO        351 TEAL PLAZA
     670  NEW YORK             MATTHEW GREEN           900 WALL STREET
     890  YONKERS              ZILYA KOLKER            610 OSIO LANE
      13  CORNING              JOE GROSSMAN            ONE FEDERAL PLAZA


CUSTOMER:

CUST_SOC_SEC  CUST_NAME          CUST_DATE_OF_BIRTH  CUST_BRANCH  CUST_RATING
---------+---------+---------+---------+---------+---------+---------+---------+
   111111111  PHYLLIS ELKIND     1962-03-29                   12            4
   222222222  JAY RANADE         1960-09-21                  890            8
   333333333  RICHARD GREEN      1947-08-15                   12            7
   444444444  ------------------ 1965-12-25                  670            9
   555555555  HEIDI SCHMIDT      1942-06-04                  890            2
   666666666  MUKESH SEHGAL      1957-10-24                  300            5
   777777777  LAI-HA NG          1970-01-01                  450            7
   888888888  GEORGE SCHMIDT     1950-07-04                   12            2


ACCOUNT:

ACCT_NO   ACCT_BALANCE  ACCT_CREDIT_BAL  ACCT_CUST_ID  ACCT_START_DATE
---------+---------+---------+---------+---------+---------+---------+---------+
AE11         12000.94           500.00     111111111  1987-03-17
AE12           500.00           500.00     555555555  1979-12-25
AE21            77.53          2000.00     888888888  1980-01-01
AB21              .00           180.55     444444444  1989-02-12
BB12         12001.35          3300.00     222222222  1989-02-14
BB13           646.01            25.00     666666666  1986-10-31
CE21         35100.98           100.00     333333333  1985-06-14
DE11            20.00            25.00     777777777  1979-05-20
DB11            75.00              .00     555555555  1980-11-11


TRANSACTION:

TXN_TYPE  TXN_TIMESTAMP                   TXN_AMOUNT  TXN_ACCT_NO
---------+---------+---------+---------+---------+---------+---------+
CREDIT    1989-01-01-12.12.12.000000          200.50  BB12
CREDIT    1989-01-01-13.13.13.000000         1200.00  BB12
OPENACCT  1989-02-02-16.16.16.000000  -------------   AE11
CREDIT    1989-02-02-17.17.17.000000           50.75  AE21
DEBIT     1989-02-03-18.18.18.000000          100.00  AE21
CREDIT    1989-02-03-19.19.19.000000         2000.00  AE11
DEBIT     1989-02-04-20.20.20.000000         1200.55  DE11
```

Figure 3.2 The sample tables.

action. Not every account is associated with one of the seven transactions in the table, but some accounts are associated with more than one.

Each table has a primary key—the column or columns which ensure the row's uniqueness (Fig. 3.3). In our tables, each branch has a branch ID (BRANCH_ID) which uniquely identifies the branch, each customer is uniquely identified by his or her social security number (CUST_SOC_SEC), and each account has a unique account number (ACCT_NO). A key made up of more than one column is a *composite key*. The transaction table's primary key, consisting of TXN_ACCT_NO, TXN_TYPE, and TXN_TIMESTAMP, is a composite key.

BRANCH:
PRIMARY KEY

BRANCH_ID	BRANCH_CITY	BRANCH_MGR	BRANCH_ADDR
12	NEW YORK	HIRO TANAKA	43 WEST 57 STREET
300	YONKERS	BRUCE HOFFMAN	7 MORANI STREET
450	ROCHESTER	ANGELA VALENTINO	351 TEAL PLAZA
670	NEW YORK	MATTHEW GREEN	900 WALL STREET
890	YONKERS	ZILYA KOLKER	610 OSIO LANE
13	CORNING	JOE GROSSMAN	ONE FEDERAL PLAZA

CUSTOMER:
PRIMARY KEY

CUST_SOC_SEC	CUST_NAME	CUST_DATE_OF_BIRTH	CUST_BRANCH	CUST_RATING
111111111	PHYLLIS ELKIND	1962-03-29	12	4
222222222	JAY RANADE	1960-09-21	890	8
333333333	RICHARD GREEN	1947-08-15	12	7
444444444	------------------	1965-12-25	670	9
555555555	HEIDI SCHMIDT	1942-06-04	890	2
666666666	MUKESH SEHGAL	1957-10-24	300	5
777777777	LAI-HA NG	1970-01-01	450	7
888888888	GEORGE SCHMIDT	1950-07-04	12	2

ACCOUNT:
PRIMARY KEY

ACCT_NO	ACCT_BALANCE	ACCT_CREDIT_BAL	ACCT_CUST_ID	ACCT_START_DATE
AE11	12000.94	500.00	111111111	1987-03-17
AE12	500.00	500.00	555555555	1979-12-25
AE21	77.53	2000.00	888888888	1980-01-01
AB21	.00	180.55	444444444	1989-02-12
BB12	12001.35	3300.00	222222222	1989-02-14
BB13	646.01	25.00	666666666	1986-10-31
CE21	35100.98	100.00	333333333	1985-06-14
DE11	20.00	25.00	777777777	1979-05-20
DB11	75.00	.00	555555555	1980-11-11

TRANSACTION: PRIMARY KEY

TXN_TYPE	TXN_TIMESTAMP	TXN_AMOUNT	TXN_ACCT_NO
CREDIT	1989-01-01-12.12.12.000000	200.50	BB12
CREDIT	1989-01-01-13.13.13.000000	1200.00	BB12
OPENACCT	1989-02-02-16.16.16.000000	------------	AE11
CREDIT	1989-02-02-17.17.17.000000	50.75	AE21
DEBIT	1989-02-03-18.18.18.000000	100.00	AE21
CREDIT	1989-02-03-19.19.19.000000	2000.00	AE11
DEBIT	1989-02-04-20.20.20.000000	1200.55	DE11

Figure 3.3   Each table in the sample database has a primary key.

You'll remember that relationships between tables are established through the tables' primary and foreign keys. Our CUSTOMER, AC-COUNT, and TRANSACTION tables contain foreign keys which link them to their associated parent tables. BRANCH is the parent of CUSTOMER, CUSTOMER is the parent of ACCOUNT, and AC-COUNT is the parent of TRANSACTION. Figure 3.4 shows the relationships between the tables' primary and foreign keys. Starting at the bottom of the hierarchy with the TRANSACTION table, TXN_ACCT_NO is a foreign key that points to the primary key column of the ACCOUNT table, ACCT_NO. Both columns contain the account identification number. In the ACCOUNT table,

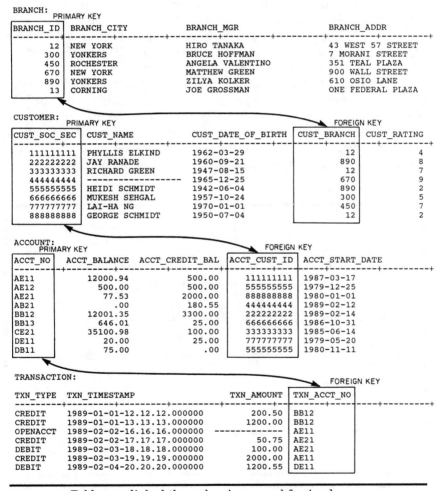

Figure 3.4   Tables are linked through primary and foreign keys.

ACCT_CUST_ID is the foreign key that points to the primary key column of the CUSTOMER table, CUST_SOC_SEC. The customer's social security number is found in both columns. And finally, in the CUSTOMER table, the CUST_BRANCH column is the foreign key that points to the primary key column of the BRANCH table, BRANCH_ID. Both hold the branch identification number. Notice that in each case the foreign key points to the primary key of its parent table.

3.3   SPUFI

We'll use SPUFI to submit the statements that create the sample database. SPUFI enables you to dynamically execute SQL statements from your TSO terminal. In your application development work, you can use SPUFI to test or debug SQL statements before you insert them into your programs. You will be using it here to submit the statements which create and load our sample DB2 tables and in Chaps. 4, 5, and 6 to execute SQL retrieval and update statements.

The flow of a SPUFI session is quite straightforward. By placing your SQL statements in a sequential dataset or PDS member, SPUFI can submit them to DB2 dynamically. It formats the SQL results and returns them and the messages generated in a browsable sequential dataset. A nice feature of SPUFI is that it makes use of ISPF EDIT for input and ISPF BROWSE for output. SPUFI is intended for DP per-

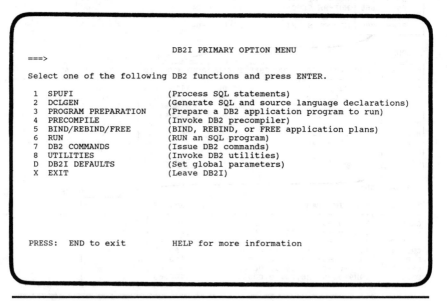

```
                          DB2I PRIMARY OPTION MENU
   ===>

   Select one of the following DB2 functions and press ENTER.

       1  SPUFI                  (Process SQL statements)
       2  DCLGEN                 (Generate SQL and source language declarations)
       3  PROGRAM PREPARATION    (Prepare a DB2 application program to run)
       4  PRECOMPILE             (Invoke DB2 precompiler)
       5  BIND/REBIND/FREE       (BIND, REBIND, or FREE application plans)
       6  RUN                    (RUN an SQL program)
       7  DB2 COMMANDS           (Issue DB2 commands)
       8  UTILITIES              (Invoke DB2 utilities)
       D  DB2I DEFAULTS          (Set global parameters)
       X  EXIT                   (Leave DB2I)




       PRESS:   END to exit          HELP for more information
```

Figure 3.5   DB2I menu.

sonnel who are already familiar with ISPF commands; there is nothing new to learn to produce the input file or to read the output file. All you have to do is understand how to use the options on the SPUFI main panel. You'll see how this works as we step through the process of creating and populating our tables.

SPUFI is accessed through DB2I (the I stands for Interactive), which is the set of ISPF panels provided with DB2 for interactive functions. The DB2I Primary Option Menu (Fig. 3.5) is accessed either from the ISPF Primary Option Menu, an installation-written submenu (e.g., Relational Products Menu), or a CLIST. This will depend on how your company accesses DB2. Option 1 on the DB2I panel brings you to the SPUFI panel (Fig. 3.6).

3.3.1 Input and Output Datasets

Items 1, 2, and 3 in SPUFI are used to define the input dataset (Fig. 3.7). The dataset may be either a sequential file or a PDS, but it must already be allocated. PDSs are often used instead of sequential datasets because they can hold several related members. For example, we will have a separate member for each table in our sample database.

Items 2 and 3 in the illustration are optional. You must enter a volume serial number for uncataloged datasets and a dataset password if

```
                        SPUFI
===>

Enter the input data set name:      (Can be sequential or partitioned)
  1  DATA SET NAME ... ===>
  2  VOLUME SERIAL ... ===>         (Enter if not cataloged)
  3  DATA SET PASSWORD ===>         (Enter if password protected)

Enter the output data set name:     (Must be a sequential data set)
  4  DATA SET NAME ... ===>

Specify processing options:
  5  CHANGE DEFAULTS   ===>         (Y/N - Display SPUFI defaults panel?)
  6  EDIT INPUT ...... ===>         (Y/N - Enter SQL statements?)
  7  EXECUTE ......... ===>         (Y/N - Execute SQL statements?)
  8  AUTOCOMMIT ...... ===>         (Y/N - Commit after successful run?)
  9  BROWSE OUTPUT ... ===>         (Y/N - Browse output data set?)




  PRESS: ENTER to process    END to exit    HELP for more information
```

Figure 3.6 SPUFI panel.

```
                           SPUFI
===>
┌─────────────────────────────────────────────────────────────────┐
│ Enter the input data set name:       (Can be sequential or partitioned)
│ 1   DATA SET NAME ... ===> 'USER1.DB2.SAMPLE(BRANCH)'
│ 2   VOLUME SERIAL ... ===>           (Enter if not cataloged)
│ 3   DATA SET PASSWORD ===>           (Enter if password protected)
└─────────────────────────────────────────────────────────────────┘
   Enter the output data set name:     (Must be a sequential data set)
   4   DATA SET NAME ... ===>

   Specify processing options:
   5   CHANGE DEFAULTS   ===>          (Y/N - Display SPUFI defaults panel?)
   6   EDIT INPUT ...... ===>          (Y/N - Enter SQL statements?)
   7   EXECUTE ......... ===>          (Y/N - Execute SQL statements?)
   8   AUTOCOMMIT ...... ===>          (Y/N - Commit after successful run?)
   9   BROWSE OUTPUT ... ===>          (Y/N - Browse output data set?)



   PRESS: ENTER to process     END to exit    HELP for more information
```

Figure 3.7   SPUFI input dataset specification.

```
                           SPUFI
===>
   Enter the input data set name:       (Can be sequential or partitioned)
   1   DATA SET NAME ... ===> 'USER1.DB2.SAMPLE(BRANCH)'
   2   VOLUME SERIAL ... ===>           (Enter if not cataloged)
   3   DATA SET PASSWORD ===>           (Enter if password protected)
┌─────────────────────────────────────────────────────────────────┐
│ Enter the output data set name:       (Must be a sequential data set)
│ 4   DATA SET NAME ... ===> OUTPUT
└─────────────────────────────────────────────────────────────────┘
   Specify processing options:
   5   CHANGE DEFAULTS   ===>          (Y/N - Display SPUFI defaults panel?)
   6   EDIT INPUT ...... ===>          (Y/N - Enter SQL statements?)
   7   EXECUTE ......... ===>          (Y/N - Execute SQL statements?)
   8   AUTOCOMMIT ...... ===>          (Y/N - Commit after successful run?)
   9   BROWSE OUTPUT ... ===>          (Y/N - Browse output data set?)



   PRESS: ENTER to process     END to exit    HELP for more information
```

Figure 3.8   SPUFI output dataset specification.

it is required by your installation. We have preallocated an 80-byte PDS, USER1.DB2.SAMPLE, and have specified the first member, BRANCH. As with any other PDS, ISPF allows you to dynamically create a new member for an existing PDS.

The output dataset name is entered in item 4 on the panel (Fig. 3.8). Unlike the input dataset, this must be a sequential dataset, and it does not have to be preallocated. If it already exists, SPUFI will reuse it; otherwise, SPUFI will allocate it dynamically. When specifying both input and output datasets, remember that TSO appends your user ID as the high-level qualifier to dataset names not enclosed in quotes. We've called the output dataset OUTPUT, but you may use whatever name you wish for item 4.

The remaining items on the SPUFI panel refer to SPUFI's processing options. For each option, you must enter either YES or NO. When you press Enter, SPUFI executes the first option for which a YES is specified. We've entered YES for all options (Fig. 3.9).

3.3.2 SPUFI Defaults

Pressing Enter processes the first option, CHANGE DEFAULTS, and takes you to the panel CURRENT SPUFI DEFAULTS (Fig. 3.10). The first item on this panel, ISOLATION LEVEL, determines the extent

```
                           SPUFI
    ===>

    Enter the input data set name:        (Can be sequential or partitioned)
      1  DATA SET NAME ... ===> 'USER1.DB2.SAMPLE(BRANCH)'
      2  VOLUME SERIAL ... ===>           (Enter if not cataloged)
      3  DATA SET PASSWORD ===>           (Enter if password protected)

    Enter the output data set name:       (Must be a sequential data set)
      4  DATA SET NAME ... ===> OUTPUT

    Specify processing options:
      5  CHANGE DEFAULTS    ===> YES      (Y/N - Display SPUFI defaults panel?)
      6  EDIT INPUT ...... ===> YES       (Y/N - Enter SQL statements?)
      7  EXECUTE ......... ===> YES       (Y/N - Execute SQL statements?)
      8  AUTOCOMMIT ...... ===> YES       (Y/N - Commit after successful run?)
      9  BROWSE OUTPUT ... ===> YES       (Y/N - Browse output data set?)



    PRESS: ENTER to process     END to exit     HELP for more information
```

Figure 3.9   SPUFI processing options.

```
                       CURRENT SPUFI DEFAULTS
===>
Enter the following to control your SPUFI session:
  1  ISOLATION LEVEL   ===> CS          (RR=Repeatable Read, CS=Cursor Stability)
  2  MAX SELECT LINES  ===> 250         (Maximum number of lines to be
                                           returned from a SELECT)
Output data set characteristics:
  3  RECORD LENGTH ... ===> 4092        (LRECL=Logical record length)
  4  BLOCK SIZE ...... ===> 4096        (Size of one block)
  5  RECORD FORMAT ... ===> VB          (RECFM=F, FB, FBA, V, VB, or VBA)
  6  DEVICE TYPE ..... ===> SYSDA       (Must be DASD unit name)

Output format characteristics:
  7  MAX NUMERIC FIELD ===> 20          (Maximum width for numeric fields)
  8  MAX CHAR FIELD .. ===> 80          (Maximum width for character fields)
  9  COLUMN HEADING .. ===> NAMES       (NAMES, LABELS, ANY or BOTH)




PRESS: ENTER to proceed      END to exit     HELP for more information
```

Figure 3.10   SPUFI defaults panel.

to which other programs can use the tables that your request is accessing. For our purposes, this should be set to CS (cursor stability), which allows greater concurrent access than RR (repeatable read). An explanation of repeatable read and cursor stability is in Chap. 12. The second item, MAX SELECT LINES, determines the number of lines SPUFI will return from your SQL statement. You may set this to any integer, but the default, 250, will be fine for our examples. If your SQL statement were to request all of the rows of a 2000-row table, however, you would only see the first 250 rows unless you changed this option.

Items 3 through 6 are used to define the output dataset's characteristics: RECORD LENGTH, BLOCK SIZE, RECORD FORMAT, and DEVICE TYPE. These are the same parameters that you use to define any other dataset. We've used SPUFI's defaults. For RECORD LENGTH, this is 4092 and for BLOCK SIZE, 4096. RECORD FORMAT may be V, VB, VBA, F, FB, or FBA. These stand for combinations of variable, fixed, and blocked. The FBA and VBA formats put printer control characters in your output. We've used the default, VB. The DEVICE TYPE may be any MVS DASD device, and again, we've used the SPUFI default, SYSDA.

The last three items on the default panel define characteristics that SPUFI uses to format the output data. Items 7 and 8 specify the maximum width for numeric and character fields. If numeric data is wider than the maximum numeric field specified, the numeric data is either partially displayed or replaced with asterisks. Character data is truncated from the right. The defaults, 20 for numeric and 80 for character, have been filled in.

Item 9 on the default panel has to do with the column headings SPUFI will use when it formats the results. If NAMES is specified, the column names are used. Columns may also have labels associated with them; they are created with a LABEL ON statement. These will be used for headings if LABELS is specified. ANY means that a column will be headed with a label, column name, or blanks (in that order of precedence), depending on which exists. BOTH will display both column names and labels, if both exist. We've used NAMES.

3.3.3 Edit and Execute

The End key takes you back to SPUFI's main panel. Once the defaults panel has been processed, SPUFI replaces the YES next to option 5 on the SPUFI panel with an asterisk (Fig. 3.11). Pressing Enter initiates EDIT INPUT, the next option for which a YES is specified. You are taken into ISPF EDIT for the input dataset specified on the first SPUFI panel, USER1.DB2.SAMPLE(BRANCH) (Fig. 3.12). Copy the statements from this figure into your own dataset. These are the SQL statements you need to create the BRANCH table and populate it with data. The explanations of these statements are in later chapters

```
                            SPUFI
    ===>
    DSNE800A NO DEFAULT VALUES WERE CHANGED. PRESS ENTER TO CONTINUE
    Enter the input data set name:      (Can be sequential or partitioned)
      1  DATA SET NAME ... ===> 'USER1.DB2.SAMPLE(BRANCH)'
      2  VOLUME SERIAL ... ===>          (Enter if not cataloged)
      3  DATA SET PASSWORD ===>          (Enter if password protected)

    Enter the output data set name:     (Must be a sequential data set)
      4  DATA SET NAME ... ===> OUTPUT

    Specify processing options:
      5  CHANGE DEFAULTS    ===> *       (Y/N - Display SPUFI defaults panel?)
      6  EDIT INPUT ......  ===> YES     (Y/N - Enter SQL statements?)
      7  EXECUTE .........  ===> YES     (Y/N - Execute SQL statements?)
      8  AUTOCOMMIT ......  ===> YES     (Y/N - Commit after successful run?)
      9  BROWSE OUTPUT ...  ===> YES     (Y/N - Browse output data set?)




    PRESS: ENTER to process      END to exit     HELP for more information
```

Figure 3.11 An asterisk replaces the YES when a processing option is completed.

```
EDIT ---- USER1.DB2.SAMPLE(BRANCH) 01.99 ------------------- COLUMNS 001 072
COMMAND ===>                                                SCROLL ===> CSR
****** **************************** TOP OF DATA ****************************
          CREATE TABLE BRANCH
                 (BRANCH_ID     SMALLINT      NOT NULL WITH DEFAULT,
                  BRANCH_CITY   CHAR    (20)  NOT NULL WITH DEFAULT,
                  -- THE FOLLOWING FIELD ACCEPTS NULLS
                  BRANCH_MGR    CHAR    (25)  ,
                  -- THE FOLLOWING FIELD HAS A VARCHAR DATA TYPE
                  BRANCH_ADDR   VARCHAR (25)  NOT NULL WITH DEFAULT,
          PRIMARY KEY(BRANCH_ID));

          CREATE UNIQUE INDEX XBRANCH ON BRANCH
                 (BRANCH_ID);

          INSERT INTO BRANCH
          VALUES (012, 'NEW YORK', 'HIRO TANAKA', '43 WEST 57 STREET');

          INSERT INTO BRANCH
          VALUES (300,'YONKERS', 'BRUCE HOFFMAN', '7 MORANI STREET');

****** *************************** BOTTOM OF DATA *************************
```

Figure 3.12 EDIT INPUT takes you to ISPF EDIT.

in the book. For now, we must jump ahead of ourselves and give you the statements you need and let the explanation follow later. We have shown INSERT statements for the first two rows in the BRANCH table. Look back at Fig. 3.2 to see the data for the remaining rows, and follow the same format.

Notice that SPUFI allows you to submit multiple SQL statements in one execution but that each statement must be separated with a semicolon. You may begin your SQL statements in any position on a line. SQL statements are free in form. A statement may be coded on one or many lines with each line indented to any position. Individual words may not be divided between lines. Feel free to use whatever editing tricks you know to make the typing job go faster but make sure you copy this exactly, commas and all. Since SPUFI ignores everything that follows two dashes on a line, we've used this to add comments.

When you have completed inputting these SQL statements, press your End key to return to the SPUFI panel, which will now have an asterisk next to EDIT INPUT. If the next item, EXECUTE, is marked YES, pressing Enter will cause SPUFI to submit the SQL statements within the input dataset to DB2. If this is successful, you will have created the BRANCH table and the XBRANCH index and will have inserted six rows of data into the table.

We have specified YES for option 8, AUTOCOMMIT. This option determines whether SPUFI will automatically save (COMMIT) or erase (ROLLBACK) the results of your session. The concepts of COMMIT and ROLLBACK are discussed in detail in Chap. 10. Specifying YES for AUTOCOMMIT means that at the end of a successful session, SPUFI will automatically issue a COMMIT, telling DB2 to write all changes to the database. Specifying NO allows you to look at the results of the session and decide at that point, via a separate screen which SPUFI displays, whether to COMMIT or ROLLBACK your changes or DEFER the decision. DEFER holds the changes in limbo while you process another input dataset.

3.3.4 Browse

Once the statements have executed, you are automatically taken to BROWSE because you entered YES for option 9, BROWSE OUTPUT. Figure 3.13 shows the information SPUFI includes in USER1.OUTPUT. Each SQL statement in USER1.DB2.SAMPLE(BRANCH) is followed by a processing summary. This includes the status of SQLCODE, a field which DB2 updates following each execution of an SQL statement. In the case of INSERT, it also reports the number of rows affected, that is, one for each insert.

Use Figs. 3.14, 3.15, and 3.16, and the data in Fig. 3.2 to create and execute the CUSTOMER, ACCOUNT, and TRANSACTION PDSs in the same way. If any of the SQL statements executed in a session re-

```
BROWSE  - USER1.OUTPUT----------------------------- LINE 000000 COL 001 080
COMMAND ===>                                              SCROLL ===> CSR
***************************** TOP OF DATA  ********************************
--------+---------+---------+---------+---------+---------+---------+-------
CREATE TABLE BRANCH
      (BRANCH_ID    SMALLINT        NOT NULL WITH DEFAULT,
       BRANCH_CITY  CHAR     (20)   NOT NULL WITH DEFAULT,
       -- THE FOLLOWING FIELD ACCEPTS NULLS
       BRANCH_MGR   CHAR     (25)  ,
       -- THE FOLLOWING FIELD HAS A VARCHAR DATA TYPE
       BRANCH_ADDR  VARCHAR  (25)   NOT NULL WITH DEFAULT,
PRIMARY KEY(BRANCH_ID));
--------+---------+---------+---------+---------+---------+---------+-------
DSNE616I STATEMENT EXECUTION WAS SUCCESSFUL, SQLCODE IS 0
--------+---------+---------+---------+---------+---------+---------+-------

CREATE UNIQUE INDEX XBRANCH ON BRANCH
      (BRANCH_ID);
--------+---------+---------+---------+---------+---------+---------+-------
DSNE616I STATEMENT EXECUTION WAS SUCCESSFUL, SQLCODE IS 0
--------+---------+---------+---------+---------+---------+---------+-------

INSERT INTO BRANCH
VALUES (012, 'NEW YORK', 'HIRO TANAKA', '43 WEST 57 STREET');
```

Figure 3.13 BROWSE OUTPUT takes you to ISPF BROWSE.

```
---------+---------+---------+---------+---------+---------+---------+-------
DSNE615I NUMBER OF ROWS AFFECTED IS 1
DSNE616I STATEMENT EXECUTION WAS SUCCESSFUL, SQLCODE IS 0
---------+---------+---------+---------+---------+---------+---------+-------

INSERT INTO BRANCH
VALUES (300, 'YONKERS', 'BRUCE HOFFMAN', '7 MORANI  STREET');
---------+---------+---------+---------+---------+---------+---------+-------
DSNE615I NUMBER OF ROWS AFFECTED IS 1
DSNE616I STATEMENT EXECUTION WAS SUCCESSFUL, SQLCODE IS 0
---------+---------+---------+---------+---------+---------+---------+-------

---------+---------+---------+---------+---------+---------+---------+-------
DSNE617I COMMIT PERFORMED, SQLCODE IS 0
DSNE616I STATEMENT EXECUTION WAS SUCCESSFUL, SQLCODE IS 0
---------+---------+---------+---------+---------+---------+---------+-------
DSNE601I SQL STATEMENTS ASSUMED TO BE BETWEEN COLUMNS 1 AND 72
DSNE620I NUMBER OF SQL STATEMENTS PROCESSED IS 4
DSNE621I NUMBER OF INPUT RECORDS READ IS 19
DSNE622I NUMBER OF OUTPUT RECORDS WRITTEN IS 40
******************************BOTTOM OF DATA ******************************
```

Figure 3.13   (*Continued*)

```
EDIT ---- USER1.DB2.SAMPLE(CUSTOMER) 01.99 ----------------- COLUMNS 001 072
COMMAND ===>                                                 SCROLL ===> CSR
****** **************************** TOP OF DATA ****************************
        CREATE TABLE CUSTOMER
            (CUST_SOC_SEC        INTEGER   NOT NULL WITH DEFAULT,
            --THE FOLLOWING FIELD ACCEPTS NULLS
            CUST_NAME           CHAR (18) ,
            CUST_DATE_OF_BIRTH DATE       NOT NULL WITH DEFAULT,
            CUST_BRANCH         SMALLINT  NOT NULL WITH DEFAULT,
            CUST_RATING         SMALLINT  NOT NULL WITH DEFAULT,
        PRIMARY KEY (CUST_SOC_SEC),
        FOREIGN KEY RCCUST  (CUST_BRANCH)  REFERENCES BRANCH);

        CREATE UNIQUE INDEX XCUSTOMER ON CUSTOMER
            (CUST_SOC_SEC);

        INSERT INTO CUSTOMER
        VALUES (111111111, 'PHYLLIS ELKIND', '1962-03-29', 12, 4);

        INSERT INTO CUSTOMER
        VALUES (222222222, 'JAY RANADE', '1960-09-21', 890, 8);

****** **************************** BOTTOM OF DATA****************************
```

Figure 3.14   Input for the CUSTOMER table.

```
EDIT ---- USER1.DB2.SAMPLE(ACCOUNT) 01.99 ------------------ COLUMNS 001 072
COMMAND ===>                                                   SCROLL ===> CSR
****** *************************** TOP OF DATA ****************************
          CREATE TABLE ACCOUNT
                    (ACCT_NO          CHAR    (04)      NOT NULL WITH DEFAULT,
                     ACCT_BALANCE     DECIMAL (11,2)    NOT NULL WITH DEFAULT,
                     -- THE FOLLOWING FIELD ACCEPTS NULLS
                     ACCT_CREDIT_BAL  DECIMAL (11,2),
                     ACCT_CUST_ID     INTEGER           NOT NULL WITH DEFAULT,
                     ACCT_START_DATE  DATE              NOT NULL WITH DEFAULT,
          PRIMARY KEY (ACCT_NO),
          FOREIGN KEY RCACCT (ACCT_CUST_ID) REFERENCES CUSTOMER);

          CREATE UNIQUE INDEX XACCOUNT ON ACCOUNT
                (ACCT_NO);

          INSERT INTO ACCOUNT
          VALUES ('AE11', 12000.94, 500, 111111111, '1987-03-17');


          INSERT INTO ACCOUNT
          VALUES ('AE12', 500, 500, 555555555, '1979-12-25');

****** *************************** BOTTOM OF DATA ****************************
```

Figure 3.15   Input for the ACCOUNT table.

```
EDIT ---- USER1.DB2.SAMPLE(TRANS) 01.99 ------------------- COLUMNS 001 072
COMMAND ===>                                                   SCROLL ===> CSR
****** *************************** TOP OF DATA ***************************
          CREATE TABLE TRANSACTION
                    (TXN_TYPE         CHAR (08)       NOT NULL WITH DEFAULT,
                     TXN_TIMESTAMP    TIMESTAMP       NOT NULL WITH DEFAULT,
                     --THE FOLLOWING FIELD ACCEPTS NULLS
                     TXN_AMOUNT          DECIMAL (11,2),
                     TXN_ACCT_NO      CHAR (04)       NOT NULL WITH DEFAULT,
          PRIMARY KEY (TXN_ACCT_NO, TXN_TYPE, TXN_TIMESTAMP),
          FOREIGN KEY RCTXN  (TXN_ACCT_NO)  REFERENCES ACCOUNT);

          CREATE UNIQUE INDEX XTRANSACTION ON TRANSACTION
                (TXN_ACCT_NO, TXN_TYPE, TXN_TIMESTAMP);

          INSERT INTO TRANSACTION
          VALUES ('CREDIT', '1989-01-01-12.12.12', 200.50, 'BB12');

          INSERT INTO TRANSACTION
          VALUES ('DEBIT', '1989-02-03-18.18.18', 100, 'AE21');

****** *************************** BOTTOM OF DATA***************************
```

Figure 3.16   Input for the TRANSACTION table.

ceives an error code, the statements which follow it are ignored. SPUFI will automatically tell DB2 to rollback any of the changes which preceded the error statement since we specified AUTOCOMMIT. Get back into EDIT, correct your errors, and resubmit the entire PDS member.

With these sample tables in place, either physically or mentally (for those without access to DB2), we can get on with learning how to access and update DB2 data. The next three chapters use the sample database tables to illustrate the DML component of SQL.

Data Manipulation Language

4

The SELECT Statement

4.1 INTRODUCTION

The data manipulation part of SQL (abbreviated DML for Data Manipulation Language) enables you to retrieve, update, insert, and delete data from DB2 tables. Chapters 4, 5, and 6 are devoted to this topic. Chapters 4 and 5 focus on the variety of ways in which you can use SELECT, SQL's statement for data retrieval. Updating, inserting, and deleting data are described in Chap. 6, as are the peculiarities of manipulating DATE and TIME data types and the constraints imposed by referential integrity. In these chapters we give examples of each language element discussed. For full syntax diagrams, we refer you to App. C.

The examples in these chapters are what you need for interactive data access, as with SPUFI or QMF. In Part 4 of this book, "Application Programming," you will see how the syntax is modified for inclusion in programs. On some examples of incorrect syntax, we include the error code and message that SQL would return. SQL's error codes begin with a negative sign (e.g., -811).

All of the examples in these chapters use the tables from the sample application described in Chap. 3. Figure 4.1 presents these tables and is repeated at the beginning of each chapter for reference. You may want to use SPUFI, as described in the previous chapter, to try the examples yourself. As you proceed, it would be interesting to imagine the COBOL coding that would be required to perform the same processing. This will demonstrate the economy of an SQL statement and will clarify the processing implied by the statement.

4.1.1 The SELECT Statement Format

You can think of the SELECT statement as, in some ways, the heart of SQL. The clauses of the SELECT statement are:

BRANCH:

BRANCH_ID	BRANCH_CITY	BRANCH_MGR	BRANCH_ADDR
12	NEW YORK	HIRO TANAKA	43 WEST 57 STREET
300	YONKERS	BRUCE HOFFMAN	7 MORANI STREET
450	ROCHESTER	ANGELA VALENTINO	351 TEAL PLAZA
670	NEW YORK	MATTHEW GREEN	900 WALL STREET
890	YONKERS	ZILYA KOLKER	610 OSIO LANE
13	CORNING	JOE GROSSMAN	ONE FEDERAL PLAZA

CUSTOMER:

CUST_SOC_SEC	CUST_NAME	CUST_DATE_OF_BIRTH	CUST_BRANCH	CUST_RATING
111111111	PHYLLIS ELKIND	1962-03-29	12	4
222222222	JAY RANADE	1960-09-21	890	8
333333333	RICHARD GREEN	1947-08-15	12	7
444444444	------------------	1965-12-25	670	9
555555555	HEIDI SCHMIDT	1942-06-04	890	2
666666666	MUKESH SEHGAL	1957-10-24	300	5
777777777	LAI-HA NG	1970-01-01	450	7
888888888	GEORGE SCHMIDT	1950-07-04	12	2

ACCOUNT:

ACCT_NO	ACCT_BALANCE	ACCT_CREDIT_BAL	ACCT_CUST_ID	ACCT_START_DATE
AE11	12000.94	500.00	111111111	1987-03-17
AE12	500.00	500.00	555555555	1979-12-25
AE21	77.53	2000.00	888888888	1980-01-01
AB21	.00	180.55	444444444	1989-02-12
BB12	12001.35	3300.00	222222222	1989-02-14
BB13	646.01	25.00	666666666	1986-10-31
CE21	35100.98	100.00	333333333	1985-06-14
DE11	20.00	25.00	777777777	1979-05-20
DB11	75.00	.00	555555555	1980-11-11

TRANSACTION:

TXN_TYPE	TXN_TIMESTAMP	TXN_AMOUNT	TXN_ACCT_NO
CREDIT	1989-01-01-12.12.12.000000	200.50	BB12
CREDIT	1989-01-01-13.13.13.000000	1200.00	BB12
OPENACCT	1989-02-02-16.16.16.000000	-------------	AE11
CREDIT	1989-02-02-17.17.17.000000	50.75	AE21
DEBIT	1989-02-03-18.18.18.000000	100.00	AE21
CREDIT	1989-02-03-19.19.19.000000	2000.00	AE11
DEBIT	1989-02-04-20.20.20.000000	1200.55	DE11

Figure 4.1   The sample tables.

```
SELECT ...
   FROM ...
   WHERE ...
   GROUP BY ...
   HAVING ...
   ORDER BY ...
```

The clauses must follow this sequence but only the SELECT and
FROM clauses are required. The full syntax is shown in App. C. The
result of the SELECT is a subset of data from an existing table or view
or from more than one table or view. SELECTs from multiple tables
are described in the next chapter.

The FROM clause tells DB2 the name of the table or view from which you are selecting data. If you created the table yourself, as in our sample database, you may refer to the table by its simple name, e.g., CUSTOMER. If, however, you wish to access a table that was created by someone else, you must use its fully qualified name. For example, if someone with the ID USER1 had created the CUSTOMER table, you would have to refer to it as USER1.CUSTOMER in your request. If DB2 does not see a period in the name, it assumes that it is a simple name and affixes the ID of the user who is logged on.

4.1.2   The Result Table—A Subset of Your Data

In a relational system, *the result of any operation on a table(s) is a new table, the result table.* It will include some or all of the columns and some or all of the rows of the original table(s).

While the actual data is stored in objects called tables, a result table is not stored on any physical device and cannot be found in DB2's Catalog. It is a conceptual file whose existence is temporary. When you access DB2 through SPUFI, you are able to view the formatted result table in your output dataset. SPUFI puts column names in the heading, shows null values with dashes, etc., so that the table is readable. You can save your SPUFI output dataset which shows the result table, but there is no way to save the result table itself. Note, however, that we will see an exception to this when we get to QMF in Part 3 of this book.

Let's look at an example of a SELECT statement and its associated result table as formatted by SPUFI:

```
SELECT CUST_SOC_SEC
    FROM CUSTOMER

RESULT TABLE:

CUST_SOC_SEC
--------+---
   111111111
   222222222
   333333333
   444444444
   555555555
   666666666
   777777777
   888888888
```

This statement retrieves customer social security number data from the CUSTOMER table. We can describe the result table as having eight rows, each of one attribute, CUST_SOC_SEC. But other than looking at this table in our output dataset, we cannot access it or find it in DB2's Catalog.

When processing complex queries, DB2 may create intermediate result sets. These are also conceptual, but unlike a result table, they are never visible to the user. It is sometimes helpful to visualize the intermediate sets in order to understand how DB2 arrives at the result table you finally see.

4.2   THE SELECT CLAUSE

In general, what you specify in the SELECT clause of the SELECT statement determines the columns that will be returned in the result table from the table identified in the FROM clause.

4.2.1   *, Columns, Literals

An * is a wild card character and will return all columns as in the following:

```
SELECT *
   FROM CUSTOMER

RESULT TABLE:
```

CUST_SOC_SEC	CUST_NAME	CUST_DATE_OF_BIRTH	CUST_BRANCH	CUST_RATING
111111111	PHYLLIS ELKIND	1962-03-29	12	4
222222222	JAY RANADE	1960-09-21	890	8
333333333	RICHARD GREEN	1947-08-15	12	7
444444444	------------------	1965-12-25	670	9
555555555	HEIDI SCHMIDT	1942-06-04	890	2
666666666	MUKESH SEHGAL	1957-10-24	300	5
777777777	LAI-HA NG	1970-01-01	450	7
888888888	GEORGE SCHMIDT	1950-07-04	12	2

All of the columns in the CUSTOMER table are returned in the order that was specified when the table was defined. If you wanted to specify the whole list, you would receive the same result with:

```
SELECT CUST_SOC_SEC, CUST_NAME, CUST_DATE_OF_BIRTH,
       CUST_BRANCH, CUST_RATING
   FROM CUSTOMER
```

Notice that when you list more than one column, you must separate them with commas.

While the * is a convenient way to retrieve all columns without having to type or even know their names, it should only be used in interactive queries. If your application program expects certain columns, table changes may cause your query with an * to produce unexpected and undesirable results. To be safe, make explicit SELECT requests from a program.

Suppose you wanted to see the columns in a different order or wanted only some of the columns returned? The order of the columns listed in the SELECT clause dictates the order of the retrieved columns. What you say is what you get:

```
SELECT CUST_NAME, CUST_SOC_SEC, CUST_BRANCH
   FROM CUSTOMER
```

RESULT TABLE:

CUST_NAME	CUST_SOC_SEC	CUST_BRANCH
PHYLLIS ELKIND	111111111	12
JAY RANADE	222222222	890
RICHARD GREEN	333333333	12
----------------	444444444	670
HEIDI SCHMIDT	555555555	890
MUKESH SEHGAL	666666666	300
IAI-HA NG	777777777	450
GEORGE SCHMIDT	888888888	12

Although our original table had CUST_SOC_SEC first followed by CUST_NAME, the columns that will be returned will have CUST_NAME followed by CUST_SOC_SEC as we specified in the SELECT clause. In addition, our result table will *not* contain CUST_DATE_OF_BIRTH or CUST_RATING because they were not SELECTed.

On occasion, you may want to specify that columns which do not exist in the base table be returned with your data. You can do this with a literal:

```
SELECT CUST_SOC_SEC, 'IS SOCIAL SECURITY FOR',
       CUST_NAME
   FROM CUSTOMER
```

RESULT TABLE:

CUST_SOC_SEC		CUST_NAME
111111111	IS SOCIAL SECURITY FOR	PHYLLIS ELKIND
222222222	IS SOCIAL SECURITY FOR	JAY RANADE
333333333	IS SOCIAL SECURITY FOR	RICHARD GREEN
444444444	IS SOCIAL SECURITY FOR	------------------
555555555	IS SOCIAL SECURITY FOR	HEIDI SCHMIDT
666666666	IS SOCIAL SECURITY FOR	MUKESH SEHGAL
777777777	IS SOCIAL SECURITY FOR	IAI-HA NG
888888888	IS SOCIAL SECURITY FOR	GEORGE SCHMIDT

There is no heading on the column that is returned in the result table because the literal is not a column in the CUSTOMER table. Literals in the SELECT can be used to explain output or to identify the source of data in complex queries. We will use this second technique in the next chapter.

4.2.2 DISTINCT

The keyword DISTINCT may be used in the SELECT clause to eliminate what would be duplicate rows. It acts upon the intermediate result set so that when you get your result table, each row is unique. Although DISTINCT may only be specified in the SELECT clause, unlike the other options discussed so far, it affects the rows that are returned, not the columns. The default is its opposite, ALL, which returns *all* rows, including duplicates. Compare the following two statements and their results:

```
SELECT TXN_TYPE
   FROM TRANSACTION

RESULT TABLE:

  TXN_TYPE
  --------+
  CREDIT
  CREDIT
  OPENACCT
  CREDIT
  DEBIT
  CREDIT
  DEBIT

SELECT DISTINCT TXN_TYPE
   FROM TRANSACTION

RESULT TABLE:

  TXN_TYPE
  ---------
  CREDIT
  DEBIT
  OPENACCT
```

You can see that the result of the second statement differs from that of the first in that DB2 has eliminated the duplicate rows.

4.3 THE WHERE CLAUSE

Just as the SELECT clause specifies the columns to be returned in the result table, *the WHERE clause determines the rows to be returned.*

This clause contains a search condition which must be satisfied by each row returned in the result table. Those rows that qualify form an intermediate set which is then processed further according to the specifications in the SELECT clause. Comparison operators and the operators AND, OR, BETWEEN, IN, and LIKE may only be used on the WHERE clause and, with some differences, on the HAVING clause, which is described later in this chapter. Let's begin with comparison operators.

4.3.1 Comparison Operators

The search condition in the WHERE clause contains one or more predicates which specify a comparison between two values. It is quite common for a column's value to be compared to a fixed value (constant) as in the following:

```
SELECT CUST_SOC_SEC
   FROM CUSTOMER
   WHERE CUST_BRANCH = 890

RESULT TABLE:

CUST_SOC_SEC
----------+--
   222222222
   555555555
```

This SELECT causes each row in the CUSTOMER table to be evaluated to determine if the value of the CUST_BRANCH column in that row is equal to the value 890. If it is, the row is selected and the column specified in the SELECT clause is returned to the result table. In addition to constants, either side of a comparison may be a column value, an expression (you will see this later in this chapter), or a variable field in a program, called a host variable in DB2.

The two sides of a comparison must be of compatible data types. CUST_BRANCH is defined as a numeric field; therefore it may only be compared with a numeric constant, a numeric column value, etc. Numeric constants, we have said, are notated without quotes. When a comparison takes place, the algebraic values of numbers are compared whereas character strings are compared on a character by character basis with the EBCDIC value determining the collating sequence.

In the above SQL statement, CUST_BRANCH = 890 is the predicate. The comparison operator is = . DB2 supports the following comparison operators:

Operator	Meaning
=	equal
⌐ = or < >	not equal
>	greater than
⌐ > or < =	not greater than
<	less than
⌐ < or > =	not less than

If there are no rows that satisfy the condition specified in the WHERE clause, no rows are returned. For example:

```
SELECT CUST_SOC_SEC
   FROM CUSTOMER
   WHERE CUST_BRANCH = 100
```

RESULT TABLE:

```
CUST_SOC_SEC
--------+---
```

Since our table has no branches identified as 100, SPUFI returns the heading with no rows beneath it.

4.3.2   AND, OR

A WHERE clause may contain several predicates connected by the Boolean operators AND and OR. AND specifies that the clauses on either side of the AND must both be true. Using OR indicates that either of the two clauses must be true. Let's look at how this works.

```
SELECT CUST_NAME
   FROM CUSTOMER
   WHERE CUST_BRANCH = 890
      AND CUST_RATING > 2
```

RESULT TABLE:

```
CUST_NAME
---------+--------
JAY RANADE
```

In the above statement, only rows which satisfy *both* the condition that CUST_BRANCH equals 890 *and* the condition that CUST_RATING is greater than 2 are selected. Since we've only asked for CUST_NAME in the SELECT clause, you can see that only that one column is returned.

If you want to find the rows that satisfy *either* condition you would code:

```
SELECT CUST_NAME
   FROM CUSTOMER
   WHERE CUST_BRANCH = 890
      OR CUST_RATING > 2
```

RESULT TABLE:

```
CUST_NAME
---------+-------
PHYLLIS ELKIND
JAY RANADE
RICHARD GREEN
------------------
HEIDI SCHMIDT
MUKESH SEHGAL
LAI-HA NG
```

This results in a table that contains all of the rows with a value of 890 in CUST_BRANCH as well as all of the rows where CUST_RATING > 2. If either condition is true, the row is selected and returned. Notice that one of the rows returned is null for CUST_NAME. SPUFI shows this with dashes.

4.3.3 BETWEEN, IN

BETWEEN is an operator that's probably new to you. It is used in a WHERE clause to specify a condition that is satisfied if a value is equal to or between two other values:

```
SELECT CUST_NAME, CUST_RATING
   FROM CUSTOMER
   WHERE CUST_RATING BETWEEN 1 AND 5
```

RESULT TABLE:

```
CUST_NAME           CUST_RATING
---------+----------+----------+-
PHYLLIS ELKIND            4
HEIDI SCHMIDT             2
MUKESH SEHGAL             5
GEORGE SCHMIDT            2
```

For a row to pass this selection criteria, the value in its CUST_RATING column must be greater than or equal to 1 and less than or equal to 5. You can see that in this example a CUST_RATING of 5 is returned as well as the values that are between 1 and 5. The same result would be generated with the following statement:

```
SELECT CUST_NAME, CUST_RATING
  FROM CUSTOMER
  WHERE CUST_RATING >= 1
    AND CUST_RATING <= 5
```

RESULT TABLE:

CUST_NAME	CUST_RATING
PHYLLIS ELKIND	4
HEIDI SCHMIDT	2
MUKESH SEHGAL	5
GEORGE SCHMIDT	2

Notice that if you use this longer format, you must repeat the column name in each comparison. You may not say WHERE CUST_RATING > = 1 AND < = 5.

DB2 checks for greater than or equal to the first boundary and less than or equal to the second boundary, so when using the BETWEEN keyword, specify the lower boundary first. If you specify the upper boundary first, DB2 will not give you an error message, but you will not get any results.

Similar to the BETWEEN keyword, IN is a form of shorthand for one or more ORs. Consider the following selection condition:

```
WHERE CUST_BRANCH = 012
  OR CUST_BRANCH = 890
  OR CUST_BRANCH = 670
```

The same column is used in all three comparisons, so DB2 allows you to express the same statement in a briefer and more easily understood WHERE clause using IN:

```
WHERE CUST_BRANCH IN (012, 890, 670)
```

The parentheses are required. This can be read as "Where CUST_BRANCH is equal to one of the items in the list (012, 890, 670)."

4.3.4 LIKE

Comparisons in the WHERE clause can be made more generic using the keyword LIKE. *LIKE allows you to compare similar values through the use of wild card characters.* A percent sign (%) is the wild card for any string of zero or more characters. An underscore (_) is the wild card for any single character. Look at the following example:

```
SELECT ACCT_CUST_ID, ACCT_NO
   FROM ACCOUNT
   WHERE ACCT_NO LIKE 'AE%'
```

RESULT TABLE:

```
ACCT_CUST_ID  ACCT_NO
---------+----------+-
   111111111  AE11
   555555555  AE12
   888888888  AE21
```

In this example, a row passes the selection criteria if the value in that row's ACCT_NO column begins with the characters AE. The percent sign indicates that any number of other characters, including none, may follow the AE and that we don't care what they are.

The underscore (_) is used in a similar way but indicates *one character only*:

```
SELECT ACCT_CUST_ID, ACCT_NO
   FROM ACCOUNT
   WHERE ACCT_NO LIKE '_B%'
```

RESULT TABLE:

```
ACCT_CUST_ID  ACCT_NO
---------+----------+-
   444444444  AB21
   222222222  BB12
   666666666  BB13
   555555555  DB11
```

Here, we don't care what the first character of ACCT_NO's value is, but the second character must be a B, followed by zero to more other characters.

LIKE may only be used to compare character data. When using it, be sure to account for trailing blanks because DB2 pads fixed-length character strings with blanks. A column X, defined as CHAR(4), containing the value AB actually contains two blanks after the AB. The condition WHERE X = _B is comparing a 2-byte string, _B, to the 4-byte string AB,blank,blank. DB2 does not consider these to be equivalent. Fields that are defined as variable in length, VARCHAR, are not padded with blanks, so AB,blank,blank would actually be stored as AB and would, therefore, be selected using the same WHERE condition.

4.3.5 Negative Conditions

Negative search conditions may be specified in the WHERE clause with NOT or ¬. There are, however, some idiosyncracies to be aware of. The keyword NOT is used differently from the not symbol (¬) when using comparison operators. The keyword NOT must precede the entire search condition:

```
WHERE NOT BRANCH_ID = 890
```

while the not symbol (¬) precedes the comparison operator:

```
WHERE BRANCH ¬ = 890
```

The distinction between NOT and ¬ is strictly syntactical; the processing is identical.

However, to indicate a negative condition in comparisons using IN, BETWEEN, or LIKE, you must use the keyword NOT rather than the symbol ¬, but you may put the keyword in either position:

```
WHERE NOT CUST_BRANCH IN (012, 890, 670)
WHERE CUST_BRANCH NOT IN (012, 890, 670)
```

Either of these formats is acceptable and they will be evaluated identically.

4.3.6 Parentheses and Precedence

As in any other language, when you create a complicated command, you must be careful that the condition you specify is interpreted by the system as you intended it to be. For example:

```
SELECT ACCT_NO, ACCT_BALANCE, ACCT_CREDIT_BAL
   FROM ACCOUNT
   WHERE ACCT_BALANCE < 1000
     AND ACCT_CREDIT_BAL < 500
     OR ACCT_NO LIKE '_E%'
```

Which rows will be returned from this statement? Does DB2 interpret this to mean:

ACCT_BALANCE < 1000

AND

ACCT_CREDIT_BAL < 500 OR
ACCT_NO LIKE '_E%'

Or does DB2 think it means:

ACCT_BALANCE < 1000 AND
ACCT_CREDIT BAL < 500

OR

ACCT_NO LIKE '_E%'

The answer is the latter interpretation. DB2 evaluates Boolean operators in this order: NOT, AND, OR. Therefore, DB2 applies the AND before the OR as in the second example. The set of rows for which this example is true are:

RESULT TABLE:

ACCT_NO	ACCT_BALANCE	ACCT_CREDIT_BAL
AE11	12000.94	500.00
AE12	500.00	500.00
AE21	77.53	2000.00
AB21	.00	180.55
BB13	646.01	25.00
CE21	35100.98	100.00
DE11	20.00	25.00
DB11	75.00	.00

If, however, your intention was to find the accounts which satisfied the criteria in the first example, you need to use parentheses in your statement. DB2 evaluates statements within parentheses before the Boolean operators. To achieve this interpretation, the new statement and its result would be:

```
SELECT ACCT_NO, ACCT_BALANCE, ACCT_CREDIT_BAL
   FROM ACCOUNT
   WHERE ACCT_BALANCE < 1000
      AND (ACCT_CREDIT_BAL < 500
      OR ACCT_NO LIKE '_E%')
```

RESULT TABLE:

ACCT_NO	ACCT_BALANCE	ACCT_CREDIT_BAL
AE12	500.00	500.00
AE21	77.53	2000.00
AB21	.00	180.55
BB13	646.01	25.00
DE11	20.00	25.00
DB11	75.00	.00

You can see that the result is a completely different set of accounts.

4.4   COLUMN FUNCTIONS AND GROUPS

SQL provides you with a number of built-in functions to simplify or automate some types of processing. Built-in functions are classified as either column or scalar functions. You will find a discussion of scalar functions in Sec. 4.6.

Column functions are used in the SELECT clause but they differ from the SELECT clause options we have seen so far in that they return a single value to the result table rather than a series of rows or columns. They operate on the entire column to produce one value in the result table. If the SELECT statement contains a WHERE clause, the column function is applied to only those rows that meet the conditions of the clause and have been included in the intermediate result set.

4.4.1 SUM, AVG, MIN, MAX, COUNT

The following table summarizes the column functions that are available, what they do, and any restrictions on their use:

Function	Description	Restrictions
SUM	Sum of values in column	Numeric data only
AVG	Average of values in column	Numeric data only
MIN	Minimum value within column	
MAX	Maximum value within column	
COUNT	Counts the number of rows	

Suppose you want to know the average account balance, the maximum account balance, and the total number of rows for the accounts with a credit balance under 500 dollars. You can combine the column functions in a single statement and say:

```
SELECT AVG(ACCT_BALANCE), MAX(ACCT_BALANCE), COUNT(*)
   FROM ACCOUNT
   WHERE ACCT_CREDIT_BAL < 500
```

RESULT TABLE:

```
--------+---------+---------+---------+-----
  7168.398000      35100.98          5
```

The result table shows that five of the nine rows in the ACCOUNT table satisfy the condition in the WHERE clause. For those five rows, the average account balance and the maximum account balance are determined, as is the number of rows (COUNT) in this intermediate result set. Unlike the other column functions, the argument of COUNT is an asterisk. It is counting the rows, rather than operating on any particular column. Because the arguments of AVG and MAX are decimal in this example, the results are decimal. If the argument was an integer, the result would be an integer and any fractional part of the average would be lost.

Notice that the columns generated by a column function do not have headings in the result table because they are not existing columns in the base table. They are displayed in the order requested in the SELECT clause.

When you apply a column function to one column in a SELECT clause, it results in a single row, therefore, you may not also SELECT on a condition that will result in many rows. The following is not possible:

```
SELECT AVG(ACCT_BALANCE), ACCT_CUST_ID
    FROM ACCOUNT
```

This SELECT clause contains both a column function, AVG(ACCT_BALANCE), and a column name, ACCT_CUST_ID. It is asking for one value in one row, the average account balance, and for one value in many rows, all customer IDs. This is not allowed in DB2 because the result of the query would not be a table.

You may want to combine the keyword DISTINCT with column functions. This will cause DB2 to eliminate duplicate values before passing the set of values to the column function. Note the difference in results between the following two statements:

```
SELECT SUM(ACCT_CREDIT_BAL)
    FROM ACCOUNT
```

RESULT TABLE:

```
---------+-------
    6630.55
```

```
SELECT SUM(DISTINCT ACCT_CREDIT_BAL)
    FROM ACCOUNT
```

RESULT TABLE:

```
---------+-------
    6105.55
```

As you can see, DISTINCT must be placed within the parentheses. The values of ACCT_CREDIT_BAL in the ACCOUNT table are:

```
 500.00
 500.00
2000.00
 180.55
3300.00
  25.00
 100.00
  25.00
    .00
```

The sum of all of these values is the value returned by the first statement, 6630.55.

The second statement generates a table of the values of ACCT_CREDIT_BAL with duplicate values eliminated:

```
    .00
  25.00
 100.00
 180.55
 500.00
2000.00
3300.00
```

The sum of these values is the value returned by the second statement.

We've described the COUNT(*) function, which counts all of the rows. But suppose you were interested in the total number of DISTINCT values in the column of a table. For this you can use COUNT(DISTINCT *columnname*). DISTINCT cannot be used with COUNT(*); it can only be used when the argument of COUNT is a column name. Here is an example which answers the question, How many different credit balances are there in our ACCOUNT table?

```
SELECT COUNT(DISTINCT ACCT_CREDIT_BAL)
   FROM ACCOUNT

RESULT TABLE:

   ---------+-
            7
```

All of the rows from the ACCOUNT table are considered, but the rows with duplicate information in the ACCT_CREDIT_BAL column are eliminated and the number of remaining rows is then counted.

DISTINCT may be used with MIN and MAX to find the smallest or largest value within the column, but it makes no sense since it will not affect the result. The MIN or MAX of a column remains the same no matter how many duplicate values appear in the column.

4.4.2   GROUP BY

Column functions return a result based on all of the rows in the intermediate result set. It is also possible to group rows based on some criteria and return a result for each group within the intermediate result set. This is done with the GROUP BY clause.

GROUP BY is an optional clause in the SELECT statement that causes the rows in the intermediate result set to be grouped according to the values in the column(s) specified in the GROUP BY clause. It follows the WHERE clause, if there is one, and is most commonly used when the SELECT clause contains one or more column functions. Let's look at an example to make this a little clearer:

```
SELECT MAX(CUST_RATING)
   FROM CUSTOMER
```

RESULT TABLE:

```
------
   9
```

```
SELECT MAX(CUST_RATING)
   FROM CUSTOMER
   GROUP BY CUST_BRANCH
```

RESULT TABLE:

```
------
   7
   5
   7
   9
   8
```

The result of the first statement is that all of the rows in the CUSTOMER table are evaluated together to determine the highest CUST_RATING. In the second statement, all of the rows of the table are first grouped according to the values in the CUST_BRANCH column. The highest CUST_RATING for each group (CUST_BRANCH) is then determined. This results in as many MAX CUST_RATINGs as there are distinct values in CUST_BRANCH.

If we could see the intermediate grouping, it would look like this:

INTERMEDIATE RESULT:

111111111	PHYLLIS ELKIND	1962-03-29	12	4
333333333	RICHARD GREEN	1947-08-15	12	7
888888888	GEORGE SCHMIDT	1950-07-04	12	2
666666666	MUKESH SEHGAL	1957-10-24	300	5
777777777	LAI-HA NG	1970-01-01	450	7
444444444	------------------	1965-12-25	670	9
222222222	JAY RANADE	1960-09-21	890	8
555555555	HEIDI SCHMIDT	1942-06-04	890	2

The highest CUST_RATING is then found for each group, giving us the five rows we see in the result table.

The result table would be more meaningful if we knew the CUST_BRANCH value for each MAX value. This can be done by specifying CUST_BRANCH in the SELECT clause in addition to the column function. If a column name (e.g., CUST_BRANCH) appears in the GROUP BY clause, it may be used along with the column function(s) in the SELECT clause. When we add the column to the SELECT clause, the new statement and its result table look like this:

```
SELECT CUST_BRANCH, MAX(CUST_RATING)
    FROM CUSTOMER
    GROUP BY CUST_BRANCH
```

RESULT TABLE:

```
CUST_BRANCH
----------+---------
      12    7
     300    5
     450    7
     670    9
     890    8
```

You may specify more than one column in the GROUP BY clause. However, the SELECT clause may only contain columns which are the argument of a column function or are named in the GROUP BY clause. GROUP BY is the only exception to the rule which says that column function and simple columns may not be combined in a SELECT clause.

4.4.3 HAVING

HAVING specifies a condition which each group of rows must satisfy in order to be passed to the column function. It follows the GROUP BY clause and is optional. HAVING is to groups as WHERE is to rows.

The syntax for a HAVING clause is very much like that of the WHERE clause with one major difference: column functions may be used in the HAVING clause but not in the WHERE clause. We will modify our GROUP BY example to illustrate the use of HAVING:

```
SELECT CUST_BRANCH, MAX(CUST_RATING)
  FROM CUSTOMER
  GROUP BY CUST_BRANCH
  HAVING COUNT(*) >= 2
```

RESULT TABLE:

```
CUST_BRANCH
---------+---------
      12      7
     890      8
```

To understand how DB2 derived the result table, look again at our representation of the intermediate result:

INTERMEDIATE RESULT:

					CUST_BRANCH	
111111111	PHYLLIS ELKIND	1962-03-29			12	4
333333333	RICHARD GREEN	1947-08-15			12	7
888888888	GEORGE SCHMIDT	1950-07-04			12	2
666666666	MUKESH SEHGAL	1957-10-24			300	5
777777777	LAI-HA NG	1970-01-01			450	7
444444444	------------------	1965-12-25			670	9
222222222	JAY RANADE	1960-09-21			890	8
555555555	HEIDI SCHMIDT	1942-06-04			890	2

The rows in the CUSTOMER table are grouped by the value in the CUST_BRANCH column. Three rows are in branch 12, one row is in branch 300, one in branch 450, one in branch 670, and two in branch 890. By including the HAVING clause, we are asking that the MAX customer rating be returned for each group which has two or more rows in it. Only branches 12 and 890 satisfy this condition. The result table, therefore, contains the maximum rating for only those two branches.

4.5 ARITHMETIC OPERATIONS

In the SQL statements we have looked at so far, we have seen column names, constants, and functions used to express values. Values may also be derived from arithmetic operations. Arithmetic operations may be associated with both the SELECT and WHERE clause and can only be performed on numeric data types.

4.5.1 +, − , *, /

SQL's arithmetic operators are:

Operator	Meaning
+	Addition
−	Subtraction
*	Multiplication
/	Division

In complex expressions, as in most programming languages, expressions in parentheses are evaluated first beginning with the innermost pair if they're nested; multiplication and division are evaluated before addition and subtraction. The column that is generated takes its data type from the operands in the expression. When there are mixed operands, the order of precedence is decimal, integer, small integer.

4.5.2 In the SELECT Clause

Arithmetic operators in the SELECT clause enable you to display not only data stored in your table but also information derived from that ⁓data. They may be used alone in a SELECT clause or in combination with column names, as in the following example:

```
SELECT ACCT_NO, ACCT_BALANCE + ACCT_CREDIT_BAL
  FROM ACCOUNT

RESULT TABLE:

ACCT_NO
----------+----------+---
AE11          12500.94
AE12           1000.00
AE21           2077.53
AB21            180.55
BB12          15301.35
BB13            671.01
CE21          35200.98
DE11             45.00
DB11             75.00
```

This query shows us the total balance for each account (regular balance plus credit balance). As you saw with other derived columns, there is no heading for the calculated column in the result table.

Arithmetic expressions may be used in the SELECT clause with column functions:

```
SELECT MAX(ACCT_BALANCE) - AVG(ACCT_BALANCE)
FROM ACCOUNT
```

RESULT TABLE:

```
-----------+--------
  28387.445556
```

This statement gives you the difference between the largest account balance and the average account balance by first determining the maximum balance and the average balance and then calculating the difference and returning that figure to the result table.

4.5.3 In the WHERE Clause

Arithmetic expressions may also be included in the search condition of a WHERE clause:

```
SELECT ACCT_NO, ACCT_CUST_ID,
       ACCT_BALANCE + ACCT_CREDIT_BAL
  FROM ACCOUNT
 WHERE ACCT_BALANCE + ACCT_CREDIT_BAL > 2000
```

RESULT TABLE:

```
ACCT_NO   ACCT_CUST_ID
-----------+-----------+---------+-------
AE11      111111111        12500.94
AE21      888888888         2077.53
BB12      222222222        15301.35
CE21      333333333        35200.98
```

To be passed to the intermediate result set, a row in the account table must satisfy the condition that the sum of its regular balance plus the credit balance is greater than 2000.

4.6 SCALAR FUNCTIONS AND CONCATENATION

In addition to the column functions we've been talking about throughout this chapter, SQL provides a second category of built-in functions called scalar functions. Like a column function, a scalar function produces a single value as a result. The difference between them lies in the arguments they accept. The argument of a column function is all of the values in a column for multiple rows, while the argument of a scalar function is one column value in a single row. Also, unlike column functions, which can be used only in a SELECT or HAVING clause, scalar functions can be used in a WHERE clause as well.

A scalar function operates on one row at a time, producing one result for each row that is passed to it. Thus, scalar functions, unlike column functions, may be specified in a SELECT clause along with simple column names.

4.6.1 SUBSTR, LENGTH

SUBSTR enables you to extract a subset of a string of characters. For instance, to see only the first two characters in the column ACCT_NO, you would say:

```
SELECT SUBSTR(ACCT_NO,1,2), ACCT_CUST_ID
    FROM ACCOUNT
```

RESULT TABLE:

	ACCT_CUST_ID
AE	111111111
AE	555555555
AE	888888888
AB	444444444
BB	222222222
BB	666666666
CE	333333333
DE	777777777
DB	555555555

The first argument within the parentheses (ACCT_NO) names the column that will be operated on and must be defined as a character data type. The second argument (1) specifies where in the original string you want to begin the substring (the first character), and the third argument (2) specifies the length of the substring to be extracted. Thus, in the result table from this sample we see only the first two characters of the account number.

Here is an example of SUBSTR in a WHERE clause:

```
SELECT ACCT_NO, ACCT_CUST_ID
FROM ACCOUNT
WHERE SUBSTR(ACCT_NO,2,1) = 'E'
```

RESULT TABLE:

```
ACCT_NO  ACCT_CUST_ID
---------+----------+-
AE11        111111111
AE12        555555555
AE21        888888888
CE21        333333333
DE11        777777777
```

This statement gets the account number and customer ID for each account whose account number has an E in the second position. The argument of the SUBSTR function here specifies that the substring beginning at the second byte of ACCT_NO, extending for 1 byte, be extracted.

The same result is obtained with the statement:

```
SELECT ACCT_NO, ACCT_CUST_ID
FROM ACCOUNT
WHERE ACCT_NO LIKE '_E%'
```

RESULT TABLE:

```
ACCT_NO  ACCT_CUST_ID
---------+----------+-
AE11        111111111
AE12        555555555
AE21        888888888
CE21        333333333
DE11        777777777
```

Here the predicate uses LIKE to find accounts whose account numbers have any character in the first position, E in the second position, and any character(s) following the E.

The LENGTH function is used to find the length of a value of any data type. For character data it returns the length of the string, including blanks. For a variable-length string it returns the actual length rather than the maximum length. For other data types the length returned will be:

Data type	Length returned
Small integer	2
Large integer	4
Decimal numbers with precision p	p / 2 (any remainder is truncated) + 1
DATE	4
TIME	3
TIMESTAMP	10

4.6.2 Conversion

SQL facilitates data conversion with the scalar functions DECIMAL, INTEGER, DIGITS, HEX, FLOAT, and VARGRAPHIC. FLOAT and VARGRAPHIC are used infrequently and will not be discussed here.

DECIMAL is used to convert any number to a decimal representation with a specified precision. The first argument specifies a numeric column or expression. The second and third arguments specify the total number of digits for the result and the number of digits to the right of the decimal point. Imagine a table containing a SALARY_PER_YEAR column which is defined as integer. To see semiannual incomes, the following statement could be used:

```
SELECT DECIMAL(SALARY_PER_YEAR/2,6,2)
   FROM IMAGINARY_TABLE
```

The first argument is the value in the salary column divided by 2; notice that you can use arithmetic expressions in column functions. The second argument says the total length of the result should be six digits, including the digits to the right of the decimal point, and the third says there should be two digits to the right of the decimal point. The results might look like this:

```
9003.45
 850.00
1900.30
```

INTEGER works similarly to DECIMAL, converting any number to an integer. Any digits to the right of the decimal point are truncated; no rounding takes place:

```
SELECT INTEGER(AVG(ACCT_BALANCE))
    FROM ACCOUNT
```

RESULT TABLE:

```
----------+-
      6713
```

This returns the average of all account balances as a whole number. The decimal portion is chopped off. Since INTEGER truncates decimals, to obtain a rounded number you must add 0.5:

```
SELECT INTEGER(ACCT_BALANCE + 0.5)
    FROM ACCOUNT
```

RESULT TABLE:

```
----------+-
     12001
       500
        78
         0
     12001
       646
     35101
        20
        75
```

This statement returns the account balance rounded up to the nearest whole number.

The DIGITS function converts numeric values to characters. The leading zeroes are included; the sign and the decimal point are not. DIGITS can be used to convert numeric data so that it can be used in functions that require character data. For example:

```
SELECT CUST_BRANCH, DIGITS(CUST_BRANCH)
    FROM CUSTOMER
    WHERE SUBSTR(DIGITS(CUST_BRANCH),5,1) = '0'
```

RESULT TABLE:

```
CUST_BRANCH
----------+---------
       890  00890
       670  00670
       890  00890
       300  00300
       450  00450
```

In this example, we want to select all branches whose branch number ends with zero. The CUST_BRANCH column has a data type of integer. Applying the DIGITS function to CUST_BRANCH makes it possible to use the SUBSTR function, which expects character data. Notice that DIGITS translates a small integer value to five characters. As with the other scalar functions, DIGITS may be used in both the SELECT and WHERE clauses.

The scalar function HEX, as you might expect, returns a result in hexadecimal format. Numeric and character data are both acceptable arguments of the function. In the following example, we show how you can apply this function to both a column defined as integer (ACCT_CUST_ID) and a column defined as character (ACCT_NO):

```
SELECT ACCT_CUST_ID, HEX(ACCT_CUST_ID), ACCT_NO,
       HEX(ACCT_NO)
  FROM ACCOUNT
```

RESULT TABLE:

ACCT_CUST_ID		ACCT_NO	
111111111	069F6BC7	AE11	C1C5F1F1
555555555	211D1AE3	AE12	C1C5F1F2
888888888	34FB5E38	AE21	C1C5F2F1
444444444	1A7DAF1C	AB21	C1C2F2F1
222222222	0D3ED78E	BB12	C2C2F1F2
666666666	27BC86AA	BB13	C2C2F1F3
333333333	13DE4355	CE21	C3C5F2F1
777777777	2E5BF271	DE11	C4C5F1F1
555555555	211D1AE3	DB11	C4C2F1F1

In each row you first see the customer ID and its hex counterpart, then the account number and its counterpart.

4.6.3 Concatenation

The concatenation operator (||) allows you to combine character values into one string. You can use this to create a new value from two or more existing values. This might be useful as a formatting tool on a report:

```
SELECT BRANCH_ADDR || ', ' || BRANCH_CITY
  FROM BRANCH
```

RESULT TABLE:

```
--------+---------+-------
43 WEST 57 STREET, NEW YORK
7 MORANI STREET, YONKERS
351 TEAL PLAZA, ROCHESTER
900 WALL STREET, NEW YORK
610 OSIO LANE, YONKERS
ONE FEDERAL PLAZA, CORNING
```

For each row in the BRANCH table, DB2 takes the values in the address column, appends a comma and a blank, and then appends the value in the city column. You could also use this in combination with the SUBSTR function to create a value from parts of two existing values.

4.7   ORDERING THE RESULT

The sequence in which the rows of the results table are presented can be specified by using the ORDER BY clause. You'll remember that rows are returned in the order in which they are stored physically. While they may start out in some order, update activity is sure to change it. If you don't use ORDER BY, there is no way, in DB2, to guarantee the order of the rows returned by a query.

4.7.1   ORDER BY Column Name

When it is used, ORDER BY is the last clause in the SELECT statement. The rows of the result table are returned in the order of the column name specified. The default is ascending order. In the following example, the rows will be returned in CUST_BRANCH sequence beginning with the lowest branch number:

```
SELECT CUST_BRANCH, CUST_NAME,
       CUST_DATE_OF_BIRTH
  FROM CUSTOMER
  ORDER BY CUST_BRANCH
```

RESULT TABLE:

CUST_BRANCH	CUST_NAME	CUST_DATE_OF_BIRTH
12	PHYLLIS ELKIND	1962-03-29
12	RICHARD GREEN	1947-08-15
12	GEORGE SCHMIDT	1950-07-04
300	MUKESH SEHGAL	1957-10-24
450	LAI-HA NG	1970-01-01
670	-----------------	1965-12-25
890	JAY RANADE	1960-09-21
890	HEIDI SCHMIDT	1942-06-04

There's no doubt that there will be times when you want to sort by more than one key. You may list more than one sort key in the ORDER BY clause. For example, we can modify our last statement as follows:

```
SELECT CUST_BRANCH, CUST_NAME,
       CUST_DATE_OF_BIRTH
  FROM CUSTOMER
 ORDER BY CUST_BRANCH, CUST_DATE_OF_BIRTH DESC
```

RESULT TABLE:

```
CUST_BRANCH  CUST_NAME            CUST_DATE_OF_BIRTH
---------+---------+---------+---------+---------+-
        12  PHYLLIS ELKIND       1962-03-29
        12  GEORGE SCHMIDT       1950-07-04
        12  RICHARD GREEN        1947-08-15
       300  MUKESH SEHGAL        1957-10-24
       450  LAI-HA NG            1970-01-01
       670  ------------------   1965-12-25
       890  JAY RANADE           1960-09-21
       890  HEIDI SCHMIDT        1942-06-04
```

The rows are first placed in order by CUST_BRANCH. If there is more than one row for a particular branch, the rows for that branch are then subordered by CUST_DATE_OF_BIRTH. DESC is used to indicate that the order for CUST_DATE_OF_BIRTH is descending, meaning that the most recent birthdate is listed first. ASC (ascending) or DESC (descending) may follow each sort key, indicating which order that particular sort sequence should take.

The only restriction on ORDER BY is that all columns named in the ORDER BY clause must also be named in that statement's SELECT clause. This is required because DB2 satisfies an order by clause by sorting the intermediate result set. The column(s) that DB2 must sort by will only be present in the intermediate result if you have included them in the SELECT clause. The following would be illegal:

```
SELECT CUST_RATING
  FROM CUSTOMER
 WHERE CUST_BRANCH > 100
 ORDER BY CUST_BRANCH
```

ERROR MESSAGE:
-208 THE ORDER BY CLAUSE IS INVALID BECAUSE COLUMN CUST_
BRANCH IS NOT PART OF THE RESULT TABLE

Here we see the SQL error code (− 208) and the accompanying error message.

4.7.2   ORDER BY Column Number

We have seen that information in a result table may be derived from the data in existing columns. Recall the following example:

```
SELECT ACCT_NO, ACCT_BALANCE + ACCT_CREDIT_BAL
   FROM ACCOUNT
```

RESULT TABLE:

```
ACCT_NO
---------+----------+---
AE11           12500.94
AE12            1000.00
AE21            2077.53
AB21             180.55
BB12           15301.35
BB13             671.01
CE21           35200.98
DE11              45.00
DB11              75.00
```

The second column in this result table is derived information, since it has no heading in the result table. You may want to sequence the rows of the result table by this derived column. This can be done by specifying the position of the column in the SELECT statement. Let's say we wanted a table returned to us in ascending account balance order. It is the second column named in the SELECT statement, so we would request:

```
SELECT ACCT_NO, ACCT_BALANCE + ACCT_CREDIT_BAL
   FROM ACCOUNT
   ORDER BY 2
```

RESULT TABLE:

```
ACCT_NO
---------+----------+---
DE11              45.00
DB11              75.00
AB21             180.55
BB13             671.01
AE12            1000.00
AE21            2077.53
AE11           12500.94
BB12           15301.35
CE21           35200.98
```

In fact, any column in the SELECT may be referred to by position rather than name in the ORDER BY clause. This is convenient when column names are long.

4.8   NULL CONSIDERATIONS

We have said that nulls can be used to represent missing information. In our sample tables, the following columns are defined to allow nulls: BRANCH_MGR in the BRANCH table, CUST_NAME in the

CUSTOMER table, ACCT_CREDIT_BAL in the ACCOUNT table, and TXN_AMOUNT in the TRANSACTION table. A branch doesn't have to have a manager; a customer may open an account without specifying a name; an account doesn't have to have a credit line attached to it; and some transactions may not have a dollar amount associated with them.

Let's take one of these, ACCT_CREDIT_BAL, and see why null might be used in place of a value. Suppose an account had no credit line account and therefore no credit line balance. Putting zeroes in this account's credit balance to indicate no credit line may confuse this account with one which has a credit line but has a balance of zero. Null is a more accurate way to differentiate between no applicable value and a value that happens to be $0.00. Unfortunately, the following, somewhat confusing, set of rules must be taken into account when using columns which may contain null values.

4.8.1 Comparisons, Arithmetic, ORDER BY, Column Functions

Comparisons appear in WHERE or HAVING clauses. When one of the operands is null, every comparison will always evaluate to false. For example:

```
SELECT TXN_TYPE
   FROM TRANSACTION
   WHERE TXN_AMOUNT ¬ = 1200

RESULT TABLE:

   TXN_TYPE
   ---------
   CREDIT
   CREDIT
   DEBIT
   CREDIT
   DEBIT
```

This query selects transaction types in the rows whose transaction amount is not equal to 1200. Only five rows are returned. The row in which the TXN_AMOUNT column contains nulls has not satisfied the conditional predicate.

Special syntax is used to formulate a comparison when you are to specifically include or exclude null values:

```
SELECT TXN_TYPE, TXN_AMOUNT
FROM TRANSACTION
WHERE TXN_AMOUNT IS NULL
```

RESULT TABLE:

```
TXN_TYPE     TXN_AMOUNT
---------+----------+---
OPENACCT    -------------
```

Only those rows in which the contents of TXN_AMOUNT is null satisfy the condition. The condition may also be formulated *"columnname* IS NOT NULL" to signify all rows that do not contain a NULL value. Arithmetic operations may be performed on columns that can contain nulls, but if the column value is null, the result will always be null.

When DB2 performs a sort, as it does with ORDER BY, nulls are considered highest in the sort sequence so that if you sort in ascending order, they will be at the end of the list:

```
SELECT CUST_NAME
FROM CUSTOMER
ORDER BY 1
```

RESULT TABLE:

```
CUST_NAME
---------+-------
GEORGE SCHMIDT
HEIDI SCHMIDT
JAY RANADE
LAI-HA NG
MUKESH SEHGAL
PHYLLIS ELKIND
RICHARD GREEN
-------------
```

The row in the CUSTOMER table in which the CUST_NAME column is null is listed last.

The last consideration in this list of null restrictions concerns column functions. Other than COUNT(*), all column functions ignore nulls:

```
SELECT TXN_AMOUNT
FROM TRANSACTION
```

RESULT TABLE:

```
TXN_AMOUNT
---------+---
    200.50
   1200.00
-------------
     50.75
    100.00
   2000.00
   1200.55
```

```
SELECT MAX(TXN_AMOUNT), MIN(TXN_AMOUNT)
   FROM TRANSACTION
```

RESULT TABLE:

```
---------+---------+--------
    2000.00         50.75
```

The first statement shows us the values of TXN_AMOUNT in the TRANSACTION table. The second statement shows that the null values in TXN_AMOUNT are not considered in the column function.

4.8.2 VALUE

The VALUE function is helpful when handling nulls. It allows you to get around some of the restrictions we've just discussed. Two or more arguments (of compatible data types) are specified in parentheses. The result of the VALUE function on these arguments will be the first argument in the list that is a non-null value. When a null value is found, it is replaced with the second argument. An example will help show this function's usefulness:

```
SELECT VALUE(CUST_NAME, 'UNKNOWN')
   FROM CUSTOMER
```

RESULT TABLE:

```
---------+-------
PHYLLIS ELKIND
JAY RANADE
RICHARD GREEN
UNKNOWN
HEIDI SCHMIDT
MUKESH SEHGAL
LAI-HA NG
GEORGE SCHMIDT
```

The first argument is CUST_NAME. If there is a non-null value in that column, it is returned. If not, the second argument, 'UNKNOWN,' is returned to the results table.

SQL's SELECT statement is a powerful tool with many options. You've seen how to retrieve information from all or some of a table's columns and all or some of a table's rows. Some of the powerful built-in features should also be familiar to you now. The next chapter continues the discussion of DML, looking at more advanced uses of the SELECT statement.

5

Subqueries, UNIONs, Joins

This chapter continues the discussion of data retrieval through SQL's SELECT statement. The three areas covered here are subqueries, UNIONs, and joins. Subqueries are also covered in the next chapter in relation to update operations. The concepts and examples included in this chapter show SQL's ability to link information from multiple tables or views together and to perform complex sets of procedures with a single statement. We present the sample tables (Fig. 5.1) again and recommend that you use them to follow each example. If possible, use SPUFI to try the queries and to create your own variations. As in Chap. 4, we show the SQL error code and message which DB2 returns for syntactically incorrect queries.

5.1 SUBQUERY

At times, your ability to answer one question depends on first answering another. For instance, if your daughter says, "Can I have everything for my birthday that Betty Jane got for hers?," you cannot answer until you first determine what Betty Jane got. Or, moving to our sample application, suppose that you want to know which customers have credit ratings higher than the average credit rating.

As with Betty Jane's presents, you must first determine the average credit rating. The following two SQL statements would provide the information you need:

```
SELECT_AVG(CUST_RATING)
    FROM CUSTOMER
```

RESULT TABLE:

```
----------+-
    5
```

```
BRANCH:

BRANCH_ID  BRANCH_CITY      BRANCH_MGR          BRANCH_ADDR
---------+---------+-------+---------+---------+---------+---------+
       12  NEW YORK         HIRO TANAKA         43 WEST 57 STREET
      300  YONKERS          BRUCE HOFFMAN       7 MORANI STREET
      450  ROCHESTER        ANGELA VALENTINO    351 TEAL PLAZA
      670  NEW YORK         MATTHEW GREEN       900 WALL STREET
      890  YONKERS          ZILYA KOLKER        610 OSIO LANE
       13  CORNING          JOE GROSSMAN        ONE FEDERAL PLAZA
```

```
CUSTOMER:

CUST_SOC_SEC  CUST_NAME        CUST_DATE_OF_BIRTH  CUST_BRANCH  CUST_RATING
---------+---------+---------+---------+---------+---------+---------+
   111111111  PHYLLIS ELKIND   1962-03-29                  12            4
   222222222  JAY RANADE       1960-09-21                 890            8
   333333333  RICHARD GREEN    1947-08-15                  12            7
   444444444  ----------------  1965-12-25                 670            9
   555555555  HEIDI SCHMIDT    1942-06-04                 890            2
   666666666  MUKESH SEHGAL    1957-10-24                 300            5
   777777777  LAI-HA NG        1970-01-01                 450            7
   888888888  GEORGE SCHMIDT   1950-07-04                  12            2
```

```
ACCOUNT:

ACCT_NO   ACCT_BALANCE  ACCT_CREDIT_BAL  ACCT_CUST_ID  ACCT_START_DATE
--------+---------+---------+---------+---------+---------+---------+
AE11         12000.94          500.00     111111111    1987-03-17
AE12           500.00          500.00     555555555    1979-12-25
AE21            77.53         2000.00     888888888    1980-01-01
AB21              .00          180.55     444444444    1989-02-12
BB12         12001.35         3300.00     222222222    1989-02-14
BB13           646.01           25.00     666666666    1986-10-31
CE21         35100.98          100.00     333333333    1985-06-14
DE11            20.00           25.00     777777777    1979-05-20
DB11            75.00             .00     555555555    1980-11-11
```

```
TRANSACTION:

TXN_TYPE   TXN_TIMESTAMP                    TXN_AMOUNT  TXN_ACCT_NO
---------+---------+---------+---------+---------+---------+---------+
CREDIT     1989-01-01-12.12.12.000000          200.50  BB12
CREDIT     1989-01-01-13.13.13.000000         1200.00  BB12
OPENACCT   1989-02-02-16.16.16.000000    -------------  AE11
CREDIT     1989-02-02-17.17.17.000000           50.75  AE21
DEBIT      1989-02-03-18.18.18.000000          100.00  AE21
CREDIT     1989-02-03-19.19.19.000000         2000.00  AE11
DEBIT      1989-02-04-20.20.20.000000         1200.55  DE11
```

Figure 5.1   The sample tables.

followed by

```
SELECT CUST_NAME
   FROM CUSTOMER
   WHERE CUST_RATING > 5
```

RESULT TABLE:

```
CUST_NAME
---------+---------
JAY RANADE
RICHARD GREEN
-------------------
LAI-HA NG
```

The first gives you an average credit rating of 5. The second SELECT makes use of the result of the first to generate the table of customers whose rating is greater than 5. Writing two separate statements works, but QMF, for example, accepts only one statement at a time as input. SQL provides an alternative, the ability to nest SELECT statements. We can get the same information from the following single statement:

```
SELECT CUST_NAME
   FROM CUSTOMER
   WHERE CUST_RATING >
       (SELECT AVG(CUST_RATING)
          FROM CUSTOMER)

RESULT TABLE:

CUST_NAME
---------+---------
JAY RANADE
RICHARD GREEN
-------------------
LAI-HA NG
```

The SELECT statement within parentheses is a subquery. It can also be referred to as the inner select, while the select in which it is embedded is the outer select.

A subquery is used in the search condition of an outer select's WHERE or HAVING clause. For simplicity, we will show it in the WHERE clause in our examples and discussion. But remember, whatever we say about using it in the WHERE clause also applies to the HAVING clause.

In the last chapter you learned that the WHERE clause contains the search condition which each row must satisfy to be passed to the SELECT clause. A row will not be tested against the search condition until the search condition's subquery has been processed. In the above example, the search condition contains a subquery, SELECT AVG(CUST_RATING) FROM CUSTOMER. DB2 processes the subquery and then uses its result (5) to construct the search condition (CUST_RATING > 5). Each row in the outer select can then be tested against this search condition.

DB2 supports multiple levels of nesting as in the following example:

```
SELECT ACCT_NO
  FROM ACCOUNT
  WHERE ACCT_BALANCE >
    (SELECT AVG(ACCT_BALANCE)
     FROM ACCOUNT
     WHERE ACCT_CUST_ID IN
       (SELECT CUST_SOC_SEC
        FROM CUSTOMER
        WHERE CUST_BRANCH = 890))
```

RESULT TABLE:

```
ACCT_NO
-------
AE11
BB12
CE21
```

This query is trying to find accounts whose balance is higher than the average account balance of customers belonging to branch 890. First the list of customers from branch 890 is determined (the innermost select—SELECT CUST_SOC_SEC FROM CUSTOMER WHERE CUST_BRANCH = 890):

INTERMEDIATE RESULT:

```
222222222
555555555
```

The next outer SELECT can now be formulated as SELECT AVG (ACCT_BALANCE) FROM ACCOUNT WHERE ACCT_CUST_ID IN (222222222, 555555555). The rows in the ACCOUNT table whose ACCT_CUST_ID is 222222222 or 555555555 are :

INTERMEDIATE RESULT:

```
AE12      500.00      500.00   555555555  1979-12-25
BB12    12001.35     3300.00   222222222  1989-02-14
DB11       75.00         .00   555555555  1980-11-11
```

Next the average account balance for these accounts is calculated as:

```
4192.1166
```

The outer select now reads SELECT ACCT_NO FROM ACCOUNT WHERE ACCT_BALANCE > 4192.1166. Now apply the query to the following ACCOUNT table.

ACCT_NO	ACCT_BALANCE	ACCT_CREDIT_BAL	ACCT_CUST_ID	ACCT_START_DATE
AE11	12000.94	500.00	111111111	1987-03-17
AE12	500.00	500.00	555555555	1979-12-25
AE21	77.53	2000.00	888888888	1980-01-01
AB21	.00	180.55	444444444	1989-02-12
BB12	12001.35	3300.00	222222222	1989-02-14
BB13	646.01	25.00	666666666	1986-10-31
CE21	35100.98	100.00	333333333	1985-06-14
DE11	20.00	25.00	777777777	1979-05-20
DB11	75.00	.00	555555555	1980-11-11

You can see how the final result table of accounts whose account balance is higher than this average is arrived at:

RESULT TABLE:

ACCT_NO

AE11
BB12
CE21

Any number of SELECTs may be nested. However, beyond five SELECTs, performance is degraded, as is your sanity. Notice that subqueries do not have to be based on the same table or view that the outer select uses.

5.1.1   After a Comparison Operator

A value in a comparison can be expressed as a constant, a column name, an arithmetic expression, or, we will now see, as a subquery. Subqueries can only follow a comparison operator if they return just one value. That is, the subquery must return one row containing one column. The following is not permitted:

```
SELECT ACCT_NO
   FROM ACCOUNT
   WHERE ACCT_BALANCE >
      (SELECT ACCT_CREDIT_BAL
       FROM ACCOUNT)
```

ERROR MESSAGE:
   -811 THE RESULT OF AN EMBEDDED SELECT STATEMENT IS
         A TABLE OF MORE THAN ONE ROW, OR THE RESULT OF
         THE SUBQUERY OF A BASIC PREDICATE IS MORE
         THAN ONE VALUE

A SQL code of -811 is returned for this query. Let's see why this statement is impossible for DB2 to execute. The intermediate result from the subquery is many rows, each containing a value for ACCT_CREDIT_BAL:

INTERMEDIATE RESULT:

```
ACCT_CREDIT_BAL
------------+---
        500.00
        500.00
       2000.00
        180.55
       3300.00
         25.00
        100.00
         25.00
           .00
```

SQL's syntax does not allow you to use a comparison operator (e.g., >) to compare one value with multiple values. Nor does it make sense to ask, as this example does, for the accounts whose account balance is greater than multiple values (the values of ACCT_CREDIT_BAL).

The following SQL statements all return one value and would therefore all be valid as subqueries following a comparison operator. The first gets the balance for account AE11:

```
(SELECT ACCT_BALANCE
   FROM ACCOUNT
  WHERE ACCT_NO = 'AE11')
```

RESULT TABLE:

```
ACCT_BALANCE
--------+---
    12000.94
```

The next finds the sum of the account and credit line balances for the account AE11:

```
(SELECT ACCT_BALANCE + ACCT_CREDIT_BAL
   FROM ACCOUNT
  WHERE ACCT_NO = 'AE11')
```

RESULT TABLE:

```
--------+----
    12500.94
```

The last returns the highest credit line balance for the accounts in the table:

```
(SELECT MAX(ACCT_CREDIT_BAL)
    FROM ACCOUNT)
```

RESULT TABLE:

```
----------+---
    3300.00
```

All three examples return one column in one row. In the second, the column is derived from an arithmetic expression. The third example uses a column function which, by definition, always returns a single value. Therefore, the information returned by these queries can be used as selection criteria in WHERE clause comparisons:

```
SELECT *
    FROM ACCOUNT
    WHERE ACCT_BALANCE ¬=
        (SELECT ACCT_BALANCE
            FROM ACCOUNT
            WHERE ACCT_NO = 'AE11')
```

RESULT TABLE:

ACCT_NO	ACCT_BALANCE	ACCT_CREDIT_BAL	ACCT_CUST_ID	ACCT_START_DATE
AE12	500.00	500.00	555555555	1979-12-25
AE21	77.53	2000.00	888888888	1980-01-01
AB21	.00	180.55	444444444	1989-02-12
BB12	12001.35	3300.00	222222222	1989-02-14
BB13	646.01	25.00	666666666	1986-10-31
CE21	35100.98	100.00	333333333	1985-06-14
DE11	20.00	25.00	777777777	1979-05-20
DB11	75.00	.00	555555555	1980-11-11

The inner select tells us that the value of account balance for account AE11 is 12000.94. The outer select returns the rows from the ACCOUNT table whose account balance is not equal to that figure.

In the next example, we nest our second query:

```
SELECT *
    FROM ACCOUNT
    WHERE ACCT_BALANCE >
        (SELECT ACCT_BALANCE + ACCT_CREDIT_BAL
            FROM ACCOUNT
            WHERE ACCT_NO = 'AE11')
```

RESULT TABLE:

ACCT_NO	ACCT_BALANCE	ACCT_CREDIT_BAL	ACCT_CUST_ID	ACCT_START_DATE
CE21	35100.98	100.00	333333333	1985-06-14

Here, the inner select calculates the total of account balance and account line balance for account AE11—12,500.94. Rows from the ACCOUNT table are returned if their account balance is greater than 12,500.94.

Now let's look at our example using a function.

```
SELECT *
   FROM ACCOUNT
   WHERE ACCT_BALANCE + ACCT_CREDIT_BAL <
   (SELECT MAX(ACCT_CREDIT_BAL)
      FROM ACCOUNT)
```

RESULT TABLE:

ACCT_NO	ACCT_BALANCE	ACCT_CREDIT_BAL	ACCT_CUST_ID	ACCT_START_DATE
AE12	500.00	500.00	555555555	1979-12-25
AE21	77.53	2000.00	888888888	1980-01-01
AB21	.00	180.55	444444444	1989-02-12
BB13	646.01	25.00	666666666	1986-10-31
DE11	20.00	25.00	777777777	1979-05-20
DB11	75.00	.00	555555555	1980-11-11

The maximum account credit balance is 3300.00. The outer select returns rows from the ACCOUNT table if the sum of their account balance and account credit balance is less than 3300.00.

We've said that only subqueries which return single values can follow comparison operators. Subqueries which return multiple values can follow IN, ANY, SOME, and ALL.

5.1.2 IN

In the last chapter, we used IN to compare one value with a set of values:

```
SELECT CUST_NAME
   FROM CUSTOMER
   WHERE CUST_RATING IN (2, 4, 5).
```

RESULT TABLE:

```
CUST_NAME
---------+---------
PHYLLIS ELKIND
HEIDI SCHMIDT
MUKESH SEHGAL
GEORGE SCHMIDT
```

Names are returned for customers whose rating is 2 or 4 or 5. When it follows the keyword IN, a subquery may return multiple values:

```
SELECT *
  FROM BRANCH
  WHERE BRANCH_ID IN
    (SELECT CUST_BRANCH
     FROM CUSTOMER
     WHERE CUST_RATING > 7)
```

RESULT TABLE:

BRANCH_ID	BRANCH_CITY	BRANCH_MGR	BRANCH_ADDR
670	NEW YORK	MATTHEW GREEN	900 WALL STREET
890	YONKERS	ZILYA KOLKER	610 OSIO LANE

The above statement gives us information about branches whose customers have credit ratings greater than 7. DB2 evaluates the subquery first, returning an intermediate result of two values (the value of CUST_BRANCH in the two rows which satisfy the condition):

INTERMEDIATE RESULT:

```
CUST_BRANCH
----------+-
       890
       670
```

By substituting the intermediate result for the subquery, the outer select can now be thought of as:

```
SELECT *
  FROM BRANCH
  WHERE BRANCH_ID IN (890, 670)
```

5.1.3 ANY, SOME, ALL

ANY, SOME, and ALL are operators that may be used only with subqueries. All three are of highly questionable value since the same results can be obtained with other, less confusing operators.

ANY and SOME are identical in the way in which they function and are therefore interchangeable. When SOME or ANY is specified in a condition, the condition is satisfied if the specified relationship is true for at least one value returned by the subselect. In this example, we are using ANY to select customers whose rating is greater than any other customer rating, that is, customers with all but the lowest rating:

```
SELECT CUST_SOC_SEC, CUST_RATING
  FROM CUSTOMER
  WHERE CUST_RATING > ANY
      (SELECT CUST_RATING
        FROM CUSTOMER)
```

RESULT TABLE:

```
CUST_SOC_SEC   CUST_RATING
---------+----------+-----
   111111111        4
   222222222        8
   333333333        7
   444444444        9
   666666666        5
   777777777        7
```

A row from the CUSTOMER table will be returned if its customer rating is greater than at least one of the values of the customer ratings in the table. Performing the subquery first, we get a table of CUST_RATINGs:

INTERMEDIATE RESULT:

```
CUST_RATING
---------+-
     4
     8
     7
     9
     2
     5
     7
     2
```

The outer select is then evaluated and returns all rows from the CUS-TOMER table except those with the lowest rating. The only rows not returned are the rows of customers 555555555 and 888888888 whose customer rating is 2, the lowest customer rating.

We can achieve the same result by using the MIN function and the following statement:

```
SELECT CUST_SOC_SEC, CUST_RATING
  FROM CUSTOMER
  WHERE CUST_RATING >
      (SELECT MIN(CUST_RATING)
        FROM CUSTOMER)
```

RESULT TABLE:

```
CUST_SOC_SEC   CUST_RATING
---------+----------+-----
   111111111        4
   222222222        8
   333333333        7
   444444444        9
   666666666        5
   777777777        7
```

The two statements are equivalent; we find the second much easier to understand.

ALL is used in a similar way. When ALL is specified in a condition, the condition is satisfied if the specified relationship is true for every value returned by the subselect or if the subselect returns no values. Here is an example which uses ALL:

```
SELECT ACCT_NO, ACCT_BALANCE
  FROM ACCOUNT
  WHERE ACCT_BALANCE > ALL
    (SELECT ACCT_CREDIT_BAL
     FROM ACCOUNT)
```

RESULT TABLE:

ACCT_NO	ACCT_BALANCE
AE11	12000.94
BB12	12001.35
CE21	35100.98

Here we are looking for accounts whose account balance is greater than every credit line balance in the table. In this case, the following equivalent statement could be used:

```
SELECT ACCT_NO, ACCT_BALANCE
  FROM ACCOUNT
  WHERE ACCT_BALANCE >
    (SELECT MAX(ACCT_CREDIT_BAL)
     FROM ACCOUNT)
```

RESULT TABLE:

ACCT_NO	ACCT_BALANCE
AE11	12000.94
BB12	12001.35
CE21	35100.98

We have seen four ways to qualify subqueries that return multiple values: IN, ANY, SOME, and ALL. You've probably noticed that in all of these, the multiple values returned are from a single column within multiple rows, not multiple columns within a row. The following is not permitted:

```
SELECT *
  FROM ACCOUNT
  WHERE ACCT_BALANCE IN
    (SELECT ACCT_BALANCE, ACCT_CREDIT_BAL
       FROM ACCOUNT
       WHERE ACCT_NO LIKE 'E%')
```

ERROR MESSAGE:

    -412   THE SELECT CLAUSE OF A SUBQUERY SPECIFIES
           MULTIPLE COLUMNS

Subqueries that return multiple values may include GROUP BY and HAVING clauses. ORDER BY and UNION may not be used in subqueries of any kind.

5.2   CORRELATED SUBQUERY

The subqueries we have described so far are sometimes called simple subqueries to distinguish them from correlated subqueries. In a simple subquery, the subquery is executed once and its result is substituted into the outer select's search condition. The outer select is then processed, and each row which satisfies the search condition is returned to the result table. Sometimes, however, you may need to formulate a query in which information for the subquery is contained in the rows of the outer select. In these cases you will use a correlated subquery.

In a correlated subquery, the subquery contains a reference to a value from a higher select, the correlated reference. It is not possible to execute the subquery just once. Instead it must be executed repeatedly, once for each row from the outer select because the value of the correlated reference will change with each row.

As with simple subqueries, a correlated subquery does not have to be based on the same table or view that the outer select uses. We will first look at a subquery which accesses a table different from the table of the outer select.

5.2.1   Correlated Subquery with Different Tables

The following statement uses information from the BRANCH and CUSTOMER table to find the names of the managers of the branches that have customers with a customer rating of 2:

```
SELECT BRANCH_MGR
   FROM BRANCH
   WHERE 2 IN
      (SELECT CUST_RATING
         FROM CUSTOMER
         WHERE CUST_BRANCH = BRANCH.BRANCH_ID)
```

RESULT TABLE:

```
BRANCH_MGR
---------+-------
HIRO TANAKA
ZILYA KOLKER
```

To process the outer select, DB2 must test each row to see if it satisfies the search condition—that 2 is one of the customer ratings for that branch's customers. However, the search condition contains a subquery, so the specifics of the search condition are unknown until the result of the subquery is known. And in order to find the result of the subquery—find customer ratings for customers whose branch is the same as the current branch—DB2 must resolve "current branch" by looking at the value of BRANCH_ID in the current row of the BRANCH table. BRANCH.BRANCH_ID is the correlated reference and refers to a column from a table at a higher level.

This is a little complicated to understand, so let's look at the logic along with the sample tables. First DB2 processes the inner select. It finds a correlated reference (BRANCH.BRANCH_ID), so it obtains the first row in the outer select's BRANCH table:

BRANCH_ID	BRANCH_CITY	BRANCH_MGR	BRANCH_ADDR
12	NEW YORK	HIRO TANAKA	43 WEST 57 STREET

The value of BRANCH_ID in this row (that is, the value of BRANCH.BRANCH_ID) is 12. DB2 substitutes this value into the correlated reference of the inner select which can now be thought of as:

```
(SELECT CUST_RATING
   FROM CUSTOMER
   WHERE CUST_BRANCH = 12)
```

INTERMEDIATE RESULT:

```
CUST_RATING
---------+-
        4
        7
        2
```

The result of this subquery is then substituted into the search condition which becomes:

```
WHERE 2 IN (4, 7, 2)
```

DB2 can now evaluate the current row from the BRANCH table to see if it satisfies this search condition. 2 is in (4, 7, 2). The condition evaluates to true and the value of BRANCH_MGR in this row (HIRO TANAKA) is returned to the result table.

Going back to the outer select's BRANCH table, DB2 obtains the next row:

BRANCH_ID	BRANCH_CITY	BRANCH_MGR	BRANCH_ADDR
300	YONKERS	BRUCE HOFFMAN	7 MORANI STREET

The value of BRANCH_ID in this row is 300. DB2 substitutes this value into the correlated reference of the inner select which is now evaluated as:

```
(SELECT CUST_RATING
   FROM CUSTOMER
  WHERE CUST_BRANCH = 300)
```

INTERMEDIATE RESULT:

```
CUST_RATING
-----------+-
        5
```

When the result of this subquery is substituted into the search condition, it becomes:

```
WHERE 2 IN (5)
```

DB2 can now evaluate the current row from the BRANCH table to see if it satisfies this search condition. 2 is not in (5). The condition evaluates to false and the value of BRANCH_MGR in this row (BRUCE HOFFMAN) is not returned to the result table.

It is in this manner that the outer and inner selects pass required information back and forth until each row from the outer select has been processed.

5.2.2 Correlation Names

The name of a column which acts as a correlated reference must be qualified with the name of its table. In the previous example, the correlated reference was BRANCH.BRANCH_ID. DB2 permits you to specify an alternate (often shorthand) correlation name for a table or view in the FROM clause which can then be used to qualify a column name. DB2 recognizes that you are specifying a correlation name by its position after a table name:

```
SELECT A.NAME, A.ADDRESS
   FROM CLIENTHOMETABLE A
```

Correlation names, A in the SELECT above, are used as a short-hand way of referring to table or view names which may be long and cumbersome to type, as is CLIENTHOMETABLE. They also help to avoid ambiguity in situations where it is not clear which table a column name refers to. We will use more examples of correlation names in the rest of this chapter, but let's look now at an example of a correlation name in a correlated reference:

```
SELECT BRANCH_MGR
   FROM BRANCH XYZ
   WHERE 2 IN
      (SELECT CUST_RATING
         FROM CUSTOMER
         WHERE CUST_BRANCH = XYZ.BRANCH_ID)
```

In this example, XYZ is the correlation name for the BRANCH table. Now, everywhere that we would have used the BRANCH table name, we can use XYZ instead. The BRANCH_ID column name of the BRANCH table is qualified with XYZ, the correlation name for the table. The correlated reference is XYZ.BRANCH_ID instead of BRANCH.BRANCH_ID.

5.2.3 Correlated Subquery with the Same Table

In our discussion of simple subqueries, we used the following example to find customers with credit ratings higher than the average credit rating:

```
SELECT CUST_NAME
   FROM CUSTOMER
   WHERE CUST_RATING >
      (SELECT AVG(CUST_RATING)
         FROM CUSTOMER)
```

Suppose we needed, instead, to find customers with credit ratings higher than their branch's average credit rating. This involves a correlated subquery because the inner select, which finds the average, will have to be executed repeatedly for each customer's branch.

In this correlated subquery all of the information we need is in the CUSTOMER table, so the CUSTOMER table is specified in the FROM clause of both the outer and inner selects:

```
SELECT CUST_NAME
   FROM CUSTOMER OUTER
   WHERE CUST_RATING >
      (SELECT AVG(CUST_RATING)
        FROM CUSTOMER INNER
        WHERE INNER.CUST_BRANCH = OUTER.CUST_BRANCH)
```

RESULT TABLE:

```
CUST_NAME
---------+--------
JAY RANADE
RICHARD GREEN
```

We've used correlation names in both FROM clauses. Rather than using arbitrary aliases, we have used INNER and OUTER to help clarify the comparison in the subquery.

Use the sample tables to follow the discussion of the example. DB2 obtains the first row of the outer select's CUSTOMER table:

CUST_SOC_SEC	CUST_NAME	CUST_DATE_OF_BIRTH	CUST_BRANCH	CUST_RATING
111111111	PHYLLIS ELKIND	1962-03-29	12	4

The value of CUST_BRANCH in this row (that is, the value of OUTER.CUST_BRANCH) is 12. DB2 substitutes this value for the correlated reference of the inner select, resulting in:

```
(SELECT AVG(CUST_RATING)
   FROM CUSTOMER INNER
   WHERE INNER.CUST_BRANCH = 12)
```

INTERMEDIATE RESULT:

```
---------+-
      4
```

The average credit rating for branch 12 is 4, so the outer select's search condition becomes:

```
WHERE CUST_RATING > 4
```

DB2 evaluates the current row of the outer select's CUSTOMER table to see if it satisfies this search condition. The value of CUST_RATING in the current row is 4; 4 > 4 evaluates to false and the value of CUST_NAME in this row (PHYLLIS ELKIND) is not returned to the result table. To make sure you understand it, try to apply this same logic to the next rows.

When DB2 calculates the result of the inner select (in this case, the average credit rating for branch 12), it saves the result so that the next time it encounters a row in the outer SELECT with a BRANCH of 12, it won't have to recalculate the value. It can only do this if the subquery returns a single value, as with column functions.

5.2.4 EXISTS

In the subqueries we have looked at so far, DB2 evaluates the subquery either once or repetitively and substitutes the result into the WHERE clause of the outer select. Another way to use a subquery is with the keyword EXISTS. With EXISTS, DB2 also evaluates the subquery once or repetitively (depending on whether the subquery is simple or correlated). However, rather than using the value(s) of the subquery's result, DB2 instead evaluates the subquery only to determine if it returns zero or more rows. There are only two possibilities: yes, at least one row is returned, or no, no rows are returned. Because it is the existence of rows rather than any particular values within the rows that is important, the SELECT clause in the subquery is usually ·coded SELECT * rather than SELECT *columnname(s)*. Let's look at an example:

```
SELECT *
   FROM TRANSACTION
   WHERE EXISTS
     (SELECT *
        FROM TRANSACTION
        WHERE TXN_TYPE = 'SYSTEMERROR')

RESULT TABLE:

TXN_TYPE  TXN_TIMESTAMP                TXN_AMOUNT  TXN_ACCT_NO
--------+---------+---------+---------+---------+---------+---------+-------
```

This lets us look at all transactions if there has been a system error on any transaction. This is an example of using EXISTS with a simple, rather than correlated, subquery. The subquery is executed once and finds that no row satisfies the condition TXN_TYPE = 'SYSTEMERROR'. Therefore, the EXISTS condition evaluates to false and no rows from the outer select are returned. If the subquery had read WHERE TXN_TYPE = 'OPENACCT', the EXISTS condition would evaluate to true and all the rows from the TRANSACTION table would be returned to the result table.

The use of EXISTS with a simple subquery is supported but is not very common in practice because there are few situations in which it

is applicable. The usefulness of EXISTS and its opposite, NOT EX-
ISTS, is more evident in correlated subqueries. Let's say we want to
find all of the managers of the branches that have customers with a
credit rating of 4:

```
--The correlation name BR is used for BRANCH
    SELECT BRANCH_MGR, BRANCH_CITY
    FROM BRANCH BR
    WHERE EXISTS
      (SELECT *
        FROM CUSTOMER
        WHERE CUST_BRANCH = BR.BRANCH_ID
        AND CUST_RATING = 4)
```

RESULT TABLE:

BRANCH_MGR	BRANCH_CITY
HIRO TANAKA	NEW YORK

DB2 recognizes this as a correlated subquery because the subquery
has a correlated reference, BR.BRANCH_ID, whose value is drawn
from the table of the outer select.

DB2 obtains the first row of the outer select's BRANCH table:

BRANCH_ID	BRANCH_CITY	BRANCH_MGR	BRANCH_ADDR
12	NEW YORK	HIRO TANAKA	43 WEST 57 STREET

The value of BRANCH_ID in this row (that is, the value of
BR.BRANCH_ID) is 12. DB2 substitutes this value for the correlated
reference of the inner select, resulting in:

```
(SELECT *
    FROM CUSTOMER
    WHERE CUST_BRANCH = 12
    AND CUST_RATING = 4)
```

INTERMEDIATE RESULT:

CUST_SOC_SEC	CUST_NAME	CUST_DATE_OF_BIRTH	CUST_BRANCH	CUST_RATING
111111111	PHYLLIS ELKIND	1962-03-29	12	4

One row is returned from this subquery. Therefore, the EXISTS condition evaluates to true and the values of BRANCH_MGR and
BRANCH_CITY in the current row (HIRO TANAKA, NEW YORK)
are returned to the result table.

DB2 obtains the next row of the outer select's BRANCH table:

BRANCH_ID	BRANCH_CITY	BRANCH_MGR	BRANCH_ADDR
300	YONKERS	BRUCE HOFFMAN	7 MORANI STREET

The value of BRANCH_ID in this row is 300. DB2 substitutes this value for the correlated reference of the inner select, which can now be thought of as:

```
(SELECT *
   FROM CUSTOMER
   WHERE CUST_BRANCH = 300
     AND CUST_RATING = 4)
```

INTERMEDIATE RESULT:

CUST_SOC_SEC	CUST_NAME	CUST_DATE_OF_BIRTH	CUST_BRANCH	CUST_RATING

Since no rows were returned from this subquery, the EXISTS condition evaluates to false and the values of BRANCH_MGR and BRANCH_CITY in the current row (BRUCE HOFFMAN, ALBANY) are not returned to the result table.

The keyword EXISTS can be modified by the keyword NOT to produce a result based on the fact that the inner select results in no rows being selected. For example, this will find all of the branches that have no customers:

```
SELECT BRANCH_ID
   FROM BRANCH BBB
   WHERE NOT EXISTS
       (SELECT *
          FROM CUSTOMER
          WHERE CUST_BRANCH = BBB.BRANCH_ID)
```

RESULT TABLE:

```
BRANCH_ID
---------
    13
```

The only row returned is the one in which BRANCH_ID = 13. Let's see why. When 13 is substituted for BBB.BRANCH_ID in the subquery, the subquery becomes:

```
(SELECT *
   FROM CUSTOMER
   WHERE CUST_BRANCH = 13)
```

RESULT TABLE:

CUST_SOC_SEC	CUST_NAME	CUST_DATE_OF_BIRTH	CUST_BRANCH	CUST_RATING

There are no customers with CUST_BRANCH of 13, so no rows are returned from the subquery. The condition NOT EXISTS evaluates to true and the value 13 from the outer select is returned to the result table. All other BRANCH_IDs in the BRANCH table are associated with at least one customer, so they fail the NOT EXISTS condition.

EXISTS and NOT EXISTS may only be used in connection with subqueries.

5.3   UNION

UNION is used to merge the results of two or more SELECT statements into one result table. When DB2 finds the keyword UNION, it processes each SELECT statement individually and then merges the intermediate result table of each into one result table, removing any duplicate rows. Here is an example in which UNION is used to identify accounts having a balance or credit balance greater than 750:

```
SELECT ACCT_NO, ACCT_BALANCE, 'Balance'
   FROM ACCOUNT
   WHERE ACCT_BALANCE > 750
UNION
SELECT ACCT_NO, ACCT_CREDIT_BAL, 'Credit'
   FROM ACCOUNT
   WHERE ACCT_CREDIT_BAL > 750
```

RESULT TABLE:

ACCT_NO	ACCT_BALANCE	
AE11	12000.94	BALANCE
AE21	2000.00	CREDIT
BB12	3300.00	CREDIT
BB12	12001.35	BALANCE
CE21	35100.98	BALANCE

We've included a literal column in each SELECT to identify the source of the rows in the combined result table. We could have phrased this query without UNION, by using an OR (WHERE ACCT_BALANCE > 750   OR   ACCT_CREDIT_BAL > 750). This would not, however, let us see the Balance or Credit distinction that we can see with our UNION example.

As long as each SELECT clause has the same number of columns, any number of SELECT statements may be UNIONed. In addition, columns in the same relative position must be of compatible data types (see Chap. 4 for a discussion of data type compatibility).

If you want the result table sorted in a particular sequence, you can include an ORDER BY clause in the last SELECT statement. Let's say you wanted the results of the above query to be in descending order of the balance in regular and credit amounts. To accomplish this, use the following:

```
SELECT ACCT_NO, ACCT_BALANCE, 'Balance'
  FROM ACCOUNT
  WHERE ACCT_BALANCE > 750
UNION
SELECT ACCT_NO, ACCT_CREDIT_BAL, 'Credit'
  FROM ACCOUNT
  WHERE ACCT_CREDIT_BAL > 750
ORDER BY 2 DESC
```

RESULT TABLE:

```
ACCT_NO    ACCT_BALANCE
--------+----------+----------+-
CE21          35100.98  BALANCE
BB12          12001.35  BALANCE
AE11          12000.94  BALANCE
BB12           3300.00  CREDIT
AE21           2000.00  CREDIT
```

As you can see, the result table appears in descending order of the amount in the balance column. When used with UNION, ORDER BY must specify the position of a column in the SELECT clause rather than a column name. In this case, the second column in the SELECT statement refers to both the regular and credit balances.

Suppose you wanted to see the duplicate rows or that you know that there won't be any so you want to avoid the overhead of sorting the result set. Using UNION ALL produces a union in which duplicates are not discarded. The result tables from the following statements show the difference between a UNION and UNION ALL:

```
SELECT ACCT_BALANCE, ACCT_NO
  FROM ACCOUNT
  WHERE ACCT_BALANCE BETWEEN 100 AND 700
UNION
SELECT ACCT_CREDIT_BAL, ACCT_NO
  FROM ACCOUNT
  WHERE ACCT_CREDIT_BAL BETWEEN 100 AND 700
ORDER BY 2
```

RESULT TABLE:

```
ACCT_BALANCE  ACCT_NO
--------+----------+--
    180.55  AB21
    500.00  AE11
    500.00  AE12
    646.01  BB13
    100.00  CE21
```

```
SELECT ACCT_BALANCE, ACCT_NO
  FROM ACCOUNT
  WHERE ACCT_BALANCE BETWEEN 100 AND 700
UNION ALL
SELECT ACCT_CREDIT_BAL, ACCT_NO
  FROM ACCOUNT
  WHERE ACCT_CREDIT_BAL BETWEEN 100 AND 700
ORDER BY 2
```

RESULT TABLE:

```
ACCT_BALANCE   ACCT_NO
----------+-----------+--
    180.55   AB21
    500.00   AE11
    500.00   AE12
    500.00   AE12
    646.01   BB13
    100.00   CE21
```

Notice that in the second result table, the duplicate rows have not been removed.

You may combine several SELECT statements using UNION, UNION ALL, or a combination of the two. When a combination is used, however, the order of the SELECT statements will affect the result and you may need to use parentheses to clarify at which points you want duplicates discarded.

5.4 JOIN

With the keyword UNION, you can combine information from more than one table or view, with rows from different tables or views combined "vertically" in the result table. That is, rows from the different sources follow one another. Now let's look at the join operation, which also makes it possible to combine information from more than one table or view by appending information from one table or view to the information in the other. Rows, or portions of rows, from different tables or views are concatenated "horizontally." Figure 5.2 illustrates the difference. In the UNION, rows XXX, YYY, ZZZ, and VVV are stacked, while in the join they are connected to make two longer rows.

5.4.1 Simple Joins

The ability to join tables is central to relational processing. In the first chapter, we compared relational to nonrelational systems. We said that in an RDBMS, relationships between entities, or tables, are made by establishing common columns between tables. The SQL operation used to link tables together through these common columns is the join.

Union:

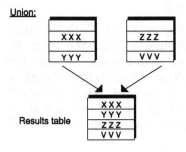

Join:

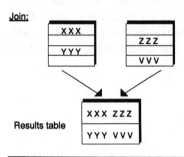

Figure 5.2 The differrence between a UNION and a join.

Unlike UNION, there is no comparable join keyword. The join operation is implied by naming more than one table or view in the FROM clause of a SELECT statement:

```
SELECT BRANCH_ID, BRANCH_ADDR, CUST_SOC_SEC,
       CUST_BRANCH
   FROM BRANCH, CUSTOMER
   WHERE BRANCH_ID = CUST_BRANCH
```

RESULT TABLE:

BRANCH_ID	BRANCH_ADDR	CUST_SOC_SEC	CUST_BRANCH
12	43 WEST 57 STREET	111111111	12
890	610 OSIO LANE	222222222	890
12	43 WEST 57 STREET	333333333	12
670	900 WALL STREET	444444444	670
890	610 OSIO LANE	555555555	890
300	7 MORANI STREET	666666666	300
450	351 TEAL PLAZA	777777777	450
12	43 WEST 57 STREET	888888888	12

Although it is not required, joins normally contain a conditional clause which identifies the columns through which rows can be linked. In the above example, BRANCH_ID, the primary key of the BRANCH table, and CUST_BRANCH, the foreign key in the CUSTOMER table, although named differently, contain information from the same domain. Therefore, they can be used to link each branch row with the customer rows belonging to that branch. The linkage is often based on equality, but any comparison operator may be used. When a join column contains nulls, that row will not satisfy the condition and will not appear in the result table since a comparison which involves a null value always evaluates to false.

The result of a join in which you do not specify a linkage condition is a Cartesian product, which is a set, constructed from two given sets, containing all pairs of elements from both sets. When no match condition is specified, the result table includes all possible combinations of rows. The size of a Cartesian product is the number of rows in table 1 multiplied by the number of rows in table 2, and so on, if more than two tables participate in the join.

Look again at our first example:

```
SELECT BRANCH_ID, BRANCH_ADDR, CUST_SOC_SEC,
       CUST_BRANCH
  FROM BRANCH, CUSTOMER
 WHERE BRANCH_ID = CUST_BRANCH
```

To conceptualize how this join is processed, first imagine an intermediate table which is the cartesian product of the BRANCH and CUSTOMER tables specified in the FROM clause. Figure 5.3 illustrates this.

When the specified condition (BRANCH_ID = CUST_BRANCH) is applied to this large table, rows which do not satisfy the condition are removed and the result table remains. A good way to understand the join operation is to first imagine the cartesian product and then apply the selection criteria to it.

Some of the statements we've used as examples of correlated subqueries could be rewritten as joins. Here's one of our previous examples and its join equivalent:

```
SELECT BRANCH_MGR
  FROM BRANCH
 WHERE 2 IN
      (SELECT CUST_RATING
         FROM CUSTOMER
        WHERE CUST_BRANCH = BRANCH.BRANCH_ID)
```

We used this subquery to find the managers of branches having customers with a rating of 2. We can accomplish the same thing with the following join:

```
BRANCH_ID  BRANCH_ADDR                     CUST_SOC_SEC  CUST_BRANCH
---------+---------+---------+---------+---------+---------+---
      12  43 WEST 57 STREET                 111111111          12
      12  43 WEST 57 STREET                 222222222         890
      12  43 WEST 57 STREET                 333333333          12
      12  43 WEST 57 STREET                 444444444         670
      12  43 WEST 57 STREET                 555555555         890
      12  43 WEST 57 STREET                 666666666         300
      12  43 WEST 57 STREET                 777777777         450
      12  43 WEST 57 STREET                 888888888          12
     300  7 MORANI STREET                   111111111          12
     300  7 MORANI STREET                   222222222         890
     300  7 MORANI STREET                   333333333          12
     300  7 MORANI STREET                   444444444         670
     300  7 MORANI STREET                   555555555         890
     300  7 MORANI STREET                   666666666         300
     300  7 MORANI STREET                   777777777         450
     300  7 MORANI STREET                   888888888          12
     450  351 TEAL PLAZA                    111111111          12
     450  351 TEAL PLAZA                    222222222         890
     450  351 TEAL PLAZA                    333333333          12
     450  351 TEAL PLAZA                    444444444         670
     450  351 TEAL PLAZA                    555555555         890
     450  351 TEAL PLAZA                    666666666         300
     450  351 TEAL PLAZA                    777777777         450
     450  351 TEAL PLAZA                    888888888          12
     670  900 WALL STREET                   111111111          12
     670  900 WALL STREET                   222222222         890
     670  900 WALL STREET                   333333333          12
     670  900 WALL STREET                   444444444         670
     670  900 WALL STREET                   555555555         890
     670  900 WALL STREET                   666666666         300
     670  900 WALL STREET                   777777777         450
     670  900 WALL STREET                   888888888          12
     890  610 OSIO LANE                     111111111          12
     890  610 OSIO LANE                     222222222         890
     890  610 OSIO LANE                     333333333          12
     890  610 OSIO LANE                     444444444         670
     890  610 OSIO LANE                     555555555         890
     890  610 OSIO LANE                     666666666         300
     890  610 OSIO LANE                     777777777         450
     890  610 OSIO LANE                     888888888          12
      13  ONE FEDERAL PLAZA                 111111111          12
      13  ONE FEDERAL PLAZA                 222222222         890
      13  ONE FEDERAL PLAZA                 333333333          12
      13  ONE FEDERAL PLAZA                 444444444         670
      13  ONE FEDERAL PLAZA                 555555555         890
      13  ONE FEDERAL PLAZA                 666666666         300
      13  ONE FEDERAL PLAZA                 777777777         450
      13  ONE FEDERAL PLAZA                 888888888          12
```

Figure 5.3   A Cartesian product results from the unqualified join.

```
SELECT BRANCH_MGR
  FROM BRANCH B, CUSTOMER C
 WHERE B.BRANCH_ID = C.CUST_BRANCH
   AND C.CUST_RATING = 2
```

We've used correlation names for both tables in this join example. This was not, in fact, required because the column names used in our sample tables follow a naming standard which ensures that each column name is unique. It is very possible, however, that both columns containing branch ID information in different tables would have the same name. In that case, the columns would need to be qualified with either their table names or correlation names.

5.4.2   Joining a Table to Itself

SQL allows you to join a table to itself by specifying the same table twice in the FROM clause. Correlation names, in this case, are required to distinguish the two references to the same table. This example finds transactions which have both the same transaction type and the same account number:

```
SELECT A.TXN_TYPE, A.TXNACCT_NO, A.TXN_TIMESTAMP,
       B.TXN_TYPE, B.TXNACCT_NO, B.TXN_TIMESTAMP
  FROM TRANSACTION A, TRANSACTION B
 WHERE A.TXN_TYPE = B.TXN_TYPE
   AND A.TXN_ACCT_NO = B.TXN_ACCT_NO
```

Figure 5.4 shows the result table from this query. The Cartesian product of joining the TRANSACTION table to itself should be a result table with 49 rows (7 * 7). The conditional clause has selected only nine rows in which the same transaction type and same account number appear on both sides of the result table row. However, the first half of the seven rows are a mirror image of the second half. In Fig. 5.5 we have boxed those rows.

To eliminate this duplication of rows we could add the condition:

```
AND A.TXN_TIMESTAMP ⌐ = B.TXN_TIMESTAMP
```

This would discard all of the "boxed" rows from the result table above and we would be left with the result table shown in Fig. 5.6. However, these two rows are actually similar to each other. We can eliminate the boxed rows and at the same time eliminate a row's "reverse" by specifying:

```
AND A.TXN_TIMESTAMP < B.TXN_TIMESTAMP
```

The statement is now:

```
SELECT A.TXN_TYPE, A.TXNACCT_NO, A.TXN_TIMESTAMP,
       B.TXN_TYPE, B.TXNACCT_NO, B.TXN_TIMESTAMP
  FROM TRANSACTION A, TRANSACTION B
 WHERE A.TXN_TYPE = B.TXN_TYPE
   AND A.TXN_ACCT_NO = B.TXN_ACCT_NO
   AND A.TXN_TIMESTAMP < B.TXN_TIMESTAMP
```

Figure 5.7 shows the result table generated by this SELECT. Only account BB12 has two transactions of the same type that occurred at different times.

```
TXN_TYPE   TXN_ACCT_NO   TXN_TIMESTAMP              TXN_TYPE   TXN_ACCT_NO   TXN_TIMESTAMP
--------+----------+----------+---------+----------+----------+---------+---------+---------+
CREDIT     BB12          1989-01-01-12.12.12.000000   CREDIT     BB12          1989-01-01-12.12.12.000000
CREDIT     BB12          1989-01-01-12.12.12.000000   CREDIT     BB12          1989-01-01-13.13.13.000000
CREDIT     BB12          1989-01-01-13.13.13.000000   CREDIT     BB12          1989-01-01-12.12.12.000000
CREDIT     BB12          1989-01-01-13.13.13.000000   CREDIT     BB12          1989-01-01-13.13.13.000000
OPENACCT   AE11          1989-02-02-16.16.16.000000   OPENACCT   AE11          1989-02-02-16.16.16.000000
CREDIT     AE21          1989-02-02-17.17.17.000000   CREDIT     AE21          1989-02-02-17.17.17.000000
DEBIT      AE21          1989-02-03-18.18.18.000000   DEBIT      AE21          1989-02-03-18.18.18.000000
CREDIT     AE11          1989-02-03-19.19.19.000000   CREDIT     AE11          1989-02-03-19.19.19.000000
DEBIT      DE11          1989-02-04-20.20.20.000000   DEBIT      DE11          1989-02-04-20.20.20.000000
```

Figure 5.4   Joining a table to itself.

```
TXN_TYPE   TXN_ACCT_NO   TXN_TIMESTAMP                            TXN_TYPE   TXN_ACCT_NO   TXN_TIMESTAMP
--------+----------+----------+---------+---------+----------+----------+---------+---------+---------+
CREDIT     BB12          1989-01-01-12.12.12.000000   CREDIT     BB12          1989-01-01-13.13.13.000000
CREDIT     BB12          1989-01-01-12.12.12.000000   CREDIT     BB12          1989-01-01-13.13.13.000000
CREDIT     BB12          1989-01-01-13.13.13.000000   CREDIT     BB12          1989-01-01-12.12.12.000000
CREDIT     BB12          1989-01-01-13.13.13.000000   CREDIT     BB12          1989-01-01-13.13.13.000000
OPENACCT   AE11          1989-02-02-16.16.16.000000   OPENACCT   AE11          1989-02-02-16.16.16.000000
CREDIT     AE21          1989-02-02-17.17.17.000000   CREDIT     AE21          1989-02-02-17.17.17.000000
DEBIT      AE21          1989-02-03-18.18.18.000000   DEBIT      AE21          1989-02-03-18.18.18.000000
CREDIT     AE11          1989-02-03-19.19.19.000000   CREDIT     AE11          1989-02-03-19.19.19.000000
DEBIT      DE11          1989-02-04-20.20.20.000000   DEBIT      DE11          1989-02-04-20.20.20.000000
```

Figure 5.5   Redundant information in the result of the join.

```
TXN_TYPE   TXN_ACCT_NO   TXN_TIMESTAMP              TXN_TYPE   TXN_ACCT_NO   TXN_TIMESTAMP
--------+----------+----------+---------+----------+----------+---------+---------+---------+
CREDIT     BB12          1989-01-01-12.12.12.000000   CREDIT     BB12          1989-01-01-13.13.13.000000
CREDIT     BB12          1989-01-01-13.13.13.000000   CREDIT     BB12          1989-01-01-12.12.12.000000
```

Figure 5.6   Two rows as mirrors of each other.

```
TXN_TYPE   TXN_ACCT_NO   TXN_TIMESTAMP              TXN_TYPE   TXN_ACCT_NO   TXN_TIMESTAMP
--------+----------+----------+---------+----------+----------+---------+---------+---------+
CREDIT     BB12          1989-01-01-12.12.12.000000   CREDIT     BB12          1989-01-01-13.13.13.000000
```

Figure 5.7   A single row results from the join.

5.4.3 Outer Join

In the joins we have looked at so far, we have been able to join rows
when values from the joined tables can be matched in some way.
There are situations in which you need to also find those rows which
do not have matching values; for this you would use an outer join,
which makes use of three concepts we have already looked at: join,
UNION, and correlated subquery with NOT EXISTS.

Suppose we wanted to produce a list of all our accounts along with
the transactions for each account. Using a join to do this would only
show us the accounts that had transactions:

```
SELECT ACCT_NO, TXN_TYPE, TXN_AMOUNT
    FROM ACCOUNT, TRANSACTION
    WHERE ACCT_NO = TXN_ACCT_NO
```

The following example will provide a result table with all accounts and their associated transactions. The list, however, will include accounts that have transactions to be processed as well as those that don't:

```
SELECT ACCT_NO, TXN_TYPE, TXN_AMOUNT
  FROM ACCOUNT, TRANSACTION
  WHERE ACCT_NO = TXN_ACCT_NO
UNION ALL
SELECT ACCT_NO, 'NO TXN', 0
  FROM ACCOUNT
  WHERE NOT EXISTS
    (SELECT *
      FROM TRANSACTION
      WHERE TXN_ACCT_NO = ACCOUNT.ACCT_NO)
```

RESULT TABLE:

ACCT_NO	TXN_TYPE	TXN_AMOUNT
AE11	OPENACCT	----------
AE11	CREDIT	2000.00
AE21	CREDIT	50.75
AE21	DEBIT	100.00
BB12	CREDIT	1200.00
BB12	CREDIT	200.50
DE11	DEBIT	1200.55
AE12	NO TXN	.00
AB21	NO TXN	.00
BB13	NO TXN	.00
CE21	NO TXN	.00
DB11	NO TXN	.00

The first SELECT statement is a join of the ACCOUNT and TRANSACTION tables in which the join condition is made through account number (ACCT_NO = TXN_ACCT_NO). The second SELECT statement contains a correlated subquery with NOT EXISTS, which finds the accounts with no transactions. This subquery contains a correlated reference, ACCOUNT.ACCT_NO. (Note that we have chosen to qualify the column with its table name rather than a correlation name.) The outer SELECT passes the account number of each row to the subquery, which determines if there are any transactions for that account number. If no transaction rows are returned, the NOT EXISTS condition is satisfied and that account's row is returned with the literal NO TXN and an amount of 0.

The results of this SELECT statement are then UNIONed with those of the first. UNION ALL prevents duplicates from being discarded (an account might have more than one transaction of the same type and amount), and the desired list is generated in the result table.

You've now been introduced to subqueries and their cousins, correlated subqueries; UNIONs; joins; and outer joins. With this under your belt, you should now see the power of SQL's ability to combine information from more than one table.

Update Operations and Date and Time Support

The last two chapters were devoted to aspects of the SELECT statement. In this chapter, we move on to update operations with the INSERT, DELETE, and UPDATE operators of SQL's DML component. But first let's turn to a discussion of date and time support in DB2. Refer to Fig. 6.1 throughout the chapter; it shows the tables of our sample database.

6.1 DATE AND TIME

With release 1.3, DB2 added date and time support to its implementation of SQL, including date, time, timestamp data types (described in Chap. 2), special registers, and new scalar functions. Through these features, you can decrease the amount of coding required for date and time conversions and for date and time arithmetic.

When you use date and time values in SQL statements, you are using them in their character representations. One of the different formats available (Fig. 6.2) can be chosen at precompile or installation time. DB2's default is ISO, so that is the format we use in our examples.

6.1.1 Special Registers

DB2 has a set of six storage areas, or special registers, which may be referenced by SQL. Four of these registers maintain date and time data. The CURRENT DATE, CURRENT TIME, and CURRENT TIMESTAMP registers contain the values indicated by their names when the SQL statement referencing the registers is executed. Therefore, if any of these is referenced more than once in the same SQL statement, they will be based on a single clock reading. However, as

BRANCH:

BRANCH_ID	BRANCH_CITY	BRANCH_MGR	BRANCH_ADDR
12	NEW YORK	HIRO TANAKA	43 WEST 57 STREET
300	YONKERS	BRUCE HOFFMAN	7 MORANI STREET
450	ROCHESTER	ANGELA VALENTINO	351 TEAL PLAZA
670	NEW YORK	MATTHEW GREEN	900 WALL STREET
890	YONKERS	ZILYA KOLKER	610 OSIO LANE
13	CORNING	JOE GROSSMAN	ONE FEDERAL PLAZA

CUSTOMER:

CUST_SOC_SEC	CUST_NAME	CUST_DATE_OF_BIRTH	CUST_BRANCH	CUST_RATING
111111111	PHYLLIS ELKIND	1962-03-29	12	4
222222222	JAY RANADE	1960-09-21	890	8
333333333	RICHARD GREEN	1947-08-15	12	7
444444444	------------------	1965-12-25	670	9
555555555	HEIDI SCHMIDT	1942-06-04	890	2
666666666	MUKESH SEHGAL	1957-10-24	300	5
777777777	LAI-HA NG	1970-01-01	450	7
888888888	GEORGE SCHMIDT	1950-07-04	12	2

ACCOUNT:

ACCT_NO	ACCT_BALANCE	ACCT_CREDIT_BAL	ACCT_CUST_ID	ACCT_START_DATE
AE11	12000.94	500.00	111111111	1987-03-17
AE12	500.00	500.00	555555555	1979-12-25
AE21	77.53	2000.00	888888888	1980-01-01
AB21	.00	180.55	444444444	1989-02-12
BB12	12001.35	3300.00	222222222	1989-02-14
BB13	646.01	25.00	666666666	1986-10-31
CE21	35100.98	100.00	333333333	1985-06-14
DE11	20.00	25.00	777777777	1979-05-20
DB11	75.00	.00	555555555	1980-11-11

TRANSACTION:

TXN_TYPE	TXN_TIMESTAMP	TXN_AMOUNT	TXN_ACCT_NO
CREDIT	1989-01-01-12.12.12.000000	200.50	BB12
CREDIT	1989-01-01-13.13.13.000000	1200.00	BB12
OPENACCT	1989-02-02-16.16.16.000000	-------------	AE11
CREDIT	1989-02-02-17.17.17.000000	50.75	AE21
DEBIT	1989-02-03-18.18.18.000000	100.00	AE21
CREDIT	1989-02-03-19.19.19.000000	2000.00	AE11
DEBIT	1989-02-04-20.20.20.000000	1200.55	DE11

Figure 6.1   The sample tables.

FORMAT	DATE	TIME
USA (IBM USA Standard)	MM/DD/YYYY 03/29/1947	HH:MM AM 02:15 AM
EUR (European Standard)	DD.MM.YYYY 29/03/1947	HH.MM.SS 02:15:10
ISO (International Standards Organization)	YYYY-MM-DD 1947-03-29	HH.MM.SS 02:15:10
JIS (Japanese Industrial Standard Christian Era)	(same as ISO)	

Figure 6.2   Date and time formats.

with other programming languages, referencing the registers else-where in the program will produce a different reading. DB2 uses these registers for default values. When a column has a date/time data type, and NOT NULL WITH DEFAULT is specified in the definition, the default used to fill the columns will be the current value in the corresponding special register. For example, the default for the DATE data type is the value in CURRENT DATE.

The CURRENT TIMEZONE register contains a time duration between -24 and 24 hours. It can be used to convert a local time into Greenwich Mean Time by subtracting CURRENT TIMEZONE from a local TIME value.

6.1.2   Date and Time Functions

In previous chapters we saw several scalar functions provided by SQL (e.g., DECIMAL and INTEGER). There are several other scalar functions that are specifically related to date and time. They are used to convert date/time data and, like other scalar functions, can be specified in either the SELECT or WHERE clauses of a statement.

The functions DATE, TIME, and TIMESTAMP return, as you would expect, a date, time, or timestamp. Among the arguments accepted by DATE are a timestamp, a character representation of a date (e.g., 1989-01-10), or a character string in the form $yyyynnn$, where nnn is the nth day of that year. The function takes the argument and converts it to a date. For example:

```
SELECT DATE(TXN_TIMESTAMP),TXN_TIMESTAMP
    FROM TRANSACTION
    WHERE TXN_TYPE = 'CREDIT'
```

RESULT TABLE:

```
                           TXN_TIMESTAMP
---------+---------+---------+--------
1989-02-03   1989-02-03-19.19.19.000000
1989-02-02   1989-02-02-17.17.17.000000
1989-01-01   1989-01-01-12.12.12.000000
1989-01-01   1989-01-01-13.13.13.000000
```

```
SELECT DATE('1989001'), ACCT_NO
    FROM ACCOUNT WHERE
    ACCT_CUST_ID IN (222222222, 555555555)
```

RESULT TABLE:

```
              ACCT_NO
---------+---------
1989-01-01   AE12
1989-01-01   BB12
1989-01-01   DB11
```

In the first example, the DATE function returns the date portion of the timestamp data. In the second, it converts a character string to one of the date data types (e.g., USA, ISO, etc.); which type is determined at installation or precompile time.

The TIME and TIMESTAMP functions perform similarly. The arguments that TIME operates on may be a timestamp, time, or character representation of a time. Here we're extracting the time from a timestamp:

```
SELECT TIME(TXN_TIMESTAMP), TXN_TIMESTAMP
   FROM TRANSACTION
   WHERE TXN_TYPE = 'CREDIT'

RESULT TABLE:

            TXN_TIMESTAMP
---------+----------+----------+------
19.19.19   1989-02-03-19.19.19.000000
17.17.17   1989-02-02-17.17.17.000000
12.12.12   1989-01-01-12.12.12.000000
13.13.13   1989-01-01-13.13.13.000000
```

When one value is used, TIMESTAMP operates like DATE and TIME, accepting a timestamp, character representation of a timestamp, or character string in the form *yyyymmddhhmmss* and returning a timestamp data type.

TIMESTAMP may also be used with a pair of values to convert them into a timestamp. The first must be a date or character representation of a date and the second, a time or character representation of a time. The function merges them into a timestamp made up of the specified date and time. The microsecond portion will be equal to zero.

The functions YEAR, MONTH, DAY, HOUR, MINUTE, SECOND, and MICROSECOND all extract that portion of the argument implied by the name of the function and return an integer. The arguments for YEAR, MONTH, and DAY can be a date, timestamp, or date duration (we will explain the duration concept later in this chapter). HOUR, MINUTE, and SECOND will accept a time, timestamp, or time duration, and MICROSECOND will accept only a timestamp for an argument. Here's an example of how they're used:

```
SELECT  YEAR(CUST_DATE_OF_BIRTH), MONTH(CUST_DATE_OF_BIRTH),
        CUST_DATE_OF_BIRTH
    FROM CUSTOMER
```

RESULT TABLE:

```
                              CUST_DATE_OF_BIRTH
---------+----------+----------+----
    1962       3    1962-03-29
    1960       9    1960-09-21
    1947       8    1947-08-15
    1965      12    1965-12-25
    1942       6    1942-06-04
    1957      10    1957-10-24
    1970       1    1970-01-01
    1950       7    1950-07-04
```

As you can see, the YEAR function extracted the year from
CUST_DATE_OF_BIRTH, while the MONTH function extracted the
MONTH.

Now, suppose you wanted to know how many days it is until a specific
date. You could use these functions and get the DAY and MONTH and
try to do some fancy arithmetic, or you could use the DAYS function (not
to be confused with DAY). The arguments that are supported are date,
timestamp, or character representation of a date. DAYS returns a number representing the number of days between December 31, 0000, and
the date specified in the argument. While you will rarely be interested in
this number, you can use the DAYS function in an arithmetic expression
to find the number of days between two dates:

```
SELECT  CURRENT DATE, ACCT_START_DATE,
        DAYS(CURRENT DATE) - DAYS(ACCT_START_DATE)
    FROM ACCOUNT
```

RESULT TABLE:

```
              ACCT_START_DATE
----------+----------+----------+----------+
1989-05-20  1987-03-17              795
1989-05-20  1979-12-25             3434
1989-05-20  1980-01-01             3427
1989-05-20  1989-02-12               97
1989-05-20  1989-02-14               95
1989-05-20  1986-10-31              932
1989-05-20  1985-06-14             1436
1989-05-20  1979-05-20             3653
1989-05-20  1980-11-11             3112
```

This statement gives you the number of days that each account has existed as of today's date.

The last function we will describe is CHAR. CHAR converts a date/time value into a character string. It is most commonly used with two arguments. The first is the date/time value and the second is the abbreviation which indicates the format for the result. Look again at Fig. 6.2 for the format choices. The following statement shows how the same field can be represented in different formats:

```
SELECT CHAR(CUST_DATE_OF_BIRTH, USA),
       CHAR(CUST_DATE_OF_BIRTH, EUR)
  FROM CUSTOMER
```

RESULT TABLE:

```
---------+---------+--
03/29/1962   29.03.1962
09/21/1960   21.09.1960
08/15/1947   15.08.1947
12/25/1965   25.12.1965
06/04/1942   04.06.1942
10/24/1957   24.10.1957
01/01/1970   01.01.1970
07/04/1950   04.07.1950
```

We will see more examples of these functions as we describe other aspects of date and time operations.

6.1.3 Duration

DB2 provides the facilities that enable you to represent the concept of time and date durations. Duration is a number which indicates an interval of time. There are three types of durations: labeled, date, and time.

A labeled duration is represented by a number plus a keyword. The keyword may be YEAR, MONTH, DAY, HOUR, MINUTE, SECOND, OR MICROSECOND (or the plural of each); 10 HOURS, 2 MINUTES, and 1 MONTH are all examples of labeled durations.

A date duration is represented by eight digits and a decimal point in the format *yyyymmdd.* and is used to express an interval of time. The date duration 00200000., for example, is equivalent to the labeled duration, 20 YEARS, that is, 0020 years, 00 months, and 00 days, and 01000504. is equivalent to 100 YEARS, 5 MONTHS, and 4 DAYS. Similarily, a time duration, represented by six digits and a decimal point in the format *hhmmss.*, can be used to express an interval of time; 002505. expresses the interval of 25 minutes and 5 seconds.

A column in a table may contain a date or time duration but must be defined as DECIMAL (8,0) or (6,0), respectively. The fact that a duration is represented depends on the context in which it is used. For instance, our ACCOUNT table might have had a column OVERDRAWN_DAYS, indicating the number of days that an account can be overdrawn. If the value in this column were used in an arithmetic expression with another date value, it would be interpreted as a date duration. For instance, on the day that an account was overdrawn you could determine when to start withholding payment by coding:

```
SELECT CURRENT DATE + OVERDRAWN_DAYS
  FROM ACCOUNT
```

Here the value in OVERDRAWN_DAYS is treated as a duration and is added to the date in the special register, CURRENT DATE. If the CURRENT DATE was 1989-07-04 and the value in an account's OVERDRAWN_DAYS was 00000015, the result would be 1989-07-19. Incidentally, to show the resulting date on a report in the USA format, you could have used the CHAR function as follows:

```
SELECT CHAR((CURRENT DATE + OVERDRAWN_DAYS), USA)
  FROM ACCOUNT
```

Now the result would appear as 07/19/1989.

6.1.4 Arithmetic and Comparisons

Our last example used a date and a duration in an arithmetic expression. The rules, and exceptions to the rules, involving date/time data in arithmetic expressions are complex. For those particulars we refer you to IBM manuals. There is much, however, that we can say which will have many practical applications.

The only arithmetic operations valid for date/time values are addition and subtraction. Addition may be performed only when one operand is a duration. The other operand must be a date, time, or timestamp and the result will be a date, time, or timestamp. The order of the operands is optional. For example:

```
SELECT ACCT_START_DATE, (ACCT_START_DATE + 10 DAYS),
       (ACCT_START_DATE - 00000015.)
    FROM ACCOUNT
```

RESULT TABLE:

ACCT_START_DATE		
1987-03-17	1987-03-27	1987-03-02
1979-12-25	1980-01-04	1979-12-10
1980-01-01	1980-01-11	1979-12-17
1989-02-12	1989-02-22	1989-01-28
1989-02-14	1989-02-24	1989-01-30
1986-10-31	1986-11-10	1986-10-16
1985-06-14	1985-06-24	1985-05-30
1979-05-20	1979-05-30	1979-05-05
1980-11-11	1980-11-21	1980-10-27

In the above, we've used a column value with a labeled duration (10 DAYS) and a column value with a date duration (00000015.).

One peculiarity to be aware of is the inconsistency which results when a MONTH duration is used in an expression. Since the length of a month varies, asking DB2 to add or subtract any number of months from a date will produce erroneous results. You'd be better off explicitly adding or subtracting a number of days instead.

In addition to expressions in which one operand is a duration, you can also subtract a date from a date or a time from a time to get the span of time between two dates or two times. The result will be a date duration or time duration. For example, the difference between 03/01/80 and 03/01/88 is 8 YEARS. Addition of dates or times does not make sense, so for addition, one operand must be a duration. SQL does not have a timestamp duration, so timestamps may not be subtracted from timestamps. Let's see what happens when we subtract one date from another. In this example, we're going to determine the customer's age at the time that the account was opened:

```
SELECT ACCT_NO, (ACCT_START_DATE - CUST_DATE_OF_BIRTH)
    FROM CUSTOMER, ACCOUNT
    WHERE CUST_SOC_SEC = ACCT_CUST_ID
```

RESULT TABLE:

ACCT_NO	
AE11	241119.
BB12	280423.
CE21	370930.
AB21	230118.
DB11	380507.
AE12	370621.
BB13	290007.
DE11	90419.
AE21	290528.

The way we determine the customer's age is to first subtract their date of birth from the open date of the account. We've joined information from two tables, CUSTOMER and ACCOUNT. The result of subtracting the date of birth from the account start date is a date duration, which shows the number of years, months, and days between the customer's birth and the account's start date. To translate that into the customer's age when the account was opened, we could extract the years portion of the result by modifying the same statement to read:

```
SELECT ACCT_NO,  YEAR(ACCT_START_DATE - CUST_DATE_OF_BIRTH)
FROM CUSTOMER, ACCOUNT
WHERE CUST_SOC_SEC = ACCT_CUST_ID
```

RESULT TABLE:

ACCT_NO	
AE11	24
BB12	28
CE21	37
AB21	23
DB11	38
AE12	37
BB13	29
DE11	9
AE21	29

This statement determines the difference between the two dates but only presents the difference in years. This, of course, is the age of the customer.

In a subtraction statement, you may substitute a character representation of a date or time value for one, and only one, of the operands. The following expression, therefore, is not valid:

```
'10.30.00' - '10.15.00'
```

However, since the TIME function converts a character string to a TIME value, we can use it to create the following valid expression:

```
TIME('10.30.00') - '10.15.00'
```

The result of this expression will be the time duration 001500., or 15 minutes.

6.2 MODIFYING THE DATABASE

In the preceding two chapters, we explained the options available with SQL's SELECT statement. Undoubtedly, your work will also require that you make changes to a database, and for that, the DML component of SQL has three operations in addition to retrieval: INSERT, DELETE, and UPDATE. All three will modify a database, but with them, only one table or view may be the object of modification.

6.2.1 View Restrictions

If you want to modify a view, the view itself must be derived from a single base table. That is, it may not be based on a join of two or more tables. An additional restriction is that the view may not have been defined using the column functions GROUP BY or DISTINCT. For INSERT and UPDATE only, a view may not contain any column which is defined with an arithmetic expression or scalar function.

6.2.2 INSERT

INSERT is the statement used to add rows to an existing table or view. It always operates on an entire row because, unlike SELECT, where you can work with part of a row, you cannot INSERT part of a row.

You can insert a single row by specifying the values for the row or insert multiple rows by specifying a subset of an existing table. The first is a simple insert; the second is a mass insert.

The following format is used to insert a single row:

```
INSERT INTO table or view
    (list of column names)
    VALUES (list of values)
```

The position of the values in the list of values must correspond exactly to the position of the column names to which they apply. In addition, the values in the VALUE clause must always be compatible with the data type and length of the corresponding columns. If a column has been defined as NULL, you may specify NULL in the VALUE clause. If a column has been defined as NOT NULL WITH DEFAULT, you may use a positional comma in the VALUE clause to set a column to its default value.

The list of column names is optional because DB2 will automatically include all of the columns when it adds the row. Column names are not included in the following example (after each INSERT example we include a display of the table as it appears after the INSERT):

```
INSERT INTO BRANCH
VALUES (700, 'SUE LAIDLER', '12 MAIDEN LANE')
```

RESULT TABLE:

BRANCH_ID	BRANCH_CITY	BRANCH_MGR	BRANCH_ADDR
12	NEW YORK	HIRO TANAKA	43 WEST 57 STREET
300	YONKERS	BRUCE HOFFMAN	7 MORANI STREET
450	ROCHESTER	ANGELA VALENTINO	351 TEAL PLAZA
670	NEW YORK	MATTHEW GREEN	900 WALL STREET
890	YONKERS	ZILYA KOLKER	610 OSIO LANE
13	CORNING	JOE GROSSMAN	ONE FEDERAL PLAZA
700		SUE LAIDLER	12 MAIDEN LANE

Here we have inserted a single row into the BRANCH table. Notice that although we did not include a list of column names, DB2 inserted all of the column values, ordered as they exist in the BRANCH table definition. Because we specified no value for BRANCH_CITY, its default, spaces, has been inserted.

The following example includes a list of column names:

```
INSERT INTO CUSTOMER
    (CUST_BRANCH, CUST_SOC_SEC, CUST_DATE_OF_BIRTH)
VALUES (670, 100000000, '1989-01-01')
```

RESULT TABLE:

CUST_SOC_SEC	CUST_NAME	CUST_DATE_OF_BIRTH	CUST_BRANCH	CUST_RATING
111111111	PHYLLIS ELKIND	1962-03-29	12	4
222222222	JAY RANADE	1960-09-21	890	8
333333333	RICHARD GREEN	1947-08-15	12	7
444444444	----------------	1965-12-25	670	9
555555555	HEIDI SCHMIDT	1942-06-04	890	2
666666666	MUKESH SEHGAL	1957-10-24	300	5
777777777	LAI-HA NG	1970-01-01	450	7
888888888	GEORGE SCHMIDT	1950-07-04	12	2
100000000	----------------	1989-01-01	670	0

Here we've only named three of the table's six columns and have specified an order different from the table's column order. Since we cannot add a partial row, the columns we have not specified will still be included in the new row, but they will be filled with their default values. The columns CUST_FIRST_NAME and CUST_LAST_NAME are defined as NULL in our database. Therefore, in the new row they are displayed as null (meaning their null indicator has been set to hex 'FF'). CUST_RATING, defined in the database as NOT NULL WITH DEFAULT, has been filled with its default value, zero, since it has a numeric data type.

If any of our columns had been defined as NOT NULL, we would have gotten an error if we had excluded them from our INSERT statement because a value is required. Therefore, the definition of a column as NOT NULL should be used with care.

The following general format is used to insert a subset of data from one table into another (a mass insert):

```
INSERT INTO table or view
    (list of column names)
    subselect
```

Again the list of column names is optional. The subselect may be any valid SELECT statement, but the columns in the SELECT clause must correspond to the explicit or implicit list of column names in the INSERT statement.

This technique can be quite useful for creating a test, or temporary, table. Let's suppose we've already created a table called TEST_TRANSACTION whose columns match those of the TRANSACTION table in data type and size. We can insert a subset of the TRANSACTION table into our new table with the following INSERT statement:

```
INSERT INTO TEST_TRANSACTION
    SELECT *
      FROM TRANSACTION
     WHERE TXN_TYPE = 'DEBIT'
```

We're adding all of the debit transactions into the TEST_TRANSACTION table. Our table would now contain the following data:

TSTTX_TYPE	TSTTX_TIMESTAMP	TSTTX_AMOUNT	TSTTX_ACCT_NO
DEBIT	1989-02-03-18.18.18.000000	100.00	AE21
DEBIT	1989-02-04-20.20.20.000000	1200.55	DE11

A mass insert can also be used to load a table with information from two tables. Assume that we have a new table called CUSTOMER_MGR and that it contains the columns SOC_SEC and MANAGER, which correspond to CUST_SOC_SEC in the CUSTOMER table and BRANCH_MGR in the BRANCH table. The table will provide a cross-reference to the customer's branch manager by the customer's social security number. The table could be loaded by coding the following statement:

```
INSERT INTO CUSTOMER_MGR
   (CUSTMGR_SOC_SEC, CUSTMGR_MANAGER)
   SELECT CUST_SOC_SEC, BRANCH_MGR
   FROM BRANCH, CUSTOMER
   WHERE BRANCH_ID = CUST_BRANCH
```

RESULT TABLE:

```
CUSTMGR_SOC_SEC   CUSTMGR_MANAGER
----------+-----------+---------+---
   888888888   HIRO TANAKA
   111111111   HIRO TANAKA
   333333333   HIRO TANAKA
   666666666   BRUCE HOFFMAN
   777777777   ANGELA VALENTINO
   444444444   MATTHEW GREEN
   100000000   MATTHEW GREEN
   222222222   ZILYA KOLKER
   555555555   ZILYA KOLKER
```

Here we are inserting rows into CUSTOMERMGR by selecting the corresponding columns from the join of BRANCH and CUSTOMER. We have included the column name list in the INSERT statement for documentation purposes. The new base table contains data joined from our two original tables. You've probably noticed that when doing a mass insert from one or more tables into a new table, the new table does not have to have all of the columns of the tables from which it is receiving data.

6.2.3 DELETE

DELETE is used to remove rows from a table. Like INSERT, SQL's DELETE statement operates on an entire row at once. The result of a DELETE is the removal of zero to many rows from a table or view. The general format of the DELETE statement is:

```
DELETE
FROM table or view
WHERE search condition
```

The WHERE clause here is like the SELECT statement's WHERE clause. It is optional, and it contains a search condition which each row must satisfy to be, in this case, deleted. Just as a SELECT statement with no WHERE clause will select all of the rows from a table, a DELETE statement with no WHERE clause will delete all of the rows from a table. This is not what you usually mean to do, so beware of leaving it out by mistake.

The following statement will delete the row that we added from the BRANCH table in our earlier INSERT example:

```
DELETE
  FROM BRANCH
  WHERE BRANCH_ID = 700
```

RESULT TABLE:

BRANCH_ID	BRANCH_CITY	BRANCH_MGR	BRANCH_ADDR
12	NEW YORK	HIRO TANAKA	43 WEST 57 STREET
300	YONKERS	BRUCE HOFFMAN	7 MORANI STREET
450	ROCHESTER	ANGELA VALENTINO	351 TEAL PLAZA
670	NEW YORK	MATTHEW GREEN	900 WALL STREET
890	YONKERS	ZILYA KOLKER	610 OSIO LANE
13	CORNING	JOE GROSSMAN	ONE FEDERAL PLAZA

In this case, we have only one row that satisfies the condition that BRANCH_ID = 700. You can see that it has been deleted.

All of the options available on the SELECT statement's WHERE clause may be used here, including a subquery or correlated subquery. The only difference is that when the outer statement is a DELETE, a subquery or correlated subquery must reference a different table from the table that is the object of the DELETE statement. The following is an example of a DELETE statement which contains a subquery:

```
DELETE
  FROM CUSTOMER
  WHERE CUST_RATING < 4 AND CUST_BRANCH IN
    (SELECT BRANCH_ID
       FROM BRANCH
       WHERE BRANCH_MGR = 'MATTHEW GREEN')
```

RESULT TABLE:

CUST_SOC_SEC	CUST_NAME	CUST_DATE_OF_BIRTH	CUST_BRANCH	CUST_RATING
111111111	PHYLLIS ELKIND	1962-03-29	12	4
222222222	JAY RANADE	1960-09-21	890	8
333333333	RICHARD GREEN	1947-08-15	12	7
444444444	-------------	1965-12-25	670	9
555555555	HEIDI SCHMIDT	1942-06-04	890	2
666666666	MUKESH SEHGAL	1957-10-24	300	5
777777777	LAI-HA NG	1970-01-01	450	7
888888888	GEORGE SCHMIDT	1950-07-04	12	2

As with a SELECT statement, DB2 first processes the subquery SELECT BRANCH_ID FROM BRANCH WHERE BRANCH_MGR = 'MATTHEW GREEN'. This gets the ID for Matthew Green's branch, 670. This value is passed to the outer DELETE and substituted into the condition in the WHERE clause. The statement now says to delete customers in branch 670 whose rating is less than 4. The row which meets the condition CUST_RATING < 4 AND CUST_BRANCH IN (670) is deleted from the CUSTOMER table. This, it turns out, is a row we added with a previous INSERT.

6.2.4 UPDATE

The fourth and last operator of SQL's DML is UPDATE. Like INSERT and DELETE, it involves modifying the database. However, unlike them, it may be used to operate on specific columns within a row or set of rows.

The general format of the UPDATE statement is:

```
UPDATE table or view
   SET column1 = value1, column2 = value2 . . .
   WHERE search condition
```

The UPDATE clause identifies the table or view to be modified. The SET clause identifies one or more columns and the values with which they should be replaced. Remember, in an INSERT, DELETE, or UPDATE, only one table or view may be the object of the operation.

Like DELETE, a WHERE clause is optional in the UPDATE statement. If you use WHERE, however, only the columns in those rows which satisfy the condition in the WHERE clause will be updated. The WHERE clause may contain a subquery or correlated subquery. If it does, the table or view of the outer UPDATE must be different from that of the subquery. If there is no WHERE clause, the updates will be applied to all of the rows in the table.

The first example we'll look at updates one row's account balance and credit balance:

```
UPDATE ACCOUNT
   SET ACCT_BALANCE = 80.00, ACCT_CREDIT_BAL = 1000.00
   WHERE ACCT_NO = 'AE21'
```

RESULT TABLE:

ACCT_NO	ACCT_BALANCE	ACCT_CREDIT_BAL	ACCT_CUST_ID	ACCT_START_DATE
AE11	12000.94	500.00	111111111	1987-03-17
AE12	500.00	500.00	555555555	1979-12-25
AE21	80.00	1000.00	888888888	1980-01-01
AB21	.00	180.55	444444444	1989-02-12
BB12	12001.35	3300.00	222222222	1989-02-14
BB13	646.01	25.00	666666666	1986-10-31
CE21	35100.98	100.00	333333333	1985-06-14
DE11	20.00	25.00	777777777	1979-05-20
DB11	75.00	.00	555555555	1980-11-11

As you can see, the values for ACCT_BALANCE and ACCT_CREDIT_BAL have been replaced in only one row, the one with ACCT_NO AE21.

In the next example, several rows satisfy the WHERE condition and are thus updated according to the SET clause's specification:

```
UPDATE ACCOUNT
    SET ACCT_BALANCE = ACCT_BALANCE + 5000
    WHERE ACCT_NO LIKE '_B%'

RESULT TABLE:
```

ACCT_NO	ACCT_BALANCE	ACCT_CREDIT_BAL	ACCT_CUST_ID	ACCT_START_DATE
AE11	12000.94	500.00	111111111	1987-03-17
AE12	500.00	500.00	555555555	1979-12-25
AE21	80.00	1000.00	888888888	1980-01-01
AB21	5000.00	180.55	444444444	1989-02-12
BB12	17001.35	3300.00	222222222	1989-02-14
BB13	5646.01	25.00	666666666	1986-10-31
CE21	35100.98	100.00	333333333	1985-06-14
DE11	20.00	25.00	777777777	1979-05-20
DB11	5075.00	.00	555555555	1980-11-11

In a generous mood, we've just added $5000 to the account of everyone with a B in the second position of their account number. While we used constants in the first example, in this one the value in the SET clause is an arithmetic expression. You may also use a column name which will replace the column's current value with the value of a different column in the same row, or you can use a special register. Here's an example which uses both of these alternatives:

```
UPDATE ACCOUNT
    SET ACCT_BALANCE = ACCT_CREDIT_BAL,
        ACCT_START_DATE = CURRENT DATE
    WHERE ACCT_NO = 'AE21'

RESULT TABLE:
```

ACCT_NO	ACCT_BALANCE	ACCT_CREDIT_BAL	ACCT_CUST_ID	ACCT_START_DATE
AE11	12000.94	500.00	111111111	1987-03-17
AE12	500.00	500.00	555555555	1979-12-25
AE21	1000.00	1000.00	888888888	1989-05-20
AB21	5000.00	180.55	444444444	1989-02-12
BB12	17001.35	3300.00	222222222	1989-02-14
BB13	5646.01	25.00	666666666	1986-10-31
CE21	35100.98	100.00	333333333	1985-06-14
DE11	20.00	25.00	777777777	1979-05-20
DB11	5075.00	.00	555555555	1980-11-11

This statement updates the row for account AE11 in the ACCOUNT table. The value in ACCT_BALANCE will be changed to the value in ACCT_CREDIT_VAL.

If you have been following along with your own database, you can return it to its original state for use in future chapters. The following UPDATEs will undo all of our previous changes:

```
UPDATE ACCOUNT
  SET ACCT_BALANCE = 77.53,
      ACCT_CREDIT_BAL = 2000,
      ACCT_START_DATE = '1980-01-01'
  WHERE ACCT_NO = 'AE21';

UPDATE ACCOUNT
  SET ACCT_BALANCE = ACCT_BALANCE - 5000
  WHERE ACCT_NO LIKE '_B%'
```

6.3   REFERENTIAL INTEGRITY WITH INSERT, DELETE, AND UPDATE

When a table is defined, the referential constraints associated with that table are specified. *Referential constraints specify the relationships between the primary and foreign keys of parent and dependent tables and the actions to take to maintain those relationships during update operations.* Once defined, these relationships are automatically maintained by DB2 in order to preserve the database's referential integrity. Referential constraint violations may occur during the execution of INSERT, UPDATE, or DELETE statements.

6.3.1   INSERT

When you insert a row into a dependent table, the values in that row's foreign key columns must either be null or have corresponding values in the parent table's primary key columns.

The BRANCH table is a parent table to the CUSTOMER table. CUST_BRANCH is the foreign key in CUSTOMER, relating to the BRANCH table's primary key, BRANCH_ID. The following INSERT statement results in the error message below it:

```
INSERT INTO CUSTOMER
  (CUST_SOC_SEC, CUST_BRANCH)
  VALUES (111111112, 999)
```

ERROR MESSAGE:

```
-530 THE INSERT OR UPDATE VALUE OF FOREIGN KEY RCCUST
     IS INVALID
```

In the above INSERT statement, we have specified a value for the foreign key which does exist in the BRANCH table. This not only violates referential integrity, but common sense as well. How can a customer belong to a branch that does not exist?

6.3.2   DELETE

Deleting a row from a parent table will have different results depending on the DELETE option specified in the table's referential constraints. The options are restrict (the default), set null, and cascade. If DELETE RESTRICT has been specified, your DELETE will fail if you attempt to delete a row from a parent table when there are still rows in the dependent table whose foreign key corresponds to the primary key of the parent table. In other words, as long as one foreign key containing a value in the row to be deleted still exists, DELETE RESTRICT will prevent you from deleting the row in the parent table. This is the option used throughout the book for our sample database. The following is an example of an invalid DELETE statement:

```
DELETE
    FROM BRANCH
    WHERE BRANCH_ID = 12

ERROR MESSAGE:

    -532 THE RELATIONSHIP RCCUST RESTRICTS THE DELETION
         OF ROW WITH RID X'00000201'
```

The CUSTOMER table, a dependent of the BRANCH table, still has rows in which the value of the foreign key column, CUST_BRANCH, is 12. Therefore, it would violate referential integrity to delete that row from the parent table. Incidentally, you may have noticed that the error message refers to the row by its internal RID (row identifier).

If DELETE SET NULL has been specified, deleting a row from a parent table will cause the nullable columns in the dependent table's foreign key to be set to null. When creating the table, SET NULL can only be specified if at least one column in the foreign key allows nulls.

If DELETE CASCADE has been specified, deleting a row from a primary table will cause the associated rows in all dependent tables to be deleted as well. This will propagate down to tables which are dependents of the dependent table as well if DELETE CASCADE has also been specified for those relationships.

In our sample database, if DELETE CASCADE had been specified instead of DELETE RESTRICT for the database's referential constraints, the previous DELETE statement would not be in error but would, instead, affect all of the tables in our database:

```
DELETE
    FROM BRANCH
    WHERE BRANCHID = 12
```

Figure 6.3 shows the BRANCH, CUSTOMER, ACCOUNT, and TRANSACTION tables after such a delete. If you compare them to the tables in Fig. 6.1, you'll see that by deleting the row for branch 12, we have also deleted the rows for customers 111111111, 333333333, and 888888888 and, in turn, the rows for accounts AE11, AE32, and CE21 and, in turn again, the transactions for those accounts. Remember, this is hypothetical since we did not specify DELETE CASCADE in our definitions, but it should serve to alert you to the potential power of DELETE when DELETE CASCADE is defined as the referential constraint.

6.3.3 UPDATE

The only option for referential integrity supported by DB2 for UPDATE is RESTRICT. If you are updating a row in the parent table,

BRANCH:

BRANCH_ID	BRANCH_CITY	BRANCH_MGR	BRANCH_ADDR
300	YONKERS	BRUCE HOFFMAN	7 MORANI STREET
450	ROCHESTER	ANGELA VALENTINO	351 TEAL PLAZA
670	NEW YORK	MATTHEW GREEN	900 WALL STREET
890	YONKERS	ZILYA KOLKER	610 OSIO LANE
13	CORNING	JOE GROSSMAN	ONE FEDERAL PLAZA

CUSTOMER:

CUST_SOC_SEC	CUST_NAME	CUST_DATE_OF_BIRTH	CUST_BRANCH	CUST_RATING
222222222	JAY RANADE	1960-09-21	890	8
444444444	------------------	1965-12-25	670	9
555555555	HEIDI SCHMIDT	1942-06-04	890	2
666666666	MUKESH SEHGAL	1957-10-24	300	5
777777777	LAI-HA NG	1970-01-01	450	7

ACCOUNT:

ACCT_NO	ACCT_BALANCE	ACCT_CREDIT_BAL	ACCT_CUST_ID	ACCT_START_DATE
AE12	500.00	500.00	555555555	1979-12-25
AB21	.00	180.55	444444444	1989-02-12
BB12	12001.35	3300.00	222222222	1989-02-14
BB13	646.01	25.00	666666666	1986-10-31
DE11	20.00	25.00	777777777	1979-05-20
DB11	75.00	.00	555555555	1980-11-11

TRANSACTION:

TXN_TYPE	TXN_TIMESTAMP	TXN_AMOUNT	TXN_ACCT_NO
CREDIT	1989-01-01-12.12.12.000000	200.50	BB12
CREDIT	1989-01-01-13.13.13.000000	1200.00	BB12
DEBIT	1989-02-04-20.20.20.000000	1200.55	DE11

Figure 6.3 The result of a DELETE CASCADE.

you may not modify the primary key columns if rows with those values exist in a dependent table:

```
UPDATE BRANCH
   SET BRANCH_ID = 312
   WHERE BRANCH_ID = 300
```

ERROR MESSAGE:

```
-531  THE PRIMARY KEY IN A PARENT ROW CANNOT BE
      UPDATED
```

Because the CUSTOMER table contains a row in which the value of the foreign key column, CUST_BRANCH, is 300, this UPDATE has failed. Similarly you cannot update a dependent table's foreign key column to a value which does not have a corresponding value in the parent table. This may cause a problem if the ID of your branch does, in fact, change. However, there are ways around this. For example, the referential constraints linking the tables can be dropped, or a dummy primary key can be maintained in the parent table and used in a two-step update of the foreign key.

Remember, these constraints and referential integrity, in general, are optional. It is hoped that future releases of DB2 will support additional UPDATE options.

Query Management Facility

Part

3

Query Management Facility

7

QMF Overview

Query Management Facility (QMF) is an interactive facility offered by IBM to supplement SPUFI. Like SPUFI, QMF enables you to dynamically submit SQL statements that retrieve and modify data in DB2 tables. Having read Chaps. 4, 5, and 6 of this book, which describe SQL's Data Manipulation Language (DML), you are well on your way to also knowing QMF. Data Definition and Data Control statements, described in Chap. 14, may also be submitted through QMF, but its main use is as a query tool with DML SELECT statements. QMF differs from SPUFI in two major ways. First, it is meant to be more of an end-user facility than SPUFI, which is designed solely for DP personnel, and second, QMF provides sophisticated report formatting facilities.

QMF is designed for a variety of users and their differing needs. For DP personnel, QMF offers 4GL-type productivity gains. The combination of QMF and SQL makes it easy to look at test data in different ways, e.g., generating control totals, counting the number of distinct values, etc. It is also possible to create production reports in a fraction of the time it would take with COBOL or any other 3GL programming language. Modifications to reports are equally easy. It must also be noted, however, that as with any other 4GL report writer, QMF cannot provide as much flexibility as a COBOL report program and furthermore, QMF will have more overhead. Your management and users will have to decide if the reduced development and maintenance costs merit a compromise in report format flexibility and operational overhead. QMF can be used to replace CICS inquiry programs, but here, too, the operational overhead and limited flexibility must be balanced with the pluses.

QMF is also meant to be a tool for end-user ad hoc queries, although the degree to which it succeeds in this is open to debate. While QMF's basic options are not hard to learn, can a user easily pick up the SQL syntax required for formulating a query? Although SQL is a higher-level language than COBOL, it is still basically a programmer's language.

To help with this, QMF provides two alternatives to SQL for writing queries, QBE (Query By Example) and Prompted Query. The choice of language, QBE, SQL, or Prompted Query, is made on the QMF Profile Panel, which is reached from the Home Panel. Since this book is intended for DP professionals, our discusion of QMF will focus on the SQL interface. Our queries will be identical to those we submitted through SPUFI. The only difference is that QMF will only accept one query at a time, so we may not submit several queries separated by semicolons as we did in SPUFI. At the end of the chapter we will take a brief look at QMF's alternatives to SQL, QBE and Prompted Query.

7.1 FIRST STEPS

How you get to QMF will depend on how it has been installed at your site. It may be a choice on your ISPF Menu, a choice on one of its submenus, a CLIST, etc. When you invoke QMF, you are presented with the QMF Home Panel. From there you will navigate to other QMF panels through a combination of commands and PF keys. Let's start by looking at QMF's Home Panel.

7.1.1 Home Panel

Figure 7.1 shows the QMF Home Panel. There is a command line at the bottom and a set of PF key assignments above it. Messages from QMF will appear above the command line. From this panel you can go to the panels associated with writing queries (PF6 = QUERY), formatting the output of queries (PF9 = FORM), writing procedures (PF10 = PROC), viewing a formatted report (PF12 = REPORT), modifying your QMF profile (PF11 = PROFILE), or viewing the output of a query as a chart (PF5 = CHART). The ability to display charts depends on your installation's configuration of software and hardware. We will not discuss charts in this book. The other PF keys on the Home Panel are shorthand ways of executing the QMF commands HELP, RETRIEVE, LIST, and SHOW. You will learn more about these commands shortly, but before we explain any operations in detail, let's first get an overview of QMF.

7.1.2 QMF Overview

For our first look at QMF we will write a query, look at the default report that QMF produces for it, modify the report format, and then

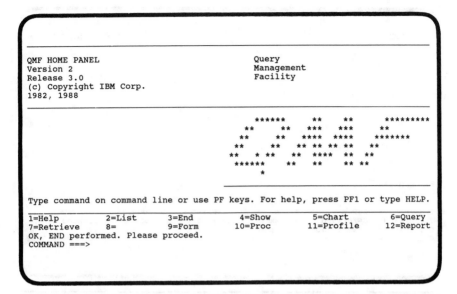

Figure 7.1   QMF Home Panel.

save both the query and the modified format. Starting at the QMF Home Panel, press PF6 to display a blank SQL Query Panel (Fig. 7.2). The Enter key acts as a toggle between each panel's command line and panel area. Press Enter to get to the panel area and type the following:

```
-- WE ARE USING THIS QUERY TO TRY OUT QMF
--
SELECT BRANCH_MGR, BRANCH_ID, BRANCH_CITY
   FROM BRANCH
```

Notice that you can enter comments with dashes as you did in SPUFI. The entry part of the panel can be edited by using the INSERT and DELETE PF keys, which insert or delete lines on the panel. With long queries you may want to use ISPF's editor. It can be invoked by typing EDIT QUERY on the command line and pressing Enter. This transforms the panel area into ISPF EDIT mode and the PF key assignments are now those of your ISPF profile. Now you can use all of the line commands you are used to for deleting, copying, or repeating lines. Another useful aspect of EDIT mode is that you can use PF1 to access the help screen as you would in a TSO session. PF3 will end the ISPF EDIT mode, which you'll need to do when you want to tell QMF to run your query. Of course, the same DB2 authorizations will apply here as with SPUFI when you attempt to access data. Using QMF it-

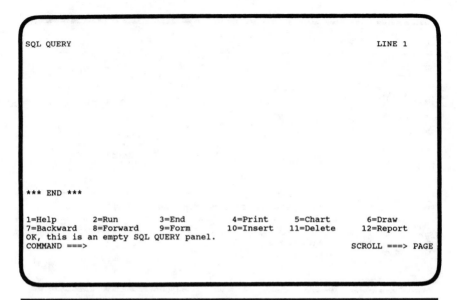

Figure 7.2   The SQL Query Panel.

self also requires DB2 authority, but many installations grant this privilege to PUBLIC, meaning that everyone can use it.

Having typed the query, you are now ready to execute it. The QMF command for submitting a query to DB2 is RUN QUERY, which can be typed on the command line or issued through PF2 = RUN. After submitting the query you are presented with the Data Base Status Panel and a cost estimate for your request (Fig. 7.3). This estimate reflects the amount of database work your query will involve. While you cannot take this figure literally, you can get an idea of the amount of overhead that will be involved and decide, if it is excessive (let's say four digits or greater), to interrupt the query by pressing the Reset key and then PA1. You will then be presented with the choice to continue, cancel, or debug the command. In our own experience, we have found the cost estimate to be so approximate that it is not very help-

```
                         DATA BASE STATUS PANEL

         Your request is currently being processed by the Data Base Manager.

           The relative cost estimate for your request is: 5
```

Figure 7.3   The Data Base Status Panel estimates the cost.

ful. There is also a QMF Governor and a DB2 Governor which can automatically cancel queries which exceed the installation-set time limit or the installation-set maximum number of rows retrieved limit.

The results of your query are displayed using QMF's default format (Fig. 7.4), which is quite similar to SPUFI's. The difference between SPUFI and QMF is that with the latter you can modify the format, a topic we will go into in some detail later in this chapter. For now, let's make a simple change. We are on the Report Panel, as noted in the upper left-hand corner of the screen. Notice that PF keys differ from panel to panel. Here, PF9=FORM takes you to the FORM.MAIN Panel from which you can modify your report format (Fig. 7.5). We will make a simple change and add a heading to our report:

```
HEADING ===> MY FIRST QMF REPORT
```

If you now press PF12=REPORT, you will be taken back to the Report Panel where the report will reflect the heading you specified on the Form Panel (Fig. 7.6).

If we ended our QMF session now, we would lose our query and our modified report format. Let's assume we'll want to run this query again next month. Toggle to the command line by pressing Enter and type:

```
SAVE QUERY AS MYQUERY
```

```
REPORT                                    LINE 1      POS 1     79


    BRANCH                  BRANCH   BRANCH
      MGR                     ID     CITY
    -------------------------  ------   --------------------
    HIRO TANAKA                  12   NEW YORK
    BRUCE HOFFMAN               300   YONKERS
    ANGELA VALENTINO            450   ROCHESTER
    MATTHEW GREEN               670   NEW YORK
    ZILYA KOLKER                890   YONKERS
    JOE GROSSMAN                 13   CORNING


    *** END ***



    1=Help          2=          3=End       4=Print      5=Chart      6=Query
    7=Backward    8=Forward     9=Form     10=Left      11=Right     12=
    OK, this is the REPORT from your RUN command.
    COMMAND ===>                                        SCROLL ===> PAGE
```

Figure 7.4   QMF's default report for the Query.

```
FORM.MAIN

COLUMNS:                    Total Width of Report Columns: 57
  NUM COLUMN HEADING                                USAGE  INDENT WIDTH EDIT  SEQ
  --- ------------------------------------------- ------- ------ ----- ----- ---
    1 BRANCH_MGR                                       2      25   C      1
    2 BRANCH_ID                                        2       6   L      2
    3 BRANCH_CITY                                      2      20   C      3
      *** END ***


PAGE:      HEADING   ===>
           FOOTING   ===>
FINAL:     TEXT      ===>
BREAK1:    NEW PAGE FOR BREAK? ===> NO
           FOOTING   ===>
BREAK2:    NEW PAGE FOR BREAK? ===> NO
           FOOTING   ===>
OPTIONS: OUTLINE? ===> YES                 DEFAULT BREAK TEXT? ===> YES

1=Help      2=Check    3=End        4=Show         5=Chart       6=Query
7=Backward 8=Forward  9=           10=Insert      11=Delete     12=Report
OK, FORM is displayed.
COMMAND ===>                                          SCROLL ===> PAGE
```

Figure 7.5   FORM.MAIN is used to modify format.

```
REPORT                                      LINE 1      POS 1     79
               MY FIRST QMF REPORT

    BRANCH                      BRANCH  BRANCH
      MGR                         ID    CITY
    ------------------------    ------  --------------------
    HIRO TANAKA                     12  NEW YORK
    BRUCE HOFFMAN                  300  YONKERS
    ANGELA VALENTINO              450  ROCHESTER
    MATTHEW GREEN                 670  NEW YORK
    ZILYA KOLKER                  890  YONKERS
    JOE GROSSMAN                   13  CORNING


*** END ***




1=Help      2=         3=End        4=Print        5=Chart       6=Query
7=Backward 8=Forward  9=Form       10=Left        11=Right      12=
OK, this is the REPORT from your RUN command.
COMMAND ===>                                          SCROLL ===> PAGE
```

Figure 7.6   A heading is added to the report.

Use whatever name you'd like following AS. Assuming that we will also want our modified form, we can type:

SAVE FORM AS MYFORM.

Next month when we want to run this query again we will type:

RUN MYQUERY (FORM=MYFORM

Notice, no right parenthesis is required. This overview has now touched on several topics that are worth taking a closer look at. The first is QMF's use of temporary and permanent objects.

7.2 TEMPORARY AND PERMANENT OBJECTS

In the overview, you entered a query on the Query Panel and then modified and viewed its output on the Report and Form Panels. While still on the Report Panel, you issued the command SAVE QUERY AS MYQUERY, and QMF saved the query you had previously typed on the Query Panel. This is because a query entered on the Query Panel is held in a temporary storage area where it remains until one of three things happens: you type in a different query, you issue the RESET command, or you leave QMF. QUERY is one of QMF's five temporary storage areas. The others are DATA, FORM, PROC, and PROFILE. So when you typed SAVE QUERY AS MYQUERY, you told QMF to save the contents of the QUERY temporary storage area in a file named MYQUERY.

Temporary storage areas can be thought of as temporary objects. Each is cleared at the end of a QMF session and only one of each may exist at any given moment during a session. QUERY, FORM, PROC, and PROFILE all have panels of the same name associated with them; DATA does not. As you'll soon see, DATA is viewed through the Report Panel. The commands SHOW or DISPLAY bring you to the appropriate panel. In our example above, if you issued the command SHOW QUERY, you would be brought to the Query Panel. SHOW FORM would take you to the Form Panel, which holds your most recent modifications. PF keys can also be used to navigate to these panels. When you begin a QMF session, the temporary storage areas and, therefore, the panels are empty. When you enter or change the contents of one of those panels, you change the contents of the associated temporary storage area.

As you saw in the overview, temporary objects may be made permanent by issuing the SAVE command. Later, you'll see how permanent objects can be recalled into temporary storage through several different commands. The home for permanent objects is the DB2 database.

The QMF objects, QUERY, FORM, PROC, and PROFILE, are stored as rows in the QMF tables, which hold information about QMF objects. DATA is stored as its own DB2 base table. When a permanent object is retrieved, it is copied into the appropriate temporary storage area where you can modify it without affecting the permanent object. If you save the modified version using the same name, you will replace the old version. The command used to clear a temporary storage area is RESET. RESET has no effect on the permanent objects you have created. Now let's take a brief look at each object.

7.2.1 QUERY

As we've mentioned, QUERY holds a single SQL statement, most commonly a SQL SELECT statement. You may use DISPLAY or SHOW to see the contents of QUERY on the Query Panel and RESET to clear it. RUN QUERY will submit the contents of QUERY for execution. To create a permanent QUERY object, code:

    SAVE QUERY AS queryname

7.2.2 DATA

A QMF query, like any other SQL SELECT statement, returns a subset of data in a result table. In QMF, that subset of data is put into the DATA temporary storage area. Unlike the other temporary objects, DATA is not associated with a panel, so you cannot DISPLAY or SHOW data directly. Instead you would use SHOW REPORT or DISPLAY REPORT. They will bring you to the Report Panel where you can see the contents of DATA formatted by FORM. You can enter a RESET DATA command to clear the temporary storage area and a SAVE DATA AS dataname to save it. SAVE DATA is different from the other QMF SAVE commands. It does not add a row to the QMF object table but, instead, actually creates a new base table in the tablespace specified in your profile. You must have the authority to create a table in this tablespace. The problem with the SAVE DATA command is that the creation of a table causes a lock on its database, and if several QMF users do this at the same time, it could grind the system to a halt. As a result, it is not uncommon to limit the SAVE DATA privilege to a small group of users.

7.2.3 FORM

The temporary storage area FORM holds the formatting instructions for DATA. There are actually several panels associated with FORM. Right now we'll concentrate on the primary one. You may use SHOW

FORM or DISPLAY FORM to go to the first Form Panel, FORM.MAIN. When you execute a query, a FORM, appropriate to that data, is created in the temporary storage area. As with the other panels, you can change the contents of FORM through the Form panels. For example, in our earlier example we added a heading. If you then issue the RUN QUERY command, the contents of temporary storage area FORM are replaced with QMF's default format values again. If you want to run the query and use the current contents of FORM, you must use the following command:

```
RUN QUERY (FORM=FORM
```

RESET behaves a little differently with FORM. With QUERY, DATA and, as we will see, PROC, RESET clears a temporary storage area. With FORM, it doesn't empty the temporary storage area; it returns it to QMF's default format values for the current contents of DATA. FORM may be saved in the same way as QUERY.

7.2.4 PROC

We turn now to the object PROC. A PROC, or procedure, is an object which contains QMF commands. SHOW PROC or DISPLAY PROC takes you to the Proc Panel. A procedure may contain one or more QMF commands and can be executed by a single RUN command. We might construct a procedure which contains the following commands:

```
RUN MYQUERY (FORM=MYFORM
PRINT REPORT
```

Running this procedure changes the contents of the PROC, QUERY, and FORM temporary storage areas. The RESET and SAVE commands are the same for PROC as they are for QUERY and FORM. See Chap. 8 for a more detailed look at PROCs.

7.2.5 PROFILE

The last object on our list is PROFILE. Each user has one and only one PROFILE associated with his or her ID. PROFILE holds the characteristics of your QMF session and is the only temporary storage area that is not empty when you begin a QMF session. It is automatically refreshed with the last saved version of your PROFILE. The SAVE command for PROFILE differs from that of other objects in that you cannot SAVE a PROFILE with a particular name. This is because there may be only one PROFILE for any user ID. RESET PROFILE also behaves differently from some of the other QMF objects because rather than clearing the PROFILE temporary storage area, it replaces any modifications you have made with the last saved PROFILE in the database.

There are two ways to modify your PROFILE. You may either use the SET PROFILE command or make the changes on the Profile Panel. To use the panel, type DISPLAY PROFILE or SHOW PROFILE at any QMF command line to go to the Profile Panel (Fig. 7.7). Two of the more useful options are CONFIRM and LANGUAGE. CONFIRM determines whether or not you are shown a confirmation panel after submitting a statement to modify a DB2 table. Many QMF commands also allow you to override your PROFILE's specification by including a CONFIRM clause such as the following:

```
RUN QUERY (CONFIRM=YES
```

Your PROFILE will not be changed, but you will be shown a Confirm Panel for the execution of this command.

LANGUAGE allows you to choose PROMPTED, SQL, or QBE. You may change from one to another of these options with the SET PROFILE command. If you are on the Query Panel and want to write a query using QBE, just type the following on the command line:

```
SET PROFILE (LANG=QBE
```

QBE will become the language setting for this QMF session until you exit or issue a RESET PROFILE or RESET QUERY. RESET undoes

```
PROFILE

General Operands:
      CASE      ===> UPPER      Enter UPPER, STRING, or MIXED.
      DECIMAL   ===> PERIOD     Enter PERIOD, COMMA, or FRENCH.
      CONFIRM   ===> NO         Enter YES or NO.
      LANGUAGE  ===> SQL        Enter SQL, QBE, or PROMPTED.

Defaults for printing:
      WIDTH     ===> 132        Number of characters per line.
      LENGTH    ===> 60         Number of lines per page.
      PRINTER   ===>            Printer to be used for output.

QMF Administration Operands:   (Not usually changed)
      SPACE     ===> "DSQDBDEF"."DSQTSDEF"
                           Enter the name of DB2 DATABASE or TABLESPACE in which
                           tables will be saved by the SAVE DATA command.
      TRACE     ===> NONE
                           Enter ALL, NONE or a character string of function-id,
                           trace-level pairs.
1=Help         2=Save         3=End        4=Print       5=Chart       6=Query
7=             8=             9=Form       10=           11=           12=Report
OK, PROFILE is shown.
COMMAND ===>
```

Figure 7.7   The Profile Panel displays your current profile.

the modifications made to your temporary PROFILE storage area and resets them to the values of the permanent PROFILE object in the database. If you change a value and issue the SAVE PROFILE command, you will replace the permanent object with this new PROFILE. Notice that no clause is used to name the profile you are saving because there is only one per user.

7.3 QMF COMMANDS

We've mentioned several QMF commands in the process of introducing you to QMF. Let's go back for a more detailed look at some of these commands and take a first look at some additional ones.

7.3.1 SAVE

The SAVE command creates a permanent object from the contents of a temporary storage area. With the exception of the object PROFILE, it associates a name with the saved object. Suppose you want other QMF users to be able to use your QUERYs, PROCs, FORMs, or Data. If you include the SHARE parameter when you save, then other IDs will have access to the saved object. For example, to save a PROC that others will use you would code:

```
SAVE PROC AS MYPROC (SHARE=YES,COMMENT='ACCOUNT REPT'
```

If you omit the SHARE parameter, only your ID will be able to access MYPROC in the future. We've also included the COMMENT parameter in this example. A comment must be enclosed in single quotation marks and may be up to 57 characters long, including the quotation marks. You cannot use COMMENT with PROFILE and neither PROFILE nor DATA use the SHARE parameter. COMMENT lets you document the objects you create so other users can understand their use.

7.3.2 DISPLAY

We used DISPLAY and SHOW to navigate through QMF's panels and display the contents of temporary storage areas. DISPLAY has a second function. It can be used to retrieve permanent objects from the QMF database and replace the contents of the temporary storage area with them. The syntax is:

```
DISPLAY name
```

The name part of the command is the object's name as it was specified in the AS *objectname* clause of the SAVE command. You may specify the type of object (QUERY, FORM, PROC, or TABLE) before the

name but it is not required. When DATA is saved, it becomes a TA-
BLE, so to display it you would issue a DISPLAY command such as:

```
DISPLAY TABLE MYDATA
```

or

```
DISPLAY MYDATA
```

Each object is displayed on its associated panel. A table is displayed on
the Report Panel. DISPLAY TABLE can be used to display any table
for which you have SELECT authority. It is analogous to issuing a SE-
LECT * FROM *table name* from the Query Panel.

7.3.3 RUN

RUN, like DISPLAY, can also be used with permanent objects from
the database. The syntax is very similar:

```
RUN name
```

Again, the name may be preceded by object type, but it isn't necessary.
For RUN this will be either QUERY or PROC, the only types of objects that can be submitted for execution. Earlier, when we wanted to
run a QUERY using the contents of FORM to format the output, we
coded:

```
RUN QUERY (FORM=FORM
```

Since you've learned how to save the form permanently, we can specify not only a permanent query to run, but also a permanent FORM to
format it with. For instance we could code:

```
RUN CHGQUERY (FORM=CHGFORM,CONFIRM=YES
```

Notice that we also used the optional CONFIRM parameter to override the CONFIRM value in our PROFILE for the duration of this
command. This means that a confirmation panel will appear when we
submit this command, giving us the option of continuing, or cancel-
ling, the command which would have modified rows in the database.

We should mention the QMF Command Prompt Panels. They are
quite useful for syntax help when submitting a command. Type the
command followed by a question mark and an appropriate panel is
displayed. For example, if you type:

```
RUN ?
```

A RUN command Prompt Panel is displayed on which you can specify
the type of object (QUERY or PROC) and, if it is a saved object, the
object name (Fig. 7.8). If it is a QUERY you are running, a second

```
                        RUN Command Prompt

    type ===>

    name ===>

                To run an object from temporary storage, enter its type:
                QUERY or PROC.

                To run an object from the data base, enter its name (and
                optionally its type).  Type can be QUERY or PROC.

                Press ENTER to execute the command from this panel.

                If QUERY is entered, the RUN QUERY prompt panel is
                displayed.




    PF 1=Help        3=End

    ISPF Command ===>
```

Figure 7.8 The RUN command Prompt Panel.

panel will then be displayed where you can optionally specify the FORM and CONFIRM parameters.

7.3.4 IMPORT, EXPORT, PRINT, ERASE, RETRIEVE

You've seen how it is possible to share QUERYs, FORMs, etc., with other users of the same QMF system by using the SHARE parameter. At times, you might also want to transport your objects to users on a different system, perhaps from test to production. The IMPORT and EXPORT commands make this possible by letting you pass information between the TSO or CMS environments and QMF. We'll assume we're using a TSO environment for the purposes of our discussion. IMPORT and EXPORT also make it possible to modify objects outside of QMF and apply non-QMF processes to them. Both commands can be used with QMF's temporary storage areas or with QMF's permanent database objects. Let's see how this works with IMPORT first.

IMPORT can be used to bring a QUERY into the QUERY temporary storage area. For example:

```
IMPORT QUERY FROM 'USERID.QUERY.LIBRARY'
    (MEMBER=QUERY1
```

We are importing from a dataset external to DB2. The QUERY temporary   storage   area   now   holds   the   contents   of

USERID.QUERY.LIBRARY(QUERY1). The same format is used to IMPORT FORMs, PROCs, and DATA; the type of object must be specified.

With the query in temporary storage, you can now issue the SAVE command to create a permanent query in the new environment. You can also do this with the IMPORT command directly. We'll modify the command to include the name that the object will have in the database. For example:

```
IMPORT QUERY MYQUERY FROM 'USERID.QUERY.LIBRARY'
(MEMBER=QUERY1
```

This statement brings member QUERY1 into temporary storage and, at the same time, stores it permanently as MYQUERY. If MYQUERY already exists, it will be replaced; otherwise it will be created. You may do the same with FORMs, PROCs, and TABLEs.

To IMPORT data into temporary storage, use the object type DATA. To IMPORT data into the database, use TABLE. A restriction specific to IMPORT DATA or IMPORT TABLE is that the data must be in either QMF or IXF format. These, you will see, are the two options for data format on the EXPORT command. QMF is the default. There are a few other things to be aware of with the IMPORT command. One is that QMF expects each line in a QUERY or PROC to be 79 characters long and will truncate or pad with blanks if your dataset records are not this length. The limit for a QUERY or PROC is 409 lines, a maximum that is hard to exceed.

EXPORT is similar in syntax to IMPORT. From temporary storage you may EXPORT QUERY, FORM, PROC, or REPORT. Notice that REPORT is an object that you can EXPORT but not IMPORT. You may also EXPORT DATA, but there is an additional data format clause that must be specified as either IXF or QMF. The IXF format should be used to export data to products other than QMF. For example:

```
EXPORT DATA TO EXPDATA (DATAFORMAT=IXF
```

Now let's turn to the PRINT command. It can be used to PRINT a QUERY, FORM, PROC, PROFILE, or REPORT either from temporary storage or from the database. Its most common use is to PRINT a REPORT that has been created by running a QUERY or PROC. The format for the command is:

```
PRINT REPORT (DATETIME=NO
```

We have included one of the PRINT command's options, DATETIME. If your report does not specify that you want both the date and time in its heading or text, DB2 automatically prints the system date and time in the footing. You can suppress this with DATETIME=NO, as we have in our example. Similarily, if you do not specify that you want a page number, a page number will be automatically printed. You can suppress this with PAGENO = NO.

The ERASE command should be used with care. It is used to erase permanent objects, that is, QUERY, FORM, PROC, or TABLE. This example erases a FORM called MYFORM:

```
ERASE FORM MYFORM (CONFIRM=YES
```

The object type, in this example FORM, is optional, as is the confirm clause. You may only erase objects for which you have the necessary authority.

The QMF RETRIEVE command is quite similar to the RETRIEVE command of ISPF. It is used to redisplay the last command entered at the command prompt. A question mark may be used for the same purpose. Up to 22 RETRIEVES or ?s will recall commands entered that many generations back.

QMF also has a very thorough set of Help panels which you can access by using the HELP PF key or by issuing the HELP command on the command line.

7.3.5 LIST

QMF keeps information about QUERYs, FORMs, and PROCs in tables called Q.OBJECT_DIRECTORY and Q.OBJECT_DATA. It keeps a separate table, Q.PROFILES, for information about PROFILEs and uses the Catalog tables for information about TABLEs, the permanent objects for DATA. The LIST command retrieves information from these tables. Its format is LIST followed by an object type or the word ALL, meaning all object types. There is also an optional OWNER clause to limit the list to those objects owned by specific user IDs and a NAME clause to limit the list to objects of specific names. ALL may be specified for either. The default OWNER is the signed-on user ID and the default for NAME is ALL. Here is an example of the LIST command:

```
LIST ALL (OWNER=USER1, NAME=MY%
```

This example will produce a list of all QUERYs, FORMs, PROCs, and TABLEs whose owner is USER1 and have names beginning with the characters MY. We have used the percent sign as a wild card for the NAME option. The wild card underscore (_) may also be used. The percent sign indicates any number of characters, while the underscore indicates a single character. This, you may remember, is the same as SQL's use of wild cards on the LIKE clause. You may also use wild cards for the OWNER option. The most recently generated list is kept in temporary storage until a different LIST command is issued. Therefore, if you have already issued a LIST command and you want to go back and look at the results again, you may reissue it by simply typing LIST, with no other specifications.

Figure 7.9 shows the output from the above LIST command. Object Name, Object Owner, and Object Type are self-explanatory. Object Subtype shows the language of a QUERY (SQL, QBE, or PROMPTED) and indicates if a table is real or a view (T or V). There are no tables or views in this example. The Restricted column reflects the SHARE = Y/N option with which the object was saved. If an object was saved with COMMENTS, you may view them by pressing PF12/24. A Comments column will be displayed in the place of Owner, Type, Subtype, and Retricted columns. PF12/24 acts as a toggle, so pressing it again will return the initial columns. Notice the ISPF command line on the bottom of the LIST panel, which means that QMF is using Dialog Manager for this function, and ISPF commands, rather than QMF commands, will be recognized.

The QMF Command column on the Data Base Object List is used to execute commands specific to a particular object. Some of the commands that may be specified here are DISPLAY, ERASE, EXPORT, IMPORT, RUN, and SAVE. You can type a command across the entire width of the screen, overlaying portions of the list. The same syntax rules and options apply for each command as they did for execution

```
Enter a QMF command next to the name you want to specify and press ENTER.
You may use a "/" to insert the object name into your command.

QMF                           Object    Object    Object
Command   Object Name         Owner     Type      Subtype   Restricted
--------  ------------------  --------  --------  --------  --------------------
          MYFORM              USER1     FORM                Y
          MYPROC              USER1     PROC                N
          MYQUERY             USER1     QUERY     SQL       Y
*****************************  BOTTOM OF DATA  *****************************




PF 1=Help      2=           3=End List  4=SortName  5=SortOwnr  6=SortType
PF 7=Backward  8=Forward    9=List ?   10=Clear    11=Refresh  12=Comments
OK, your data base object list is displayed.
ISPF Command ===>                                           SCROLL ===>
```

Figure 7.9   LIST shows you QMF objects that are in the database.

from the command line. Since the object name for the command is indicated by the placement of the command on the same line, you can use a slash (/) in place of it. For example you could type the following command on the MYQUERY line:

```
RUN / (FORM=MYFORM
```

This would execute the query and use the values in MYFORM to format the report. After you've viewed the report, you can type LIST on the command line of the Report Panel to return to the Data Base Object List. An asterisk will be inserted at the beginning of the QMF Command column on MYQUERY's line to indicate that an action was just performed on that object.

It's been our experience that it's sometimes difficult to fit a command and its parameter on one line or on the command line of a panel. It is useful, therefore, to know the acceptable abbreviations for QMF commands. There is, unfortunately, no particular rhyme or reason to the abbreviation scheme that is used by the product. In fact, the same word may be abbreviated one way on one command and a different way with another command. For example, the shortest abbreviation for CONFIRM is C when used with EXPORT, CON when used with IMPORT, and CO when used with SET PROFILE. Figure 7.10 lists the commands we have discussed so far and the abbreviations you may use for them. Where there is more than one way to abbreviate a word, we show the shortest common denominator among the abbreviations.

7.4 FORMATTING REPORTS

QMF provides a wide range of options through which you can satisfy your users' report requests. Release 2.3 of QMF increased these options tremendously. The base data for any report, of course, is created

Command	Abbreviation
DISPLAY	DI
ERASE	ER
EXPORT	EXP
HELP	H
IMPORT	IM
LIST	LI
PRINT	P
RETRIEVE	RET
RUN	RU
SAVE	SA
CONFIRM=YES/NO	CON=Y/N
COMMENT=	COM=
SHARE=YES/NO	S=Y/N

Figure 7.10 Abbreviations for QMF commands.

by the query that you write. Here, we're talking about report format only. Formatting is done through QMF's FORM panels. So far, we've only spoken of FORM.MAIN. In fact, FORM.MAIN is one of a possible 13 panels that you can use to format a report. Every value on FORM.MAIN is reflected on a subordinate panel. The opposite is not true; the subordinate panels have many more options than FORM.MAIN. FORM.MAIN is a kind of condensed version of what is possible, and for limited changes it's sufficient by itself. Rather than explaining each panel and each option, we will look instead at two reports to see how you can produce them with QMF. This should give you a feeling for what is possible. Necessity can then be the mother of your future QMF inventions.

7.4.1 Headings, Edit Codes, Usage Codes, Control Breaks

The query for our first example selects four columns from the TRANS-ACTION table and orders the rows by account number:

```
SELECT TXN_TYPE, TXN_TIMESTAMP, TXN_AMOUNT,
       TXN_ACCT_NO
   FROM TRANSACTION
ORDER BY TXN_ACCT_NO
```

We issue the following SAVE command so that we can rerun this query later without having to retype it:

```
SAVE QUERY AS MYQUERY2 (S=Y,COM='TEST QUERY'
```

Notice that we've used abbreviations for SHARE and COMMENT.

Running this query produces the report shown in Fig. 7.11. Now we can modify this format to make it more usable. Let's start with a heading. In the example in the overview, we used the heading field on FORM.MAIN to give our report a title. Now we'll get a little fancier and use the panel FORM.PAGE to generate a heading (Fig. 7.12). To get to FORM.PAGE you can type the command SHOW FORM.PAGE or DISPLAY FORM.PAGE or you can press PF4. PF4 gives you the command prompt panel for the SHOW command (Fig. 7.13). You can also get this by typing SHOW ?. There are so many Form panels that you may very well need this panel in order to remember their different names.

FORM.PAGE is where you can specify a heading and/or footing for each page. Our user wants the following information in the heading:

```
TODAY'S DATE      BANKER'S BANK        PAGE: N
                 TRANSACTION REPORT
```

```
REPORT                                    LINE 1      POS 1      79


                                          TXN
   TXN          TXN                   TXN  ACCT
   TYPE         TIMESTAMP             AMOUNT  NO
   --------     --------------------------  ---------------  ----
   OPENACCT     1989-02-02-16.16.16.000000          -    AE11
   CREDIT       1989-02-03-19.19.19.000000    2000.00    AE11
   CREDIT       1989-02-02-17.17.17.000000      50.75    AE21
   DEBIT        1989-02-03-18.18.18.000000     100.00    AE21
   CREDIT       1989-01-01-13.13.13.000000    1200.00    BB12
   CREDIT       1989-01-01-12.12.12.000000     200.50    BB12
   DEBIT        1989-02-04-20.20.20.000000    1200.55    DE11


*** END ***


1=Help          2=           3=End        4=Print       5=Chart        6=Query
7=Backward      8=Forward    9=Form       10=Left       11=Right       12=
OK, this is the REPORT from your RUN command.
COMMAND ===>                                          SCROLL ===> PAGE
```

Figure 7.11   The output of MYQUERY2.

```
FORM.PAGE

Blank Lines Before Heading ===> 0        Blank Lines After Heading ===> 2
LINE   ALIGN    PAGE HEADING TEXT
----   ------   ----+----1----+----2----+----3----+----4----+----5----+
1      CENTER
2      CENTER
3      CENTER
4      CENTER
                 *** END ***
Blank Lines Before Footing ===> 2        Blank Lines After Footing ===> 0
LINE   ALIGN    PAGE FOOTING TEXT
----   ------   ----+----1----+----2----+----3----+----4----+----5----+
1      CENTER
2      CENTER
3      CENTER
4      CENTER
                 *** END ***

1=Help    2=Check    3=End       4=Show        5=Chart        6=Query
7=Backward 8=Forward 9=          10=Insert     11=Delete      12=Report
OK, FORM.PAGE is shown.
COMMAND ===>                                          SCROLL ===> PAGE
```

Figure 7.12   FORM.PAGE is used for headings and footings.

```
                        SHOW Command Prompt

     Enter the name or number of the panel to show  ===>

            Panel                  Description
        1.  PROFile                Current user profile
        2.  PROC                   Current procedure
        3.  Query                  Current query
        4.  Report                 Current report
        5.  Chart                  Default chart
        6.  Form                   Current form
        7.     Form.Main              Basic report formatting
        8.     Form.COlumns           Column attributes
        9.     Form.CAlc              User-defined calculations
       10.     Form.Page              Page heading and footing text
       11.     Form.Detail            Detail text
       12.     Form.Final             Final footing text
       13.     Form.BreakN            BreakN text (where N is 1 to 6)
                                         Example: FORM.BREAK2 = F.B2 = 13.2
       14.     Form.Options           Choices about a report's appearance

     PF 1=Help        3=End
     Please follow the directions on the command prompt panel.
     ISPF Command ===>
```

Figure 7.13   The SHOW command Prompt Panel.

Figure 7.14 illustrates how to fill in FORM.PAGE to get such a heading. The heading specified will appear on the top of each printed page. The first column on the screen enables you to indicate on which line you want the text that follows to appear. The first three entries all appear on line 1; one is aligned left, one is centered, and one is right aligned. The second line of the heading is centered. The user wants the date the report is run and page numbers at the top of each page. These variables are specified with &DATE and &PAGE. The format of the date was specified at DB2 installation time. Unlike dates that appear in the body of a report, you cannot specify editing options for &DATE. If you need to get around this, you can do so by including the CURRENT DATE register in your SELECT statement. You can then use the available formatting options on that date. FORM.PAGE is also used to specify a footing. Footings, if used, will appear at the bottom of each printed page.

Now let's modify the columns of the report and their headings. SHOW FORM.COLUMNS takes you to the panel shown in Fig. 7.15. The screen provides enough room for the first eight columns of your report. PF8 is used to view more, if necessary. Our report has only four columns, so we could just as easily have used FORM.MAIN, which shows the first five columns and can also be scrolled forward with PF8.

The columns are listed in the order specified in the corresponding

```
FORM.PAGE                                      MODIFIED

Blank Lines Before Heading ===> 0        Blank Lines After Heading ===> 2
LINE  ALIGN   PAGE HEADING TEXT
----  ------  ----+----1----+----2----+----3----+----4----+----5----+
1     LEFT    &DATE
1     CENTER  BANKER'S BANK
1     RIGHT   PAGE: &PAGE
2     CENTER  TRANSACTION REPORT
              *** END ***

Blank Lines Before Footing ===> 2        Blank Lines After Footing ===> 0
LINE  ALIGN   PAGE FOOTING TEXT
----  ------  ----+----1----+----2----+----3----+----4----+----5----+
1     CENTER
2     CENTER
3     CENTER
4     CENTER
              *** END ***

1=Help     2=Check   3=End         4=Show        5=Chart         6=Query
7=Backward 8=Forward 9=            10=Insert      11=Delete       12=Report
OK, FORM is displayed.
COMMAND ===>                                      SCROLL ===> PAGE
```

Figure 7.14   FORM.PAGE is filled in to produce a heading.

```
FORM.COLUMNS                                   MODIFIED

                  Total Width of Report Columns: 60
NUM COLUMN HEADING                           USAGE   INDENT WIDTH EDIT  SEQ
--- ---------------------------------------- ------- ------ ----- ----- ---
  1 TXN_TYPE                                          2      8    C     1
  2 TXN_TIMESTAMP                                     2      26   TSI   2
  3 TXN_AMOUNT                                        2      14   L2    3
  4 TXN_ACCT_NO                                       2      4    C     4
    *** END ***

1=Help     2=Check   3=End         4=Show        5=Chart         6=Query
7=Backward 8=Forward 9=            10=Insert      11=Delete       12=Report
OK, FORM.COLUMNS is shown.
COMMAND ===>                                      SCROLL ===> PAGE
```

Figure 7.15   FORM.COLUMNS is used to modify column format.

query. There are two columns on the panel that are associated with column order, NUM on the left of the panel and SEQ on the right. NUM will always correspond to the order of columns in the original query. We will see how variables that refer to a column by this number can be constructed. SEQ is what you use to reorder the way the columns appear on a report.

The WIDTH for each column is calculated according to the data type of the column and the length of its heading. If you change a column heading or data type so that the data or heading exceeds the specified width, it will be truncated or, with numeric data, will be replaced with asterisks. You must adjust the width specifications as needed. The default for a column heading is the name of the column. QMF treats an underscore in a heading as an instruction to start a new line. Look back at Fig. 7.11. TXN_ACCT_NO is placed on three column heading lines. You can change any column heading by typing the new name over the default in the COLUMN HEADING area. It is also possible to completely replace the headings with your own heading area. That is done on the FORM.DETAIL panel which we will look at in our next example. For this example, we will leave the column headings as they are.

The EDIT column on this panel refers to the format used to display data. Figure 7.16 lists some of the edit codes along with a brief description of each. The default for character data is C, which we see in Fig. 7.15 for TXN_TYPE, and TXN_ACCT_NO. Some of the character edit codes you'll probably find useful are those which allow for wrapping. It is not uncommon to have a remarks or comments column which may be up to 254 bytes long. If you display that in a character column with a width of 50, the last 204 bytes will be truncated. The

```
CHARACTER DATA:

C    - Default
CW   - Wraps at width of column
CT   - Wraps according to text; after a blank
       when possible
CDx  - Wraps according to delimiter, x specifies
       delimiter


NUMERIC DATA - DECIMAL NOTATION:

Dn  - Includes negative sign, thousands
      separators, currency symbol
In  - Includes leading zeroes, negative sign
Jn  - Includes leading zeroes
Kn  - Includes negative sign, thousands
      separators
Ln  - Includes negative sign
Pn  - Includes negative sign, thousands
      separators, percent sign

In all of the above numeric edit codes, n = number
of places after the decimal point.
```

Figure 7.16   Edit codes for column data.

edit codes CW, CT, and CD*x* will wrap the data within the column. For example, CT will wrap according to the text in the column, breaking after a blank whenever possible. A comments field in a 15-byte QMF report column might look like this if CT was specified as its edit code:

```
This customer
is opening his
account under
the name
Jinglehemershch
midt. Please
process
accordingly.
```

We use a numeric edit code for the TXN_AMOUNT column in Fig. 7.15. We want to see the data with a currency symbol, separators for thousands, and negative signs. Therefore we use D2 as the edit code. The 2 controls how many digits will follow the decimal point. If the raw data has more numbers after the decimal point than are specified in the edit code, it is rounded. Let's also change the spacing of columns across the report. We do this by changing the indent for each column from 2, the default, to 3. Before we make more changes to this report, let's see what our modifications look like so far. PF12 or SHOW REPORT will show us our modified report (Fig. 7.17). From the Report Panel, PF9 returns you to whichever Form panel you were on most recently.

Now let's make some further changes to make the report more useful. The USAGE column allows you to define how each column's data

```
REPORT                                    LINE 1      POS 1      79

1989-08-04                 BANKER'S BANK                  PAGE: 1
                        TRANSACTION REPORT


                                              TXN
   TXN          TXN                    TXN    ACCT
   TYPE         TIMESTAMP              AMOUNT  NO
  --------     -------------------    -------  ----
   OPENACCT    1989-02-02-16.16.16.000000         -     AE11
   CREDIT      1989-02-03-19.19.19.000000   $2,000.00   AE11
   CREDIT      1989-02-02-17.17.17.000000      $50.75   AE21
   DEBIT       1989-02-03-18.18.18.000000     $100.00   AE21
   CREDIT      1989-01-01-13.13.13.000000   $1,200.00   BB12
   CREDIT      1989-01-01-12.12.12.000000     $200.50   BB12
   DEBIT       1989-02-04-20.20.20.000000   $1,200.55   DE11

1
 1=Help        2=          3=End      4=Print     5=Chart      6=Query
 7=Backward    8=Forward   9=Form     10=Left     11=Right     12=
OK, REPORT is displayed.
COMMAND ===>                                      SCROLL ===> PAGE
```

Figure 7.17 The transaction report as it appears now.

should be used in the report. We will use the OMIT usage code for TXN_TIMESTAMP since we do not need this data on our report. Other USAGE options include AVG, COUNT, FIRST, LAST, MAXIMUM, MINIMUM, STDEV (standard deviation), and SUM. All of these summarize the values in a column and display the result at the subtotal and total lines.

Most of the time, we want to see report data that is grouped according to common values in one or more fields. In data processing parlance this is a control break report. If you've written COBOL batch programs, you've probably had to create such reports. QMF makes this chore remarkably simple. As with any report with control breaks, the data coming into it must be sorted on the break field(s). In DB2 we do this by using a query with an ORDER BY clause. The query for our report is ordered by TXN_ACCT_NO, so in the USAGE column for that field we'll type BREAK1, another option of USAGE. You can have up to six breaks in a single report (BREAK1, BREAK2, etc.). It only makes sense that if you're going to group data together, you'll also want to see subtotals associated with each control break and a final total at the end. To create subtotals for transactions within each account we type SUM for TXN_AMOUNT in the USAGE column. Traditionally, the break column is printed on the left of a report with the columns to be totalled on the right. We can do this by changing the SEQ numbers on FORM.COLUMN or by specifying YES for Automatic Reordering of Report Columns on the FORM.OPTIONS panel (Fig. 7.18). When Auto-

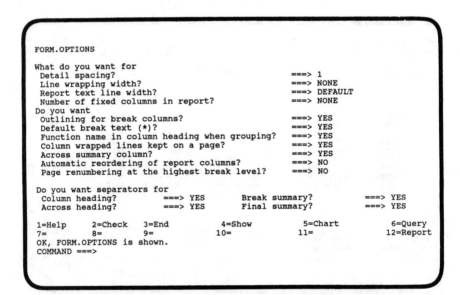

Figure 7.18 FORM.OPTIONS lets you specify automatic reordering.

matic Reordering is selected, QMF reorders the report's columns so that any break columns are on the left, followed by any GROUP BY columns. Columns whose USAGE is AVG, COUNT, SUM, etc., are placed on the right side of the report.

For every break specified in the usage codes, QMF creates an associated panel. SHOW FORM.BREAK1 takes us to that panel (Fig. 7.19). The panel permits you to specify whether to start a new page at each break or whether to have a heading or footing associated with each break. For our report we'll use a break footing. Each subtotal will have the text:

SUM OF MONIES TRANSACTED BY *nnnn* ===>

We want the account number associated with the subtotal to be filled in for the variable *nnnn*. The panel is filled in like FORM.PAGE and is shown in Fig. 7.20. The TXN_ACCT_NO column was the fourth column in our query, so &4 will be replaced with the contents of that column at each control break. To keep the report clear and easy to read, we'll leave two blank lines after each break footing.

In order to put a legend next to our grand total, we must go to FORM.FINAL. Figure 7.21 shows how we fill it in to get a final line of text. Now when we view the report by pressing PF12, it will look like the report in Fig. 7.22. Remember, if you want to use this format for your query again, be sure to save it.

```
FORM.BREAK1                                    MODIFIED

New Page for Break?          ===> NO    Repeat Detail Heading?    ===> NO
Blank Lines Before Heading ===> 0       Blank Lines After Heading ===> 0
LINE   ALIGN    BREAK 1 HEADING TEXT
----   ------   ----+----1----+----2----+----3----+----4----+----5----+
1      LEFT
2      LEFT
3      LEFT
                *** END ***

New Page for Footing?        ===> NO    Put Break Summary at Line ===> 1
Blank Lines Before Footing ===> 0       Blank Lines After Footing ===> 1
LINE   ALIGN    BREAK 1 FOOTING TEXT
----   ------   ----+----1----+----2----+----3----+----4----+----5----+
1      RIGHT
2      RIGHT
3      RIGHT
                *** END ***

1=Help       2=Check     3=End      4=Show      5=Chart       6=Query
7=Backward 8=Forward   9=         10=Insert   11=Delete     12=Report
OK, FORM.BREAK1 is shown.
COMMAND ===>                                    SCROLL ===> PAGE
```

Figure 7.19 FORM.BREAK1 is used to format the first control break.

```
FORM.BREAK1                                       MODIFIED

New Page for Break?          ===> NO      Repeat Detail Heading?    ===> NO
Blank Lines Before Heading ===> 0         Blank Lines After Heading ===> 0
LINE   ALIGN     BREAK 1 HEADING TEXT
----   ------    ----+----1----+----2----+----3----+----4----+----5----+
1      LEFT
2      LEFT
3      LEFT
                 *** END ***

New Page for Footing?        ===> NO      Put Break Summary at Line ===> 1
Blank Lines Before Footing ===> 0         Blank Lines After Footing ===> 2
LINE   ALIGN     BREAK 1 FOOTING TEXT
----   ------    ----+----1----+----2----+----3----+----4----+----5----+
1      LEFT      SUM OF MONIES TRANSACTED BY &4
2      RIGHT
3      RIGHT
                 *** END ***

1=Help      2=Check     3=End          4=Show         5=Chart        6=Query
7=Backward 8=Forward    9=             10=Insert       11=Delete      12=Report
OK, FORM is displayed.
COMMAND ===>                                              SCROLL ===> PAGE
```

Figure 7.20   FORM.BREAK1 is filled in to put a footing with each subtotal.

```
FORM.FINAL                                        MODIFIED

New Page for Final Text?     ===> NO      Put Final Summary at Line ===> 1
Blank Lines Before Text      ===> 0
LINE   ALIGN     FINAL TEXT
----   ------    ----+----1----+----2----+----3----+----4----+----5----+
1      LEFT      * TOTAL OF TRANSACTED MONIES *
2      RIGHT
3      RIGHT
4      RIGHT
5      RIGHT
6      RIGHT
7      RIGHT
8      RIGHT
9      RIGHT
10     RIGHT
11     RIGHT
12     RIGHT
13     RIGHT
                 *** END ***
1=Help      2=Check     3=End          4=Show         5=Chart        6=Query
7=Backward 8=Forward    9=             10=Insert       11=Delete      12=Report
OK, FORM.FINAL is shown.
COMMAND ===>                                              SCROLL ===> PAGE
```

Figure 7.21   FORM.FINAL is filled in to put a legend with the grand total.

```
1989-08-04                      BANKER'S BANK
                             TRANSACTION REPORT


      TXN
      ACCT          TXN                       TXN
       NO           TYPE                     AMOUNT
      ----         --------               --------------
      AE11         OPENACCT                     -
                   CREDIT                   $2,000.00

SUM OF MONIES TRANSACTED BY AE11             $2,000.00


      AE21         CREDIT                     $50.75
                   DEBIT                     $100.00

SUM OF MONIES TRANSACTED BY AE21              $150.75


      BB12         CREDIT                   $1200.00
                   CREDIT                     200.50

SUM OF MONIES TRANSACTED BY BB12             $1400.50


      DE11         DEBIT                    $1200.55

SUM OF MONIES TRANSACTED BY DE11             $1200.55

                                          ----------
* TOTAL OF TRANSACTED MONIES *              $4,751.80
```

Figure 7.22   The transaction report is finished.

7.4.2   FORM.CALC, FORM.DETAIL

Our second example uses two tables in its query:

```
SELECT ACCT_NO, ACCT_BALANCE, ACCT_CREDIT_BAL,
       ACCT_CUST_ID, CUST_NAME
  FROM ACCOUNT, CUSTOMER
 WHERE ACCT_CUST_ID = CUST_SOC_SEC
 ORDER BY ACCT_CUST_ID
```

Here, we're showing account information along with the customer's name. QMF's default report for this query is shown in Fig. 7.23. Our user's requirements for this report, however, are quite different. The user wants to use QMF to send out a personalized letter to each customer showing him or her the total amount of regular and credit line balances for all accounts. While this request would have been impossible to satisfy with releases prior to QMF 2.3, it is now quite feasible.

First, let's calculate the sum of the account's regular balance (ACCT_BALANCE) and credit line balance (ACCT_CREDIT_BAL) by using the FORM.CALC panel (Fig. 7.24). We identify this arithmetic expression with an ID (1) so that we can refer to it in our formatting panels. The ID must be an integer from 1 to 999. This sum could also be generated by putting the same arithmetic expression in the SELECT query.

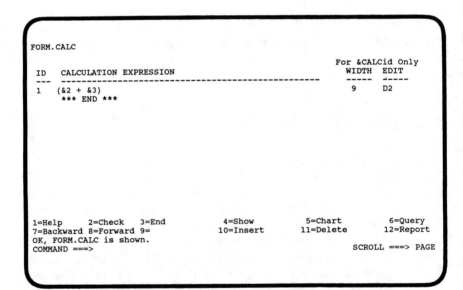

```
REPORT                                    LINE 1       POS 1      79


                             ACCT         ACCT
         ACCT       ACCT     CREDIT       CUST   CUST
          NO      BALANCE     BAL          ID    NAME
         ----   ------------ ------------ ------------ --------------------
         AE11     12000.94     500.00    111111111  PHYLLIS ELKIND
         BB12     12001.35    3300.00    222222222  JAY RANADE
         CE21     35100.98     100.00    333333333  RICHARD GREEN
         AB21         0.00     180.55    444444444  -
         DB11        75.00       0.00    555555555  HEIDI SCHMIDT
         AE12       500.00     500.00    555555555  HEIDI SCHMIDT
         BB13       646.01      25.00    666666666  MUKESH SEHGAL
         DE11        20.00      25.00    777777777  LAI-HA NG
         AE21        77.53    2000.00    888888888  GEORGE SCHMIDT


*** END ***
1=Help       2=            3=End        4=Print       5=Chart      6=Query
7=Backward   8=Forward     9=Form      10=Left       11=Right     12=
OK, this is the REPORT from your RUN command.
COMMAND ===>                                        SCROLL ===> PAGE
```

Figure 7.23   QMF's default report for the query.

```
FORM.CALC

                                                   For &CALCid Only
   ID    CALCULATION EXPRESSION                       WIDTH    EDIT
   ---   -------------------------------------------- -----    -----
   1     (&2 + &3)                                      9       D2
         *** END ***








1=Help      2=Check    3=End         4=Show       5=Chart      6=Query
7=Backward 8=Forward 9=            10=Insert     11=Delete    12=Report
OK, FORM.CALC is shown.
COMMAND ===>                                      SCROLL ===> PAGE
```

Figure 7.24   FORM.CALC is filled in to calculate a total.

Now, to perform our report magic, we turn to FORM.DETAIL. Figure 7.25 shows how to set up a freeform letter or report. We do not want headings, so we specify NO to the panel's first question. We want to have each account, i.e., row in the result, on its own page so we answer YES to "New Page for Detail Block?" The other important option here is the option which specifies the line number on which the report data should start or, in our case, the word NONE to indicate that no rows of data should be printed. On the bottom half of the panel, we've written our text using column variables within it. The variable &5 will provide the customer's name, &CALC1 will show the sum of the customer's balances, and &1 gives the account number. In the align column we have used integers to place the lines of text horizontally on the page. We'll leave a margin of 10 characters on the left and indent an additional 5 for the paragraph indent. Figure 7.26 shows the output of this form—a "personalized" letter for each account.

Date, time, and page number are printed by default at the bottom of each page. In order to suppress them, specify DATETIME = NO and PAGENO = NO. We save the QUERY as QACCOUNT and the FORM as FACCOUNT. We can then write the following PROC to run the query and print the report:

```
-- PROC FOR ACCOUNT LETTER
RUN QACCOUNT (FORM=FACCOUNT
PRINT REPORT (DATETIME=NO, PAGENO=YES
```

```
FORM.DETAIL                                     MODIFIED

Include Column Headings with Detail Heading? ===> NO
LINE  ALIGN    DETAIL HEADING TEXT
----  ------   ----+----1----+----2----+----3----+----4----+----5----+
1     LEFT
2     LEFT
3     LEFT
               *** END ***

New Page for Detail Block? ===> YES    Repeat Detail Heading?   ===> NO
Keep Block on Page?        ===> NO     Blank Lines after Block  ===> 0
Put Tabular Data at Line (Enter 1-999 or NONE) ===> NONE
LINE  ALIGN    DETAIL BLOCK TEXT
----  ------   ----+----1----+----2----+----3----+----4----+----5----+
1     10       DEAR &5 :
3     15       AS A SPECIAL SERVICE THIS MONTH WE ARE
4     10       OFFERING SPECIAL BONUS POINTS TO CUSTOMERS
5     10       WHOSE COMBINED BALANCES EXCEED &CALC1 .
6     10       CONGRATULATIONS, ACCOUNT,  &1 !

1=Help     2=Check   3=End       4=Show       5=Chart       6=Query
7=Backward 8=Forward 9=          10=Insert    11=Delete     12=Report
OK, cursor positioned.
COMMAND ===>                                     SCROLL ===> PAGE
```

Figure 7.25   FORM.DETAIL is filled in to produce a free-form report.

DEAR PHYLLIS ELKIND :

    AS A SPECIAL SERVICE THIS MONTH WE ARE
OFFERING SPECIAL BONUS POINTS TO CUSTOMERS
WHOSE COMBINED BALANCES EXCEED $12,499.94 .
CONGRATULATIONS ON YOUR ACCOUNT, AE11 !

Figure 7.26   The output of our free-form report.

In this chapter we have used SQL in all our examples. Let's take a brief look at the other ways QMF can be used.

7.5   QUERY BY EXAMPLE

QBE presents the user with an empty form which can be filled in and then executed. For example, say you wanted to find the transaction type, amount, and account number for transactions of an amount greater than $1000. You would first issue the command, DRAW TRANSACTION, which displays a blank version of the TRANSACTION table for you, with column names only. You could then construct your query by entering P. (for print) under each column you wish returned (TXN TYPE, TXN_AMOUNT, and TXN_ACCT_NO) and the condition > 1000 in the TXN_AMOUNT column (Fig. 7.27). This is equivalent to typing:

```
QBE QUERY                                    MODIFIED    LINE 1

TRANSACTION ° TXN_TYPE ° TXN_TIMESTAMP    ° TXN_AMOUNT  ° TXN_ACCT_NO
------------+----------+-------------------+-------------+------------
            °   P.    °                   °   P.       °   P. > 1000

*** END ***




1=Help        2=Run        3=End       4=Enlarge    5=Reduce      6=Draw
7=Backward    8=Forward    9=Form      10=Left      11=Right      12=Report
OK, example table created by DRAW.
COMMAND ===>                                        SCROLL ===> PAGE
```

Figure 7.27   The DRAW TRANSACTION template can submit queries and updates.

```
SELECT TXN_TYPE, TXN_ACCOUNT, TXN_ACCT_NO
   FROM TRANSACTION
   WHERE TXN_AMOUNT > 1000
```

QBE has never been a widely used option, and its usefulness is even more questionable with the addition to QMF of Prompted Query.

7.6 PROMPTED QUERY

QMF, like DB2 itself, has been improved with each release. Prompted Query is an enhancement of QMF version 2.3. It is meant to broaden the audience that can use QMF by prompting the user with step by step guides to writing a query. Prompted Query is only used for data retrieval, that is, SELECT statement formulation. When you work with QMF through Prompted Query, a series of dialog panels appear in the upper right-hand corner of your screen. In Fig. 7.28, the Tables Dialog Panel is displayed on the right of the screen. PF4 will LIST the tables available to you or you can simply type in TRANSACTION on the first line and then press Enter. You see the name of the table you selected echoed on the left of the screen and a new dialog panel, the Specify Panel, shown on the right (Fig. 7.29). The Specify Dialog Panel is a menu from which you can specify columns, predicates for the WHERE clause, and ORDER BY and DISTINCT clauses. Remember, these panels are provided for users who do not know SQL syntax.

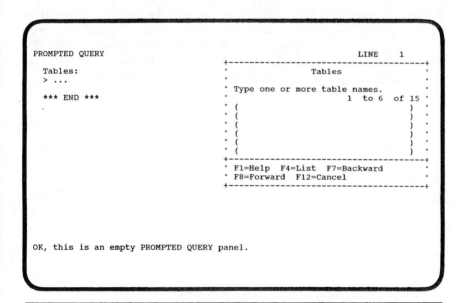

Figure 7.28   Prompted query shows you a table's Dialog Panel.

```
PROMPTED QUERY                        MODIFIED   LINE    1
                              +-------------------------+
  Tables:                     .           Specify       .
    TRANSACTION               .                         .
                              . Select an item.         .
  Columns:                    .                         .
    ALL                       . 2 1. Tables...          .
                              .   2. Columns...         .
  *** END ***                 .   3. Row Conditions...  .
                              .   4. Sort....           .
                              .   5. Duplicate Rows...  .
                              +-------------------------+
                              . F1=Help  F12=Cancel     .
                              +-------------------------+




  OK, ENTER performed. Please proceed.
```

Figure 7.29   Choose SQL options on the Specify Panel.

All of the options are already available to you through SQL. When you have finished with the dialog panels, PF12 cancels Prompted Query and leaves you with the options you have chosen in the echo area on the left side of your screen. PF4 or SHOW SQL displays the SQL equivalent, which makes this a nice way to learn SQL. From this point on, QMF functions the same as it does without Prompted Query.

This should give you some idea of what you can do with QMF. In Chap. 8, we continue our discussion of QMF, turning to the issue of how to prepare queries and procedures that end users can use.

8

Using QMF to Support
End-User Applications

In Chap. 7 we explained the features of QMF from the perspective of a programmer. We touched on QBE and Prompted Query, which can help a user formulate ad hoc queries. In this chapter, we focus our attention on the ways QMF can be used to provide canned QUERYs, PROCs, and applications for an end-user audience.

8.1 QUERY

When you write QUERYs for the use of others, it is particularly important that you include comments in them. They must be saved with SHARE = YES or only you will be able to use them. Tables named in QUERYs should be given their fully qualified names. Otherwise, users of the QUERY will have their IDs used by DB2 as the high-level qualifiers of the tables, which is probably not what you want to happen.

Perhaps the most important way to increase the usefulness of QUERYs is to make them flexible by writing them with variables. A variable starts with an ampersand (&), can appear anywhere in a QUERY, and can represent anything that can be in a QUERY—a word, clause, table name, column name, etc. For example, a manager might want a QUERY that shows all of the customers in a particular branch. You could write the following:

```
SELECT * FROM CUSTOMER WHERE CUST_BRANCH = 50
```

Using this format, a new QUERY will be needed to see customers from a different branch. A more flexible solution is to use a variable for the value of branch:

```
--This is QUERY1. It contains a QUERY variable,
--&QBRANCH.
SELECT * FROM CUSTOMER WHERE CUST_BRANCH = &QBRANCH
```

When the QUERY is run, the user supplies a value for the variable, which is substituted into the QUERY so that the appropriate rows are returned. There are two ways to supply the value. It can be input on the RUN statement, by entering:

```
RUN QUERY1 (&QBRANCH=50
```

Or, alternatively, you can type:

```
RUN QUERY1
```

QMF will then prompt you with a panel on which you can enter the value of the variable or variables (Fig. 8.1). The panel has space for multiple variables; QMF will only pay attention to the first n entries, where n is the number of variables you actually have in your QUERY.

Variables for numeric literals are straightforward; you just enter the value. Variables for nonnumeric literals, however, require that the user put quotes around the value. Let's look at QUERY2:

```
--This is QUERY2.
SELECT * FROM ACCOUNT WHERE ACCT_NO = &ACCT
```

ACCT_NO is a CHAR column so the user would have to code a RUN statement like:

```
              RUN Command Prompt -- Values of Variables

       Your RUN command runs a query or procedure with variables that need
       values.  Fill in a value after the arrow for each variable named below:


       &QBRANCH           ===>
                          ===>
                          ===>
                          ===>
                          ===>
                          ===>
                          ===>
                          ===>
                          ===>
                          ===>


       Press ENTER to execute the command from this panel.



       PF 1=Help      3=End
       Please give a value for each variable name.
       ISPF Command ===>
```

Figure 8.1   The RUN command prompt—Value of Variables Panel.

```
RUN QUERY2 (&ACCT='AE11'
```

SQL syntax requires that quotes be placed around nonnumeric literals. This may be confusing for end users, especially because they probably won't know which columns have been defined as numeric and which as character. You might be tempted to try to solve the problem by writing the query:

```
SELECT * FROM ACCOUNT WHERE ACCT_NO = '&ACCT'
```

but this won't work because the quotes around the variable will tell QMF not to make any substitutions, just to look for an account number consisting of the characters &, A, C, C, T. We will soon see the way around this, which involves putting the QUERY into a PROC.

8.2   PROC

PROCs provide an added measure of flexibility and convenience for end users. PROCs written for others, like QUERYs, must be saved with SHARE = YES and should have meaningful comments throughout. All QMF objects used in them should be given fully qualified names, as explained above for QUERYs. Several QMF commands can be combined in one PROC. For instance, say you have three QUERYs, QUERYA, QUERYB, and QUERYC, and you've coded and saved special FORMs for each QUERY, named FORMA, FORMB, and FORMC. You could write a PROC that would run all of the QUERYs, with their FORMs, and print the output automatically. A PROC like this would relieve a user of having to remember FORM names and individual QUERY names. The PROC would be coded:

```
--This PROC will run three queries.
RUN QUERYA
+ (FORM=FORMA
PRINT REPORT
RUN QUERYB (FORM=FORMB
PRINT REPORT
RUN QUERYC (FORM=FORMC
PRINT REPORT
```

We've illustrated the use of comment lines in this PROC by using two hyphens to start our comment, just as we did in our QUERYs. Also, note that a command can be continued on a new line if the continuation character, +, is the first character on the new line. QUERYs, in contrast, can be continued line to line without a continuation character.

PROCs may contain variables, called PROC variables, just as QUERYs can contain QUERY variables. For example:

```
--This is PROCA. It includes a PROC variable, &FORM.
RUN QUERYA (FORM=&FORM
PRINT REPORT
```

This PROC can be run, substituting FORMA for the variable, with the command:

```
RUN PROCA (&FORM=FORMA
```

You also can type:

```
RUN PROCA
```

and you will be prompted with the RUN COMMAND PROMPT—VALUE OF VARIABLES panel, the same one used to prompt for QUERY variable values (Fig. 8.1). Instead of &QBRANCH, &FORM will be displayed. You can enter FORMA on the corresponding line to substitute that value for the PROC variable.

It is also possible for PROCs, with or without PROC variables, to run QUERYs which themselves contain variables. QMF first scans the PROC and resolves any PROC variable it finds by substituting the value specified in the RUN PROC command. If QMF finds no values specified for the variable, it displays the RUN COMMAND PROMPT—VALUE OF VARIABLES panel (Fig. 8.1). Next, QMF scans the first QUERY in the PROC and resolves any QUERY variable it finds by substituting the value specified for the variable in the RUN QUERY command. Again, if it finds no value, it displays the variable prompt panel.

Let's look again at QUERY1:

```
--This is QUERY1. It contains a QUERY variable,
--&QBRANCH.
SELECT * FROM CUSTOMER WHERE CUSTOMER = &QBRANCH
```

Our RUN statement for QUERY1 was:

```
RUN QUERY1 (&QBRANCH=50
```

What will happen if we try to include this RUN statement within a PROC?

```
--This is PROC1. It will not work.
RUN QUERY1 (&QBRANCH=50
```

Even though this is the same RUN statement we used to run QUERY1, it will not work when embedded in a PROC. When QMF sees the ampersand in the PROC, it assumes it's a PROC variable. If you have only said RUN PROC1, it finds no value specified for the variable, so it prompts you with the variable panel. What if you type in a value, say 50? QMF will then substitute that value into the PROC which will now read:

```
RUN QUERY1 (50=50
```

This is not a valid statement and the PROC will not run. Luckily, there is a way around this: QMF can recognize a variable in a PROC as a QUERY variable if it is preceded by a double, rather than single, ampersand (&&). So we modify PROC1 as follows:

```
--This is PROC1, corrected format.
RUN QUERY1 (&&QBRANCH=50
```

Now when you say RUN PROC1, QMF scans the PROC and finds no PROC variables to resolve. It then scans the QUERY and finds the QUERY variable, QBRANCH, which it resolves by substituting the value specified in the PROC's RUN QUERY statement, 50.

PROC1 has the value 50 hard coded into it. If we want to modify the PROC so that it instead accepts a value at run-time, we need a PROC variable. This is what it looks like:

```
--This is PROC2, a variation of PROC1
Run QUERY1 (&&QBRANCH=&PBRANCH
```

The PROC variable &PBRANCH is used in place of the value 50. Now we can run PROC2 by saying:

```
RUN PROC2 (&PBRANCH=10
```

QMF first scans the PROC, finds the PROC variable &PBRANCH, and substitutes the value from the RUN PROC statement, 10. Then it scans the QUERY, finds the variable &QBRANCH in it, and substitutes the value specified in the RUN QUERY statement, &&QBRANCH=10.

We mentioned earlier that PROCs can solve the problem of users having to enclose nonnumeric literals in quotes to have them work properly in queries. The solution involves concatenating variables, one of which uses a single quotation mark ('). Let's recode QUERY2 as:

```
SELECT * FROM ACCOUNT WHERE ACCT_NO =
        &QUOTE&ACCT&QUOTE
```

Notice that there are two variables: &QUOTE and &ACCT. The variable &QUOTE appears twice. We'll hard code a value for &QUOTE in the PROC itself. PROC3 can be coded:

```
--This is PROC3
RUN QUERY2 (&ACCT=&&ACCT, &QUOTE='
```

The user can now run the PROC without enclosing the variable value in quotes:

```
RUN PROC3 (&ACCT=AE11
```

With all of these substitutions in place, the QUERY that would be executed is:

```
SELECT * FROM ACCOUNT WHERE ACCT_NO = 'AE11'
```

In using this trick, the variable containing the ' (&QUOTE) must be the last variable in the RUN QUERY statement, or QMF will try to make the ' a delimiter and you will get a syntax error.

8.3 THE LIST COMMAND

If you develop canned QUERYs and PROCs, your users can use the LIST command to produce a list of all of the objects they are authorized to use. We explained the syntax of LIST in Chap. 7. Users can, for instance, type LIST PROC and get a list of all of the PROCs they are eligible to use; similarly, they can type LIST QUERIES or LIST FORMS. To see all of the QMF objects they are eligible to use, they can type LIST ALL. From the Data Base Object List Panel, which displays the output of LIST, users can look at the comments you've saved, associated with the QUERYs, by pressing PF24.

8.4 BATCH EXECUTION OF QMF

Canned QUERYs and PROCs can also be submitted as batch jobs. The most common use for batch QMF is to run PROCs that produce reports, particularly when the QUERY in the PROC is long-running. Many installations also use QMF PROCs in batch to produce production reports as an alternative to coding COBOL programs. The JCL for running QMF in batch is somewhat involved, quite lengthy, and installation-specific, so we suggest that you ask your DBA about how the QMF jobs are run in your shop. We will mention that the way you tell a QMF batch job which PROC to run is by supplying an input file of 80-byte records.

The fact that the QMF batch job relies on a file to tell it which PROC to run restricts your ability to supply variables as symbolics in the JCL. Usually, the best you can do is to have several PDS members containing different variations of the input file to accommodate the variety of runs you'll have to make. For example, there may be one for a month-end report and one for regular reports. JCL symbolics could be used for the member names. Another possibility is to write a program that would accept a JCL parm and use it to write a temporary file containing the run-time variables and the information necessary to run the appropriate QMF PROC.

8.5   A QMF APPLICATION

Suppose your boss comes up to you and says, "Our senior vice president wants to see a demo of what our new DB2 database can do. He has no patience for learning new software or systems—he's an old-time banker. We don't have the time or money for CICS menus or CO-BOL programs. Can you put up something using QMF that won't require him to know anything about the software and have it ready next week?"

QMF is certainly a faster tool than COBOL for producing a report about DB2 data, but just how user-friendly is QMF? Providing users with canned QUERYs and PROCs relieves them of having to know SQL. But they still have to know something about navigating the database in QMF. They have to know how to use the LIST command and how to display the COMMENTS column. Once they find the PROC or QUERY they want, they have to know how to answer the variable prompts, if the PROC or QUERY contains any variables. The answer to our question, therefore, is that QMF is not necessarily friendly enough for a real end user. Fortunately, QMF provides another solution. It provides you with the facilities to embed QMF commands (including those that run PROCs and QUERYs) in a more user-friendly front end.

To give you an idea of what this might look like, we have designed a sample application that uses a CLIST/Dialog Manager front end to run three QMF PROCs that in turn run three QMF QUERYs. If you have used CLISTs and Dialog Manager before, you will be able to use this sample as a model from which you can clone new applications. If CLIST and Dialog Manager are new to you, the sample will still be useful because it will give you an idea of what can be done with QMF, even if you yourself do not code the CLIST or Dialog Manager components.

Our sample application will be used by upper management to view the bank's branches and their managers (ordered by branch or by manager) or to see a particular branch's customers. For this, the ID of the branch will be entered by the user.

Figure 8.2 shows the flow of the application. From QMF, the user invokes the CLIST, BRANCH by typing TSO BRANCH. TSO is a QMF command that enables you to run any TSO command, including

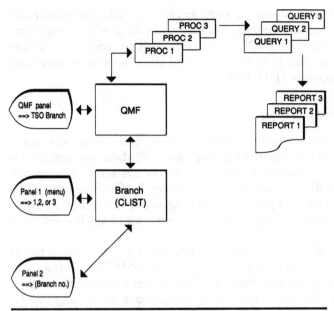

Figure 8.2. A sample CLIST/QMF application.

a CLIST, from QMF. The CLIST displays PANEL1, which is the main menu (Fig. 8.3). The user enters 1, 2, or 3 at the arrow. For option 3, a branch number is required so the CLIST displays PANEL2 (Fig. 8.4) if option 3 is chosen. The CLIST then has QMF run PROC1, PROC2, or PROC3, depending on the option entered. Each PROC runs the corresponding QUERY, displays the report, and returns to the CLIST, which displays the main menu again.

Let's look at the components that make up this application. We'll

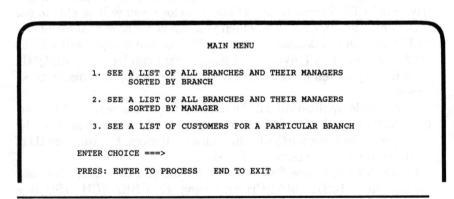

Figure 8.3 The CLIST puts out a menu.

```
ENTER BRANCH ID ===>
```

Figure 8.4   A second panel is used to specify the branch.

look at the coding for the QUERYs, the PROCs, the Dialog Manager Panels, and finally, the CLIST.

The first query is associated with option 1 on the menu which says:

1. SEE A LIST OF ALL BRANCHES AND THEIR MANAGERS SORTED BY BRANCH

QUERY1 looks like this:

```
--This is QUERY1
SELECT BRANCH_ID, BRANCH_MGR
   FROM BRANCH
   ORDER BY BRANCH_ID
```

The second option on the menu reads:

2. SEE A LIST OF ALL BRANCHES AND THEIR MANAGERS SORTED BY MANAGER

The QUERY for this choice is:

```
--This is QUERY2
SELECT BRANCH_ID, BRANCH_MGR
   FROM BRANCH
   ORDER BY BRANCH_MGR
```

And option 3 on the menu is:

3. SEE A LIST OF CUSTOMERS.FOR A PARTICULAR BRANCH

The QUERY for choice 3, QUERY3, references the variable QBRANCH, which will contain the branch number the user wants to select:

```
--This is QUERY3
SELECT CUST_SOC_SEC, CUST_NAME, CUST_BRANCH
   FROM CUSTOMER
   WHERE CUST_BRANCH = &QBRANCH
   ORDER BY CUST_SOC_SEC
```

Each QUERY is run by a corresponding PROC, all three of which will be similar. The first command in each will run the respective QUERY. The third command, TSO, will reinvoke the original CLIST, BRANCH. This will accomplish the application loop. Without it, the user would be out of the application after getting the report and would have to manually type in TSO BRANCH to get back

```
) BODY
%                         BANKERS BANK
%                          MAIN MENU
+
+
+    1. SEE A LIST OF ALL BRANCHES AND THEIR MANAGERS
+          SORTED BY BRANCH
+
+    2. SEE A LIST OF ALL BRANCHES AND THEIR MANAGERS
+          SORTED BY MANAGER
+
+    3. SEE A LIST OF CUSTOMERS FOR A PARTICULAR BRANCH
+
+
%ENTER CHOICE ===>_C+

+PRESS: ENTER TO PROCESS    END TO EXIT
) PROC
   VER (&C,NB,LIST,1,2,3)
) END
```

Figure 8.5 The Dialog Manager code for PANEL1.

```
) BODY
+
+      ENTER BRANCH ID ===>_BRNO+
) PROC
   VER (&BRNO,NB,NUM)
) END
```

Figure 8.6 The Dialog Manager code for PANEL2.

to the application menu. We need an additional command between these two. If we code each PROC with the RUN QUERY command followed by the TSO BRANCH command, we will get the menu and enter a choice, but instead of seeing the report, we will get the menu again. This is because by default QMF applications do not show the interactive QMF panels such as, in this case, the Report Panel. To allow our users to see the Report Panel from within the application, we will have to code a new QMF command in our PROC, INTERACT. This command will allow the user to INTERACT with native QMF from within an application.

Now, let's look at each PROC. PROC1 is coded:

```
--This is PROC1
RUN QUERY QUERY1
INTERACT
TSO BRANCH
```

PROC2 is coded:

```
--This is PROC2
RUN QUERY QUERY2
INTERACT
TSO BRANCH
```

PROC3, which must pass a variable to the QUERY, contains the necessary QUERY variable and PROC variable:

```
--This is PROC3
RUN QUERY QUERY3(&&QBRANCH=&PBRANCH
INTERACT
TSO BRANCH
```

Note that our PROCs will use the default FORMs for the reports they produce. If we had wanted to, we could have coded customized FORMs and specified them in the PROC RUN statements.

The panel components of our sample application are created through Dialog Manager. In Figs. 8.5 and 8.6 we present the coding for these panels. In each panel, the % character is an attribute byte meaning the field following is BRIGHT PROTECTED, the + character means NORMAL PROTECTED, and the _ means an INPUT field. The VER operand in the PROC section of each panel is used to edit the input fields. In Fig. 8.5, VER(&C,NB,LIST,1,2,3) means that the variable C on the panel must be NONBLANK and must contain one of the values following the word LIST. In Fig. 8.6, VER(&BRNO,NB,NUM) means that BRNO must be nonblank and numeric.

Now that you've taken a look at the panels, QUERYs, and PROCs needed for our application, let's take a look at the CLIST that drives it.

```
/*Line 1 displays the first panel */

    1.    ISPEXEC DISPLAY PANEL(PANEL1)

/*Hitting the End key sets &LASTCC to a value greater than
   zero. Line 2 gets out of the CLIST if the user hits the
   End key.*/

    2.    IF &LASTCC > 0 THEN GOTO ENDIT

/*Lines 3 and 4 mean that if the user enters 1, the QMF
   command interface will be invoked to run PROC1 */

    3.    IF &C = 1 THEN -
    4.        ISPEXEC SELECT PGM(DSQCCI) PARM(RUN PROC1)

/*Lines 5 and 6 mean that if the user enters 2, the QMF
   command interface will be invoked to run PROC2.*/

    5.    IF &C = 2 THEN -
    6.        ISPEXEC SELECT PGM(DSQCCI) PARM(RUN PROC2)

/*Lines 7-10 mean that if the user enters 3, panel2 will
   be displayed to get the user's choice of a branch
   number. The QMF command interface will then be invoked
   to run PROC3, using the branch number entered by the
   user */

    7.    IF &C = 3 THEN DO
    8.        ISPEXEC DISPLAY PANEL(PANEL2)
    9.        ISPEXEC SELECT PGM(DSQCCI) -
   10.            PARM(RUN PROC3 (&&&&PBRANCH=&BRNO))
   11.    END
   12.    ENDIT: EXIT
```

Let's take a closer look at line 10. BRNO is the name of the variable on PANEL2 where the user enters the branch number of the customers he or she wishes to select. &PBRANCH is the name of the PROC variable. If the user picks choice 3 and enters a branch number of 50, &BRNO in line 10 will be equal to 50. We need to pass a parm to QMF of:

```
RUN PROC3 (&PBRANCH=50
```

To get the value of &BRNO into &PBRANCH, we have to start with &&&&PBRANCH. The CLIST interface substitutes a single ampersand for each double ampersand, giving us &&PBRANCH. Then the ISPF interface substitutes a single ampersand for each double ampersand, giving us &PBRANCH!

To make this application work, the CLIST and the panels have to be placed in the appropriate libraries. You may need to find out how your installation has this set up.

Applications of much greater complexity than this sample are possible. You can run COBOL programs as QMF applications or even run COBOL programs which in turn run CLISTs. Consult Dialog Manager manuals if you are interested in these possibilities.

QMF allows other kinds of customization. For instance, you can customize the legends on QMF panels and customize PF keys. You could arrange things so that users who got into QMF would see a Home Panel legend such as

```
PRESS PF4 TO RUN BRANCH APPLICATION
```

Then, when the user hits PF4, the command TSO BRANCH would be executed to run a CLIST named BRANCH.

QMF has been made very powerful and flexible and can be made extremely user friendly. However, there may be considerable programming effort and maintenance involved in developing this user friendliness. In particular, we find that CLISTs, especially nested CLISTs, are considerably harder to maintain and debug than are COBOL programs. Customizing QMF commands, PF keys, and panels should also be undertaken with care. Each installation will have to determine how much customization is worth the maintenance and, on the other hand, how much end users will be required to adapt themselves to QMF.

In the future, IBM may well provide the ability to create user-friendly panels directly in QMF, without requiring the sort of programming effort we have described in this chapter. Should this happen, QMF's ease of use will be greatly enhanced.

Application Programming

Accessing DB2 from an Application Program— Introduction to Embedded SQL

We've discussed accessing DB2 interactively using SPUFI or QMF. DB2 can also be accessed from application programs. In the next three chapters we'll introduce the coding that enables you to access DB2 from host programs written in COBOL, Assembler, PL/I, Fortran, and C. We'll be using COBOL for our examples and illustrations. Each chapter includes a sample program. For the sake of clarity and space, we have included only the source code of the sample programs in these chapters.

DB2 handles its data management itself, keeping it essentially transparent to the user. For the programmer, this means that file definitions (FDs), OPENs, CLOSEs, READs, WRITEs, and REWRITEs are not needed to access DB2 data. SQL statements are directly embedded into a program and then translated by DB2's Precompiler component into source language calls to DB2. As you'll see in Chap. 12, precompile is part of a series of steps called "program preparation." We will repeat PROGRAM1, including the output from its compile step, at that time.

If you are a programmer, you already know how to write programs. Now you will learn how to modify your programs so that they can access DB2. We will begin by describing four new features that are required for DB2: table declarations, the SQLCA, the SQL statements themselves, and host variables. You will often see these features collectively referred to as embedded SQL.

9.1 TABLE DECLARATIONS

A table declaration specifies the columns of a table and the attributes of those columns (e.g., data type and length). The WORKING-

STORAGE section of your program will normally include a DE-
CLARE TABLE statement for each table accessed by the program.

9.1.1 DECLARE TABLE Statement

The SQL DECLARE TABLE statement defines the table and its columns. For the BRANCH table, the statement would be (remember,
this is for a COBOL program):

```
EXEC SQL
    DECLARE BRANCH TABLE
        (BRANCH_ID      SMALLINT  NOT NULL WITH DEFAULT,
        BRANCH_CITY     CHAR (20), NOT NULL WITH DEFAULT,
        BRANCH_MGR      CHAR (25),
        BRANCH_ADR      VARCHAR (25) NOT NULL WITH DEFAULT)
END-EXEC
```

Notice how closely this resembles the statement used to create the
same table in Chap. 3 (Fig. 9.1).

Strictly speaking, the table declaration is optional, but it really
should always be used. It serves as program documentation and, in
addition, is used by the Precompiler to verify that table and column
names used in your SQL statements are valid. The DB2
Precompiler runs independently of DB2. It can be run when DB2 is
not up and can even be run on a system that does not have DB2.
Consequently, the Precompiler cannot use the DB2 Catalog to validate table or column names. Instead it uses the table declaration to
verify these names.

9.1.2 DCLGEN

If you code SQL's DECLARE TABLE statement yourself, the table
definition checked by the Precompiler will be only as accurate as
your own typing. DB2 provides a declaration generator called
DCLGEN (pronounced deck-el-jen) to automatically produce accurate DECLARE TABLE code. It may be invoked from DB2I (DB2
Interactive), or through the DCLGEN subcommand of the DSN
command processor, or as a JCL job. DB2I is the simplest and most
often used method.

```
CREATE TABLE BRANCH
    (BRANCH_ID     SMALLINT     NOT NULL WITH DEFAULT,
    BRANCH_CITY CHAR (20)       NOT NULL WITH DEFAULT,
    BRANCH_MGR  CHAR (25        ,
    BRANCH_ADDR VARCHAR (25) NOT NULL WITH DEFAULT)
```

Figure 9.1 The DDL to create the
BRANCH table.

```
                         DB2I PRIMARY OPTION MENU
===>

Select one of the following DB2 functions and press ENTER.

    1  SPUFI                (Process SQL statements)
    2  DCLGEN               (Generate SQL and source language declarations)
    3  PROGRAM PREPARATION  (Prepare a DB2 application program to run)
    4  PRECOMPILE           (Invoke DB2 precompiler)
    5  BIND/REBIND/FREE     (BIND, REBIND, or FREE application plans)
    6  RUN                  (RUN an SQL program)
    7  DB2 COMMANDS         (Issue DB2 commands)
    8  UTILITIES            (Invoke DB2 utilities)
    D  DB2I DEFAULTS        (Set global parameters)
    X  EXIT                 (Leave DB2I)




    PRESS:  END to exit          HELP for more information
```

Figure 9.2   DB2I menu.

Figure 9.2 is the DB2I menu. Choosing the second option brings you to the DCLGEN panel (Fig. 9.3). Enter the table name (BRANCH) and the destination dataset name ('USERID.DCLGNLIB(BRANCH)'). The destination dataset is most commonly a partitioned dataset and requires 80-byte records. The dataset must have been allocated already, but you can add a member through the DCLGEN panel. We have given the member the same name as the table, but this is purely a matter of choice.

One quirk of DCLGEN is that it expects the lowest-level qualifier of the dataset named in 'Destination Data Set' to be COBOL (or whichever language has been specified on the DB2I defaults panel), e.g., SAMPLE.COBOL(BRANCH). As with other datasets, your ID is appended as the high-level qualifier. If the destination dataset name that you've defined ends in a word other than COBOL, you must enclose the entire dataset name in single quotes as we have in our example. If you don't, DCLGEN will append COBOL as the low-order qualifier and will not, therefore, find your dataset.

DCLGEN reads the SYSIBM.SYSCOLUMNS Catalog table, extracts the information it needs about the columns of the named table (BRANCH), and constructs the DECLARE TABLE code. In addition, DCLGEN generates a host language record layout for a row of the table. This record layout is convenient to use as a work area for passing table rows between DB2 and your program. The output of DCLGEN,

```
                              DCLGEN
===>

Enter table name for which declarations are required:
  1  SOURCE TABLE NAME ===> BRANCH
  2  AT LOCATION.......===>                        (Optional)

Enter destination data set:          (Can be sequential or partitioned)
  3  DATA SET NAME ... ===> 'USER1.DCLGNLIB(BRANCH)'
  4  DATA SET PASSWORD ===>           (If password protected)

Enter options as desired:
  5  ACTION .......... ===> ADD       (ADD new or REPLACE old declaration)
  6  COLUMN LABEL .... ===> NO        (Enter YES for column label)
  7  STRUCTURE NAME .. ===>                         (Optional)
  8  FIELD NAME PREFIX ===>                         (Optional)




  PRESS: ENTER to process     END to exit      HELP for more information
```

Figure 9.3   DCLGEN panel.

as it will appear in your program after precompilation, is shown in Fig. 9.4.

To insert this into your program, you would code:

```
EXEC SQL
    INCLUDE BRANCH
END-EXEC
```

Note that the use of a period following END-EXEC is optional and depends on the COBOL in which it is embedded. For example, if the SQL statement is embedded in a COBOL IF statement, END-EXEC would be followed by a period only if the range of the IF is to be ended; otherwise, it would not be followed by a period.

The INCLUDE statement causes the Precompiler to fetch the named member and merge it into the source code at precompile time. This is analogous to the way the COBOL compiler fetches COBOL copy members and merges them into the source code at compile time.

The other options on the DCLGEN panel allow you to:

- Specify a location for tables in a distributed network.

- Specify a password if the destination dataset is password protected.

- Replace an existing member.

- Insert column labels.

```
************************************************************************
* DCLGEN  TABLE(BRANCH)                                                *
*         LIBRARY(USER1.DCLGENLIB(BRANCH))                             *
*         APOST                                                        *
* ... IS THE DCLGEN COMMAND THAT MADE THE FOLLOWING STATEMENTS         *
************************************************************************

*****EXEC SQL DECLARE BRANCH TABLE
*****( BRANCH_ID                     SMALLINT NOT NULL,
*****  BRANCH_CITY                   CHAR(20) NOT NULL,
*****  BRANCH_MGR                    CHAR(25),
*****  BRANCH_ADDR                   VARCHAR(25) NOT NULL
*****) END-EXEC.
************************************************************************
* COBOL DECLARATION FOR TABLE BRANCH                                   *
************************************************************************
  01  DCLBRANCH.
      10 BRANCH-ID                   PIC S9(4) USAGE COMP.
      10 BRANCH-CITY                 PIC X(20).
      10 BRANCH-MGR                  PIC X(25).
      10 BRANCH-ADDR.
         49 BRANCH-ADDR-LEN          PIC S9(4) USAGE COMP.
         49 BRANCH-ADDR-TEXT         PIC X(25).
************************************************************************

* THE NUMBER OF COLUMNS DESCRIBED BY THIS DECLARATION IS 4             *
************************************************************************
```

Figure 9.4   DCLGEN generates a DECLARE TABLE and a record layout.

■ Specify the 01 level name (the default is the table name preceded by DCL—in our example, DCLBRANCH).

■ Specify the field names (the default is the table's column names; if you specify a prefix of XXX, field names will be generated sequentially as XXX01, XXX02, etc.).

The names that DCLGEN generates will be the same for like-named columns in different tables. Having two fields in your Data Division with the same name will produce a COBOL error when you make an unqualified reference to one of them in your program. In our sample application, we've been using a naming standard that prefixes each column name in a table with an identifier unique to that table (e.g., CUST_SOC_SEC, CUST_DATE_OF_BIRTH). Column names are therefore unique across tables and we will not have this problem.

If columns in different tables do have identical names, you will have to get around this in your COBOL program. One way is to use an editor to change the DCLGEN names. However, this may cause maintenance problems down the line. Another solution is to use COBOL qualified data names, e.g., FIELDA OF RECORDB, in your COBOL statements. Note that the use of a qualified name within an embedded SQL statement requires a different syntax. Instead of the above, you would reference the fields as RECORDB.FIELDA in a SQL statement.

9.2   SQL COMMUNICATIONS AREA
(SQLCA)

The second item required to access DB2 from a program is a SQLCA. The Precompiler will insert this if you code:

```
EXEC SQL
   INCLUDE SQLCA
END-EXEC
```

The SQLCA contains a set of fields that DB2 updates after each SQL statement is executed. It indicates the results of executing the statement. In a COBOL program they will be a combination of binary and alphanumeric fields. The SQLCA is analogous to an extended file status area for VSAM files or a PCB Mask for IMS.

Figure 9.5 shows the SQLCA for a COBOL program with an explanation of each field. The most important field in it is SQLCODE, a binary fullword field that is updated with a SQL return code after each SQL statement. This is the same return code that is returned by SPUFI (SPUFI also returns an accompanying explanation for the code). If a SQL statement is successful, this field is set to zero. If a SELECT returns no rows, it is set to +100. If an error is found, it is set to the appropriate negative SQL code. In some warning conditions, it may be set to another positive value. There are hundreds of possible SQLCODEs. For information on them see IBM's *DB2 Messages and Codes* manual.

After a SQL statement is executed, it is important that your application program interrogate the SQLCODE. If you want to display it, it should be moved to a numeric edited field because it is a binary number and possibly negative. Otherwise, it may appear as letters or other non-numeric characters. If you look at a negative SQLCODE directly in a dump or with the CEDF transaction in CICS, it will be displayed in hex twos complement form, the decoding of which is obscure to most COBOL programmers. Moving the SQLCODE to a COBOL field of PIC Z(8)9- will make debugging easier.

Most of the other fields in the SQLCA are used rarely, but you may find two of them to be useful. SQLWARN0 will contain a W if any of the other six warning fields are set to W. These warnings indicate conditions such as possible truncation when moving DB2 column data into your program. The other field of interest is SQLERRD(3). This contains the number of rows affected after an INSERT, UPDATE, or DELETE SQL statement.

```
01 SQLCA.
   05 SQLCAID     PIC X(8).
   This field contains the literal 'SQLCA'; it is intended to make
   it easier to spot the SQLCA in a dump.
   05 SQLCABC     PIC S9(9) COMP-4.
   This field contains 136, the length of the SQLCA.
   05 SQLCODE     PIC S9(9) COMP-4.
   This field contains the SQL return code.
   05 SQLERRM.
      49 SQLERRML PIC S9(4) COMP-4.
      49 SQLERRMC PIC X(70).
   This field contains parts of error messages.
   05 SQLERRP     PIC X(8).
   This field contains diagnostic information such as an
   internal DB2 program name.
   05 SQLERRD     OCCURS 6 TIMES
                  PIC S9(9) COMP-4.
   SQLERRD (1) contains a Relational Data System error code.
   SQLERRD (2) contains a Data Manager error code.
   SQLERRD (3) contains the number of rows inserted, updated or
               deleted by the last SQL statement.
   SQLERRD (4) not applicable to static SQL.
   SQLERRD (5) not applicable to static SQL.
   SQLERRD (6) contains a Buffer Manager error code.
   05 SQLWARN.
      10 SQLWARN0 PIC X.
      This field is blank if the other 6 SQLWARN fields are blank.
      If at least one other SQLWARN field has a 'W' in it,
      SQLWARN0 contains 'W'.
      10 SQLWARN1 PIC X.
      This field contains 'W' if a CHAR or VARCHAR column was
      truncated when moved into a host variable.
      10 SQLWARN2 PIC X.
      This field contains 'W' if null values are eliminated from
      the argument of a function.
      10 SQLWARN3 PIC X.
      This field contains 'W' if the number of columns is larger
      than the number of host variables.
      10 SQLWARN4 PIC X.
      Not applicable to static SQL.
      10 SQLWARN5 PIC X.
      This field contains 'W' if the SQL statement wasn't run
      because it is a SQL/DS statement that isn't valid in DB2.
      10 SQLWARN6 PIC X.
      This field contains 'W' if a date or timestamp was changed
      to correct an invalid date resulting from arithmetic.
      10 SQLWARN7 PIC X.
      Not currently used by DB2.
   05 SQLEXT       PIC X(8).
   Not currently used by DB2.
```

Figure 9.5 Annotated SQLCA for a COBOL program.

9.3 EMBEDDED SQL STATEMENTS

The same SQL that you've used with DB2's interactive facilities can
be used in your programs with some modification.

9.3.1 Delimiters

SQL statements are enclosed in delimiters so that the Precompiler can
distinguish them from the host language statements. In COBOL the
delimiters are EXEC SQL and END-EXEC. If you are familiar with
CICS, you will notice that this is analogous to the EXEC CICS and

END-EXEC delimiters for CICS statements. A typical statement might look like:

```
EXEC SQL
   UPDATE CUSTOMER
      SET CUST_NAME = 'HEATHER NEWMAN'
      WHERE CUST_SOC_SEC = 444444444
END-EXEC
```

SQL statements are coded in columns 12 through 72. Other than DE-CLARE and INCLUDE, which are not executable statements, SQL statements are put in the PROCEDURE DIVISION of a COBOL program. The only syntax requirement is that the words of the opening delimiter, EXEC SQL, appear together on one line.

9.3.2 SELECT INTO

With SPUFI and QMF, you were able to retrieve information directly with the SELECT statement. The output was also automatically formatted and returned to you as a result table, displayed with headings, numeric editing, etc. With embedded SQL, you must supply a storage area into which DB2 can place the information by adding a new clause to the SELECT statement. For a program to retrieve DB2 data, the syntax must be SELECT...INTO. The INTO clause names the CO-BOL field(s) that will be used to receive the data that was retrieved.

We know that a SELECT statement will return a results table consisting of zero, one, or more rows. The SELECT...INTO feature works only if zero or one row is returned in the results table. If the SELECT statement is such that the result is more than one row in the table, it will fail with a negative SQL code (-811) and will retrieve no data. When you expect multiple rows in the results table, you must use a cursor, which points to one row at a time. This is described in Chap. 10.

Let's look at how to use SELECT...INTO:

```
EXEC SQL
   SELECT CUST_SOC_SEC, CUST_DATE_OF_BIRTH
      INTO SSNUM, BIRTHDATE
      FROM CUSTOMER
      WHERE CUST_SOC_SEC = 111111111
END-EXEC
```

SSNUM and BIRTHDATE are data items in your host program. Their characteristics must correspond to CUST_SOC_SEC and CUST_DATE_OF_BIRTH, respectively. DB2 will place the values it retrieves into these data items so that your program can manipulate them as needed (e.g., move them to a report line). Notice that only one row is returned by this statement; thus it is valid for SELECT...INTO. Also note that the order of the INTO variables corresponds to the order of the SELECT columns.

9.4   HOST VARIABLES

In the SELECT...INTO example, SSNUM and BIRTHDATE are fields in the host program. Fields in your program's working-storage or linkage sections that are referenced in SQL statements are called host variables. They are preceded by a colon (:) when they are used in a SQL statement. Although the colon is not always required (as in the example above), it is always used in practice for clarity. The above example *should* have been coded:

```
EXEC SQL
   SELECT CUST_SOC_SEC, CUST_DATE_OF_BIRTH
      INTO :SSNUM, :BIRTHDATE
      FROM CUSTOMER
      WHERE CUST_SOC_SEC = 111111111
END-EXEC
```

The colon distinguishes a host variable from a DB2 table or column name. The order of the columns selected and host variables specified must correspond, as should their data types.

9.4.1   Variable-Length Columns

If you are retrieving fixed-length columns, elementary COBOL data items can be used as host variables. However, if you are retrieving columns defined in the database as VARCHAR, the corresponding host variable must be a group-level data item with two elementary items. The elementary items must be level 49. The first, a binary halfword, PIC S9(4) COMP, holds the length of the character string; the second, a fixed-length data item equal in length to the maximum length of the VARCHAR column holds the value (data) of the column. When the column is retrieved, the first elementary item is set to the length of the value in the retrieved column and that number of bytes of data is moved into the fixed-length data item. For instance, BRANCH_ADDR in the sample database's BRANCH table is defined as VARCHAR (25). A suitable host variable for this column would be:

```
05  BRANCH-ADDR.
    49  ADDRESS-LEN        PIC S9(4) COMP.
    49  ADDRESS-TEXT       PIC X(25).
```

AAAAAAAAAAAAAAAAAAAAAAAAA	ADDRESS-TEXT IS INITIALIZED TO A'S
AAAAAAAAAAAAAAAAAAAAAAAAA	ADDRESS-TEXT AFTER WE RETRIEVE A ROW WITH NO DATA IN IT. ADDRESS-LEN = 0.
BBBBBBBBBBBBBBBBBBBBBAAAAA	ADDRESS-TEXT AFTER WE RETRIEVE A ROW WITH 20 B'S IN IT. ADDRESS-LEN = 20.
CCCCCCCCCCCCCCCBBBBBAAAAA	ADDRESS-TEXT AFTER WE RETRIEVE A ROW WITH 15 C'S IN IT. ADDRESS-LEN = 15.

Figure 9.6   VARCHAR column retrieval.

If a particular occurrence of this column containing 20 bytes of data was retrieved, ADDRESS-LEN would be set to 20 and the first 20 bytes of ADDRESS-TEXT would be replaced with the 20 bytes from the column. There is no padding with blanks. Therefore, before retrieving VARCHAR columns, the host variables should always be cleared.

Follow along in Fig. 9.6 to see how VARCHAR column retrieval works. Let's suppose that we initialize our ADDRESS-TEXT field to contain all As and then retrieve a row that has no data in this column. After the retrieval, ADDRESS-LEN will have a zero in it. ADDRESS-TEXT will still have our original 25 As because no data would have been moved to it. If the next row we retrieve has 20 Bs in it, we find that ADDRESS-LEN is set to 20, the first 20 bytes of ADDRESS-TEXT contain Bs, and the last 5 bytes of ADDRESS-TEXT still have the original As. Finally, suppose that the next row we retrieve has 15 Cs. ADDRESS-LEN is set to 15, the first 15 bytes of ADDRESS-TEXT have Cs, the next 5 have Bs, and the final 5 have the original As. You can see that you'll have a problem if your program just moves ADDRESS-TEXT to a report line. This is why we recommend clearing host variables before they receive data from VARCHAR columns.

9.4.2   Data Type Compatibility

DB2 requires that host variables for numeric columns be numeric, that host variables for character columns be character, and that host variables for date and time columns have the corresponding character representations. Although DB2 will perform any necessary conversion from one type of numeric field to another, it is good programming practice to provide host variables that are equivalent in data type and in scale to the columns they are to receive. Otherwise, performance degradation may result from forcing DB2 to do the required conversions. For example, columns defined as INTEGER should have host variables defined as PIC S9(9) COMP; columns defined as SMALLINT should have host variables defined as PIC S9(4) COMP; a column defined as DECIMAL (9,2) should have a host variable defined as PIC

```
-------------------------|-------------------------------------
        DB2              |               COBOL
-------------------------|-------------------------------------
FIELD_A    CHAR(n)       | 01 FIELD-A   PIC X(n)
-------------------------|-------------------------------------
FIELD_A    VARCHAR(n)    | 01 FIELD-A
                         |    49 FIELD-A-LEN   PIC S9(4)  COMP
                         |    49 FIELD-A-TEXT PIC X(n)
-------------------------|-------------------------------------
FIELD-A    SMALLINT      | 01 FIELD-A   PIC S9(4)  COMP
-------------------------|-------------------------------------
FIELD_A    INTEGER       | 01 FIELD-A   PIC S9(9)  COMP
-------------------------|-------------------------------------
FIELD_A    DECIMAL(p,q)  | 01 FIELD-A   PIC S9(a)V9(q)  COMP-3
                         |          where a = p-q
-------------------------|-------------------------------------
FIELD_A    DATE          | 01 FIELD-A   PIC X(10)
-------------------------|-------------------------------------
FIELD_A    TIME          | 01 FIELD-A   PIC X(8)
-------------------------|-------------------------------------
FIELD_A    TIMESTAMP     | 01 FIELD-A   PIC X(26)
-------------------------|-------------------------------------
```

Figure 9.7 Data type correspondence between DB2 and COBOL.

S9(7)V99 COMP-3. Figure 9.7 shows the correspondence between CO-BOL and DB2 data types. If you are using binary host variables (corresponding to INTEGER or SMALLINT columns), it is important to use the NOTRUNC COBOL compiler option. (In COBOL II version 2.3, this option is called TRUNC(OPT).) The NOTRUNC COBOL compiler option tells the compiler to allow any value that will fit into a field to stay there and not to limit the allowable value to the maximum number of digits defined in the picture clause. For example, for a PIC S9(4) COMP field, a program compiled NOTRUNC will allow the field's 2 bytes to contain 32767; if the program is compiled TRUNC, the compiler will generate code to truncate the value to 9999, four digits because the picture clause specifies four places.

9.4.3 To Supply a Value

Host variables can also be used to supply values to DB2. In an earlier example, we used a literal in the WHERE clause (where CUST_SOC_SEC = 111111111). Instead, we could have used a host variable in place of the literal:

```
WORKING-STORAGE SECTION.
.
.
01  SOC-SEC-IN      PIC S9(9) COMP.
.
PROCEDURE DIVISION.
.
RETRIEVE-DATA.
     EXEC SQL
       SELECT CUST_SOC_SEC, CUST_DATE_OF_BIRTH
         INTO :SSNUM, :BIRTHDATE
         FROM CUSTOMER
         WHERE CUST_SOC_SEC = :SOC-SEC-IN
     END-EXEC
```

SOC-SEC-IN is a host variable that contains a value that could come from an online screen, an input transaction file, or be defined as a constant in the program. Programs are different from ad hoc queries in that they are generally concerned with multiple iterations of data rather than a single literal. Host variables provide the flexibility that is usually required by application programs.

In addition to supplying values for a WHERE clause, host variables may also be used to supply a value for a SELECT clause (as a literal constant):

```
EXEC SQL
   SELECT ACCT_BALANCE + :BONUS-PRIZE
   INTO :NEW-ACCOUNT-BAL
   FROM ACCOUNT
   WHERE ACCT_ID = :ACCT-ID-IN
END-EXEC
```

as a value in an UPDATE statement's SET clause:

```
EXEC SQL
   UPDATE CUSTOMER
   SET CUST_RATING = :NEW-CUST-RATING
   WHERE CUST_ID = :CUST-ID-IN
END-EXEC
```

or in an INSERT statement's VALUES clause:

```
EXEC SQL
   INSERT INTO BRANCH
   VALUE (:ID-VALUE, :MGR-VALUE, :CITY-VALUE,
          :ADDR-VALUE)
END-EXEC
```

Host variables may not be used to represent a table, view, or column name.

When a variable-length host variable is used to supply a value, the binary field containing the length must be explicitly set to the number of bytes to be supplied. That number of bytes will then be moved to the column from the host variable field containing the data. The COBOL verb UNSTRING with the COUNT IN option can be used to extract the data portion of a field and determine its length.

9.4.4 Host Structures

It is often convenient to group several variables together into one named set, a host structure. DB2 manuals use the term "structure" to refer to COBOL group items and to record layouts. A host structure may occur within a multilevel COBOL record layout (Fig. 9.8), but the host structure itself may only have two levels. The only exceptions are

```
01 WS-BANK-RECORD.
   05 ADDRESS                PIC X(30).
   05 HISTORY.
      10 TRANSACTION.
         15 TYPE             PIC X(08).
         15 TIMESTAMP        PIC X(26).
         15 AMOUNT           PIC S9(9)V2 COMP-3.
         15 ACCT-NO          PIC X(04).
```

Figure 9.8 A multilevel layout containing
a two-level host structure.

host structures which contain variables for VARCHAR columns. In
that case, the level 49 items are a third level.

If a program contains the following structure:

```
01 BRANCH-INFO.
   05 BRANCH-ADDR.
      49 ADDRESS-LEN PIC S9(4) COMP.
      49 ADDRESS-TEXT PIC X(25).
   05 BRANCH-CITY      PIC X(20).
   05 BRANCH-MGR       PIC X(25).
```

the fields in the structure can be referenced in a SQL statement by
referring to their group name:

```
EXEC SQL
   SELECT BRANCH_ADDR, BRANCH_CITY, BRANCH_MGR
      INTO :BRANCH-INFO
      FROM BRANCH
      WHERE BRANCH_ID = 890
END-EXEC
```

Each of the selected fields will be placed in the corresponding field
within BRANCH_INFO. Note that the order of the fields within
BRANCH_INFO must correspond to the order of the fields following
SELECT.

Another example of a host structure is a record layout corresponding to one row of the table such as that produced by DCLGEN. In our
DCLGEN example it was called DCLBRANCH. The structure can be
used to either receive a row from a table or to supply a row to a table.
If we were to move the appropriate values into the host variable area,
we could execute the following statement to update the database table
with a new row:

```
EXEC SQL
   INSERT INTO BRANCH
      VALUES (:DCLBRANCH)
END-EXEC.
```

9.5 NULLS

So far, we have made no provision for handling nulls in embedded
SQL. If a host variable is used as we've described in our examples so

far, a column with a null value would not be returned and an error condition (a negative SQL code) would be set. Also, we haven't discussed how to set a column to null except for the literal null, which, like other literals, is often not very useful in a program.

To handle nulls, we need an indicator variable for each host variable that might contain a null value. It is used primarily to indicate whether or not the associated host variable actually contains a null value. The indicator variable is a halfword binary field in your host program (PIC 9(4) COMP). The association between an indicator variable and a host variable is established in the SQL statement:

```
WORKING-STORAGE SECTION.
  .
  .
01  CUST-NAME          PIC X(18).
01  CUST-DATE-OF-BIRTH PIC X(10).
01  NAME-IND           PIC S9(4) COMP.
  .
PROCEDURE DIVISION.
  .
RETRIEVE-DATA.
    EXEC SQL
      SELECT CUST_NAME, CUST_DATE_OF_BIRTH
        INTO :CUST-NAME:NAME-IND, :CUST-DATE-OF-BIRTH
        FROM CUSTOMER
        WHERE CUST_SOC_SEC = 444444444
    END-EXEC
```

CUST_NAME is defined as null in our database and is associated with NAME-IND, the indicator variable for this host variable. We know that this is an indicator variable because it begins with a colon and immediately follows the host variable in the SQL statement with no intervening comma or space.

To associate indicators with a host structure, you must use a table of indicators called an indicator structure:

```
01  INDICATOR-TABLE.
    02  CUST-IND     PIC S9(4) COMP OCCURS 5 TIMES.
```

The number of times the indicator variable occurs must be equal to the number of fields in the associated host structure. This example of an indicator structure could be used with the host structure for our CUSTOMER table, which has five fields (Fig. 9.9). Only the name column is nullable, but the indicator table must have five occurrences, one for each field.

```
CUSTOMER TABLE HOST STRUCTURE:

  01   DCLCUSTOMER.
       05   CUST-SOC-SEC            PIC S9(9) COMP.
       05   CUST-NAME               PIC X(18).
       05   CUST-DATE-OF-BIRTH      PIC X(10).
       05   CUST-BRANCH             PIC S9(4) COMP.
       05   CUST-RATING             PIC S9(4) COMP.
```

Figure 9.9   The customer table has five columns, one of which may be null.

An indicator structure, like an indicator variable, is linked to a host structure in a SQL statement:

```
EXEC SQL
    SELECT *
    INTO :DCLCUSTOMER:CUST-IND
    FROM CUSTOMER
    WHERE CUST_SOC_SEC = 111111111
END-EXEC
```

CUST-IND is used to link the indicator table with the host structure. Note that it is the field with the occurs clause and not the table name which is used to refer to the indicator structure.

When a column is retrieved into a host variable, the associated indicator variable is set to indicate different conditions. If the value in the column is null, the indicator variable is set to -1 and no data is moved to the host variable. If the value for the column is null because of an arithmetic or conversion error, the indicator variable is set to -2. If the column is not null but has been truncated, the indicator value will be set to the positive value of the number of bytes in the original column. Thus, an indicator variable containing zero after a retrieval means that the column was retrieved in its entirety and was not null, a positive value in the indicator variable means truncation has occurred, and a negative value in the indicator variable means the column is null. When data is retrieved into a host structure with an associated indicator structure, each indicator variable in the array is set according to the corresponding field. Columns that cannot be null and have no truncation or arithmetic errors will cause their indicator variables to be set to zero.

Indicator variables and structures are also used to set columns to null. When performing inserts or updates, setting the indicator variable to -1 will insert a null value into the corresponding column. For example, if you wanted to add a row to the CUSTOMER table and set the CUST_NAME column to null, you could code:

```
WORKING-STORAGE SECTION.

***********************************************************
*  COBOL DECLARATION FOR TABLE CUSTOMER               *
***********************************************************
01  DCLCUSTOMER.
    10  CUST-SOC-SEC        PIC S9(9) USAGE COMP.
    10  CUST-NAME           PIC X(18).
    10  CUST-DATE-OF-BIRTH  PIC X(10).
    10  CUST-BRANCH         PIC S9(4) USAGE COMP.
    10  CUST-RATING         PIC S9(4) USAGE COMP.


***********************************************************
*  INDICATOR STRUCTURE CONSISTS OF FIVE INDICATORS,    *
*  CUST-IND  (1) THRU CUST-IND (5)                     *
***********************************************************

01  INDICATOR-TABLE.
    02  CUST-IND           PIC S9(4) COMP OCCURS 5
                                     TIMES.


PROCEDURE DIVISION.
UPDATE-DATA.
    MOVE -1 TO CUST-IND(2)
    MOVE (any other values required to other fields)

***********************************************************
*  IN THIS INSERT STATEMENT, THE CUST-IND INDICATOR    *
*  STRUCTURE IS ASSOCIATED WITH THE DCLCUSTOMER HOST   *
*  STRUCTURE. BOTH THE INDICATOR STRUCTURE AND THE HOST*
*  STRUCTURE CONSIST OF 5 VARIABLES.                   *
***********************************************************

    EXEC SQL
        INSERT INTO CUSTOMER
        VALUES (:DCLCUSTOMER:CUST-IND)
    END-EXEC
```

9.6 ERROR HANDLING

Your program must establish the success or failure of each SQL statement's execution and should also specify the action to take upon encountering an exception. The error fields in the SQLCA and the WHENEVER statement can be used to handle errors. DSNTIAR, an IBM-supplied routine, is also an option; it will be described later in this chapter.

9.6.1 SQLCA Fields

The most straightforward way to handle errors in an application program is to interrogate the SQLCODE and SQLWARRN0 fields in the SQLCA after each SQL statement. Look back at Fig. 9.5 for the SQLCA's layout.

9.6.2   WHENEVER

DB2 has a convenient feature called WHENEVER that causes the DB2 translator to automatically generate the code needed to interrogate SQLCODE and/or SQLWARN0 after each SQL statement. An action to take is specified in the event that an error, exception, or warning exists in the SQLCA. The syntax of WHENEVER is:

```
EXEC SQL.
    WHENEVER condition action
END-EXEC
```

The *condition* can be SQLWARNING, SQLERROR, or NOT FOUND. SQLWARNING is triggered when SQLCODE is greater than zero but not equal to 100 or when SQLWARN0 = 'W'. SQLERROR is triggered when SQLCODE is negative. NOT FOUND is triggered when SQLCODE is equal to +100. This is summarized in Fig. 9.10. The *action* can either be CONTINUE or GO TO *label*. CONTINUE, as an action, means to ignore the exception and continue processing. GO TO means to branch to the paragraph or section named and begin processing the statements found there. Here are two examples of the WHENEVER clause:

```
EXEC SQL
    WHENEVER SQLWARNING GO TO PARA-B
END-EXEC

EXEC SQL
    WHENEVER NOT FOUND CONTINUE
END-EXEC
```

The WHENEVER clause is convenient and straightforward to use when the action for any condition remains the same throughout a program. But, suppose you don't want the same condition throughout the program? DB2 allows you to change the specified action at different points in a program. For example, you could code:

CONDITION	EVENT
SQLWARNING	SQLCODE > 0, but not equal to 100, OR SQLWARNING = 'W'
SQLERROR	SQLCODE < 0
NOTFOUND	SQLCODE = 100

Figure 9.10 Events that trigger the WHENEVER condition.

```
EXEC SQL
    WHENEVER NOT FOUND GO TO PARA-A
END-EXEC
```

This statement would be in effect for all SQL statements that follow it. If, at some later point in the program you code:

```
EXEC SQL
    WHENEVER NOT FOUND GO TO PARA-B
END-EXEC
```

The first GO TO will be superseded and the new one will be in effect for all subsequent SQL statements.

You must be very careful when changing the action to be taken. Unlike HANDLE CONDITION in CICS, it is the order of statements in the source code and *not* the program's execution path that determines the WHENEVER statement in effect at any moment. Thus, if the source code that follows your second WHENEVER NOT FOUND (GO TO PARA-B) includes a branch to a paragraph that precedes that WHENEVER, the first WHENEVER NOT FOUND (GO TO PARA-A) will be in effect. This is exactly the opposite of what happens in the CICS HANDLE CONDITION or the PL/I ON CONDITION; these languages will always branch to PARA-B after the second WHENEVER NOT FOUND is encountered because they always act based on the most recently executed condition.

Our recommendation is to use the WHENEVER statement for conditions that will have the same action throughout a program, otherwise you should explicitly check SQLCA fields as needed in your program.

9.6.3 DSNTIAR

Frequently, it's difficult to remember the meaning of each error code. IBM supplies a routine called DSNTIAR that can be invoked from your program to explain errors. This routine provides a table of messages from the *SQL Return Code* manual and supplies the message that corresponds to a nonzero SQLCODE. Some installations may use DSNTIAR, while others will use some other homegrown routine for this purpose.

If you want to use DSNTIAR, you will need to code some data items in your program's WORKING-STORAGE SECTION. These are in two 01-level items. The first includes a message-length field that is set to 960; this is the length of all eight of the 120-byte DSNTIAR message lines combined. After the message-length field is the 960-byte message field, which is broken into eight print lines by an OCCURS 8

TIMES clause. The second 01-level item contains 120, the length of one print line. You can code the DSNTIAR data items as follows (the names are optional):

```
01  DSNTIAR-MESSAGE.
      05  MESSAGE-LENGTH         PIC S9(4) COMP VALUE +960.
      05  DSNTIAR-MSG-TEXT       OCCURS 8 TIMES
                                 INDEXED BY DSNTIAR-INDEX
                                 PIC X(120).
01  DSNTIAR-LINE-LENGTH          PIC S9(9) COMP VALUE +120.
```

To call DSNTIAR in your PROCEDURE DIVISION, you would code:

```
CALL 'DSNTIAR' USING SQLCA DSNTIAR-MESSAGE
DSNTIAR-LINE-LENGTH.
```

You would issue this CALL when SQLCODE is not zero. This CALL uses the information from the SQLCA to produce the appropriate message. It puts the message into DSNTIAR-MSG-TEXT and identifies how long the message is in MESSAGE-LENGTH. It would be wise to check the COBOL special register RETURN-CODE to make sure DSNTIAR completed successfully. If it did, you will want to place the information DSNTIAR returned to the program someplace where you can view it. This can be done by coding:

```
IF RETURN-CODE EQUAL ZERO
   PERFORM DISPLAY-DSNTIAR-MSG VARYING DSNTIAR-INDEX
   FROM 1 BY 1 UNTIL DSNTIAR-INDEX GREATER THAN 8.
```

The paragraph, DISPLAY-DSNTIAR-MSG, could be coded:

```
DISPLAY-DSNTIAR-MSG.
IF DSNTIAR-MSG-TEXT (DSNTIAR-INDEX) NOT = SPACE
   DISPLAY DSNTIAR-MSG-TXT (DSNTIAR-INDEX).
```

This will DISPLAY the DSNTIAR output to the same DDNAME as other DISPLAYS in your program. This could be a printer or the screen. Of course, you could write the output to a file or insert it into a DB2 table instead. You might want to use a DB2 table, for example, so that you, the developer, could look at error conditions received by your users. In this situation, you would probably want the table to contain columns for program name and timestamp so that you could trace problems more effectively.

9.7 PROGRAM1

We've discussed several features of embedded SQL. Now let's turn to the first of three sample programs. This and the program in the following two chapters are meant to illustrate the material discussed in each chapter.

What does PROGRAM1 do? Our sample tables include a BRANCH table. Users will need a table maintenance program to add new branches, delete old branches, and change information about current branches, such as who the branch manager is. The program does these updates and displays messages about what it is doing for audit and control purposes. The program is meant to run in batch. To make the program simpler, we are assuming that a previous program in the system has edited the input transactions.

This program reads a file of 80-byte transaction records which are applied to the BRANCH table. Each transaction is a type A (add), C (change), or D (delete). An add transaction contains data for all four columns of the BRANCH table. It also contains a length field for the VARCHAR column BRANCH_ADDR. If the BRANCH_MGR column is to be null, an asterisk will appear in the first byte of the TRANS-BRANCH-MGR field of the transaction record; the rest of the field will be spaces. A delete transaction deletes the row identified by the value in its TRANS-BRANCH-ID field. A change transaction can only update one column; the fields corresponding to the unchanged columns will be blank.

To save space, we will not use DSNTIAR as an error routine, but we'll provide our own, which simply moves SQLCODE to a numeric edited field called EDIT-SQLCODE, displays EDIT-SQLCODE with a message, closes the transaction file, displays the record counter, and ends the program.

There is an indicator structure (INDICATOR-TABLE) to handle nulls in the INSERT and SELECT SQL statements. For the UPDATE statement that sets only the BRANCH_MGR column, we provide a single indicator variable (MGR-IND). The BRANCH_MGR column is the only column in the table that can be null. The source code for PROGRAM1 follows:

```
IDENTIFICATION DIVISION.
PROGRAM-ID. PROGRAM1.

ENVIRONMENT DIVISION.
INPUT-OUTPUT SECTION.
FILE-CONTROL.
     SELECT TRANSACTION-FILE ASSIGN TRANSFIL.

DATA DIVISION.
FILE SECTION.
FD  TRANSACTION-FILE
     LABEL RECORDS ARE STANDARD
     BLOCK CONTAINS 0 RECORDS
     RECORDING MODE IS F
     RECORD CONTAINS 80 CHARACTERS.
01  TRANSACTION-RECORD                 PIC X(80).

WORKING-STORAGE SECTION.

01  WS-TRANSACTION-RECORD.
******************************************************
*  This is the record layout for TRANSACTION-FILE, the *
*  input file.  Trans-type is A for add, C for change, *
*  D for delete.  Since the BRANCH_ADDR column is      *
*  VARCHAR, we need to provide a length field as well   *
*  as a text field for it.                              *
******************************************************
     05  TRANS-TYPE                    PIC X.
     05  TRANS-BRANCH-ID               PIC 9(4).
     05  FILLER                        PIC X.
     05  TRANS-BRANCH-CITY             PIC X(20)
     05  FILLER                        PIC X..
     05  TRANS-BRANCH-MGR              PIC X(25).
     05  FILLER                        PIC X.
     05  TRANS-BRANCH-ADDR-LEN         PIC 99.
     05  TRANS-BRANCH-ADDR-TEXT        PIC X(25).

01  SWITCHES-AND-COUNTERS.
     05  EOFSW                         PIC X VALUE SPACE.
         88  END-OF-FILE                   VALUE '1'.
     05  TRANS-CTR                     PIC S9(5) COMP-3
                                           VALUE ZERO.
```

```
********************************************************
*  EDIT-SQLCODE is a numeric-edited field to display  *
*  SQLCODE after error conditions.                    *
********************************************************
      05  EDIT-SQLCODE                PIC Z(8)9-.

********************************************************
* INDICATOR-TABLE will be associated with the         *
* DCLBRANCH record layout.  It allows us to detect    *
* branches with a null BRANCH_MGR column              *
********************************************************
  01  INDICATOR-TABLE.
      05  BRANCH-IND                  PIC S9(4) COMP
                                      OCCURS 4 TIMES.

********************************************************
* MGR-IND is a single indicator variable used to set  *
* BRANCHMGR to null when that is the change requested *
* by the input transaction.                           *
********************************************************
  01  MGR-IND                         PIC S9(4) COMP.

********************************************************
* The following two SQL statements will retrieve the  *
* SQLCA and the DCLGEN  created member, BRANCH         *
********************************************************
      EXEC SQL
        INCLUDE SQLCA
      END-EXEC.

      EXEC SQL
        INCLUDE DCLBRNCH
      END-EXEC.

  PROCEDURE DIVISION.
  1000-MAINLINE.
      EXEC SQL
        WHENEVER SQLERROR GO TO 9000-ERROR-RTN
      END-EXEC.

      EXEC SQL
        WHENEVER NOT FOUND GO TO 9000-ERROR-RTN
      END-EXEC.

      PERFORM 2000-INIT.
      PERFORM 3000-PROCESS-TRANS UNTIL END-OF-FILE.
      PERFORM 4000-EOJ.
      STOP RUN.
```

```
2000-INIT.
    OPEN INPUT TRANSACTION-FILE.
    PERFORM 5000-READ-TRANS.

3000-PROCESS-TRANS.
***********************************************************
* This is the program's main loop.  From it you will    *
* branch to the ADD, DELETE or CHANGE routines.         *
***********************************************************
        IF TRANS-TYPE = 'A'
            PERFORM 6000-ADD-BRANCH
        ELSE
            IF TRANS-TYPE = 'D'
                PERFORM 7000-DELETE-BRANCH
            ELSE
                PERFORM 8000-CHANGE-BRANCH.
        PERFORM 5000-READ-TRANS.

4000-EOJ.
    CLOSE TRANSACTION-FILE.
    DISPLAY 'RECORDS READ: ' TRANS-CTR.

5000-READ-TRANS.
    READ  TRANSACTION-FILE INTO WS-TRANSACTION-RECORD
        AT END MOVE '1' TO EOFSW.
    IF NOT END-OF-FILE
        ADD 1 TO TRANS-CTR.

6000-ADD-BRANCH.
***********************************************************
* Adding a row to the BRANCH requires formatting the    *
* row, inserting it, and displaying a message           *
***********************************************************
    PERFORM 6100-FORMAT-ROW.
    PERFORM 6200-INSERT-ROW.
    DISPLAY WS-TRANSACTION-RECORD ' **ADDED**'.
```

```
    6100-FORMAT-ROW.
***********************************************************
* This routine moves date from the input transaction    *
* record to the DCLGEN record layout so that it can be   *
* added to the table.  The length field for BRANCHADDR*  *
* is converted from display to binary by the move. If    *
* BRANCHMGR is to be null, the indicator available is    *
* set to -1.                                             *
***********************************************************
        MOVE TRANS-BRANCH-ID TO BRANCH-ID.
        MOVE TRANS-BRANCH-CITY TO BRANCH-CITY.
        IF TRANS-BRANCH-MGR = '*'
            MOVE -1 TO BRANCH-IND (3)
        ELSE
            MOVE ZERO TO BRANCH-IND (3)
            MOVE TRANS-BRANCH-MGR TO BRANCH-MGR.

        MOVE TRANS-BRANCH-ADDR-LEN TO BRANCH-ADDR-LEN.
        MOVE TRANS-BRANCH-ADDR-TEXT TO BRANCH-ADDR-TEXT.

    6200-INSERT-ROW.
        EXEC SQL
          INSERT INTO BRANCH
            VALUES (:DCLBRANCH:BRANCH-IND)
        END-EXEC.

    7000-DELETE-BRANCH.
        MOVE TRANS-BRANCH-ID TO BRANCH-ID.

        EXEC SQL
          DELETE
            FROM BRANCH
            WHERE BRANCHID = :BRANCH-ID
        END-EXEC.

        DISPLAY WS-TRANSACTION-RECORD ' **DELETED**'.
```

```
   8000-CHANGE-BRANCH.
   ********************************************************
   * This updates the BRANCH table.  From it you will    *
   * branch to the paragraph which updates the column    *
   * specified for update on the input record.  The      *
   * routine then branches to paragraphs which retrieve  *
   * and then display the changed row.                   *
   ********************************************************
         MOVE TRANS-BRANCH-ID TO BRANCH-ID.

         IF TRANS-BRANCH-CITY NOT EQUAL SPACES
             PERFORM 8100-UPDATE-CITY
         ELSE
             IF TRANS-BRANCH-MGR NOT EQUAL SPACES
                 PERFORM 8200-UPDATE-MGR
             ELSE PERFORM 8300-UPDATE-ADDR.

         DISPLAY WS-TRANSACTION-RECORD ' **CHANGE**'.
         PERFORM 8400-RETRIEVE-ROW.
         PERFORM 8500-DISPLAY-ROW.

   8100-UPDATE-CITY.
         MOVE TRANS-BRANCH-CITY TO BRANCH-CITY.

         EXEC SQL
           UPDATE BRANCH
               SET BRANCH_CITY = :BRANCH-CITY
               WHERE BRANCH_ID = :BRANCH-ID
         END-EXEC.

   8200-UPDATE-MGR.
   ********************************************************
   * This routine updates the BRANCHMGR column.  If this *
   * column is to contain nulls, the indicator variable is*
   * set to -1.                                          *
   ********************************************************
         IF TRANS-BRANCH-MGR = '*'
             MOVE -1 TO MGR-IND
         ELSE
             MOVE ZERO TO MGR-IND
             MOVE TRANS-BRANCH-MGR TO BRANCH-MGR.

         EXEC SQL
           UPDATE BRANCH
               SET BRANCH_MGR = :BRANCH-MGR:MGR-IND
               WHERE BRANCH_ID = :BRANCH-ID
         END-EXEC.
```

```
8300-UPDATE-ADDR.
    MOVE TRANS-BRANCH-ADDR-LEN TO BRANCH-ADDR-LEN.
    MOVE TRANS-BRANCH-ADDR-TEXT TO BRANCH-ADDR-TEXT.

    EXEC SQL
      UPDATE BRANCH
        SET BRANCH_ADDR = :BRANCH-ADDR
        WHERE BRANCH_ID = :BRANCH-ID
    END-EXEC.

8400-RETRIEVE-ROW.
***********************************************************
* This routine retrieves the changed row.                 *
***********************************************************
    EXEC SQL
      SELECT * INTO :DCLBRANCH:BRANCH-IND
        FROM BRANCH
        WHERE BRANCH_ID = :BRANCH-ID
    END-EXEC.

8500-DISPLAY-ROW.
***********************************************************
* This routine displays changed rows,                    *
* displaying a message if the indicator variable         *
* indicates that BRANCHMGR is null.                      *
***********************************************************
    MOVE SPACES TO WS-TRANSACTION-RECORD.
    MOVE BRANCH-ID TO TRANS-BRANCH-ID.
    MOVE BRANCH-CITY TO TRANS-BRANCH-CITY.

    IF BRANCH-IND (3) LESS THAN ZERO
        MOVE '*BRANCH MGR NOT ASSIGNED*' TO
          TRANS-BRANCH-MGR
    ELSE
        MOVE BRANCH-MGR TO TRANS-BRANCH-MGR.

    MOVE BRANCH-ADDR-LEN TO TRANS-BRANCH-ADDR-LEN.
    MOVE BRANCH-ADDR-TEXT TO TRANS-BRANCH-ADDR-TEXT.
    DISPLAY WS-TRANSACTION-RECORD '**UPDATED**'.


9000-ERROR-RTN.
***********************************************************
* This is a generalized error routine.  It displays      *
* the numeric-edited sqlcode and ends the program.       *
***********************************************************
    DISPLAY '***FATAL DB2 ERROR--PROGRAM1 ENDING'.
    MOVE SQLCODE TO EDIT-SQLCODE.
    DISPLAY 'SQLCODE = ' EDIT-SQLCODE.
    PERFORM 4000-EOJ.
    STOP RUN.
```

This program has illustrated the use of embedded SQL. It contains examples of SELECT, UPDATE, DELETE, and INSERT statements and demonstrates how to handle nulls and VARCHAR columns in application programs. Our program, however, retrieves only one row at a time. In the next chapter we will present the techniques for using embedded SQL statements that select multiple rows.

10

Embedded SQL—
Advanced Topics

In this chapter we'll continue our discussion of embedded SQL, including a discussion of the technique for coding SQL statements that retrieve and update multiple rows. Before we get to this, however, we'll look at how DB2 handles data integrity. Although data integrity is relevant to all database access, it is more of an issue to you as an application programmer when your program accesses multiple rows because there is greater potential for contention with other users for shared resources. Included in the discussion of data integrity is an explanation of the SQL statements COMMIT, ROLLBACK, and LOCK TABLE, which you may need to use in programs that retrieve and update multiple rows.

10.1 DATA INTEGRITY

Data integrity, or the accuracy of data, can be jeopardized by such things as hardware or software failures or interference by concurrent users. All major DBMSs have optional provisions for ensuring data integrity—logging update activity, making changes permanent (COMMIT) or undoing changes before they are made permanent (ROLLBACK), and some form of concurrency control or locking. Let's look at how DB2 implements each of these facilities.

10.1.1 Logging

DB2 maintains a log dataset that contains a record of all of the changes made to tables. When a change is to be made, the images of the row both before and after the change are written to the log. If it is necessary to back the change out because, for example, a related change to another table failed, the before image in the log can be used to restore the database to its original state. If the change has to be reapplied (for reasons such as the pack on which the table was written is damaged and the table has to be recovered), the after image can be used.

DB2 provides logging and a system of archiving the logs and keeping track of them as an integral part of its data management. In fact, DB2 provides dual logging; that is, it writes each log record to two separate log datasets. If one of the logs is damaged, recovery is still possible using the other.

10.1.2 COMMIT and ROLLBACK

A logical unit of work is a set of changes to data, all of which must be completed successfully to be valid. If only part of the logical unit succeeds, the changes should be backed out and the data restored to its original condition before the updates began. Let's look at an example. Suppose someone wants to transfer money from a checking account to a savings account. First, the money would be subtracted from the checking account, then added to the savings account. But what if our customer went to an automatic teller machine to execute the transfer and the subtract from checking succeeded and the add to savings failed? The subtraction from checking would have to be backed out. That is, the money would have to be added back into the checking account; otherwise our customer would end up losing money instead of transferring it.

In a batch or TSO program (CICS considerations will be discussed in Chap. 11) DB2 treats the entire execution of the program as one logical unit of work unless the programmer specifies otherwise. In other words, if the program completes successfully, all of the changes that are made are applied to the database, or committed. If the program abends at any point, any changes that were made are backed out, or rolled back. COMMIT is the process of making a change permanent; ROLLBACK is the process of undoing changes that have been made but are not yet permanent.

DB2 will automatically issue a COMMIT upon successful completion of a program. For programs that really are one logical unit of work, this is fine. But in more complicated or longer running programs, the programmer may need to issue one or more explicit COMMITs. A COMMIT frees resources (e.g., tables and plans) and saves you from having to rerun an entire job when only one part has failed. A COMMIT is issued by coding:

```
EXEC SQL COMMIT END-EXEC
```

ROLLBACKs may also be either initiated automatically or requested explicitly. DB2 will issue a ROLLBACK when a program abends or when you initiate one by coding:

```
EXEC SQL ROLLBACK END-EXEC
```

The ROLLBACK will back out all changes up to the point of the last COMMIT executed in the program. If the program has issued no COMMITs, all changes made during the current execution of the program will be backed out. DB2 will also issue a ROLLBACK if a deadlock or timeout occurs. A deadlock, also called a "deadly embrace," is a situation in which one program controls a resource (e.g., TABLE-A) and needs another resource (TABLE-B) to finish its task, while at the same time, another program controls TABLE-B and needs TABLE-A to finish its task. The resources required by both programs are unavailable so neither program can proceed. DB2 will abend the program that has the fewest log records and roll back any changes it has made.

A timeout is a situation in which a program is waiting too long for a resource. "Too long" is defined at DB2 installation time. If, for example, long-running Job A locks Job B out of a tablespace, and if Job B is forced to wait too long, it will get timed out and rolled back.

To see how COMMIT and ROLLBACK are used in a program, we'll return to the example of our customer wanting to transfer money from checking to savings. Suppose our program executes PARA-A to subtract money from checking and PARA-B to add money to savings. To make sure the customer's money doesn't disappear, we should code:

```
**************************************************
* PARA-A extracts money from checking account    *
**************************************************
    PERFORM  PARA-A.
**************************************************
* If that worked, go on to PARA-B, which adds    *
* money to savings.                              *
**************************************************
    IF SQLCODE NOT NEGATIVE
        PERFORM PARA-B.
**************************************************
* If adding the money to savings worked, the     *
* extract and add are made permanent with COMMIT, *
* Otherwise both the extract from checking and    *
* add to savings are undone with ROLLBACK.        *
**************************************************
    IF SQLCODE NOT NEGATIVE
        EXEC SQL  COMMIT  END-EXEC
    ELSE
        EXEC SQL  ROLLBACK  END-EXEC.
```

Suppose you are coding a batch update program that applies thousands or millions of transactions to a table. How often should you code COMMIT statements? DB2 locks out other users from pages that have been updated but not committed. COMMITs free these resources, increasing concurrency. Concurrency, which is increased by COMMITs, must be balanced with performance, which is degraded by COMMITs because they involve writing to the logs. There is no hard-and-fast rule, but in general, it is recommended that you COMMIT after every 100 rows have been updated. You will usually be given guidelines for this by your DBA.

One of the implications of applying many updates without a COMMIT is that if the job fails, the ROLLBACK process could, conceivably, take almost as long as the original update processing—and then you would have to restart the program from the beginning to apply the updates again.

10.1.3   What DB2 Does at Commit Time

We've said that a COMMIT makes changes permanent. At a COMMIT point, DB2 writes out the relevant log buffers to the log datasets on DASD. COMMIT *does not* initiate a write of the database buffers to the corresponding datasets on DASD. In fact, DB2 will only write out all of the changed data in its database buffers when DB2 is normally shut down. In actual operation, it writes out some of the changed buffers prior to shutdown time only when the space in the bufferpool is needed for other data.

Therefore, if DB2 or MVS crashes, the database may not reflect all committed changes accurately, but the log will. When DB2 is restarted, it reads the log and applies the changes it has recorded to the database as needed.

10.1.4   Locking

Because DB2 allows many users to share resources concurrently, there must be a mechanism—locking—to ensure that users do not inadvertently interfere with each other's changes. One aspect of locking which directly affects you as a programmer is your ability to explicitly request control of a resource. For instance, if you know that you are going to be updating a significant number of the pages in a table and you want to guarantee that your program has uninterrupted control over those pages, you may want to issue a LOCK TABLE statement. This statement locks the entire table or tablespace from the point at which it is issued, usually at the beginning of a job, until your job releases it. It is coded:

```
EXEC SQL
    OCK TABLE CUSTOMER IN EXCLUSIVE MODE
END-EXEC
```

Using IN EXCLUSIVE MODE prevents others from accessing the table or tablespace at all. If the statement is executed in SHARE mode, it will allow others to read the table but not to update it. This is coded:

```
EXEC SQL
    LOCK TABLE CUSTOMER IN SHARE MODE
END-EXEC
```

For either LOCK TABLE statement, if the requested table is not available, your job will fail when it attempts to execute the statement, but you will not have lost processing time by beginning your updates and then finding yourself in a wait or timeout situation. The locks that you impose through these statements will be in effect until you issue a COMMIT or ROLLBACK.

The LOCK TABLE statement can be useful, but if it is not used carefully, it can lock out other users needlessly and can drastically reduce concurrency. Check with your installation to see if it has rules or standards about these statements. The LOCK TABLE statement will lock an entire unsegmented tablespace but will lock only the named table in a segmented tablespace.

We have touched upon some of the features of DB2's locking mechanisms. Chapter 15 will discuss the different types of locks that DB2 uses. Let's look now at how DB2 application programs can submit SQL statements that retrieve multiple rows from a table.

10.2 CURSOR OPERATIONS

Up to now we've talked about embedded SELECT statements in which only one row at a time can be returned. COBOL and many other programming languages are oriented to processing one record (or row) at a time; they are not well suited to multiple-row processing. DB2 gets around this limitation with a facility called a cursor.

Conceptually, *a cursor is a pointer that identifies one row (the CURRENT row) of a results table.* Your program can use one or more cursors to retrieve rows sequentially, one at a time, from a results table. In order to use a cursor, it must be DECLAREd and then OPENed. To retrieve the row that the cursor points to from the results table, you FETCH it. When you have completed processing the results table, the cursor is CLOSEd.

Each SELECT embedded in your program must either be a SELECT INTO, as described in the last chapter, or must be part of a DECLARE

CURSOR statement. If you know that your SELECT may produce a results table of more than one row, you must use a cursor. Otherwise, SELECT INTO is more efficient to use.

10.2.1 Declaring the Cursor

The DECLARE CURSOR statement consists of a cursor name and the SELECT statement that will create the results table to which the named cursor will point. The SELECT statement is identical in format to the embedded SQL SELECT statements discussed in Chap. 9 except that it may not have an INTO clause. The syntax of DECLARE CURSOR is:

```
EXEC SQL
    DECLARE cursor-name CURSOR FOR
        SELECT column-1, column-2...
        FROM table-name ...
        WHERE...
END-EXEC.
```

Using our BRANCH table as an example, we could declare a cursor as follows:

```
EXEC SQL
    DECLARE BRANCH_C CURSOR FOR
    SELECT BRANCH_ID, BRANCH_CITY, BRANCH_MGR,
            BRANCH_ADDR
    FROM BRANCH
    WHERE BRANCH_CITY = :TRANS-BRANCH-CITY
END-EXEC
```

Our cursor is named BRANCH_C. It will point, in turn, to each row in the table that is returned as a result of the SELECT statement. Notice that host variables can be used as in any other embedded SQL statement.

The DECLARE CURSOR statement may be placed anywhere in your program as long as it occurs before any statements that reference it. However, the convention is to place these statements in the WORKING-STORAGE SECTION of a COBOL program. Note that if the statements refer to any host variables, the host variables must be defined before the cursor declaration in the program. The DECLARE CURSOR statement is not executable; OPENing a cursor is what causes DB2 to do the work.

10.2.2 Opening and Closing the Cursor

Until a cursor is opened, it does not point to any rows. OPEN is the statement that executes the underlying SELECT and creates the results table to which the cursor points. The syntax of OPEN CURSOR is:

```
EXEC SQL
    OPEN cursor-name
END-EXEC
```

Let's open the cursor that we just declared:

```
EXEC SQL
    OPEN BRANCH_C
END-EXEC
```

Now we can begin to process the rows of the table we just retrieved. When you are finished with the results table, you should close the cursor. The syntax of CLOSE CURSOR is:

```
EXEC SQL
    CLOSE cursor-name
END-EXEC
```

If you are only going to use a cursor once, you don't actually have to close it, although it is good practice to do so. A COMMIT, whether explicit or implicit, automatically closes all cursors.

If a query contains a variable that is entered by the user, you will need to reuse the cursor for each iteration of the query. To do this, you must close it and open it again for each new table that will be produced. For instance, suppose your program requires that the user enter a city and then it processes all of the rows in the BRANCH table for that city. You can use the DECLARE CURSOR of our previous example:

```
EXEC SQL
    DECLARE BRANCH_C CURSOR FOR
    SELECT BRANCH_ID, BRANCH_CITY, BRANCH_MGR,
        BRANCH_ADDR
    FROM BRANCH
    WHERE BRANCH_CITY = :TRANS-BRANCH-CITY
END-EXEC
```

Each time the user enters a new city, the program must open the cursor BRANCH_C, process the rows for that city, and then close the cursor. Each city will produce a different results table.

10.2.3   Retrieving a Row—FETCH

To actually bring a row of a results table into your program so that it can be processed, you must use a FETCH statement. The syntax is:

```
EXEC SQL
    FETCH cursor-name
        INTO :host-variable-name
END-EXEC.
```

The INTO clause of the FETCH statement follows the same rules as the INTO clause of a SELECT statement (discussed in Chap. 9). Either a host structure containing variables for all of the fetched columns may be used or individual host variables may be named. Null indicators should be used if nullable columns are to be retrieved.

The table resulting from an OPEN cursor is treated like a sequential file, with each fetch retrieving one row. You cannot go backward to a previously retrieved row without closing and reopening the cursor and you cannot skip a row. If a fetch fails to retrieve a row because there are no more rows to retrieve (analogous to an end of file condition), SQLCODE will be set to +100. As in ordinary sequential file processing, every FETCH statement should include a test for end of file, i.e., SQLCODE = +100. You can code your own test (IF SQLCODE = 100...) or you can use the WHENEVER NOT FOUND statement.

To see how all of this fits together, let's look at the following example, which assumes that DCLTRANSACTION is a record layout, perhaps created by DCLGEN, matching a row of the TRANSACTION table, and that TRANSACTION-IND is an indicator structure to handle the possible null values.

```
WORKING-STORAGE SECTION.
*******************************************************
*    CURSOR_TXN is DECLAREd for the SQL statement    *
*    that retrieves the rows from the TRANSACTION    *
*    table that have the same account number as      *
*    the host variable, WS-ACCT-NO                   *
*******************************************************

    EXEC SQL
        DECLARE CURSOR_TXN CURSOR FOR
        SELECT TXN_TYPE, TXN_AMOUNT, TXN_TIMESTAMP,
            TXN_ACCT_NO
        FROM TRANSACTION
        WHERE TXN_ACCT_NO = :WS-ACCT-NO
    END-EXEC
    .
    .
    .

PROCEDURE DIVISION.
0000-HOUSEKEEPING.
    EXEC SQL
        OPEN CURSOR_TXN
    END-EXEC.
```

```
   1000-MAINLINE.
   **************************************************
   *  FETCH-TRANSACTIONS is a fetch loop which      *
   *  processes the rows returned by the OPEN. When *
   *  the loop is completed (i.e., end-of-file), we *
   *  close the cursor.                             *
   **************************************************
       PERFORM FETCH-TRANSACTIONS UNTIL SQLCODE = +100.
       EXEC SQL
          CLOSE CURSOR_TXN
       END-EXEC.

   1100-FETCH-TRANSACTIONS.
   **************************************************
   *  Each time FETCH-TRANSACTIONS is executed, a row *
   *  is retrieved from the TRANSACTION table and   *
   *  placed in the COBOL host variable named       *
   *  DCLTRANSACTION. We need the indicator structure*
   *  TRANSACTION-IND because the column, TXN_AMOUNT, *
   *  can be null.                                  *
   **************************************************
       EXEC SQL
          FETCH CURSOR_TXN
          INTO :DCLTRANSACTION:TRANSACTION-IND
       END-EXEC.
       IF SQLCODE NOT = +100
          PERFORM PROCESS-ROW.
   1110-PROCESS-ROW.
   **************************************************
   *  We do not include the code for this routine;  *
   *  it could be anything.  It might move a row's   *
   *  data to a print line and write out the line,  *
   *  or you could accumulate TXN_AMOUNT, etc.      *
   **************************************************
```

10.2.4 UPDATE and DELETE

Until now we have considered cursors solely as a means of retrieving rows when more than one row may be returned in a result table. There is also a syntax that allows a cursor to be used in UPDATE and DELETE operations. This lets you retrieve multiple rows to a result table and then perform a processing loop to fetch each row, process it, update one of its columns, or delete it.

In order to UPDATE or DELETE, the DECLARE CURSOR statement names a cursor and a SELECT statement, as in retrieval operations. The cursor will point to those rows in the SELECT statement's results table that may be updated or deleted. With UPDATE, an additional clause is needed in the DECLARE CURSOR statement. Any column that you wish to update must be named in the FOR UPDATE OF clause. The syntax is:

```
EXEC SQL
   DECLARE cursor-name CURSOR FOR
   SELECT column-1, column-2 ...
      FROM table-name
      WHERE ...
      FOR UPDATE OF column-1, column-2 ...
```

A column that will be updated does not have to appear in the SELECT clause itself. DELETE does not require the FOR UPDATE OF clause.

There are some restrictions on the SELECT statements that may be used in the DECLARE CURSOR statement with UPDATE and DELETE. Consistent with the restrictions on UPDATE and DELETE statements discussed in Chap. 6, only one table or view may be specified. In addition, DISTINCT, UNION, and ORDER BY are restricted to read-only cursors. DISTINCT, you will recall, eliminates duplicate rows, UNION merges the results of two or more SELECTs, and ORDER BY sorts the results table.

The OPEN, FETCH, and CLOSE statements used with update or delete operations are identical to those used for retrieval. The SQL statements to UPDATE or DELETE rows, however, have a new clause, WHERE CURRENT OF. Their syntax is:

```
EXEC SQL
    UPDATE table-name
        SET column-1 = value-1 ...
        WHERE CURRENT OF cursor-name
END-EXEC

EXEC SQL
    DELETE FROM table-name
        WHERE CURRENT OF cursor-name
END-EXEC
```

Any columns named in the SET clause of the UPDATE statement must have been identified as a target for update in the FOR UPDATE OF clause of the DECLARE CURSOR statement. With both the UPDATE and DELETE, if the WHERE CURRENT OF clause is not specified, the entire table, rather than the row that the cursor is positioned at, will be updated or deleted.

An example will help. Suppose we want to apply corrected amounts to rows in the TRANSACTION table. First we would DECLARE the cursor:

```
EXEC SQL
    DECLARE CURSOR_TXN CURSOR FOR
    SELECT TXN_TYPE, TXN_TIMESTAMP,
        TXN_AMOUNT, TXN_ACCT_NO
    FROM TRANSACTION
    FOR UPDATE OF TXN_AMOUNT
END-EXEC
```

Notice that the only field we've identified as a candidate for update is TXN_AMOUNT.

Next, we OPEN the cursor and begin processing. As we fetch each row, we calculate the corrected amount for that row and place the figure in the host variable, WS-CORRECT-AMOUNT. Having processed the row, we can now UPDATE it:

```
EXEC SQL
    UPDATE TRANSACTION
    SET TXN_AMOUNT = :WS-CORRECT-AMOUNT
    WHERE CURRENT OF CURSOR_TXN
END-EXEC
```

Alternatively, if we had wanted to delete the row, we would have coded:

```
EXEC SQL
    DELETE FROM TRANSACTION
    WHERE CURRENT OF CURSOR_TXN
```

10.2.5 Reestablishing Cursor Position

We've said that in long-running jobs it is desirable to execute a COMMIT periodically. We have also said that COMMITs close all open cursors in a program. We need a way to keep track of a cursor's position so that we can reopen it if it's closed and resume processing at the appropriate row. With retrieval operations this is fairly straightforward. Going back to the TRANSACTION table, we could code the following DECLARE CURSOR:

```
EXEC SQL
    DECLARE CURSOR_ONE CURSOR FOR
    SELECT TXN_TYPE, TXN_AMOUNT, TXN_TIMESTAMP,
           TXN_ACCT_NO
    FROM TRANSACTION
    WHERE TXN_TIMESTAMP > :WS-COMMIT-TIMESTAMP
    ORDER BY TXN_TIMESTAMP
END-EXEC.
```

The ORDER BY clause guarantees that the results table will be in timestamp order. The WHERE clause ensures that only rows with a timestamp greater than that in WS-COMMIT-TIMESTAMP will be returned.

In order to ensure that we begin at the top of the table the first time we open the cursor, we could code:

```
MVE '0001-1-1-0.00.00' TO WS-COMMIT-TIMESTAMP.
```

This is the lowest possible value of a timestamp and ensures that our WHERE clause will produce the very first row of the table. Immediately prior to issuing a commit, we must save the last timestamp retrieved so that when we reopen the cursor, we pick up where we left off. Look at the following code:

```
MOVE TXN-TIMESTAMP TO WS-COMMIT-TIMESTAMP.
EXEC SQL
   COMMIT
END-EXEC.
EXEC SQL
   OPEN CURSOR__ONE
END-EXEC.
```

The MOVE statement puts the timestamp of the last row retrieved into WS-COMMIT-TIMESTAMP. When the cursor is opened again, the new result table will contain only the rows that have not yet been processed.

This approach cannot be used with cursors declared for update because ORDER BY is not permitted in these statements. Without an ORDER BY clause, there is no way to guarantee the order of rows in a DB2 table. When it is necessary to reestablish cursor position to update, therefore, we recommend declaring the cursor for retrieval and then issuing a separate UPDATE statement as each row is fetched. This gets around the problem of unordered rows retrieved with a cursor declared for update. Note that the UPDATE statement does not have the WHERE CURRENT OF clause:

```
EXEC SQL
    DECLARE CUST CURSOR FOR
        SELECT CUST-SOC-SEC, CUST-NAME,
            CUST-DATE-OF-BIRTH, CUST-BRANCH,
            CUST-RATING
        FROM CUSTOMER
        ORDER BY CUST-SOC-SEC
END-EXEC
    .
    .
    .
EXEC SQL
OPEN CUST
END-EXEC
    .
    .
    .
PERFORM 1000-FETCH-AND-UPDATE
    .
    .
    .
1000-FETCH-AND-UPDATE
    EXEC SQL
    FETCH CUST INTO :DCLCUSTOMER
    END-EXEC
    IF CUST-RATING = 3
        EXEC SQL
            UPDATE CUSTOMER
                SET CUST-RATING = CUST-RATING +1
                WHERE CUST-SOC-SEC = :CUST-SOC-SEC
        END-EXEC
```

10.3 DYNAMIC SQL

Until now, we have only considered static embedded SQL. DB2 provides additional flexibility with dynamic SQL. Our discussion of this topic will be brief, since it is used more by developers of software packages than by application programmers; its coding is complex and there are major limitations on its use in COBOL programs.

10.3.1 Dynamic SQL Compared to Static SQL

Static SQL statements are written and compiled in advance of their execution through the DB2 precompiler and the BIND process. As a result, execution of static SQL is efficient. No SQL parsing is done at execution time and, normally, the selection of access paths occurs prior to execution time.

But suppose you were unable to construct your SQL statements before execution time? Here's where dynamic SQL can be used. Dynamic SQL parses, processes, and binds statements on the fly at execution time. While this provides flexibility, the cost is high. Each time the program is run, the SQL has to be parsed, processed, and bound, so there is considerable overhead and performance will suffer. The difference between static and dynamic SQL is analogous to the difference between a compiled (e.g., COBOL) and interpreted (e.g., CLIST) computer language. Interpreted languages invariably have poorer performance than compiled languages and are generally not suitable for production applications.

Dynamic SQL is subject to other problems in addition to those common to interpreted computer languages. Since dynamic SQL creates and binds queries on the fly, there is no way that they can be tuned in advance; therefore they may well perform poorly and may cause problems for other users. Also, the DB2 Catalog is locked during the BIND process.

10.3.2 Examples of Dynamic SQL in DB2

Although you may never have written a dynamic SQL program, you've used one if you've used DB2's interactive facilities. Both SPUFI and QMF are IBM-written dynamic SQL programs. They enable you to construct SQL statements that are bound when you submit them. This is transparent to you, the user. In situations where ad hoc queries need the flexibility of dynamic SQL, we suggest that programmers use the powerful facilities of QMF instead of attempting to code their own dynamic SQL programs.

10.4   TESTING CONSIDERATIONS

Because DB2 does its own data management and its own access path selection, testing with DB2 differs from testing with ordinary files. One difference concerns the ability to point to different sets of data (e.g., test and production) without recompiling. With ordinary MVS files, a simple change to the JCL will feed different data to a program. In DB2, however, the JCL doesn't point to the DB2 data. Instead DB2 finds the data from the table name that is coded in your program. Therefore, we need a way to change the table names in your program without having to change and recompile the program. The SYNONYM feature of DB2 provides a solution. Other testing considerations include the comparison of test results to expected results and a means to develop test data.

10.4.1   Synonyms in Testing

A synonym is an alternate name for a table or view. Any user can create a synonym that is specific to the user who created it. Suppose user Smith had created our BRANCH table. Smith could access the table by calling it either SMITH.BRANCH (its qualified name) or BRANCH (its unqualified name), because DB2 uses the user's ID as the qualifier if none is specified.

If user Jones wants to access the table and has created no synonym for it, she has to call it SMITH.BRANCH. If she creates a synonym for it (BRANCH), she can call it simply BRANCH. Actually, she could call it any unqualified name she wants; she does not have to duplicate the original table name. Usually, however, duplicating the original table name is most convenient. To create this synonym, the user codes (probably through SPUFI):

```
CREATE SYNONYM BRANCH FOR SMITH.BRANCH
```

If Jones wants to drop the synonym, she codes:

```
DROP SYNONYM BRANCH
```

When coding programs containing embedded SQL, table names should always be coded without qualifiers, and synonyms should be used to specify the actual tables being pointed to. This approach allows programs to point to one of several test tables and enables them to be moved into production without having to be changed. Let's see how this works.

Suppose Jones wants to test her program. The table for unit testing is called UTEST.BRANCH and the table for system testing is called STEST.BRANCH. Jones codes the program so that it refers to the table only as BRANCH. For unit testing, Jones CREATEs a synonym,

BRANCH, for the table UTEST.BRANCH. When she wants to move on to system testing, she DROPs this synonym and CREATEs a new synonym, BRANCH, for the table STEST.BRANCH. The program will not have to be changed or recompiled.

The strategy of maintaining different test environments whose tables have the same unqualified names but which have been created with different high-level qualifiers is a convenient way to maintain test tables. SPUFI input datasets containing CREATE SYNONYM and DROP SYNONYM statements can be shared by all users of the data to make switching environments quick and virtually automatic. And, if the unqualified table names are the same as the production table names, the programs can then be moved to production unchanged.

10.4.2 Requirements for Test Data

Creating test data for a DB2 application poses certain problems. Making up suitable test data is always difficult because the data should, ideally, contain all of the cases that might be found in production. In non-DB2 systems, once a small amount of data has been created, it may be possible to duplicate it many times to perform volume tests. This is not necessarily so in DB2.

In DB2, the access path to the data (e.g., the use of an index) is chosen automatically by DB2's Optimizer. The Optimizer selects an access path by considering many facts about the data—the size of the table, the distribution of data values, the number of distinct values, etc.

An important goal of DB2 testing is to determine whether or not the access paths chosen by the Optimizer will provide the response time and performance required by an application. For instance, if DB2 does not plan to use an index in an online inquiry of a large table, the query may run so long that it will not be practical and may have to be rewritten. It is vital to find out about the access paths as early as possible in testing.

But in order to get an accurate picture of the access paths that the Optimizer will choose, your test data must correspond closely to your production data. It is necessary to have not only a volume of data approximating that expected in production but also to have data whose range and distribution of key values approximates that expected in production. This must be kept in mind when creating test tables. DB2 lets you "fool" the Optimizer by updating certain values in the Catalog that the Optimizer checks when determining access paths.

In testing, it is sometimes useful to clone a table. This can be done with a mass insert:

```
INSERT INTO NEWTABLE
   SELECT * FROM OLDTABLE
```

If you are creating a large table, this method is likely to be a poor performer. It would be better to use the program DSNTIAUL to unload the old table and then use the LOAD utility to load the output of DSNTIAUL to your new table. DSNTIAUL can also be used to produce flat files from DB2 tables. This is particularly useful if it becomes necessary to compare expected results to actual results. SQL itself has no comparison utility, so the flat files that are produced can be processed by standard compare utilities.

10.4.3 DSNTIAUL

DSNTIAUL is a dynamic SQL program, written in Assembler and provided by IBM with DB2. It unloads data from DB2 tables and writes it to a flat file, one record per row. The columns are put in the record in the order in which they occur in the table. In addition, another file that contains LOAD control statements is written to be used to load the unloaded flat file into a DB2 table.

DSNTIAUL is run as a DB2 batch program. We will explain the JCL for DB2 programs in Chap. 12. For now, however, we will just point out that the program we execute is the TSO Terminal Monitor Program. In other words, we execute TSO as a batch job. SYSTSIN points to input data that instructs TSO to execute the DSN command that will run the DSNTIAUL program. In the following example, DB2T is the name of the DB2 subsystem and DSNTIAL2 is the name of the corresponding plan for program DSNTIAUL. Please note that plan names for IBM-supplied programs may change with different re-leases of DB2. Accordingly, verify the plan names with your DBA before using any of the JCL examples in this book.

The following JCL will run DSNTIAUL:

```
//USERID1 JOB  (job card parameters)
//DSNTIAUL EXEC PGM=IKJEFT01,DYNAMNBR=100
//SYSTSPRT DD  SYSOUT=*
//SYSPRINT DD  SYSOUT=*
//SYSTSIN  DD  *
  DSN SYSTEM(DB2T)
  RUN PROGRAM(DSNTIAUL) PLAN(DSNTIAL2) LIB('DB2.LOADLIB')
  END
//SYSIN DD *
  (table or view specification, e.g., BRANCH)
/*
//SYSRECOO DD   DSN=(first unloaded dataset)
//SYSPUNCH DD   DSN=(load statements)
```

Up to 100 tables or views can be specified as input on the JCL's SYSIN card. WHERE or ORDER BY clauses are also permitted to qualify the table named. Each table or view specification, including the WHERE or ORDER BY clause, must be placed on its own line. Continuation characters are not recognized.

If, for example, you wanted to use DSNTIAUL to unload the entire BRANCH table, you would code one control statement for SYSIN:

```
//SYSIN DD *
  BRANCH
/*
```

Or, if you wished to unload only certain rows of the BRANCH table, your statement might be:

```
//SYSIN DD *
  BRANCH WHERE BRANCH_ID > 12
```

The statements follow the syntax of SELECT statements, but they implicitly include SELECT * FROM. You do not have to code these words.

The unloaded data resulting from the execution of the first control statement is written to *ddname* SYSREC00, from the second control statement to SYSREC01, etc. The load statements that would reload the unloaded datasets to their original tables are automatically generated by DB2 and placed in the dataset named in the SYSPUNCH card. You can use that dataset later to reload your tables. By modifying the load statements, it is also possible to load data from the original table into a new table structure or to transport data within and between subsystems. Your DBA can help you with the LOAD syntax.

One quirk of DSNTIAUL is that it blocks its unloaded datasets to a maximum of 10 records per block. Since IBM provides the source code, it may be worthwhile for someone in your shop who knows Assembler to change the code to provide a more efficient blocksize.

10.5 SUBMITTING SQL IN BATCH

Programs with embedded SQL may be run in batch under the TSO Terminal Monitor Program, but on occasion, a batch SPUFI ability is needed as well. For instance, when a new application is turned over for production, the data center operations staff may need the ability to execute DDL statements to create tables or DCL statements to grant access to users. Because SPUFI is interactive, it is hard for management to control and can be inconvenient for operations to use. A more practical solution is a batch job that can execute DDL and DCL statements similar to the way that SPUFI can but is subject to the normal data center controls, schedules, audits, etc., of other batch jobs. For this we recommend DSNTEP2 and DSNTIAD. They are IBM-supplied application programs that must be compiled and linked, usually at DB2 installation time.

10.5.1 DSNTEP2

DSNTEP2 is a dynamic SQL program written in PL/I. It can execute almost all SPUFI statements. It differs from SPUFI in that DSNTEP2 recognizes a comment line by an asterisk in column 1, while SPUFI recognizes a comment line by two hyphens. Also, DSNTEP2 issues a COMMIT after every SQL statement. The last difference is that when SPUFI encounters an error it terminates; DSNTEP2 will keep going.

The JCL to run DSNTEP2 is similar to that used to run DSNTIAUL; only the program name and plan name, pointed to by the SYSTSIN DDNAME, are different. DSNTEP2's only output file is SYSPRINT, so the other output files needed for DSNTIAUL are absent here.

The following JCL will run DSNTEP2:

```
//USERID1  JOB    (jobcard parameters)
//DSNTEP2  EXEC   PGM=IKJEFT01,DYNAMNBR=100
//SYSTSPRT DD     SYSOUT=*
//SYSPRINT DD     SYSOUT=*
//SYSTSIN  DD     *
  DSN SYSTEM(DB2T)
  RUN PROGRAM(DSNTEP2) PLAN(DSNTEP22) LIB('DB2.LOADLIB')
  END
//SYSIN DD *
  (SQL statements)
/*
//
```

The input SQL statements are part of *ddname* SYSIN. The output report is written to SYSPRINT. The SYSTEM operand names your DB2 subsystem; your DBA can tell you its name. The LIB operand points to the load library containing DSNTEP2. Check with your installation to make sure that the plan name hasn't been changed.

10.5.2 DSNTIAD

DSNTIAD, also a dynamic SQL program, is written in Assembler. It is similar to DSNTEP2 in capabilities, with two exceptions—it cannot process SELECT statements that return more than one row and it has no provision for comment lines. DSNTEP2 is recommended if your installation has PL/I; otherwise you can use DSNTIAD.

DSNTIAD uses the same JCL as DSNTEP2, except that the SYSTSIN *dd* statement is coded as follows:

```
DSN SYSTEM(DB2T)
RUN PROGRAM(DSNTIAD) PLAN(DSNTIAD2) LIB('DB2.LOADLIB')
END
```

The SYSTEM operand points to the DB2 subsystem name. The LIB statement points to the load library containing DSNTIAD. Check with your installation to make sure that the plan name is correct.

10.6 PROGRAM2

Let's return to our sample application for a practical view of how to use the features described in this chapter. One customer may have more than one account. The bank wants to offer free checking to customers who have a total of over $400 in all of their accounts combined.

One customer may have many accounts. Program2 uses a cursor on the ACCOUNT table to find customers whose account balances total over $400. It then retrieves the rows of those customers from the CUSTOMER table and updates their credit rating to 99. A report line is written containing information on each customer who falls into this category.

After every 30 updates, a COMMIT is issued and the cursor, closed by the COMMIT, is reopened. In order to reestablish the cursor position after each commit, an ORDER BY clause and a comparison of ACCT_CUST_ID with the host variable COMMIT_CUST_ID is included in the cursor declaration. The program separates retrieval and update operations rather than declaring the cursor for update.

Note that we have included an error routine in case there are orphan accounts that have no associated row in the CUSTOMER table. The automatic referential integrity of version 2.1 makes this unnecessary. We have included it for the sake of our example and for those working with earlier releases of DB2.

In 3300-FORMAT-PRINTLINE, the indicator variables are tested before moving WS-CUST-FIRST-NAME and WS-CUST-LAST-NAME to the detail line. These fields are host variables for columns that can be null.

The source code for PROGRAM2 follows:

```
IDENTIFICATION DIVISION.
PROGRAM-ID. PROGRAM2.

ENVIRONMENT DIVISION.
INPUT-OUTPUT SECTION.
FILE-CONTROL.
    SELECT REPORT-FILE ASSIGN PRINTFIL.

DATA DIVISION.
FILE SECTION.
FD  REPORT-FILE
    LABEL RECORDS ARE STANDARD
    BLOCK CONTAINS 0 RECORDS
    RECORDING MODE IS F
    RECORD CONTAINS 133 CHARACTERS.
01  REPORT-RECORD                        PIC X(133).

WORKING-STORAGE SECTION.

01  WS-DETAIL-LINE.
    05  FILLER                           PIC X.
    05  FILLER                           PIC X(14)
                                             VALUE 'CUST-SOC-SEC:'.
    05  D-SOC-SEC                         PIC 9(9).
    05  FILLER                               PIC X(6)
                                         VALUE 'NAME:'.
    05  D-NAME                               PIC X(18).
    05  FILLER                               PIC X(14)
                                         VALUE 'ACCT BAL SUM:'.
    05  D-ACCT-BAL-SUM                    PIC $Z(8)9.99-.
    05  FILLER                               PIC X(12)
                                         VALUE 'OLD RATING:'.
    05  D-OLD-RATE                        PIC Z(3)9.
    05  FILLER                               PIC X(12)
                                         VALUE 'NEW RATING:'.
    05  D-NEW-RATE                        PIC Z3(9).
```

```
01  SWITCHES-AND-COUNTERS.
    05  COMMIT-CTR                    PIC S9(4) COMP
                                          VALUE ZERO.
    05  COMMIT-CUST-ID                PIC S9(9) COMP
                                          VALUE ZERO.
    05  DISPLAY-SQLCODE               PIC Z(8)9-.

01  WS-CUSTOMER-IND-TABLE.
    05  WS-CUSTOMER-IND               PIC S9(4) COMP
                                          OCCURS 3 TIMES.
```

```
******************************************************
*  We use SQL INCLUDE to get DCLGENs for the CUSTOMER*
*  table and the ACCOUNT table, and to get the SQLCA.*
******************************************************
      EXEC SQL
        INCLUDE SQLCA
      END-EXEC.

      EXEC SQL
        INCLUDE DCLCUST
      END-EXEC.

      EXEC SQL
        INCLUDE DCLACCT
      END-EXEC.

******************************************************
*  The following DECLARE CURSOR selects the sum of   *
*  ACCT_BALANCE and the CUST_ID from the ACCOUNT     *
*  table if the sum is over 400. It selects only     *
*  accounts where the CUST_ID is greater than the    *
*  host variable COMMIT-CUST-ID. At the beginning of *
*  the program this field contains zero. Each time a *
*  COMMIT is done, this field is used to save the    *
*  CUST_ID of the last customer processed so that when*
*  the cursor is reopened, it will fetch the accounts *
*  starting with those of the next customer.         *
******************************************************
      EXEC SQL
        DECLARE BALSUM CURSOR FOR
        SELECT ACCT_CUST_ID, SUM(ACCT_BALANCE)
          FROM ACCOUNT
          WHERE ACCT_CUST_ID > :COMMIT-CUST-ID
          GROUP BY ACCT_CUST_ID
          HAVING SUM(ACCT_BALANCE) > 400
          ORDER BY ACCT_CUST_ID
      END-EXEC.
```

```
01  WS-SUM-ACCT-BAL-REC.
    05  WS-SUM-CUST-ID              PIC S9(9) COMP.
    05  WS-SUM-ACCT-BAL            PIC S9(9)V99 COMP-3.


01  WS-CUSTOMER-REC.
    05  WS-CUST-SOC-SEC            PIC S9(9) COMP.
    05  WS-CUST-NAME              PIC X(18).
    05  WS-CUST-RATING            PIC S9(4) COMP.


PROCEDURE DIVISION.
1000-MAINLINE.
    EXEC SQL
        WHENEVER SQLERROR GO TO 6000-SQL-ERROR
    END-EXEC.

    OPEN OUTPUT REPORT-FILE.
    PERFORM 2000-MAIN-PROCESS UNTIL SQLCODE = +100.
    PERFORM 5000-EOJ.
    STOP RUN.

2000-MAIN-PROCESS.
*****************************************************
*  The main loop performs 3000-FETCH-AND-UPDATE     *
*  until the whole ACCOUNT table has been           *
*  processed (SQLCODE = +100) or until accounts     *
*  totaling more than $400 have been found for 30   *
*  customers and the 30 customers have had their    *
*  credit ratings updated. COMMIT-CTR is added to   *
*  each time a customer is updated. When 30 have    *
*  been updated, a COMMIT is issued. The last line  *
*  in the paragraph, IF COMMIT-CTR > ZERO..., is to *
*  cover the situation where we have processed all  *
*  the accounts (SQLCODE=100) and we have less      *
*  than 30 left to COMMIT.                          *
*****************************************************

    EXEC SQL
        OPEN BALSUM
    END-EXEC.

    PERFORM 3000-FETCH-AND-UPDATE UNTIL
        SQLCODE = +100 OR COMMIT-CTR = 30.
    IF COMMIT-CTR > ZERO
        PERFORM 4000-COMMIT.
```

```
 3000-FETCH-AND-UPDATE.
 ****************************************************
 *  This routine performs FETCH-BALSUM which        *
 *  fetches a row from the ACCOUNT table as         *
 *  specified in the DECLARE BALSUM CURSOR.         *
 *  If an account is fetched (SQLCODE NOT = +100),  *
 *  the customer is retrieved, the printline        *
 *  is formatted, the customer row is updated, and  *
 *  the report line is written                      *
 ****************************************************
        PERFORM 3100-FETCH-BALSUM.
        IF SQLCODE NOT = +100
            PERFORM 3200-RETRIEVE-CUSTOMER
            PERFORM 3300-FORMAT-PRINTLINE
            PERFORM 3400-UPDATE-CUSTOMER
            PERFORM 3500-WRITE-REPORT.


 3100-FETCH-BALSUM.
        EXEC SQL
         FETCH BALSUM INTO :WS-SUM-ACCT-BAL-REC
        END-EXEC.


 3200-RETRIEVE-CUSTOMER.
 ****************************************************
 *  This retrieves the row from CUSTOMER for the    *
 *  CUST_ID retrieved in 3100-FETCH-BALSUM. If      *
 *  SQLCODE=+100, it means that there is no such     *
 *  CUST_ID in the CUSTOMER table. This is          *
 *  a fatal error and there is a branch to an error *
 *  routine. This error can be prevented            *
 *  automatically with referential integrity in V2.1*
 ****************************************************
        MOVE SPACES TO WS-CUSTOMER-REC.

        EXEC SQL
          SELECT CUST_SOC_SEC, CUST_NAME,
                 CUST_RATING
           INTO :WS-CUSTOMER-REC:WS-CUSTOMER-IND
           FROM CUSTOMER
           WHERE CUST_SOC_SEC = :WS-SUM-CUST-ID
        END-EXEC.

        IF SQLCODE = +100
            DISPLAY 'SS NO ' WS-SUM-CUST-ID
               ' NOT FOUND IN CUSTOMER TABLE'
            GO TO 6000-SQL-ERROR.
```

```
 3300-FORMAT-PRINTLINE.
********************************************************
*  We have to check WS-CUSTOMER-IND (2), the          *
*  indicator variable for CUST_NAME. If it is zero,   *
*  we print the name; otherwise, the name is null     *
*  for this customer and we put out a message.        *
********************************************************
     MOVE WS-SUM-CUST-ID TO D-SOC-SEC.

     IF WS-CUSTOMER-IND (2) = ZERO
         MOVE WS-CUST-NAME TO D-NAME
     ELSE
         MOVE '**N/A**' TO D-NAME.

     MOVE WS-SUM-ACCT-BAL TO D-ACCT-BAL-SUM.
     MOVE WS-CUST-RATING TO D-OLD-RATE.
     MOVE 99 TO D-NEW-RATE.

 3400-UPDATE-CUSTOMER.
********************************************************
*  This routine updates the customer row retrieved,   *
*  changing the credit rating to 99.                  *
********************************************************
     EXEC SQL
       UPDATE CUSTOMER
         SET CUST_RATING = 99
         WHERE CUST_SOC_SEC = :WS-SUM-CUST-ID
     END-EXEC.

     ADD 1 TO COMMIT-CTR.

 3500-WRITE-REPORT.
     WRITE REPORT-RECORD FROM WS-DETAIL-LINE AFTER
         ADVANCING 1 LINES.

 4000-COMMIT.
     EXEC SQL
         COMMIT
     END-EXEC.

     MOVE WS-SUM-CUST-ID TO COMMIT-CUST-ID.
     MOVE ZERO TO COMMIT-CTR.
     DISPLAY '**PROGRAM2 COMMIT PERFORMED - CUSTID='    COMMIT-CUST-ID.

 5000-EOJ.
     CLOSE REPORT-FILE.
     DISPLAY '**PROGRAM2 HAS COMPLETED SUCCESSFULLY'.

 6000-SQL-ERROR.
     DISPLAY '**FATAL DB2 ERROR - PROGRAM2 ENDING'.
     MOVE SQLCODE TO DISPLAY-SQLCODE.
     DISPLAY 'SQLCODE = ' DISPLAY-SQLCODE.
     CLOSE REPORT-FILE.
     STOP RUN.
```

This program demonstrates the use of a cursor to retrieve data from a DB2 table when the SELECT statement can return more than one row. It shows how to use the COMMIT statement and how to maintain cursor position after a COMMIT. In the next chapter we will discuss accessing DB2 data from a CICS environment.

Accessing DB2 from a CICS Program

DB2 may be accessed from online programs as well as from batch programs. Accessing DB2 data from a CICS program poses some particular considerations for the application programmer. We begin with a brief look at the architecture.

11.1 DB2-CICS ATTACHMENT ARCHITECTURE

When DB2 is accessed through TSO or batch jobs, the connection between DB2 and the user or application is a single thread or MVS task. A CICS region, on the other hand, has multiple threads connecting it to DB2, because multiple users are active simultaneously. The connection between DB2 and each CICS region is defined by a new CICS table, the Resource Control Table (RCT).

11.1.1 CICS Resource Control Table

The RCT contains information such as the name of the DB2 subsystem and the maximum number of threads (concurrent users) that the DB2-CICS connection can have. From an application programming perspective, its most significant function is that it connects transaction IDs (transids) with plans. Remember, a plan is the compiled output of the BIND.

There is one entry for each transid and each plan is associated with one or more transids. Ordinarily any given transid is associated with one and only one plan. DB2 version 2.1 provides a facility for user exit routines that can dynamically change plan names during the execution of a transaction. If your installation uses these exits, plan names do not have to be in the RCT, however, the exits have some cost in performance and maintenance. If your installation doesn't use the exits, there is only one plan per transaction in the RCT and that plan must include DBRMs from all programs that the transaction might access by LINK, CALL, or XCTL. In practice, the existence of the RCT means that when a transaction is added to a CICS application, an RCT entry for that transaction must be provided if that transaction is to access DB2.

11.1.2 Types of Threads

Each CICS region connected to DB2 has one thread, the command thread, that manages the DB2-CICS connection. In addition, there are the threads used by application transactions—dedicated threads and pool threads. These are specified in the RCT.

A dedicated thread is reserved for use by a specific transaction. A transaction may be assigned one or more dedicated threads. If a transaction is defined in the RCT as having no dedicated threads, it will use a pool thread, which can be used by any transaction. For transactions that are assigned dedicated threads, the RCT is coded with one of three options for what to do if that transaction is requested when the dedicated threads are already in use. The new transaction request can wait, be abended, or use a pool thread.

You should be aware of the performance differences between dedicated threads and pool threads. Since a thread is an MVS subtask, there is some overhead involved in setting it up. A pool thread terminates when a transaction ends or issues a CICS SYNCPOINT. Therefore, each new user of a pool thread has to wait until a thread is available before starting. A dedicated thread normally remains active between users and it therefore avoids the thread creation overhead for each execution of the transaction after the first one. The consequence is that transactions that use dedicated threads are noticeably better performers than identical transactions using pool threads. Most commonly, dedicated threads will be defined for high-volume transactions; less frequently used transactions will use pool threads.

11.1.3 Functions Provided by the DB2-CICS Attach

The DB2-CICS Attach provides an interface that allows a CICS Command Level application program to issue SQL statements. Module DSNCLI must be linked with your program to access this interface. The attachment also handles the synchronization of commit processing between DB2 and CICS. Unlike TSO or batch programs, EXEC CICS SYNCPOINT and EXEC CICS ROLLBACK are used in DB2-CICS programs instead of SQL's COMMIT and ROLLBACK statements. We will discuss these later in this chapter.

11.1.4   The DSNC Transaction

DSNC is the CICS transaction that controls the DB2-CICS Attach. It must be executed to start the DB2-CICS connection. The command format is:

```
DSNC STRT x
```

Here, x is the suffix of the RCT that you want to use. The default is 0, but your installation will tell you which one to use. Your DB2 systems programmer assembles RCTs and assigns suffixes. All RCTs start with DSNCRCT.

Suppose the RCT with suffix A is the one whose plans point to system test tables, and the RCT with suffix B is the one whose plans point to volume test tables. If the region is connected to RCT A, and you need to switch to B but don't want to bring the region down, the following statements are used:

```
DSNC STOP
DSNC STRT B
```

This STOPs or disconnects CICS and DB2 and starts it up again using another RCT.

Your installation may have your CICS region set up to execute DSNC STRT automatically when the region comes up; in that case, you won't have to execute DSNC at start-up. But if you are bringing the region down, you should execute DSNC STOP first. If you don't, the region will take much longer to come down.

Note that when you enter DSNC STOP, you are asking that currently active tasks be allowed to complete before the connection is terminated. Therefore, the STOP may not take place instantly. It is possible to issue a STOP that does not wait for tasks to complete, but this is not recommended because it can leave data in an inconsistent state that will require recovery procedures.

11.1.5   Program Flow Through the DB2-CICS Attach

When an application program issues its first SQL statement, the DB2 Language Interface module (DSNCLI), which is link-edited with the program, invokes a CICS exit that passes the request for data to the attachment facility. The attach then schedules a thread. If a dedicated thread is available, it will be used; otherwise, a new thread must be started. In the meantime, DB2 checks authorization for plan execution.

While DB2 is checking authorization and, if the authorization is successful, while it is retrieving data, the transaction is in a CICS WAIT state. When DB2 has completed its work, control is returned to the CICS exit and then to the application program. Subsequent SQL calls are treated in a similar manner except that authorization checking and thread creation are done only on the first SQL call.

11.1.6 DB2-CICS Recovery and Restart—the Two-Phase Commit

If DB2 is accessed from TSO or batch, recovery is done by DB2. When DB2 is accessed by CICS, however, there are two recovery mechanisms in operation. The first one is of CICS and the second one is of DB2. CICS must coordinate the recovery of resources belonging to itself and to other subsystems which it accesses. This is done with the two-phase commit. Some variation of this scheme is necessary whenever there are distributed resources that must be updated or backed out in synch with each other.

In the two-phase commit, CICS begins the process by telling DB2 (and, if necessary, other subsystems) to prepare to COMMIT. CICS does this when it reaches a SYNCPOINT. SYNCPOINTs may be issued explicitly by application programs and are implicitly issued when a transaction ends with an EXEC CICS RETURN.

In phase 1, preparing to COMMIT, DB2 logs its updates but does not release any locks. If the updates are logged successfully, it notifies CICS that it is ready to COMMIT. Otherwise, CICS is notified that it cannot COMMIT. If phase 1 was successful for all subsystems, CICS tells DB2 to COMMIT. If any phase 1 processing was unsuccessful, CICS tells DB2 to ROLLBACK.

In phase 2, initiated by CICS' request to DB2 to COMMIT, DB2 logs its COMMIT and releases locks on resources. If DB2 crashes after phase 2 begins, it will complete the commit when it is restarted; the necessary logging was completed in phase 1.

If CICS, DB2, or the connection between them crashes, there may be transactions whose COMMIT status is in doubt (in doubt threads). When the subsystems and connections are restarted, a resolution of in doubt threads usually takes place automatically. For example, CICS will back out any tasks that were not committed when it crashed. Occasionally, however, manual intervention is required to resolve in doubt situations. You can find out if there are any of these by issuing the command DISPLAY THREAD(*)TYPE (INDOUBT) command. Basically, DB2 can be told to COMMIT them or roll them back by using the RECOVER INDOUBT DB2 command. This command can be issued from TSO using DB2I or the DSN command processor or from CICS using the DSNC transaction. Normally, application programmers would not issue such commands; they would be issued by a DBA.

11.2   PROGRAMMING CONSIDERATIONS

CICS programs accessing DB2 are, above all, CICS programs, and the principles of good design that apply to all CICS programs apply to DB2-CICS programs. In the following section we will discuss some issues that are unique to DB2.

11.2.1   SQL Design Guidelines

CICS programs must have good response time to be usable. The guidelines for ensuring this are no different than they are for any other DB2 application; Chaps. 15 and 16 discuss these guidelines in some detail.

Two important guidelines for good performance are to utilize index access, which provides fast access to table data, and to avoid sorts. There is a DB2 facility EXPLAIN (the subject of Chap. 16) that is used to determine if indexes are being used by a particular query. Remember, the user creates indexes, but it is DB2's Optimizer that decides whether or not to use them as an access path. EXPLAIN is a window into the Optimizer's decisions.

While indexes improve performance, sorts tend to degrade performance. Sorts are much less of a performance problem than they were in earlier releases of DB2, but it is still worth noting where you may be asking DB2 to do this extra work. SQL clauses that may invoke a sort include ORDER BY, GROUP BY, and SELECT DISTINCT.

Another performance guideline for CICS is to minimize thread use. As we mentioned earlier, DB2 threads are activated and resources locked starting with the first SQL statement and ending at SYNCPOINT. In a psuedo-conversational program, this is usually at the end of your program. It is good practice to do all of your time-consuming, non-SQL processing before you issue the first SQL statement. The less time a thread is used, the more concurrency the CICS and DB2 systems can support.

Lastly, we recommend that if temporary work space is needed, you use a CICS resource such as temporary storage or transient data rather than creating a temporary DB2 table from within the program. DDL is the component of SQL used to create DB2 objects. Although DDL can be used in a CICS program, it is a poor performer and also locks the DB2 Catalog and your database's database descriptor (DBD), which is the part of the Directory that holds information on a database's objects. Each database has its own DBD. These locks mean that only one task at a time can do a CREATE or DROP in the same database. This can seriously reduce concurrency on your CICS application.

11.2.2 Cursors within Pseudo-Conversational Programs

In pseudo-conversational CICS programs, the transaction ends as soon as a map is sent to the terminal, resulting in a DB2 COMMIT which will close any open cursors. If the cursor has returned more data than can fit on one screen, there are three basic approaches to handling the excess. Suppose we have a cursor defined as follows:

```
EXEC SQL
   DECLARE SELCUST CURSOR FOR
   SELECT CUST_SOC_SEC, CUST_FIRST_NAME,
          CUST_LAST_NAME
     FROM CUSTOMER
    WHERE CUST_BRANCH = :WS-BRANCH
    ORDER BY CUST_SOC_SEC
END-EXEC.
```

If we used this cursor to display fetched rows on a map, all would go well as long as there were only as many customers for the selected branch as would fit on one screen. However, if we move the first 22 customers to the map and then execute a CICS SEND MAP followed by a CICS RETURN WITH TRANSID, the same 22 rows would be displayed the second time around, clearly not what was intended.

One solution is to fetch all of the rows that the cursor returns and to store those that won't fit on the first screen in a temporary storage queue. Each temporary storage record would be one screen of data. The COMMAREA could be used to save the number of the last page displayed. This solution has the advantage that the cursor is only opened once and the database is read only once. Since our example uses an ORDER BY clause, DB2 may need a sort; with this approach, the rows are sorted only once.

There are, however, three drawbacks to this approach. First, since all of the rows that the cursor selects are fetched before the first mapful of data is sent, there may be a long wait for the first screen. Second, if the user doesn't scroll all the way to the end of the data, more work has been done than is necessary. And finally, since the rows are put into temporary storage, the rows displayed will not necessarily reflect the current state of the database; updates may be taking place that will not be reflected in the TS queue. Of course, if the table is read only, this won't be a problem.

Another solution involves changing our cursor definition slightly:

```
EXEC SQL
    DECLARE GETCUST CURSOR FOR
    SELECT CUST_SOC_SEC, CUST_NAME, CUST_DATE_OF_BIRTH,
           CUST_RATING
    FROM CUSTOMER
    WHERE CUST_BRANCH = :WS-BRANCH-SAVE
        AND CUST_SOC_SEC > :SOC-SEC-LOW
        AND CUST_SOC_SEC <= :SOC-SEC-HIGH
    ORDER BY CUST_SOC_SEC
END-EXEC.
```

This is the method used in this chapter's sample program PROGRAM3. WS-SSNUM-SAVE is a COMMAREA field initialized to zeroes. The program opens the cursor, then fetches and moves as many rows to the map as will fit on one screen. It saves the social security number of the last customer on the map in WS-SSNUM-SAVE, sends the map, and does a CICS RETURN. The next time the user hits Enter, the program opens the cursor again, but this time the cursor's SELECT statement specifies all customers whose social security number is larger than that saved in WS-SSNUM-SAVE.

If you wanted the user to be able to scroll backward and weren't concerned about the backward scroll reflecting up-to-the-minute updates, you could also use temporary storage to save each map's rows as they are fetched.

This solution returns the first screen to the user more quickly than the first solution because it fetches only a screenful of data rather than all of the rows of the result table. The processing involved to produce the result tables is the same for both methods, but the second method has far less fetching to do. Also, on each successive fetch, fewer rows must be retrieved. The forward scroll, which does not use temporary storage, will accurately reflect changes to the database.

The third solution we'll discuss is useful when you need to be able to scroll backward and forward and need up-to-the-minute information. With this method, you will read the database each time the user needs to see a screen, even if it was just viewed. We'll change the cursor definition again:

```
EXEC SQL
  DECLARE GETCUST CURSOR FOR
  SELECT CUST_SOC_SEC, CUST_NAME, CUST_DATE_OF_BIRTH,
         CUST_RATING
    FROM CUSTOMER
    WHERE CUST_BRANCH   = :WS-BRANCH-SAVE
    AND CUST_SOC_SEC > :WS-SSNUM-SAVE
    ORDER BY CUST_SOC_SEC
END-EXEC.
```

Note that we are selecting based on a specific branch number and on a range of social security numbers.

For this solution, you will need a table of social security numbers in COMMAREA to hold the last social security number from each screen:

```
01 PAGING-AREA OCCURS n TIMES.
   05 WS-SSNUM-SAVE   PIC 9(09).
```

The value of n is the maximum number of pages (screens full of data) that you expect. Occurrence 1 of the table will hold the last social security number from screen 1, occurrence 2 will hold that of screen 2, etc. The values in this table are moved to the WHERE clause of the cursor's SELECT statement to page forward and backward as follows. On the first OPEN CURSOR, SOC-SEC-LOW is set to zeroes and SOC-SEC-HIGH is set to nines. This returns to the result table all of the rows in the CUSTOMER table for the specified branch number. Rows are fetched and moved to the map until the map is full. The last social security number on the map is moved to WS-SSNUM-SAVE (1). If the user requests forward paging, the value in WS-SSNUM-SAVE (1) is moved to SOC-SEC-LOW in the DECLARE CURSOR and all of the rows with social security numbers greater than that one are returned to the result table. The last social security number from that map is saved in WS-SSNUM-SAVE (2). Paging forward continues in this manner. If the user is on the third screen and wants to page backward, the values in WS-SSNUM-SAVE (1) are moved to SOC-SEC-LOW and WS-SSNUM-SAVE (2) to SOC-SEC-HIGH to select and then fetch only those rows required for the second screen. DB2 will only have to order one screenful of data at a time, thus saving resources.

We particularly wish to emphasize efficiency in CICS programs. After all, a CICS program has a user who can do nothing further until a result is returned on the screen. More importantly, batch programs normally run once a day, while a heavily used CICS program can be executed many thousands of times a day. Also, CICS programs that hog resources are likely to degrade the performance of the entire DB2 and CICS systems and will have a wide impact.

11.3 SECURITY CONSIDERATIONS

Both CICS and DB2 have their own security mechanisms. Working with both systems involves a combination of the two mechanisms.

11.3.1 DB2-CICS Connection

DB2 itself does no authorization checking for the DB2-CICS connection, but if your installation has RACF, ACF2, or the equivalent, these security packages can be used to limit the ability of CICS to connect to DB2.

11.3.2 Attachment Facility and DB2 Commands

The attachment facility, which is accessed via the CICS transaction DSNC, does not require any DB2 authorization. Anyone who executes this transaction can start and stop the connection between DB2 and the CICS region. CICS security must be used if access to this transaction is to be restricted. The DSNC transaction can also be used to execute DB2 commands. DB2 requires that the user be granted appropriate DB2 authority to execute them.

11.3.3 Plan Execution and User Identification

When a CICS transaction issues an SQL statement, the RCT is used to determine the level of authorization checking that should be performed to make sure that the transaction is authorized to run. For each transaction, the RCT contains the plan to be executed. In addition, the RCT specifies which id DB2 should check for authorization. There are four choices: the sign-on user ID, the termid, the transid, or a literal character string. To use the sign-on user ID, the user must have signed on using the CSSN or equivalent transaction.

Whatever id DB2 is asked to check, it must check the DB2 Catalog each time a DB2 transaction is started. In a pseudo-conversational environment, this is every time someone hits the Enter key. While the Catalog pages may already be in the buffers, authorization checking uses up a certain amount of resources. DB2 version 2.1 maintains a flag in memory that says whether or not execution on a plan is granted to public; if it is, path length (number of instructions) to check authorization is reduced by 99 percent. Of course, if authorization to execute a plan is granted to the public, any restriction on who can execute the plan must be provided by CICS security. You can also embed security checking in your application.

11.3.4 Test versus Production Environment

In test, you might want to use transaction-level authorization for DB2 plans so that testers can have security from other testers who might inadvertently cause problems.

In production, our suggestion is that CICS security be used for transactions and that plans be granted to public. This strategy will save resources and improve performance. If this strategy is not acceptable, we recommend that plan authorization be by transid or by a literal text string. The reason for this is that if termid or CICS user ID is used in a large system, the DB2 Catalog will have to have thousands of entries for the thousands of users or terminals who will at some time need to access DB2. This could degrade performance and also would require many updates to the DB2 Catalog to maintain these entries, which can cause locking and contention problems.

A CICS region can be connected to only one DB2 subsystem at a time; one DB2 system can be connected to many CICS regions. It is therefore possible to have the same version of DB2 serve both test and production regions. This is normally a bad idea because it would probably be necessary to be too restrictive to the test regions' authorizations to protect the production data. In addition, defective programs in test could degrade performance in the whole DB2 subsystem, which would then affect production.

11.4 PROGRAM3

Our sample CICS DB2 program, PROGRAM3, is a browse program that uses a cursor. It allows a user to enter a transid and receive a map on which to enter a branch number. The program returns 17 customers of that branch in social security number order. If there are more customers in the branch, it also puts out a message asking the user to hit Enter to get more customers. When it has returned all of the customers of a branch, it puts out a message saying so. At any time, if the user enters a different branch number, the program will start browsing the new branch's customers in ascending order of social security number. Fields displayed for each customer are social security number, name, birthdate, and credit rating. Figure 11.1 is the map for this program.

```
                    BRANCH CUSTOMER INQUIRY SCREEN

        ENTER BRANCH ===>

        SSNUM         NAME                   BIRTHDATE    RATING

        ---------    --------------------    ----------    ----
        ---------    --------------------    ----------    ----
        ---------    --------------------    ----------    ----
        ---------    --------------------    ----------    ----
        ---------    --------------------    ----------    ----
        ---------    --------------------    ----------    ----
        ---------    --------------------    ----------    ----
        ---------    --------------------    ----------    ----
        ---------    --------------------    ----------    ----
        ---------    --------------------    ----------    ----
        ---------    --------------------    ----------    ----
        ---------    --------------------    ----------    ----
        ---------    --------------------    ----------    ----
        ---------    --------------------    ----------    ----
        ---------    --------------------    ----------    ----
        HIT CLEAR OR PF3 TO QUIT
```

Figure 11.1   Inquiry screen for PROGRAM3.

```
IDENTIFICATION DIVISION.
PROGRAM-ID. PROGRAM3.

ENVIRONMENT DIVISION.

DATA DIVISION.

WORKING-STORAGE SECTION.

COPY DFHAID

01  WS-COMMAREA.
    05   WS-SSNUM-SAVE                PIC S9(9)  COMP   VALUE ZERO.
    05   WS-BRANCH-SAVE               PIC S9(4)  COMP   VALUE ZERO.

01  WS-COM-LENGTH                     PIC S9(4)  COMP   VALUE +6.

01  WS-LINE-SUB                       PIC S9(4)  COMP   VALUE +1.

01  WS-ERROR-MSG.
    05   FILLER                       PIC X(36)
             VALUE 'A DB2 ERROR HAS OCCURRED. SQLCODE ='.
    05   EDIT-SQLCODE                 PIC Z(8)9-.

01  NAME-IND                          PIC S9(4)  COMP.

    EXEC SQL
       INCLUDE DCLCUST
    END-EXEC.

    EXEC SQL
       INCLUDE SQLCA
    END-EXEC.
```

```
************************************************************
* This cursor selects rows from the CUSTOMER table where  *
* the CUST_SOC_SEC column > WS-SSNUM-SAVE.  WS-SSNUM-SAVE* *
* starts with zeros in it.  Each time a screenful of data* *
* is fetched, the social security number in the last row  *
* is saved in WS-SSNUM-SAVE.  This is used to maintain     *
* cursor position; the next time through the program,      *
* the DECLARE CURSOR will specify rows with social         *
* security numbers greater that that saved from the        *
* previous screen's last row.                              *
************************************************************
        EXEC SQL
            DECLARE GETCUST CURSOR FOR
            SELECT CUST_SOC_SEC, CUST_NAME,
                CUST_DATE_OF_BIRTH, CUST_RATING
            FROM CUSTOMER
            WHERE CUST_BRANCH = :WS-BRANCH-SAVE
            AND CUST_SOC_SEC >  :WS-SSNUM-SAVE
            ORDER BY CUST_SOC_SEC
        END-EXEC.

************************************************************
* The output map has been redefined as a COBOL table so   *
* 17 rows from the CUSTOMER table can be conveniently      *
* moved to the map with a loop using a subscript.          *
************************************************************
        COPY MAP1.

01  MAPTAB REDEFINES MAPXO.
    05  FILLER                      PIC X(23).
    05  LINE-TABLE.
        10  LINE-ENTRY OCCURS 17 TIMES.
            15  SSNUM-ENTRY             PIC 9(9).
            15  FILLER                  PIC X(3).
            15  NAME-ENTRY              PIC X(18).
            15  FILLER                  PIC X(4).
            15  BIRTH-ENTRY             PIC X(10).
            15  FILLER                  PIC X(4).
            15  RATE-ENTRY              PIC 9(4).
            15  FILLER                  PIC X(4).
        10  FILLER                  PIC X(50).
```

```
LINKAGE SECTION.

01  DFHCOMMAREA.
    05  SSNUM-SAVE                      PIC S9(4) COMP.
    05  BRANCH-SAVE                     PIC S9(4) COMP.

PROCEDURE DIVISION.
1000-MAINLINE.
************************************************************
* The user hits PF3 or CLEAR to get out of the program    *
* and return to CICS.                                      *
************************************************************
    IF EIBAID = DFHCLEAR OR DFHPF3
        EXEC CICS
            RETURN
        END-EXEC.

************************************************************
* If EIBCALEN = zero, it's the first time through and      *
* we send the map with a message, 'PLEASE ENTER BRANCH'    *
************************************************************
    IF EIBCALEN = ZERO
        MOVE 'PLEASE ENTER BRANCH'  TO MSG10
        MOVE ZEROS TO WS-SSNUM-SAVE, WS-BRANCH-SAVE
        GO TO 500-SEND-MAP.

    MOVE DFHCOMMAREA TO WS-COMMAREA.

************************************************************
* We receive a map on which INPUT1I is the branch for      *
* which we are to show customer information.  We           *
* initialize LINE-TABLE which is where we will format      *
* the rows of customer information to send to the map.  If *
* the branch from the map (INPUT1I) is different from the  *
* branch saved, it means that we are selecting for a new   *
* branch rather than paging forward on a previously        *
* selected branch.  If it is a new branch, we will         *
* move zeros to WS-SSNUM-SAVE so our DECLARE CURSOR will    *
* select all customers for that branch.  If we are paging  *
* forward, the DECLARE CURSOR will use WS-SSNUM-SAVE to     *
* get customers with social security numbers greater than  *
* the last customer shown on the previous screen.          *
************************************************************
```

```
      EXEC CICS
        RECEIVE MAP('MAPX') MAPSET('MAP1') INTO(MAPXI)
      END-EXEC.

      MOVE SPACES TO LINE-TABLE.

      IF WS-BRANCH-SAVE NOT EQUAL TO INPUT1I
        MOVE INPUT1I TO WS-BRANCH-SAVE
        MOVE ZEROS TO WS-SSNUM-SAVE.

  2000-OPEN-CURSOR.
  *************************************************************
  * We open the cursor and perform a fetch for the first     *
  * row. If SQLCODE = 100 after the fetch, it means we did   *
  * not find a row.  If WS-SSNUM-SAVE = ZERO, it's because   *
  * we're on a new branch and there are no customers for that*
  * branch.  Otherwise, SQLCODE = 100 means we have reached  *
  * end of data for the branch we are paging forward on.  In *
  * either case we send a map with the appropriate message.  *
  *************************************************************
      EXEC SQL
        OPEN GETCUST
      END-EXEC.

      IF SQLCODE NOT = ZERO
        PERFORM 6000-ERROR-RTN
        GO TO 5000-SEND-MAP.

      PERFORM 4000-FETCH-ROW.

      IF SQLCODE = 100
        IF WS-SSNUM-SAVE = ZEROS
          MOVE 'NO CUSTOMERS FOR SELECTED BRANCH' TO MSG1O
          GO TO 5000-SEND-MAP
        ELSE
          MOVE 'END OF SELECTED DATA' TO MSG1O
          GO TO 5000-SEND-MAP.
```

```
************************************************************
* We perform a move and fetch routine until we fill the    *
* map or reach end of data (SQLCODE = 100).  If there is   *
* more data, we save the social security number of the     *
* last customer in WS-SSNUM-SAVE.                          *
************************************************************
        PERFORM 3000-MOVE-AND-FETCH
            VARYING WS-LINE-SUB FROM 1 BY 1
            UNTIL WS-LINE-SUB > 17 OR SQLCODE = 100.

        IF SQLCODE = 100
            MOVE 'END OF SELECTED DATA' TO MSG10
            GO TO 5000-SEND-MAP
        ELSE
            MOVE 'HIT ENTER FOR MORE DATA' TO MSG10
            MOVE CUST-SOC-SEC TO WS-SSNUM-SAVE
            GO TO 5000-SEND-MAP.

    3000-MOVE-AND-FETCH.
************************************************************
* This paragraph moves the fetched data to the map line,   *
* then does another FETCH.  The indicator variable         *
* NAME-IND is checked and if the name is null, **NOT       *
* AVAILABLE** is moved to the field on the map line.       *
************************************************************
        MOVE CUST-SOC-SEC TO SSNUM-ENTRY (WS-LINE-SUB).

        IF NAME-IND NOT < ZERO
            MOVE CUST-NAME TO NAME-ENTRY (WS-LINE-SUB)
        ELSE
            MOVE '*NOT AVAILABLE*' TO NAME-ENTRY (WS-LINE-SUB).

        MOVE CUST-DATE-OF-BIRTH TO BIRTH-ENTRY (WS-LINE-SUB).
        MOVE CUST-RATING TO RATE-ENTRY (WS-LINE-SUB).

        PERFORM 4000-FETCH-ROW.

    4000-FETCH-ROW.
************************************************************
* This paragraph fetches rows from the CUSTOMER table. It  *
* needs the indicator variable, NAME-IND, because NAME can *
* be null.                                                 *
************************************************************
        EXEC-SQL
            FETCH GETCUST INTO :CUST-SOC-SEC,
                :CUST-NAME:NAME-IND, :CUST-DATE-OF-BIRTH,
                :CUST-RATING
        END-EXEC.
```

```
        IF SQLCODE = 0 OR 100
           NEXT SENTENCE
        ELSE
           PERFORM 6000-ERROR-RTN
           GO TO 5000-SEND-MAP.

    5000-SEND-MAP.
    ************************************************************
    * This sends the map and then executes a CICS RETURN with *
    * this program's TRANSID and with COMMAREA, so that the   *
    * branch and the social security of the last row retrieved*
    * can be passed to the next iteration of the program.     *
    ************************************************************
        EXEC CICS
           SEND MAP('MAPX') MAPSET('MAP1') FROM(MAPXO)
              ERASE
        END-EXEC.

        EXEC CICS
           RETURN TRANSID('TRN1') COMMAREA(WS-COMMAREA)
              LENGTH(WS-COM-LENGTH)
        END-EXEC.

    6000-ERROR-RTN.
        MOVE SQLCODE TO EDIT-SQLCODE.
        MOVE WS-ERROR-MSG TO MSG100.

    7000-GOBACK-PARAGRAPH.
        GOBACK.
```

12

Program Preparation
and Execution

As an application programmer, you are probably accustomed to writing source code and preparing it for execution through compile and link-edit steps. If you use CICS, you are also familiar with a translate step. Preparation of DB2 programs requires two additional steps—precompile and BIND—and modifications to your current RUN procedures. We will use PROGRAM1 from Chap. 9 to demonstrate how to execute these steps. But first, let's review what these steps do within DB2's architecture. Refer to Fig. 12.1 as you read for an illustration of the processes described.

You may remember from Chap. 2 that DB2 separates the application program's source language statements (COBOL in our examples) from its SQL statements. These two sets of code are then processed in two separate streams and rejoined at execution time. Precompile, BIND, and RUN are the three steps needed to do this. Precompile separates the source code into two streams, source and SQL; BIND processes the SQL statements that are the output of the precompile step; and RUN rejoins them for execution.

Let's look at precompile now in more detail. DB2's Precompiler reads the source code, comments out the SQL statements, and replaces them with calls to DB2. It also checks each SQL statement for syntax errors and compares tables and columns named in the statements against any SQL DECLARE TABLE statements in the program. The Precompiler does not refer to DB2 Catalog tables, so DB2 does not have to be up to run the Precompiler. However, this also means that its ability to find invalid references is only as good as the program's DECLARE TABLE statements. If you type your DECLARE TABLE statements yourself rather than using the output of DCLGEN, they

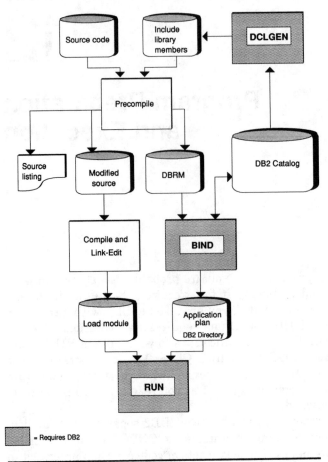

Figure 12.1   DB2 program preparation.

may not be very good. DCLGEN, the declarations generator supplied with DB2, does reference the Catalog when it produces copybook members, which is why we recommend its use prior to your program preparation. The Precompiler retrieves these and other copy members specified in SQL INCLUDE statements (like the SQLCA which DB2 supplies) and merges them into the code. The output of the Precompiler is the modified source code, a Data Base Request Module (DBRM) which holds the source code's SQL statements, and a listing which includes error messages.

The modified source code that is produced by the Precompiler must be compiled and link-edited. For CICS programs, an additional CICS translate step must also be included. The output of the link-edit step is a load module.

The DBRM that is created by the precompile step is the input to the BIND. DB2 must be up to execute a BIND, which checks SQL statements for syntax errors and compares tables and columns named in the statements against the DB2 Catalog. It also verifies the authority of the binder to perform the SQL statements specified in the program. The authorization validation process can be postponed until run-time through an option on the BIND panel. Most importantly, BIND invokes DB2's Optimizer for access path selection. The Optimizer considers indexes, table sizes, etc., to decide the paths to use in selecting data. The object code which describes how each SQL request should be satisifed is called the application plan and is the compiled output from the BIND. Application plans are stored in DB2's Directory.

The output of the link-edit step, the load module, and the output of the BIND step, the application plan, are the input to the RUN step. The sequence in which these steps must be run is as follows. DCLGEN must be run before the Precompiler, which must be run before the COBOL compiler and before the BIND. BIND may be run any time between the precompile and RUN steps. Link-edit may be run any time between the compile and RUN steps.

The separation of source language and SQL statement processing could lead to inconsistency if you changed your program, precompiled, compiled, and link-edited it without rebinding the changed DBRM. The load module and the application plan would be out of synch. DB2 prevents this through a system of timestamp comparisons (**Fig. 12.2**). When you precompile a program, a timestamp is put in the DBRM and the COBOL output. BIND passes this timestamp to the application plan just as COMPILE and LINK-EDIT pass it to the load module. During program execution, when the first call is made to DB2, DB2 compares the timestamps in the load module and the application plan. If they don't match, you get an -818 SQLCODE and an abend. To avoid the abend, whenever you change a program and execute a new precompile, compile, and link-edit, you also have to issue a BIND, even if the SQL has not changed. This puts the new timestamp into the corresponding application plan.

The steps of program preparation—DCLGEN, precompile, BIND, compile, link-edit, and RUN—can be done through batch JCL, as a TSO foreground job, or through the panels supplied by DB2I. First we'll describe DB2I, then TSO execution and batch JCL. Read the DB2I section even if you'll be using TSO or batch JCL because in it we explain the processes behind the commands.

Let's note here that the DB2I panels expect program source code to be in TSO datasets, so if your installation requires that program source be kept in another format, such as Librarian or Panvalet, you will have to move your programs to TSO datasets before using DB2I

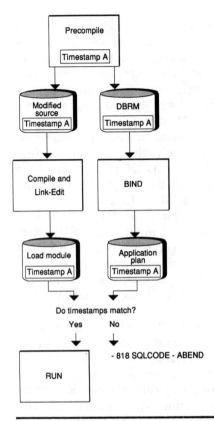

Figure 12.2 Timestamps on the load module and application plan must match.

for program preparation. If you are coding CICS programs and your installation uses Intertest or similar debugging aids, you will probably have to compile with installation-supplied JCL instead of with DB2I. Remember that these panels, like all of those supplied with DB2, have very informative HELP panels that can be accessed by typing HELP or pressing PF1.

12.1 DB2I PRIMARY OPTION MENU

When you enter DB2I, you are presented with a menu that provides you with 10 options (Fig. 12.3). SPUFI, DCLGEN, DB2 COMMANDS, and UTILITIES are discussed in other chapters. If you select option 3, PROGRAM PREPARATION, you will be able to execute any or all of the steps of program preparation—precompile, CICS translate, BIND, compile, link-edit, and RUN. DCLGEN is not included as a step, but

```
                          DB2I PRIMARY OPTION MENU
===>

Select one of the following DB2 functions and press ENTER.

   1   SPUFI                 (Process SQL statements)
   2   DCLGEN                (Generate SQL and source language declarations)
   3   PROGRAM PREPARATION   (Prepare a DB2 application program to run)
   4   PRECOMPILE            (Invoke DB2 precompiler)
   5   BIND/REBIND/FREE      (BIND, REBIND, or FREE application plans)
   6   RUN                   (RUN an SQL program)
   7   DB2 COMMANDS          (Issue DB2 commands)
   8   UTILITIES             (Invoke DB2 utilities)
   D   DB2I DEFAULTS         (Set global parameters)
   X   EXIT                  (Leave DB2I)




PRESS:   END to exit          HELP for more information
```

Figure 12.3   DB2I menu.

we recommend that you execute it as a prestep to program preparation. The DB2I Primary Option Menu also includes direct access to PRECOMPILE (option 4) and to RUN (option 6). Option 5, BIND/REBIND/FREE, lets you rebind and free a plan, something which you cannot do through option 3. We will discuss REBIND and FREE later in the chapter.

12.2   DB2I DEFAULTS

Before we dive into program preparation, let's first look at option D on the DB2I Menu, DB2I DEFAULTS. This is particularly relevant if you are using DB2I for the first time with your TSO-ID.

Figure 12.4 shows the DB2I DEFAULTS panel with the IBM-supplied default values for items 1 through 8. Item 9 is optional. The first item is DB2 NAME. Make sure this is set to the name of the DB2 subsystem on which your application runs. Your DBA can tell you what name to use. The default for item 3, APPLICATION LANGUAGE, is COBOL. Set it to COB2 for VS COBOL II. COBOL STRING DELIMITER, item 6, can cause problems. The value entered here determines the delimiters that the Precompiler will generate in its modified COBOL output. If it's in conflict with the delimiters expected by your COBOL compiler, you'll get compiler errors.

The DB2I JOB STATEMENT is optional but is needed if you plan to

```
                        DB2I DEFAULTS
===>

Change defaults as desired:

 1  DB2 NAME .............  ===> DSN      (Subsystem identifier)
 2  DB2 CONNECTION RETRIES  ===> 0        (How many retries for DB2 connection)
 3  APPLICATION LANGUAGE    ===> COBOL    (COBOL, COB2, FORT, ASM, ASMH, PLI)
 4  LINES/PAGE OF LISTING   ===> 60       (A number from 5 to 999)
 5  MESSAGE LEVEL ........  ===> I        (Information, Warning, Error, Severe)
 6  COBOL STRING DELIMITER  ===> DEFAULT  (DEFAULT, ' or ")
 7  SQL STRING DELIMITER    ===> DEFAULT  (DEFAULT, ' or ")
 8  DECIMAL POINT ........  ===> .        (. or ,)

 9  DB2I JOB STATEMENT:   (Optional if your site has a SUBMIT exit)
    ===>
    ===>
    ===>
    ===>



PRESS: ENTER to save and exit    END to exit    HELP for more information
```

Figure 12.4   DB2I Defaults Panel.

do program preparation in the background. Fill in the appropriate job card information for your installation unless your installation has a TSO SUBMIT exit that automatically creates a job card when JCL that does not contain a job card is submitted.

Most of the time, you can use the default values for the other items on the panel. Item 2, DB2 CONNECTION RETRIES, can be the default, 0, for the number of retries to execute if thread connection to DB2 fails. The default for item 4, 60, specifies the number of lines per page in the precompile listing, and item 5's default, I, specifies that both warning and error messages should be displayed on the output of the precompile. Leave SQL STRING DELIMITER as a single quote and DECIMAL POINT as a period.

12.3 PROGRAM PREPARATION PANELS

Use your End key to go back to the DB2I menu. Option 3 takes you to a DB2 PROGRAM PREPARATION screen (Fig. 12.5) that can be used as a guide to the steps of program preparation and the set of associated panels.

INPUT DATA SET NAME is where you enter the name of your source code dataset. It can be either a sequential file or a PDS member. Entry of a value is similar to that of the dataset name field on the DCLGEN panel described in Chap. 9. If you do not enclose the name

```
                     DB2 PROGRAM PREPARATION
 ===>

 Enter the following:
   1  INPUT DATA SET NAME ....  ===> 'USER1.COBOL(PROGRAM1)'
   2  DATA SET NAME QUALIFIER   ===> TEMP        (For building data set names)
   3  PREPARATION ENVIRONMENT   ===> FOREGROUND  (FOREGROUND, BACKGROUND, EDITJCL)
   4  RUN TIME ENVIRONMENT ...  ===> TSO         (TSO, CICS, IMS)
   5  STOP IF RETURN CODE >=    ===> 8           (Lowest terminating return code)
   6  OTHER OPTIONS ===>

 Select functions:              Display panel?       Perform function?
   7  CHANGE DEFAULTS ........  ===> N   (Y/N)        ............
   8  PL/I MACRO PHASE .......  ===> N   (Y/N)        ===> N   (Y/N)
   9  PRECOMPILE ............. ===> Y   (Y/N)        ===> Y   (Y/N)
  10  CICS COMMAND TRANSLATION ....  .....           ===> N   (Y/N)
  11  BIND ..................  ===> Y   (Y/N)        ===> Y   (Y/N)
  12  COMPILE OR ASSEMBLE ....  ===> Y   (Y/N)        ===> Y   (Y/N)
  13  PRELINK ...............  ===> N   (Y/N)        ===> N   (Y/N)
  14  LINK ..................  ===> Y   (Y/N)        ===> Y   (Y/N)
  15  RUN ...................  ===> N   (Y/N)        ===> N   (Y/N)


 PRESS:   ENTER to process        END to exit       HELP for more information
```

Figure 12.5   Program Preparation Panel.

in quotes, the logged on user ID is appended as the high-level qualifier and COBOL is appended as a suffix. Use the quotes and avoid confusion.

The next item, DATA SET NAME QUALIFIER, which defaults to TEMP, is used by DB2I to construct dataset names for temporary work files. The dataset names will consist of the concatenation of your user ID as the high-level qualifier, the name you specify in DATA SET NAME QUALIFIER as the second qualifier, and the low-end qualifier of the name as follows:

PCLIST for the precompiler listing

CSLIST for the CICS translator listing

COBOL for the COBOL source code output from the precompiler

LIST for the COBOL compiler listing

LINKLIST for the linkage editor listing

For example, if your user ID is YOURID and you have taken the default dataset name qualifier TEMP, the precompiler listing would be in a dataset called YOURID.TEMP.PCLIST.

The third item, PREPARATION ENVIRONMENT, allows you to execute the steps of program preparation in TSO by specifying FOREGROUND or to execute the steps as MVS batch jobs by specifying

BACKGROUND or EDITJCL . EDITJCL first takes you to an EDIT screen where you can change the JCL before issuing a SUBMIT. FOREGROUND is the default.

RUN TIME ENVIRONMENT enables you to specify whether the program will run in TSO, CICS, or IMS/DC. All programs are prepared under TSO, but they may be run from any of the three. However, if your program will be running from CICS or IMS/DC, the program cannot be submitted for execution from DB2I since you cannot execute a CICS or IMS program from TSO.

Options 7 through 15 on this panel enable you to choose which panels you want to view and possibly modify, as well as which steps to execute. You can run steps without displaying the associated panels first if the information provided on the panels was entered previously and it has not changed. You can also display panels without actually performing the function. The DB2I DEFAULT panel that we just discussed can be accessed by specifying Y for option 7 as well as from the DB2I Menu. PL/I MACRO PHASE and CICS COMMAND TRANSLATION, options 8 and 10, apply, of course, only to programs written in those languages.

Now let's use these panels to prepare PROGRAM1. First, replace INPUT DATA SET NAME with the name of the dataset containing your source code. Then, elect to display the panel and perform the function for PRECOMPILE, BIND, COMPILE OR ASSEMBLE, and LINK by putting a Y in the Display Panel and Perform Function columns for each of them. We can put an N for PRELINK because this is only applicable for programs that are written in C. Finally, let's just look at the RUN panel first by placing a Y in the Display Panel column. We won't perform the RUN function yet.

Now, pressing Enter will display each of the panels you have selected, allowing you to make changes to them. Upon completion of all of the panels, the functions will actually be performed if a Y is in the Perform Function column. Hitting PF3 at any point in the process of panel display will take you back to DB2 PROGRAM PREPARATION. Once DB2I begins to execute the functions you have selected, the only way to discontinue processing is to issue an INTERRUPT to the system by pressing the PA1 key.

12.3.1 PRECOMPILE Panel

When you press Enter the first time, you are taken to PRECOMPILE (Fig. 12.6). You could have also gone directly to the screen from the DB2I PRIMARY OPTION MENU option 4 (Fig. 12.3). Since we came through the Program Preparation Panel, however, items 1 and 3, INPUT DATA SET and DSNAME QUALIFIER, are already filled in and

```
                         PRECOMPILE
===>

Enter precompiler data sets:
 1  INPUT DATA SET .... ===> 'USER1.COBOL(PROGRAM1)'
 2  INCLUDE LIBRARY ... ===> 'USER1.DCLGNLIB'

 3  DSNAME QUALIFIER .. ===> TEMP         (For building data set names)
 4  DBRM DATA SET ..... ===> 'USER1.DBRMLIB'

Enter processing options as desired:
 5  WHERE TO PRECOMPILE ===> FOREGROUND  (FOREGROUND, BACKGROUND, or EDITJCL)
 6  OTHER OPTIONS ..... ===>
```

Figure 12.6   Precompile Panel.

are protected. If you want to change them, you must return to DB2 PROGRAM PREPARATION by pressing PF3.

Item 2 asks for the INCLUDE LIBRARY. In Chap. 9, we used DCLGEN to produce a DECLARE TABLE statement for the BRANCH table for PROGRAM1. Figure 12.7 shows the DCLGEN panel on which we directed DCLGEN's output to a dataset USER1.DCLGNLIB(BRANCH). PROGRAM1 referenced this member with the code:

```
EXEC SQL
    INCLUDE BRANCH
END-EXEC
```

```
                        DCLGEN
===>

Enter table name for which declarations are required:
 1  SOURCE TABLE NAME ===> BRANCH

Enter destination data set:          (Can be sequential or partitioned)
 2  DATA SET NAME ... ===> 'USER1.DCLGNLIB(BRANCH)'
 3  DATA SET PASSWORD ===>           (If password protected)

Enter options as desired:
 4  ACTION ......... ===> ADD        (ADD new or REPLACE old declaration)
 5  COLUMN LABEL .... ===> NO        (Enter YES for column label)
 6  STRUCTURE NAME .. ===>                         (Optional)
 7  FIELD NAME PREFIX ===>                         (Optional)




PRESS: ENTER to process    END to exit     HELP for more information
```

Figure 12.7   DCLGEN Panel.

Now we must use this library name for item 2 in Fig. 12.6 (PRECOMPILE) so that the Precompiler will merge the DCLGEN output into the program. We have therefore entered 'USER1.DCLGNLIB' in item 2.

Item 4 in Fig. 12.6, DBRM DATA SET, allows you to name the dataset into which you want the DBRM generated by the precompile step placed. If, instead, you use the default TEMP for the dataset name, DB2I will create a dataset called YOURID.TEMP.DBRM. The problem with using TEMP is that this dataset will be deleted and recreated each time you use the panels, and it is often desirable (and may be necessary) to save your DBRM library. Therefore, we recommend that you fill in the dataset name of a file that you have created previously. DBRM datasets are partitioned datasets with 80-byte records.

12.3.2 BIND Panel

The BIND panel can be accessed directly from DB2I or by electing to have it displayed, as we have, on the Program Preparation Panel. Because we've reached this panel from DB2 PROGRAM PREPARATION, items 1 and 2 are already filled in and are protected (Fig. 12.8). Item 2, MEMBER, has been filled in with the name of the program, PROGRAM1, which was the member name on the Program Preparation Panel (USER1.COBOL(PROGRAM1)). A DBRM must have the

```
                            BIND
===>

Enter DBRM data set name(s):
 1   LIBRARY(s)    ===> 'USER1.DBRM'
 2   MEMBER(s)     ===> PROGRAM1
 3   PASSWORD(s) ===>

 4   MORE DBRMS? ===> NO                     (YES to list more DBRMs)

Enter options as desired:
 5   PLAN NAME ................ ===> PROGRAM1   (Required to create a plan)
 6   ACTION ON PLAN ........... ===> REPLACE    (REPLACE or ADD)
 7   RETAIN EXECUTION AUTHORITY ===> YES         (YES to retain user list)
 8   ISOLATION LEVEL .......... ===> CS          (RR or CS)
 9   PLAN VALIDATION TIME ..... ===> BIND        (RUN or BIND)
10   RESOURCE ACQUISITION TIME  ===> USE         (USE or ALLOCATE)
11   RESOURCE RELEASE TIME .... ===> COMMIT      (COMMIT or DEALLOCATE)
12   EXPLAIN PATH SELECTION ... ===> NO          (NO or YES)
13   OWNER OF PLAN (AUTHID) ... ===>             (Leave blank for your primary ID
```

Figure 12.8   BIND Panel.

same name as the program that created it. Precompiling a program produces one DBRM and BIND produces one application plan. However, several DBRMs may be input to the BIND to produce that one plan. This is true, for example, if your program calls other subprograms that also contain SQL statements. This panel, therefore, allows you to enter more than one DBRM dataset by answering YES to MORE DBRMs, which takes you to a second screen with room for their names. Option 5, PLAN NAME, has also been filled in automatically with the program name but you may change this since a plan may have a name different from the DBRM(s) from which it is produced. Plan names must be unique across the entire DB2 subsystem.

Item 6, ACTION ON PLAN, provides BIND with instructions on what to do with the PLAN. The options are REPLACE or ADD. REPLACE overlays whatever is there or creates the plan if it doesn't exist. In effect, if there is no plan already, it is the same as specifying ADD. ADD works only if the plan does not already exist.

Before we look at the other options on the panel, we must digress for a moment to discuss authority, a topic covered more fully in Chap. 14. DB2's system of authorization includes authorities associated with creating and executing plans. A plan is created or added by binding its DBRM(s) for the first time with BIND ADD. This requires BINDADD authority. When a plan already exists, you can update or replace it by binding its DBRM(s) with BIND REPLACE. This requires BIND authority. To run a DB2 program you must execute its plan. This requires EXECUTE authority. BINDADD does not have a specific plan name associated with it while BIND and EXECUTE are always associated with a specific plan name. The ID of the person who creates a plan automatically has BIND and EXECUTE authority for that plan and may therefore replace or execute it. That authid may also grant other users BIND and EXECUTE authority for that plan. Requests for DB2 access through a program may also require DB2 authorities (e.g., SELECT on a table or UPDATE). The authid which issues a BIND ADD or a BIND REPLACE must also have all of the authorities required by the statements within the program for the BIND to be successful. Although we have not yet described REBIND, we will say at this point that REBIND requires the same authority as BIND.

The next option is RETAIN EXECUTION AUTHORITY. If you have created a plan and have granted EXECUTE authorities to other users, this option will determine whether those authorities will be retained when you do a BIND REPLACE. Normally this option should be YES, but if you change it to NO, all EXECUTE authorities previously granted on the plan will be revoked.

There is one quirk in all of this. If you create a plan and then grant BIND authority to another user, if the other user does a BIND RE-

PLACE on your plan and specifies NO for RETAIN EXECUTION authority, you will not be able to execute the plan you originally created although you will still be able to BIND it. DB2 sees a plan's owner as its last binder. You would either have to issue a BIND REPLACE yourself to regain execute authority or have the other user grant execute authority to you.

Let's skip now to option 13, OWNER OF PLAN (AUTHID). As you will see in Chap. 14, version 2.1 tries to simplify some of this ownership confusion by letting you establish a secondary authid which can be the same for a group of users, such as a project team. If you leave option 13 blank, your own authid will be assumed. Alternatively, you can use a project authid and avoid any confusion when different members of the team issue BIND REPLACE on a plan or for that matter when they leave the project and are replaced by others. At that point the ID of the person leaving would be removed from the group of IDs associated with the project ID, and the new employee's ID would be added.

Option 8, ISOLATION LEVEL, is a very important parameter because it has a powerful effect on concurrency. The values that may be entered are RR for repeatable read or CS for cursor stability. *Repeatable read means that DB2 keeps locks on all of the pages from which your plan reads data until a COMMIT or ROLLBACK is issued. Cursor stability means that DB2 only keeps locks on the page from which you are currently reading data.* For example, suppose you have a batch job that selects every row in a table. With cursor stability, only the page on which the cursor is located would be locked out to a would-be updater while with repeatable read, the whole table could be locked out. Cursor Stability is the best choice in most situations but there are times when Repeatable Read is preferable, for example, if you must prevent intervening updates to a row which is read at several points in the same program. Cursor stability and repeatable read do not affect update operations since data that is changed always remains locked until a COMMIT or a ROLLBACK is issued.

PLAN VALIDATION TIME, the next option, can be either BIND or RUN, meaning BIND time or RUN time. This controls when DB2 checks the DB2 Catalog to validate tables and columns named in the DBRM and to check the binder's authorizations. BIND is normally much preferred because with BIND, the checking is done once, at BIND time while with RUN, the checking is done each time the plan is executed. You will need to code RUN if the tables accessed in the plan do not yet exist, but we suggest that you then rebind it with BIND at PLAN VALIDATION TIME as soon as possible.

RESOURCE ACQUISITION TIME and RESOURCE RELEASE

TIME, options 10 and 11, tell DB2 when to acquire and release locks on tables and indexes. The choices for option 10 are to acquire resources at the point at which they are used (USE) or when the plan is first allocated (ALLOCATE). The choices for option 11 are to free resources when a COMMIT or ROLLBACK is issued (COMMIT) or when the plan terminates (DEALLOCATE).

In most cases, USE/COMMIT is the best combination because it maximizes concurrency. ALLOCATE/DEALLOCATE should only be considered to prevent deadlocks from occurring. With this option, the plan does not start until it has all of the resources it could need and does not release the resources until the plan terminates. This means that the plan will not encounter a situation in which it cannot get a resource it needs because another user already has it. If another user has the resource, a plan using the ALLOCATE/DEALLOCATE combination won't start. The ALLOCATE/DEALLOCATE combination holds resources longer and may also hold more resources. This is because the plan will cause all tables that might be accessed by a program to be acquired, even though some of them may not be accessed in this execution of the program. The USE/DEALLOCATE combination is permitted, but it is used infrequently. ALLOCATE/COMMIT is an invalid combination.

The next item on the BIND panel, EXPLAIN PATH SELECTION, is where you can elect for DB2 to run an SQL EXPLAIN for each SQL statement in the plan being bound. EXPLAIN shows the access paths that the Optimizer will use to satisfy the requests for data. How to access and understand the output of EXPLAIN is the subject of Chap. 16.

12.3.3 COMPILE, LINK, and RUN

Although there are separate options on the DB2 Program Preparation Panel for the COMPILE OR ASSEMBLE, LINK, and RUN panels, there is only one panel that combines all three of them (Fig. 12.9). This panel can be accessed from the DB2I menu or by opting for it on the Program Preparation Panel. It provides a means to supply information to the compiler and linkage editor. Items 1 through 3 refer to the COBOL copybook libraries that contain members named in COBOL COPY statements and to options for the COBOL compiler (e.g., NOTRUNC, OPTIMIZE). Items 4 through 7 refer to libraries where the linkage editor will look for modules and to the load library in which the linkage editor will put your link-edited program. Note that DB2I will provide the linkage editor with the DB2 load libraries and, for CICS links, with the CICS load libraries it needs. DB2I also pro-

```
                    PROGRAM PREPARATION: COMPILE, LINK, AND RUN
    ===>

    Enter compiler or assembler options:
      1   INCLUDE LIBRARY ===>
      2   INCLUDE LIBRARY ===>
      3   OPTIONS ....... ===>

    Enter linkage editor options:
      4   INCLUDE LIBRARY ===>
      5   INCLUDE LIBRARY ===>
      6   INCLUDE LIBRARY ===>
      7   LOAD LIBRARY .. ===> 'USER1.LOAD'
      8   PRELINK OPTIONS ===>
      9   OPTIONS ....... ===>

    Enter run options:
     10   PARAMETERS .... ===>
     11   SYSIN DATA SET  ===> TERM
     12   SYSPRINT DS ... ===> TERM


    PRESS: Enter to proceed     END to exit     HELP for more information
```

Figure 12.9   Compile, Link, and RUN Panel.

vides linkage editor control statements which include the necessary DB2 and CICS interface modules.

Items 8 and 9 allow you to enter PRELINK and LINK edit options. This panel also lets you specify RUN parameters, but remember, you can only perform the RUN function if you are running a TSO program. IMS and CICS programs cannot be run using DB2I. For TSO programs, however, you may supply EXEC PARMS in option 10 and SYSIN and SYSPRINT datasets in options 11 and 12. We describe the limitations of the PARMS parameter later in this chapter.

If your program uses non-DB2 files and you use the RUN option, you need to allocate the files with a CLIST or with the TSO ALLOC command before running the program. You should do this before invoking DB2I. Remember also that the file for COBOL DISPLAY output must be preallocated if your program has any DISPLAY or, in VS COBOL, EXHIBIT, or READY TRACE statements.

Once all of the panels specified on DB2 Program Preparation Panel have been displayed, DB2I will execute the steps that were specified on the panel. In our case, this will be all but the RUN step. DB2I issues messages to your screen as it finishes each step, reporting on the completion status of the step. You can then look at your output in the appropriate datasets.

Figure 12.10 illustrates what you should find in USER1.TEMP.COBOL. It is the COBOL source code output from the

```
            IDENTIFICATION DIVISION.
            PROGRAM-ID. PROGRAM1.
                .
                .
                .
            *************************************************************
            * INDICATOR-TABLE WILL BE ASSOCIATED WITH THE              *
            * DCLBRANCH RECORD LAYOUT.  IT ALLOWS US TO DETECT         *
            * BRANCHES WITH A NULL BRANCH_MGR COLUMN                   *
            *************************************************************
            01  INDICATOR-TABLE.
                05 BRANCH-IND                 PIC S9(4) COMP
                                                   OCCURS 4 TIMES.
            *************************************************************
            * MGR-IND IS A SINGLE INDICATOR VARIABLE USED TO SET       *
            * BRANCH_MGR TO NULL WHEN THAT IS THE CHANGE REQUESTED     *
            * BY THE INPUT TRANSACTION.                                *
            *************************************************************
            01  MGR-IND                       PIC S9(4) COMP.
            *************************************************************
            * THE FOLLOWING TWO SQL STATEMENTS WILL RETRIEVE THE       *
            * SQLCA AND THE DCLGEN CREATED MEMBER, BRANCH              *
            *************************************************************
-- LINE AAA --  *****EXEC SQL
--------------  *****   INCLUDE SQLCA
            *****END-EXEC.
            01 SQLCA.
                05 SQLCAID    PIC X(8).
                05 SQLCABC    PIC S9(9) COMP-4.
                05 SQLCODE    PIC S9(9) COMP-4.
                05 SQLERRM.
                   49 SQLERRML PIC S9(4) COMP-4.
                   49 SQLERRMC PIC X(70).
                05 SQLERRP    PIC X(8).
                05 SQLERRD    OCCURS 6 TIMES
                              PIC S9(9) COMP-4.
                05 SQLWARN.
                   10 SQLWARN0 PIC X.
                   10 SQLWARN1 PIC X.
                   10 SQLWARN2 PIC X.
                   10 SQLWARN3 PIC X.
                   10 SQLWARN4 PIC X.
                   10 SQLWARN5 PIC X.
                   10 SQLWARN6 PIC X.
                   10 SQLWARN7 PIC X.
                05 SQLEXT     PIC X(8).
            *****EXEC SQL
```

Figure 12.10   Program1 output from the precompiler.

precompile step. Because of space constraints, we have not included the entire source code output, but we have marked the parts of the output that illustrate topics discussed so far. Look at line AAA. The EXEC SQL INCLUDE SQLCA END-EXEC statement from the source code has been commented out and the SQLCA has been included beneath it. The same is true with the BRANCH DCLGEN which follows. Starting at line BBB you will find over 150 lines of code which bear no resemblance to our source code. This has all been inserted by the Precompiler and is the workspace that DB2 will use to do its calls to the database. You will never need to reference or even understand the meaning of these fields. Similarly, at line CCC following the Procedure Division heading, the Precompiler has added SQL-SKIP and SQL-INITIAL paragraphs. Now go down to line EEE. Notice that the Precompiler has commented out our SQL INSERT statement and has

```
*****  INCLUDE BRANCH
*****END-EXEC.
****************************************************************
* DCLGEN TABLE(BRANCH)                                         *
*          LIBRARY(SP5PEL.PHYLLIS.CNTL(BRANCH))                *
*          APOST                                               *
*  ... IS THE DCLGEN COMMAND THAT MADE THE                     *
*          FOLLOWING STATEMENTS                                *
****************************************************************
*****EXEC SQL DECLARE BRANCH TABLE
*****( BRANCH_ID            SMALLINT NOT NULL,
*****  BRANCH_CITY          CHAR(20) NOT NULL,
*****  BRANCH_MGR           CHAR(25),
*****  BRANCH_ADDR          VARCHAR(25) NOT NULL
*****) END-EXEC.
****************************************************************
* COBOL DECLARATION FOR TABLE BRANCH                           *
****************************************************************
       01  DCLBRANCH.
           10 BRANCH-ID              PIC S9(4) USAGE COMP.
           10 BRANCH-CITY            PIC X(20).
           10 BRANCH-MGR             PIC X(25).
           10 BRANCH-ADDR.
              49 BRANCH-ADDR-LEN     PIC S9(4) USAGE COMP.
              49 BRANCH-ADDR-TEXT    PIC X(25).
****************************************************************
* THE NUMBER OF COLUMNS DESCRIBED BY THIS DECLARATION IS 4 *
****************************************************************
       77 SQL-NULL        PIC S9(9) COMP-4 VALUE +0.
       77 SQL-INIT-FLAG PIC S9(4) COMP-4 VALUE +0.
        88 SQL-INIT-DONE VALUE +1.
       01 SQL-PLIST4.
          05 SQL-PLIST-CON   PIC S9(9)  COMP-4 VALUE +2654208.
          05 SQL-CALLTYPE    PIC S9(4)  COMP-4 VALUE +30.
          05 SQL-PROG-NAME   PIC X(8)          VALUE "PROGRAM1".
          05 SQL-TIMESTAMP-1 PIC S9(9)  COMP-4 VALUE +336476956.
          05 SQL-TIMESTAMP-2 PIC S9(9)  COMP-4 VALUE +22531281.
          05 SQL-SECTION     PIC S9(4)  COMP-4 VALUE +1.
          05 SQL-CODEPTR     PIC S9(9)  COMP-4.
          05 SQL-VPARMPTR    PIC S9(9)  COMP-4 VALUE +0.
          05 SQL-APARMPTR    PIC S9(9)  COMP-4 VALUE +0.
          05 SQL-STMT-NUM    PIC S9(4)  COMP-4 VALUE +159.
          05 SQL-STMT-TYPE   PIC S9(4)  COMP-4 VALUE +232.
          05 SQL-PVAR-LIST4.
             10 SQL-PVAR-SIZE  PIC S9(9) COMP-4 VALUE +52.
             10 SQL-PVAR-DESCS.
                15 SQL-PVAR-TYPE1 PIC S9(4) COMP-4 VALUE +501.
```

LINE BBB --

Figure 12.10 *(Continued)*

replaced it with code that performs SQL-INITIAL and references
fields from those 150 lines added to WORKING-STORAGE at line
BBB. Because our source code has WHENEVER statements (line
DDD), after every call to DSNHLI (the DB2 attach), the precompile
has inserted code to check SQLCODE and take the action specified in
our WHENEVER statements.

```
      15 SQL-PVAR-LEN1  PIC S9(4) COMP-4 VALUE +2.
   10 SQL-PVAR-ADDRS.
      15 SQL-PVAR-ADDR1 PIC S9(9) COMP-4.
      15 SQL-PVAR-IND1  PIC S9(9) COMP-4.
      15 SQL-PVAR-TYPE2 PIC S9(4) COMP-4 VALUE +453.
      15 SQL-PVAR-LEN2  PIC S9(4) COMP-4 VALUE +20.
      15 SQL-PVAR-ADDR2 PIC S9(9) COMP-4.
      15 SQL-PVAR-IND2  PIC S9(9) COMP-4.
      15 SQL-PVAR-TYPE3 PIC S9(4) COMP-4 VALUE +453.
      15 SQL-PVAR-LEN3  PIC S9(4) COMP-4 VALUE +25.
      15 SQL-PVAR-ADDR3 PIC S9(9) COMP-4.
      15 SQL-PVAR-IND3  PIC S9(9) COMP-4.
      15 SQL-PVAR-TYPE4 PIC S9(4) COMP-4 VALUE +449.
      15 SQL-PVAR-LEN4  PIC S9(4) COMP-4 VALUE +25.
      15 SQL-PVAR-ADDR4 PIC S9(9) COMP-4.
      15 SQL-PVAR-IND4  PIC S9(9) COMP-4.
01 SQL-PLIST5.
   05 SQL-PLIST-CON    PIC S9(9) COMP-4 VALUE +2654208.
   05 SQL-CALLTYPE     PIC S9(4) COMP-4 VALUE +30.
   05 SQL-PROG-NAME    PIC X(8)         VALUE "PROGRAM1".
   05 SQL-TIMESTAMP-1  PIC S9(9) COMP-4 VALUE +336476956.
   05 SQL-TIMESTAMP-2  PIC S9(9) COMP-4 VALUE +22531281.
   05 SQL-SECTION      PIC S9(4) COMP-4 VALUE +2.
   05 SQL-CODEPTR      PIC S9(9) COMP-4.
   05 SQL-VPARMPTR     PIC S9(9) COMP-4 VALUE +0.
   05 SQL-APARMPTR     PIC S9(9) COMP-4 VALUE +0.
   05 SQL-STMT-NUM     PIC S9(4) COMP-4 VALUE +165.
   05 SQL-STMT-TYPE    PIC S9(4) COMP-4 VALUE +233.
   05 SQL-PVAR-LIST5.
      10 SQL-PVAR-SIZE PIC S9(9) COMP-4 VALUE +16.
      10 SQL-PVAR-DESCS.
         15 SQL-PVAR-TYPE1 PIC S9(4) COMP-4 VALUE +500.
         15 SQL-PVAR-LEN1  PIC S9(4) COMP-4 VALUE +2.
      10 SQL-PVAR-ADDRS.
         15 SQL-PVAR-ADDR1 PIC S9(9) COMP-4.
         15 SQL-PVAR-IND1  PIC S9(9) COMP-4.
01 SQL-PLIST6.
   05 SQL-PLIST-CON    PIC S9(9) COMP-4 VALUE +2654208.
   05 SQL-CALLTYPE     PIC S9(4) COMP-4 VALUE +30.
   05 SQL-PROG-NAME    PIC X(8)         VALUE "PROGRAM1".
   05 SQL-TIMESTAMP-1  PIC S9(9) COMP-4 VALUE +336476956.
   05 SQL-TIMESTAMP-2  PIC S9(9) COMP-4 VALUE +22531281.
   05 SQL-SECTION      PIC S9(4) COMP-4 VALUE +3.
   05 SQL-CODEPTR      PIC S9(9) COMP-4.
   05 SQL-VPARMPTR     PIC S9(9) COMP-4 VALUE +0.
   05 SQL-APARMPTR     PIC S9(9) COMP-4 VALUE +0.
   05 SQL-STMT-NUM     PIC S9(4) COMP-4 VALUE +191.
```

Figure 12.10 *(Continued)*

```
    05 SQL-STMT-TYPE    PIC S9(4) COMP-4 VALUE +234.
    05 SQL-PVAR-LIST6.
       10 SQL-PVAR-SIZE  PIC S9(9) COMP-4 VALUE +28.
       10 SQL-PVAR-DESCS.
          15 SQL-PVAR-TYPE1 PIC S9(4) COMP-4 VALUE +452.
          15 SQL-PVAR-LEN1  PIC S9(4) COMP-4 VALUE +20.
       10 SQL-PVAR-ADDRS.
          15 SQL-PVAR-ADDR1 PIC S9(9) COMP-4.
          15 SQL-PVAR-IND1  PIC S9(9) COMP-4.
          15 SQL-PVAR-TYPE2 PIC S9(4) COMP-4 VALUE +500.
          15 SQL-PVAR-LEN2  PIC S9(4) COMP-4 VALUE +2.
          15 SQL-PVAR-ADDR2 PIC S9(9) COMP-4.
          15 SQL-PVAR-IND2  PIC S9(9) COMP-4.
 01 SQL-PLIST7.
    05 SQL-PLIST-CON   PIC S9(9) COMP-4 VALUE +2654208.
    05 SQL-CALLTYPE    PIC S9(4) COMP-4 VALUE +30.
    05 SQL-PROG-NAME   PIC X(8)           VALUE "PROGRAM1".
    05 SQL-TIMESTAMP-1 PIC S9(9) COMP-4 VALUE +336476956.
    05 SQL-TIMESTAMP-2 PIC S9(9) COMP-4 VALUE +22531281.
    05 SQL-SECTION     PIC S9(4) COMP-4 VALUE +4.
    05 SQL-CODEPTR     PIC S9(9) COMP-4.
    05 SQL-VPARMPTR    PIC S9(9) COMP-4 VALUE +0.
    05 SQL-APARMPTR    PIC S9(9) COMP-4 VALUE +0.
    05 SQL-STMT-NUM    PIC S9(4) COMP-4 VALUE +207.
    05 SQL-STMT-TYPE   PIC S9(4) COMP-4 VALUE +234.
       10 SQL-PVAR-SIZE  PIC S9(9) COMP-4 VALUE +28.
       10 SQL-PVAR-DESCS.
          15 SQL-PVAR-TYPE1 PIC S9(4) COMP-4 VALUE +453.
          15 SQL-PVAR-LEN1  PIC S9(4) COMP-4 VALUE +25.
       10 SQL-PVAR-ADDRS.
          15 SQL-PVAR-ADDR1 PIC S9(9) COMP-4.
          15 SQL-PVAR-IND1  PIC S9(9) COMP-4.
          15 SQL-PVAR-TYPE2 PIC S9(4) COMP-4 VALUE +500.
          15 SQL-PVAR-LEN2  PIC S9(4) COMP-4 VALUE +2.
          15 SQL-PVAR-ADDR2 PIC S9(9) COMP-4.
          15 SQL-PVAR-IND2  PIC S9(9) COMP-4.
 01 SQL-PLIST8.
    05 SQL-PLIST-CON   PIC S9(9) COMP-4 VALUE +2654208.
    05 SQL-CALLTYPE    PIC S9(4) COMP-4 VALUE +30.
    05 SQL-PROG-NAME   PIC X(8)           VALUE "PROGRAM1".
    05 SQL-TIMESTAMP-1 PIC S9(9) COMP-4 VALUE +336476956.
    05 SQL-TIMESTAMP-2 PIC S9(9) COMP-4 VALUE +22531281.
    05 SQL-SECTION     PIC S9(4) COMP-4 VALUE +5.
    05 SQL-CODEPTR     PIC S9(9) COMP-4.
    05 SQL-VPARMPTR    PIC S9(9) COMP-4 VALUE +0.
    05 SQL-APARMPTR    PIC S9(9) COMP-4 VALUE +0.
    05 SQL-STMT-NUM    PIC S9(4) COMP-4 VALUE +215.
```

Figure 12.10   *(Continued)*

```
 05 SQL-STMT-TYPE     PIC S9(4) COMP-4 VALUE +234.
 05 SQL-PVAR-LIST8.
    10 SQL-PVAR-SIZE  PIC S9(9) COMP-4 VALUE +28.
    10 SQL-PVAR-DESCS.
       15 SQL-PVAR-TYPE1 PIC S9(4) COMP-4 VALUE +448.
       15 SQL-PVAR-LEN1  PIC S9(4) COMP-4 VALUE +25.
    10 SQL-PVAR-ADDRS.
       15 SQL-PVAR-ADDR1 PIC S9(9) COMP-4.
       15 SQL-PVAR-IND1  PIC S9(9) COMP-4.
       15 SQL-PVAR-TYPE2 PIC S9(4) COMP-4 VALUE +500.
       15 SQL-PVAR-LEN2  PIC S9(4) COMP-4 VALUE +2.
       15 SQL-PVAR-ADDR2 PIC S9(9) COMP-4.
       15 SQL-PVAR-IND2  PIC S9(9) COMP-4.
01 SQL-PLIST9.
 05 SQL-PLIST-CON    PIC S9(9) COMP-4 VALUE +2656256.
 05 SQL-CALLTYPE     PIC S9(4) COMP-4 VALUE +30.
 05 SQL-PROG-NAME    PIC X(8)         VALUE "PROGRAM1".
 05 SQL-TIMESTAMP-1  PIC S9(9) COMP-4 VALUE +336476956.
 05 SQL-TIMESTAMP-2  PIC S9(9) COMP-4 VALUE +22531281.
 05 SQL-SECTION      PIC S9(4) COMP-4 VALUE +6.
 05 SQL-CODEPTR      PIC S9(9) COMP-4.
 05 SQL-VPARMPTR     PIC S9(9) COMP-4 VALUE +0.
 05 SQL-APARMPTR     PIC S9(9) COMP-4 VALUE +0.
 05 SQL-STMT-NUM     PIC S9(4) COMP-4 VALUE +224.
 05 SQL-STMT-TYPE    PIC S9(4) COMP-4 VALUE +231.
 05 SQL-PVAR-LIST9.
    10 SQL-PVAR-SIZE  PIC S9(9) COMP-4 VALUE +16.
    10 SQL-PVAR-DESCS.
       15 SQL-PVAR-TYPE1 PIC S9(4) COMP-4 VALUE +500.
       15 SQL-PVAR-LEN1  PIC S9(4) COMP-4 VALUE +2.
    10 SQL-PVAR-ADDRS.
       15 SQL-PVAR-ADDR1 PIC S9(9) COMP-4.
       15 SQL-PVAR-IND1  PIC S9(9) COMP-4.
 05 SQL-AVAR-LIST9.
    10 SQL-AVAR-SIZE  PIC S9(9) COMP-4 VALUE +52.
    10 SQL-AVAR-DESCS.
       15 SQL-AVAR-TYPE1 PIC S9(4) COMP-4 VALUE +501.
       15 SQL-AVAR-LEN1  PIC S9(4) COMP-4 VALUE +2.
    10 SQL-AVAR-ADDRS.
       15 SQL-AVAR-ADDR1 PIC S9(9) COMP-4.
       15 SQL-AVAR-IND1  PIC S9(9) COMP-4.
       15 SQL-AVAR-TYPE2 PIC S9(4) COMP-4 VALUE +453.
       15 SQL-AVAR-LEN2  PIC S9(4) COMP-4 VALUE +20.
       15 SQL-AVAR-ADDR2 PIC S9(9) COMP-4.
       15 SQL-AVAR-IND2  PIC S9(9) COMP-4.
       15 SQL-AVAR-TYPE3 PIC S9(4) COMP-4 VALUE +453.
       15 SQL-AVAR-LEN3  PIC S9(4) COMP-4 VALUE +25.
```

Figure 12.10 *(Continued)*

```
                    15 SQL-AVAR-ADDR3 PIC S9(9) COMP-4.
                    15 SQL-AVAR-IND3  PIC S9(9) COMP-4.
                    15 SQL-AVAR-TYPE4 PIC S9(4) COMP-4 VALUE +449.
                    15 SQL-AVAR-LEN4  PIC S9(4) COMP-4 VALUE +25.
                    15 SQL-AVAR-ADDR4 PIC S9(9) COMP-4.
                    15 SQL-AVAR-IND4  PIC S9(9) COMP-4.
-------------- PROCEDURE DIVISION.
-- LINE CCC -- SQL-SKIP.
--------------     GO TO SQL-INIT-END.
               SQL-INITIAL.
                   MOVE 1 TO SQL-INIT-FLAG.
                   CALL "DSNHADDR" USING SQL-VPARMPTR OF SQL-PLIST4 SQL-PVAR-LIS
            -      T4.
                   CALL "DSNHADDR" USING SQL-PVAR-ADDRS OF SQL-PLIST4 BRANCH-ID
                   OF  DCLBRANCH BRANCH-IND OF INDICATOR-TABLE(1) BRANCH-CITY OF
                   DCLBRANCH BRANCH-IND OF INDICATOR-TABLE(2) BRANCH-MGR OF  DC
            -      LBRANCH BRANCH-IND OF INDICATOR-TABLE(3) BRANCH-ADDR OF  DCLB
            -      RANCH BRANCH-IND OF INDICATOR-TABLE(4)
                   CALL "DSNHADDR" USING SQL-CODEPTR OF SQL-PLIST4 SQLCA.
                   CALL "DSNHADDR" USING SQL-VPARMPTR OF SQL-PLIST5 SQL-PVAR-LIS
            -      T5.
                   CALL "DSNHADDR" USING SQL-PVAR-ADDRS OF SQL-PLIST5 BRANCH-ID
                   OF DCLBRANCH SQL-NULL
                   CALL "DSNHADDR" USING SQL-CODEPTR OF SQL-PLIST5 SQLCA.
                   CALL "DSNHADDR" USING SQL-VPARMPTR OF SQL-PLIST6 SQL-PVAR-LIS
            -      T6.
                   CALL "DSNHADDR" USING SQL-PVAR-ADDRS OF SQL-PLIST6 BRANCH-CIT
            -      Y OF DCLBRANCH SQL-NULL BRANCH-ID OF DCLBRANCH SQL-NULL
                   CALL "DSNHADDR" USING SQL-CODEPTR OF SQL-PLIST6 SQLCA.
                   CALL "DSNHADDR" USING SQL-VPARMPTR OF SQL-PLIST7 SQL-PVAR-LIS
            -      T7.
                   CALL "DSNHADDR" USING SQL-PVAR-ADDRS OF SQL-PLIST7 BRANCH-MGR
                   OF DCLBRANCH MGR-IND BRANCH-ID OF DCLBRANCH SQL-NULL
                   CALL "DSNHADDR" USING SQL-CODEPTR OF SQL-PLIST7 SQLCA.
                   CALL "DSNHADDR" USING SQL-VPARMPTR OF SQL-PLIST8 SQL-PVAR-LIS
            -      T8.
                   CALL "DSNHADDR" USING SQL-PVAR-ADDRS OF SQL-PLIST8 BRANCH-ADD
            -      R OF DCLBRANCH SQL-NULL BRANCH-ID OF DCLBRANCH SQL-NULL
                   CALL "DSNHADDR" USING SQL-CODEPTR OF SQL-PLIST8 SQLCA.
                   CALL "DSNHADDR" USING SQL-VPARMPTR OF SQL-PLIST9 SQL-PVAR-LIS
            -      T9.
                   CALL "DSNHADDR" USING SQL-PVAR-ADDRS OF SQL-PLIST9 BRANCH-ID
                   OF DCLBRANCH SQL-NULL
                   CALL "DSNHADDR" USING SQL-APARMPTR OF SQL-PLIST9 SQL-AVAR-LIS
            -      T9.
                   CALL "DSNHADDR" USING SQL-AVAR-ADDRS OF SQL-PLIST9 BRANCH-ID
                   OF  DCLBRANCH BRANCH-IND OF INDICATOR-TABLE(1) BRANCH-CITY OF
```

Figure 12.10   *(Continued)*

```
                          DCLBRANCH BRANCH-IND OF INDICATOR-TABLE(2) BRA
               -          LBRANCH BRANCH-IND OF INDICATOR-TABLE(3) BRANCH-ADDR OF DCLB
               -          RANCH BRANCH-IND OF INDICATOR-TABLE(4).
                          CALL "DSNHADDR" USING SQL-CODEPTR OF SQL-PLIST9 SQLCA.
                          SQL-INIT-END.
--------------     1000-MAINLINE.
-- LINE DDD --  *****EXEC SQL
--------------  ***** WHENEVER SQLERROR GO TO 9000-ERROR-RTN
                *****END-EXEC.
                *****EXEC SQL
                ***** WHENEVER NOT FOUND GO TO 9000-ERROR-RTN
                *****END-EXEC.
                     PERFORM 2000-INIT.
                     PERFORM 3000-PROCESS-TRANS UNTIL END-OF-FILE.
                     PERFORM 4000-EOJ.
                     STOP RUN.
                         .
                         .
                         .
--------------     6200-INSERT-ROW.
-- LINE EEE --  *****EXEC SQL
--------------  *****   INSERT INTO BRANCH
                *****      VALUES (:DCLBRANCH:BRANCH-IND)
                *****END-EXEC.
                     PERFORM SQL-INITIAL UNTIL SQL-INIT-DONE
                     CALL "DSNHLI" USING SQL-PLIST4
                     IF SQLCODE < 0 GO TO 9000-ERROR-RTN ELSE
                     IF SQLCODE = 100 GO TO 9000-ERROR-RTN ELSE
                     MOVE 1 TO SQL-INIT-FLAG.
                7000-DELETE-BRANCH.
                     MOVE TRANS-BRANCH-ID TO BRANCH-ID.
                *****EXEC SQL
                *****   DELETE
                *****      FROM BRANCH
                *****      WHERE BRANCH_ID = :BRANCH-ID
                *****END-EXEC.
                     PERFORM SQL-INITIAL UNTIL SQL-INIT-DONE
                     CALL "DSNHLI" USING SQL-PLIST5
                     IF SQLCODE < 0 GO TO 9000-ERROR-RTN ELSE
                     IF SQLCODE = 100 GO TO 9000-ERROR-RTN ELSE
                     MOVE 1 TO SQL-INIT-FLAG.
                     DISPLAY WS-TRANSACTION-RECORD ' **DELETED**'.
                         .
                         .
                         .
                9000-ERROR-RTN.
                ********************************************************


                ********************************************************
                * THIS IS A GENERALIZED ERROR ROUTINE.  IT DISPLAYS   *
                * THE NUMERIC-EDITED SQLCODE AND ENDS THE PROGRAM.    *
                ********************************************************
                     DISPLAY '***FATAL DB2 ERROR--PROGRAM1 ENDING'.
                     MOVE SQLCODE TO EDIT-SQLCODE.
                     DISPLAY 'SQLCODE = ' EDIT-SQLCODE.
                     PERFORM 4000-EOJ.
                     STOP RUN.
```

Figure 12.10 *(Continued)*

12.4 BIND/REBIND/FREE

Going back to the DB2I menu (Fig. 12.3), we will now look at option 5
(BIND/REBIND/FREE), which takes you to a menu from which you
can choose one of three options (Fig. 12.11). The BIND panel is the
same as the one referenced on the Program Preparation Panels. The
only difference is that there is no information from other panels that
can be filled in or protected.

```
                        BIND/REBIND/FREE
===>

Select one of the following and press ENTER:

 1  BIND          (Add or replace an application plan)

 2  REBIND        (Rebind existing application plan or plans)

 3  FREE          (Erase application plan or plans)




PRESS:      END to exit      HELP for more information
```

Figure 12.11   BIND/REBIND/FREE Panel.

REBIND is a first cousin of BIND but it is significantly different in that REBIND does not use any DBRM as input; it only reoptimizes the SQL statements from the previous plan to produce a new plan. When DB2 structures are changed or dropped, such as when an index on a table is dropped, DB2 marks the affected plans and automatically issues a REBIND on them at execution time. At times you will want to have DB2 reoptimize a plan because you want it to take into account some change to the database in its choice of access paths, such as when a table size changes or an index is added. You may issue a REBIND by filling in up to 12 plan names in the REBIND panel (Fig. 12.12) or entering an asterisk to have all plans that you own rebound. The panel can also be used to change BIND options such as ISOLATION LEVEL or PLAN VALIDATION TIME. Incidentally, REBIND will not help you if you have gotten an −818 SQLCODE because of a timestamp mismatch. If you have precompiled but have neglected to BIND, REBIND will not update the timestamp in the application plan because it does not look at the new DBRM. Under these circumstances you must issue a BIND REPLACE.

The third option, FREE, should be used used very carefully because FREE means erase. This panel (Fig. 12.13) lets you specify up to 12 plans to erase or you may enter an asterisk to erase all of the plans that you own. For FREE and REBIND, you must have the proper authorization for your request to be executed.

```
                         REBIND
 ===>

 Enter plan name(s) to be rebound, or * for all authorized plans:
  1  ===>          4  ===>          7  ===>             10  ===>
  2  ===>          5  ===>          8  ===>             11  ===>
  3  ===>          6  ===>          9  ===>             12  ===>

 Enter options as desired:
 13  ISOLATION LEVEL ........ ===> SAME     (SAME, RR, or CS)
 14  PLAN VALIDATION TIME .... ===> SAME     (SAME, RUN, or BIND)
 15  RESOURCE ACQUISITION TIME ===> SAME     (SAME, ALLOCATE, or USE)
 16  RESOURCE RELEASE TIME ... ===> SAME     (SAME, DEALLOCATE, or COMMIT)
 17  EXPLAIN PATH SELECTION .. ===> SAME     (SAME, NO, or YES)




 PRESS:   ENTER to process     END to exit      HELP for more information
```

Figure 12.12 REBIND Panel.

```
                         FREE
   ===>

   Enter plan name(s) to be freed or * for all authorized plans:

    1  ===>          4  ===>          7  ===>          10  ===>
    2  ===>          5  ===>          8  ===>          11  ===>
    3  ===>          6  ===>          9  ===>          12  ===>









   PRESS: ENTER to process     END to exit    HELP for more information
```

Figure 12.13 FREE Panel.

12.5   STDSQL(86) and NOFOR

In order to conform more closely to ANSI SQL, DB2 provides, with version 2.2, the option STDSQL(86). The default is STDSQL(NO), which means that the regular DB2 syntax rules are followed. With STDSQL(86), several variations on DB2 syntax take effect. For example, any declaration of a host variable must be preceded and followed by BEGIN DECLARE SECTION and END DECLARE SECTION statements. With DB2 syntax, this is optional.

There are also differences in the way that the SQLCA and SQLCODE are handled. With STDSQL(86), the Precompiler automatically includes an SQLCA in your program. Issuing an INCLUDE SQLCA statement yourself will produce a warning from the Precompiler; manually inserting an SQLCA area will produce an error.

The SQLCA that is included with STDSQL(86) holds return codes from DB2 in a field called SQLCADE, in place of SQLCODE which does the same job in the DB2 version of the SQLCA. With STDSQL(86), the Precompiler also puts code into your program to move the contents of SQLCADE to SQLCODE. You must code the fullword binary field, SQLCODE, yourself. This field may not be part of any structure.

The other result of specifying STDSQL(86) is that cursor declarations for update are handled differently. This is called the NOFOR option and it may be specified explicitly or implicitly by specifying STDSQL(86). With NOFOR in effect, the FOR UPDATE CLAUSE is optional on a DECLARE CURSOR statement.

Both STDSQL(86) and NOFOR may be specified at installation time or as Precompiler options.

12.6   PROGRAM PREPARATION OUTSIDE OF DB2I

DB2I is meant to simplify the task of program preparation by eliminating the need to compose your own DB2 commands and JCL to run them. However, you will also find many installations that prefer the alternatives that bypass DB2I-TSO foreground execution and instead execute in batch. We will discuss these alternatives here, but first we'll look at the DSN Command Processor (DSN). It is DSN that DB2I, TSO, and batch JCL must invoke to execute those steps of program preparation which require access to DB2, namely DCLGEN, BIND, and RUN. DB2I invokes DSN behind the scenes. For the alternative to DB2I, you will invoke DSN explicitly. DB2 resides in address spaces different from those of your programs and TSO. Therefore, in order to communicate with DB2 you need a go-between. DB2 supplies DSN to handle this job. When you issue a BIND or RUN command through DB2I, DSN is invoked to pass that command to DB2. In fact, BIND and RUN are subcommands of DSN.

12.6.1 TSO Foreground Execution

DSN and its subcommands can be invoked directly from native TSO. From ISPF option 6 or TSO READY type:

```
DSN SYSTEM(xxxx)
```

and then hit Enter; *xxxx* is the DB2 subsystem name. DSN will then return a prompt of:

```
DSN
```

You may then type in the DSN subcommand you wish to run. The DSN subcommands used most by application programmers are RUN, to run an application program, and BIND, to bind a plan. The detailed syntax of these subcommands is given in the next section. When you have entered the subcommand and pressed Enter, DSN will again prompt you with DSN. You should type END and press Enter, ending the dialog with DSN. DSN and its subcommands can also be embedded in a CLIST.

12.6.2 Execution in Batch

The JCL to execute the compile or link-edit steps of program preparation will be familiar to you because it's the same JCL used for non-DB2 programs. The precompile step requires executing the DB2-supplied program DSNHPC. You should be able to get the JCL to run this program from your DBA. DSNHPC produces two output files. One will be passed to your compile JCL and one to your BIND JCL.

In order for your JCL to submit a BIND command to DB2, it, like DB2I and your TSO foreground job, must invoke DSN. However, the DSN command processor can only be run in a TSO environment. To run DSN in batch, therefore, you actually execute the TSO Terminal Monitor Program (TMP) and then invoke DSN. DSN, in turn, submits your command to DB2. To illustrate, let's look at submitting the RUN command to execute a program. Suppose your program is called PROGRAM1, its plan is called PLAN1, the program is in load library DB2.LOADLIB, and the DB2 subsystem name is DB2A. The JCL to run it might look like this:

```
//STEP1     EXEC  PGM=IKJEFT01,DYNAMNBR=20
//SYSTSPRT DD    SYSOUT=*
//SYSTSIN  DD *
  DSN SYSTEM(DB2A)
  RUN PROGRAM(PROGRAM1) PLAN(PLAN1) LIB('DB2.LOADLIB')
  END
//
```

IKJEFT01 is the TSO Terminal Monitor Program. DSN connects it to the DB2 subsystem named DB2A and submits the RUN command for PROGRAM1. If the plan name is the same as the program name, it can be omitted. If the program load library is named in a STEPLIB or JOBLIB DD statement, or if it is in the link list, it can also be omitted. Our JCL assumes that the load library in which DSN itself resides is in the link list. If it isn't, it has to be specified in the STEPLIB or JOBLIB DD statement. The RUN command must be on one line; if it must be continued onto a second physical line, the first line should have a continuation character (-) at the end of it.

In our sample JCL, the SYSTSIN DD statement points to what, in regular TSO, would be terminal input; the SYSTSPRT DD statement points to what would be terminal output. An alternative to having SYSTSIN followed by the DSN control statements is to have it invoke a batch CLIST, which in turn executes DSN. To execute a CLIST in batch, you need a SYSPROC DD statement which specifies the CLIST library. Then, if the CLIST you want to run is called CLIST1, your SYSTSIN input would look like this:

```
SYSTSIN DD *
%CLIST1
```

The percent sign tells TSO that the name of a CLIST follows.

No DD statements are needed to access DB2, but if your program needs other files, the JCL must contain the appropriate DD statements, as with any other batch job. If your program requires a parm, there is a PARMS(*value*) operand that is part of the RUN command. However, since this value is embedded in the SYSTSIN file, it cannot contain a symbolic parameter and cannot be overridden with each run of a job with the same ease as a JCL EXEC PARM. This is an unfortunate result of the fact that the program that the JCL is executing is IKJEFT01 and not your application program.

One feature of running DB2 programs with the above JCL is that if the program abends, the Terminal Monitor Program (IKJEFT01) will not abend; it will end with a condition code 12. The SYSTSPRT file will contain a message saying that the program ENDED DUE TO ERROR and will give the abend code. However, the job step will terminate with a condition code 12. In many installations, this may cause a problem because operations may not detect the condition code 12 as a job failure. Also, if your program writes files with a disposition of, for example, (NEW,CATLG,DELETE), the files will not be deleted even if the program abends.

The recommended way to cause an abend to the Terminal Monitor Program when your program abends is to execute IKJEFT1A instead of IKJEFT01. This is the name of another entry point in the Terminal Monitor Program. If your program abends, it will abend with a S04C abend, no matter what your program actually abended with. This will not help you understand your abend but it will, at least, be an abend.

The JCL we have presented runs batch DB2 jobs by invoking the DSN command processor and then executing the RUN subcommand. This JCL can also be used to do binds in batch by invoking DSN and executing the BIND subcommand. For example, if you wanted to bind a plan called PLAN1 that included DBRM members PROGRAM1 and PROGRAM2, which were in a DBRM library called MYID.DBRM, you could code a SYSTSIN statement as follows:

```
//SYSTSIN DD *
   DSN SYSTEM(DB2A)
   BIND PLAN(PLAN1) MEMBER(PROGRAM1, PROGRAM2)   -
   LIBRARY(MYID.DBRM)   -
   ACTION (REPLACE)   -
   RETAIN   -
   VALIDATE (BIND)   -
   ISOLATION (CS)   -
   ACQUIRE (USE)   -
   RELEASE (COMMIT)   -
   EXPLAIN (NO)
      END
```

You've probably recognized the parameters as the options on the DB2I BIND panel. Remember, DB2I is just a front end to DSN. The values that are entered into these fields are also identical to those of the DB2I BIND panel.

DSN commands other than BIND and RUN can be processed in a similar manner in batch. The DB2 Command and Utility Reference can supply detailed syntax. DCLGEN can be run this way, as can the utility commands that will be discussed in Chap. 17.

12.7 CICS CONSIDERATIONS

Preparing a CICS program involves adding the CICS translate step. It may be run before or after precompile, but running it first will result in warning messages from the CICS translator. Also, you are probably familiar with the need to do a CEMT SET NEWCOPY to get CICS to fetch a new copy of your program when you have recompiled it. Otherwise, your changes do not take effect. With a DB2 program you will, however, not just get an old version of the program; you will get a −818 SQLCODE if you have done a precompile, BIND, and compile without issuing a CEMT SET NEWCOPY. This is because the timestamp of the old load module in core will not match the timestamp in the plan you just precompiled and bound. You must issue the CEMT SET NEWCOPY before executing the BIND and compile steps.

Another possible cause of a −818 is that your transaction has a dedicated thread that is still active and using the old plan. If your installation allows it, you can use the DSNC transaction to disconnect currently active threads that are using this plan as soon as they are no longer in use by a transaction. The syntax is:

DSNC DISC *planname*

This transaction will allow the threads to start again when next requested. Note, however, that if multiple threads are actively using this plan, they will all be terminated.

Lastly, in CICS applications that use dedicated threads, the ALLOCATE/DEALLOCATE option of BIND may improve performance. This is because it takes a certain amount of time to acquire and free resources. If the dedicated threads can be allowed to keep the resources and not free them, processing will be saved. Check with your DBA to determine if the processing done in your system is suitable for this combination.

As you can see, the steps of program preparation and execution for DB2 programs involve learning new procedures and commands. We've seen how to use DB2I, TSO foreground, or batch JCL to precompile, compile, link-edit, bind, and run DB2 programs. Now we will leave these physical realities behind us as we turn to Chap. 13, whose subject is logical design.

Part

5

Design and Implementation of a Database

13

Logical Database Design

13.1 INTRODUCTION

Database design has two components, logical and physical. Physical design involves issues specific to the performance of the DBMS (e.g., indexes, storage options) and to processing requirements of online or batch applications. Physical design is rarely the province of the programmer or analyst and we will not discuss it here. Our discussion focuses instead on the logical design component that must precede physical design.

Logical database design is part of a larger endeavor—data planning. In the past, applications and data were tightly coupled; a data store was the by-product of an application requirement and design decisions were driven by an analysis of a business' application requirements. As the technology of databases developed, so did a new way of thinking, the data-driven approach to system development. In the data-driven approach, the global data requirements for the enterprise are defined without any bias toward particular processing requirements. With this approach, data is seen as a resource in itself. The strategic analysis of this resource is data planning.

At a high level, data planning includes the development of an enterprise data model. This ambitious task attempts to analyze and represent the information requirements of an entire enterprise. From that model, strategic decisions are made regarding what data can be shared, which databases should be built first, and, in general, how best to manage an enterprise's data resource.

For our purposes, we will describe a methodology geared to a less ambitious level of data planning, the development of a logical design for a particular system's database. The principles are the same. The goal is a model that reflects the inherent information requirements of the business. From this, a database that is stable and flexible and one that can be shared can be designed.

An enterprise data model is developed by a data administration group. At the system level, application programmer-analysts are often brought into the design process, with final review and acceptance provided by the data administration function. A cooperative effort between systems developers and data groups is an effective way to ensure that standardized design procedures and methodologies are disseminated and adhered to throughout an organization.

13.1.1 A Variety of Approaches and Tools

The subject of logical design has a rather confounding abundance of terminologies and methodologies associated with it. The methodology, terms, and symbols we use here are an amalgam of different approaches, tuned by our own design experiences. Just as we have made modifications to existing methodologies, so we invite you to do the same to that which we present here. It is our opinion that a methodology is a guideline and not a religion.

We break the logical design process into three phases. The first phase (identify the business information requirements) clarifies the information that is to be stored and produces a business entity relationship model. The second phase (identify the data requirements) translates the results of the first phase into data structures and produces a logical data model. The last phase (normalization) reviews the results of the second phase to increase the data structures' stability by reducing unneeded redundancy; it produces a normalized logical data model.

Our methodology, like most, relies on diagramming techniques. A diagram is able to illustrate information in a relatively clear and concise format. These diagrams also provide a common ground for communication among developers, designers, and users. While diagrams do present a fairly complete picture, alone they are insufficient. They must be augmented with more detailed specification in a manual or automated dictionary.

There are many tools on the marketplace that automate aspects of the design process. They fall under the umbrella of computer-aided software engineering (CASE). Automated tools are a boon to the design process because they facilitate revision and maintenance. Design is an iterative process; it takes many diagrams to arrive at a final model. This is much easier with an automated design tool. On the negative side, tools can also lock you into predetermined structures and methods that limit your flexibility.

Dictionaries are included with most CASE tools and can also be purchased separately. Figure 13.1 lists some of the products meant to aid in the design process and some of the automated dictionaries that can

```
            VENDOR                PRODUCT

DESIGN TOOLS:

    Chen & Associates, Inc.   ER Modeler Package
    DACOM                     Leverage
    Index Technology Corp.    Excelerator
    Knowledgeware             IEW (Integrated Engineering
                                  Workbench)
    Nastec Corp.              DesignAid
    SystemOID Inc.            Consoi-ERM, Consoi-LDM
    Yourdon                   ADTK (Analyst/Developer Toolkit


DICTIONARIES:

    BrownStone Solutions      DataDictionary Solution
    Computer Horizon          Migradata
    FSS                       RIDDCS
    IBM                       DBRAD
    OnLine Software           CASEPAC
```

Figure 13.1   Design tools and automated dictionaries.

be purchased independently. We have only included those dictionaries that interface with DB2, but any could be used.

The only tools *required* for the logical design process are paper, pencil, and eraser. Any part of this design methodology can be adapted for the CASE tools you already have in your shop. Modifications may be required, however, to satisfy the style or limits of the automated tool.

13.2   IDENTIFYING THE BUSINESS INFORMATION REQUIREMENTS

The first phase of logical design is to understand the information needs of the business. We will use the term "business" to mean the aspect of the business for which we are developing a system. At this stage we do not have to be concerned with issues concerning the physical implementation of the database. Instead, we attempt to develop an accurate picture of the business data itself, divorced from data processing realities. We interview users and analyze manual and automated documents and reports. Our goal is to represent the business information structures and rules.

13.2.1   Business Entities

First we must determine the business' entities. An entity is something of interest to the business, something about which you wish to maintain information. It could be a person, place, thing, event, or concept. The business entities for a university might include students, faculty, courses, supplies, etc. The information held about an entity are its attributes. The attributes of a student might be name, date of birth, address, etc.

The business and its "rules" will determine the entities to include. The rules are the operating principles and procedures for the business. For instance, in most databases a social security number would be an attribute of an entity and not an entity in itself. But if you were analyzing information requirements for the social security office, a social security number might very well be an entity with attributes, perhaps, of date issued, place issued, etc.

We have found that rather than asking users to list the entities of their businesses, it is more effective to let them describe the business or application and what it does or is meant to do in their own terms. From that, and pertinent documents, files, etc., we produce laundry lists of candidate entities. Through the process of reviewing these lists with users, they will begin to understand the concept of a business entity and will be able to work with us to refine the lists.

Let's assume, after meetings with users, that we arrive at the following list of business entities: branch, manager, customer, account, and transaction. These are based on our sample database with modifications where needed for the purpose of our example.

13.2.2   Relationships

Having defined a potential list of entities, the next step is to describe the relationships among them. Again, these relationships are defined in the context of the business and its rules. We are interested in the connections between entities that are meaningful to the business. In Fig. 13.2, we represent each entity in a box and each relationship as a diamond between two entities.

Relationships are defined in terms of cardinality. By cardinality we mean, answering the question, "How many?" Determining cardinality, or how many, is essential to data design because it is central to reducing data redundancy. If you know that each branch has many customers, you can store the information about each branch once, linking it to the many customers rather than repeating it for each customer. Between any two entities, a relationship may be one to one, one to many, or many to many. In our diagram, we show relationships with straight lines, using a "crow's foot" at the end of the line to indicate the many side of a relationship. It is also possible that an entity about which we wish to maintain information might have no meaningful connections to the other entities in our model. It would be depicted as a free-standing box. Figure 13.3 shows the entities of our example and their cardinal relationships.

The relationship of A to B is considered to be one to one if each oc-

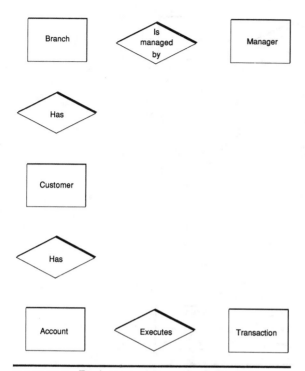

Figure 13.2   Business entities and relationships.

currence of A maps to only one occurrence of B and vice versa. In our
example, the relationship between manager and branch is one to one.
A given branch is managed by no more than one manager; a given
manager manages no more than one branch. Of course, this relationship is determined by business rules. There might very well be a bank
that has either multiple managers per branch or multiple branches
per manager.

A one to many relationship exists between A and B if one occurrence of A maps to more than one occurrence of B and one occurrence
of B maps to no more than one occurrence of A. The relationship between branches and customers is one to many. Any branch may have
more than one customer. A given customer, however, belongs to no
more than one branch. The relationship between accounts and transactions is also one to many. An account may execute more than one
transaction and any transaction must be executed by one and only one
account.

A many to many relationship exists between A and B if one occurrence of A may map to more than one occurrence of B and one
occurrence of B may map to more than one occurrence of A. The re-

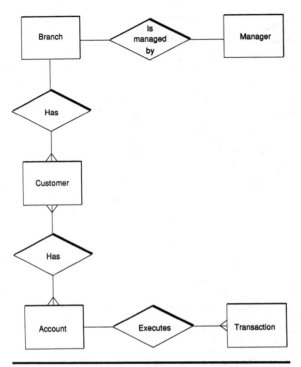

Figure 13.3   Cardinal relationships are represented.

lationship between customers and accounts is many to many. A given customer may have more than one account. One account may be owned by more than one customer, as in a joint account. Again, this relationship stems from business rules. (Note that the relationship between customer and account is one to many in our sample database; we have modified our business rule for the examples in this chapter.)

13.2.3   Conditional Relationships

In our methodology it is possible to distinguish between mandatory and optional relationships. Each side of a relationship will be one or the other. These distinctions alter the cardinality of the relationship.

   If the one side of a relationship is optional, it means that there may be zero or one occurrence of that entity in the relationship. If the one side is mandatory, there must be one occurrence of that entity in the relationship. If the many side of a relationship is optional, it means that there may be zero or more occurrences of that entity in the relationship. If the many side is mandatory, there must be at least one occurrence of that entity in the relationship.

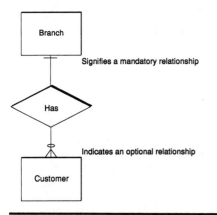

Signifies a mandatory relationship

Indicates an optional relationship

Figure 13.4   Optional and mandatory representation.

Figure 13.4 shows how these distinctions are graphically represented. A short perpendicular line indicates a mandatory relationship and a circle indicates an optional relationship. Reading down in this example, BRANCH to CUSTOMER is a one to many relationship in which the customer side of the relationship is optional (a branch may have zero to many customers). Reading up, the branch side is mandatory (a customer must belong to one branch). Figure 13.5 shows the model with all of the relationships and optional and mandatory graphic symbols included.

This is called a business entity relationship model and is the deliverable from the first phase of logical design. The term "entity relationship" (E-R) was popularized by Peter Chen in the 1970s. It is now used generically to mean a graphic representation of entities and relationships. Accompanying documentation in the dictionary should provide a definition for each business entity and relationship. Any relevant business rules should also be included.

13.3   IDENTIFY THE DATA REQUIREMENTS

Up to now, we have attempted to look at the business divorced from the realities of hardware, software, etc. For the next step, we translate these business entities and relationships into a logical data structure made up of data entities and relationships. Identifying the data requirements includes populating these entities with their primary and foreign key attributes and then with their nonkey attributes.

13.3.1   Data Entities and Relationships

Data entities are derived from business entities. We translate each business entity into a data entity. *Each data entity will eventually cor-*

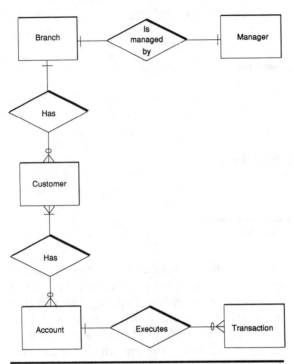

Figure 13.5   Business entity relationship model.

respond to a table. At this point, we dispense with the diamond-shaped relationships in our diagram and use only the connecting lines (Fig. 13.6).

The relationships between the data entities remain the same as their corresponding business entities in all cases except for that of the many to many relationship. Most database systems do not support many to many relationships. To do so would require much of the same data appearing in each data entity. Instead, these relationships are resolved in the design process by creating an intersection record through which the two entities are connected. In DB2 this is an associative data entity.

In our model, CUSTOMER to ACCOUNT is a many to many relationship. To resolve this, we'll create a new data entity, CUST_ACCT, which connects the two entities and can also maintain information about the association (Fig. 13.7). *This associative entity is the many side between two one to many relationships.*

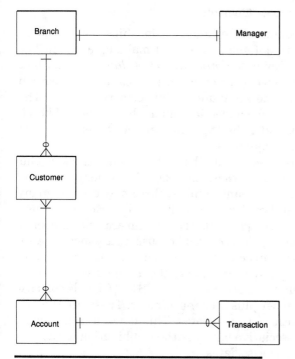

Figure 13.6 Data structure.

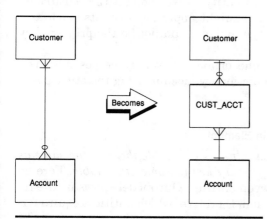

Figure 13.7 A many to many relationship
is resolved with an associative entity.

13.3.2 Define Primary Key Data Elements

Having established the data entities and relationships, we now identify the attributes (that is, data elements) that make up each entity's
primary key. *A primary key is the minimal set of data elements that
uniquely identifies an instance of an entity.* A particular customer can
be uniquely identified by one attribute, social security number. The
key would remain unique if we added last name, but we would be vi-
olating the requirement that it be the minimal set of elements; last
name is not required for uniqueness.

If a key consists of more than one attribute, it is a composite key. Our
TRANSACTION entity needs a composite key. There may be many
transactions for a particular account number; there may even be many
transactions of a particular type for an account number. However, there
will be only one transaction of a particular type for an account number at
a given time. (Transaction type is required because a customer can execute several transactions for an account at the same time.) Account number plus transaction type plus timestamp are the minimal set.

The primary key of our associative entity, CUST_ACCT, is the customer social security number plus account number. These are the primary keys of the two entities it associates. This is not a coincidence;
the primary key of an associative entity is the combination of the primary keys of the entities it associates.

To qualify as a primary key, an attribute or set of attributes must
exist for every occurrence of an entity. If we thought that customers
without social security numbers might apply for accounts (such as a
foreign citizen), social security number could not be the primary key
for the CUSTOMER entity.

In some cases, more than one primary key may be possible. You
could record this fact in your dictionary, documenting the other possibilities as alternate keys.

13.3.3 Define Foreign Key Data Elements

*A foreign key consists of those columns in a table that are the same as
the columns making up the primary key in some other table.* Foreign
keys establish the links between entities. Our model shows us the relationships between entities and, therefore, which entities require foreign key columns.

For each one to one relationship, a foreign key must exist in at least
one of the entities. BRANCH to MANAGER is a one to one relationship. The primary key of BRANCH is BRANCH_ID. We'll add this
column to the MANAGER entity where it will function as a foreign
key. In this table, the column is called MGR_BRANCH. The name of
a foreign key column can be different from its associated primary key

column. However, the domain of values that can be found in the associated columns and the type must be the same.

For each one to many relationship, the primary key of the parent entity (the one side of the relationship) must be held as a foreign key in the dependent entity (the many side of the relationship). For example, in the BRANCH to CUSTOMER relationship, the primary key of BRANCH (BRANCH_ID) must be a column in the CUSTOMER table (CUST_BRANCH). It is through the foreign key in a dependent table that a link can be made to a parent table.

An associative entity is dependent on two parents. Therefore it must contain foreign keys linking it to both of them. In our association entity, CUST_ACCT, those foreign keys, CA_SOC_SEC, and CA_ACCT_NO, are also part of the primary key.

We'll add the primary and foreign keys for all of the entities to our model (Fig. 13.8). This can now be considered the logical data model, but it should be accompanied by the specifications for nonkey data elements for each entity to be complete.

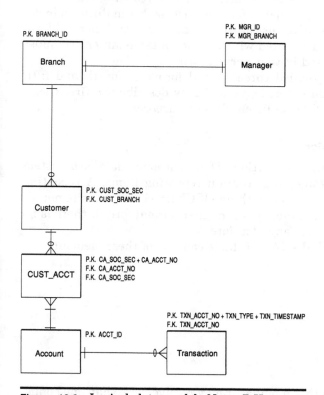

Figure 13.8 Logical data model. Note: P.K. = primary key and F.K. = foreign key.

13.3.4 Define Nonkey Data Elements

Identification of nonkey data elements is fairly straightforward. Data elements are documented separately from the model. Definitions of each element as well as length and data type information are documented through entry into a manual or automated dictionary.

The nonkey data elements make up the content of the data structure while the key data elements make up the structure itself. Having defined both, the next step is to review the now populated data entities and normalize the data model.

13.4 NORMALIZATION

Normalization is a design procedure developed by Dr. E. F. Codd in the early 1970s. Normalization, like relational theory itself, is based on mathematical theory. To put an equation into its "normal form" is to reduce it to its simplest form.

The purpose of normalization in database design is to reduce the redundant nonkey data held in a database, thereby reducing the inherent update problems that data redundancy can cause. Normalization in design involves a series of levels called normal forms. Each normal form has a set of criteria associated with it which a table (an entity) must satisfy to be considered in that normal form.

Codd originally specified three normal forms. A fourth and fifth form have since been defined. We will only describe the first three, which we believe will be sufficient for our purposes.

13.4.1 First Normal Form

The data manipulation operations of a relational database system cannot operate on tables that contain repeating items. A repeating item in COBOL is indicated with an OCCURS clause. This is not allowed within a table. A table is in the first normal form if there is no more than one value for any attribute.

The unnormalized MANAGER table consists of these elements:

```
MANAGER:
    MGR_ID
    MGR_NAME
    MGR_BRANCH
    MGR_HIRE_DATE
    MGR_BONUS
Primary Key: MGR_ID
Foreign Key: MGR_BRANCH
```

The user informs us that a manager may receive more than one bonus. This violates the first normal form, so we'll create a new table, BO-

NUS, to store the multiple bonuses of each manager. The primary key of the new table is BON_MANAGER plus BON_DATE. MANAGER to BONUS is a one to many relationship; BON_MANAGER functions as the foreign key in the BONUS table. These tables are now in first normal form:

```
MANAGER:
     MGR_ID
     MGR_NAME
     MGR_BRANCH
     MGR_HIRE_DATE
Primary Key: MGR_ID
Foreign Key: MGR_BRANCH

BONUS
     BON_MANAGER
     BON_DATE
     BON_AMOUNT
Primary Key:  BON_MANAGER + BON_DATE
Foreign Key:  BON_MANAGER
```

Although it is not physically possible to create a table with more than one value in a column, there is nothing to keep you from creating a table with three columns, BONUS1, BONUS2, BONUS3. Repeating groups across columns in this way does not violate first normal form but, in general, it should be avoided because it is inflexible; it will not work if the manager gets an extra bonus, BONUS4.

There are, however, exceptions to this rule. If the repeating group has a fixed number of occurrences, each of which is distinct in meaning from the other, it may be an advisable design. An example of this is time-related data, such as a table of monthly balances with a year's worth of data.

13.4.2 Second Normal Form

A table is in the second normal form if each nonkey attribute represents a fact about the whole key rather than only a part of the key. A table with a primary key of one column only is automatically in the second normal form.

The TRANSACTION table has a composite key. The unnormalized TRANSACTION table consists of the following elements:

```
TRANSACTION:
     TXN_TYPE
     TXN_TIMESTAMP
     TXN_AMOUNT
     TXN_ACCT_NO
     TXN_VERIFY_CODE
Primary Key:  TXN_ACCT_NO + TXN_TYPE + TXN_TIMESTAMP
Foreign Key:  TXN_ACCT_NO
```

```
TXN_TYPE   TXN_TIMESTAMP       TXN_AMOUNT  TXN_ACCT  TXN_VERIFY_CODE
--------+---------+---------+---------+---------+---------+----------
CREDIT     1989-01-01-12:12:12     200.50  B12       001
CREDIT     1989-01-01-13:13:13    1200.00  B11       001
OPENACCT   1989-02-01-15:15:15    --------  A21       002
OPENACCT   1989-02-02-16:16:15    --------  C11       002
CREDIT     1989-02-02-17:17:17      50.75  C20       001
DEBIT      1989-02-03-19:19:19    2000.50  B12       003
CREDIT     1989-02-03-19:19:19     100.50  A20       001
DEBIT      1989-02-04-20:20:20    1200.55  C10       003
```

Figure 13.9   There is redundant data in an unnormalized table.

Different types of transactions require different kinds of verification, which is indicated in the verify code. A nonkey element, TXN_VERIFY_CODE, represents a fact about a part of the key, TXN_TYPE; the table is therefore not in the second normal form.

Figure 13.9 shows a hypothetical set of data for this table. Notice that every credit transaction carries the verification code of 001, every open account, 002, and every debit, 003. This is redundant information. This redundancy will cause problems when inserting, deleting, or updating data.

For example, if the bank policy changes the verification required for a debit, the verification code will have to be changed in all rows with debits. If only some of the rows are updated, we will have what is called an update anomaly, meaning an irregularity. If all of the transactions with a certain transaction type are deleted, this transaction type and its verification code will not be stored anywhere in the database and we will have a delete anomaly. Furthermore, if bank policy identifies a new transaction type and associated verification code, it cannot be inserted until there is an instance of such a transaction. Creating a separate TRANTYPE table to hold the transaction type and its associated verification code avoids these anomalies. The following tables are now in the second normal form:

```
TRANSACTION:
      TXN_TYPE
      TXN_TIMESTAMP
      TXN_AMOUNT
      TXN_ACCT_NO
Primary Key:  TXN_ACCT_NO + TXN_TYPE + TXN_TIMESTAMP
Foreign Key:  TXN_ACCT_NO
Foreign Key:  TXN_TYPE

TRANTYPE:
      TR_TYPE
      TR_VERIFY_CODE
Primary Key:  TR_TYPE
```

TRANTYPE to TRANSACTION is a one to many relationship. One transaction type may have zero to many transactions associated with it; one transaction must have one and only one transaction type associated with it. The primary key of the one side (TR_TYPE in the TRANTYPE table) is a foreign key in the many side (TXN_TYPE in the TRANSACTION table).

13.4.3 Third Normal Form

A table is considered to be in the third normal form if each nonkey attribute represents a fact about the whole key rather than another nonkey attribute. BRANCH table contains the following elements:

```
BRANCH:
     BRANCH_ID
     BRANCH_CITY
     BRANCH_ADDR
     BRANCH_GEO_RATING
Primary Key:  BRANCH_ID
```

The geographic rating (BRANCH_GEO_RATING) is generated by the marketing department based on the number of accounts in a city. This violates the third normal form. A nonkey attribute (BRANCH_GEO_RATING) represents a fact about another nonkey attribute (BRANCH_CITY). Again there is redundancy and the accompanying possibility of update and delete anomalies. Divide and conquer is our solution again:

```
BRANCH:
     BRANCH_ID
     BRANCH_CITY
     BRANCH_ADDR
Primary Key:  BRANCH_ID
Foreign Key:  BRANCH_CITY

CITY
     CITY_NAME
     CITY_GEO_CODE
Primary Key:  CITY_NAME
```

As with TRANTYPE and TRANSACTION, there is a one to many relationship between CITY and BRANCH. CITY's primary key is a foreign key in BRANCH. Figure 13.10 shows the model which is now in the third normal form. Three tables have been added—BONUS, TRANTYPE, and CITY.

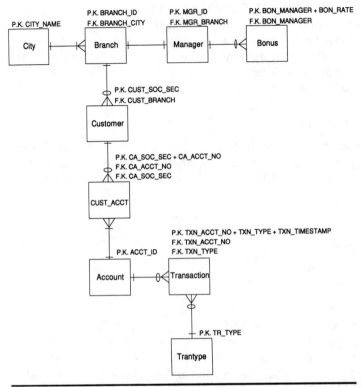

Figure 13.10 Tables are in the third normal form. Note:
P.K. = primary key and F.K. = foreign key.

The criteria for the three normal forms are summarized in Fig.
13.11. To some extent, stepping through all three normal forms is necessary only at the beginning. With experience, the process becomes integrated and it is not difficult to put a set of tables in third normal

```
A TABLE IS IN:

    FIRST NORMAL FORM
        if no more than one value exists for any attribute;

    SECOND NORMAL FORM
        if each non-key attribute represents a fact about the whole
        key, rather than only a part of the key;

    THIRD NORMAL FORM
        if each non-key attribute represents a fact about the
        whole key, rather than another non-key attribute.
```

Figure 13.11 The criteria for the three normal forms.

form in one pass. A helpful mnemonic for remembering the goal of the three normal forms is:

Let each nonkey attribute represent a fact about the key, the whole key, and nothing but the key.

13.4.4 Denormalization

Normalization results in more tables with smaller attribute sets. Retrieving data from more than one table requires a join operation, which means processing overhead. A completely normalized design, therefore, is not always the optimum solution in practice. The process of selectively combining tables by inserting redundant nonkey data columns, is called denormalization. Although this topic falls more traditionally into the realm of physical design, it is something with which you should be familiar.

The decision to denormalize is based primarily on usage. Since the objective of normalization is to eliminate update anomalies, if tables will be used only in retrieval mode, they become candidates for denormalization. For tables that will be updated, the decision to denormalize will be made by weighing factors such as usage, table size, environment, etc. Again, these decisions will probably be made in the context of the physical design phase.

13.5 REFERENTIAL INTEGRITY DECISIONS

In a relational database, relationships among data are maintained through foreign keys. Referential integrity refers to the integrity of foreign key references. Rules must be established to maintain this integrity when insert, delete, and update operations are performed. Selecting the rules appropriate to the business requirements is part of the design process.

You can choose from three possible rules to maintain referential integrity when deleting rows from a parent table: CASCADE, RESTRICT, and SET NULL. You should specify CASCADE if you want the deletion of a row from a parent table to be propagated to associated rows in dependent tables. For example, if CASCADE were defined for the BRANCH-CUSTOMER relationship, deleting a branch would mean that all of its customers would also be deleted from the database. The RESTRICT option is used if you want to prevent a row in a parent table from being deleted when associated rows still exist in dependent tables. In this case, deleting a branch would not be allowed if the database contained at least one customer who belonged to that branch. If the third option, SET NULL, is specified, the deletion of a row from a parent table will mean that a foreign key column in each associated row will be set to null. With this option, the branch attribute of the customers who belonged to a branch that was deleted would be set to null. Choosing this design option will affect the physical design of the database because at least one column in the foreign key will have to be defined as null.

The same options apply to updating a column that is part of the primary key of a parent table. However, in DB2's implementation of referential integrity, the only option supported for update is RESTRICT. If your business rules require an option other than RESTRICT, it must be implemented physically through application programs rather than through the automatic referential integrity feature of DB2.

We've described a methodology for logical database design which we think you will find a practical and useful guide. If you understand the principles of entities and relationships, normalization, and referential integrity, you should be able to produce a model of a database which the DBA group can then refine for physical requirements. Once the final database design is arrived at, the next step will be to physically create the objects that make up the database. The Data Definition Language (DDL) component of SQL is used for this purpose. Both DDL and Data Control Language (DCL) are described in the next chapter.

14

Data Definition and Data Control

In Part 2 you were introduced to the data manipulation component of SQL, Data Manipulation Language (DML). In this chapter you will learn about SQL's remaining two components, Data Definition Language (DDL) and Data Control Language (DCL). DDL is used to create, alter, and delete DB2 objects such as tables, indexes, etc. DCL controls access to DB2 objects, their underlying data, application plans, and bufferpools.

Unlike DML, which manipulates data in the database, the effect of every DDL and DCL statement is to update the DB2 Catalog. For example, anytime a DB2 object is created or altered with DDL, its description is automatically stored in the Catalog. Information about authorizations granted or revoked by DCL is maintained in the Catalog as well. Although as an applications programmer you may not need to use these statements in your own work, understanding how they function will help you communicate your needs to the DBA who uses them in your behalf.

14.1 DDL—CREATING DB2 OBJECTS

The CREATE statement is used to create DB2 objects. In Chap. 2 we described these objects—storage group, database, tablespace, table, index, and view. Now we will show you the DDL that is used to create them. Indexspace was on our list of objects in Chap. 2, but since indexspaces are created automatically by DB2 when an index is created, there is no DDL associated with their creation. We will use examples to illustrate syntax and refer you to App. C for generic syntax diagrams.

DB2 objects must be created according to the hierarchy shown in Fig. 14.1. Reading down the chart, a storage group must be created before a database, which must be created prior to the creation of a tablespace, which in turn must be created prior to the creation of a

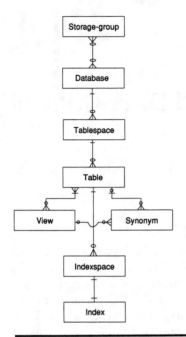

Figure 14.1   Hierarchy of DB2 objects.

table, etc. We will follow the hierarchical sequence in describing each object's CREATE statement.

The general format of the CREATE statement is:

```
CREATE objecttype objectname
    parameters
```

where *objecttype* is a valid object in DB2 and *objectname* is its name. The parameters differ for each object type. DB2 provides defaults for most of them and we will only show the more commonly used ones in our examples.

14.1.1   Storage Groups

A storage group is a set of DASD volumes. When you assign an indexspace or tablespace to a storage group, DB2 automatically creates the VSAM datasets needed for these spaces on the storage group's volumes. A storage group is created using the CREATE STOGROUP statement:

```
CREATE STOGROUP SGSAMPLE
    VOLUMES (VOL1, VOL2, VOL3)
    VCAT AAA
```

The name of the storage group here is SGSAMPLE. Any VSAM datasets created for storage group SGSAMPLE will be allocated to either VOL1, VOL2, or VOL3 by DB2. You cannot tell DB2 which volume to use. The only way to enforce placement of a dataset on a specific volume is to associate only one volume with the storage group.

The VCAT parameter is required. It identifies the user catalog in which entries will be made for the datasets created by SGSAMPLE. By definition, it is also the highest-level qualifier for each dataset name. We've called it AAA, so the name of all of the datasets created for the storage group SGSAMPLE will start with AAA. If we were to create tablespaces and indexspaces specifying storage group SGSAMPLE, DB2 would create VSAM datasets grouped under the AAA qualifier. As in any other MVS system, the high-level qualifier on a dataset name points to the VCAT which is used by the operating system to identify the location of the dataset.

14.1.2 Database

A database is a set of tables, indexes, tablespaces and indexspaces. Most often, the objects in a database are logically related to each other, as in the tables and indexes of a particular application. A database is created using the CREATE DATABASE statement:

```
CREATE DATABASE DBBANK
    STOGROUP SGSAMPLE
    BUFFERPOOL BP0
```

The name of the database will be DBBANK. All of the tablespaces and indexspaces connected with this database, unless otherwise specified, will be associated with the SGSAMPLE storage group and will use the BP0 bufferpool to access data from secondary storage. If a storage group isn't specified for the database, the database will be associated with the SYSDEFLT default storage group.

The STOGROUP and BUFFERPOOL parameters are optional. They specify the storage group and bufferpool that tablespaces and indexspaces within this database will be associated with. The subsequent CREATE statements for tablespaces and indexspaces can either explicitly specify a different storage group or bufferpool or default to the values specified in the CREATE DATABASE statement.

14.1.3 Tablespace and Table

As you may remember from Chap. 2, a tablespace can be simple, partitioned, or segmented. The DDL used to create all of these tablespaces is similar; we will describe only the creation of a simple tablespace.

The CREATE TABLESPACE statement looks like this:

```
CREATE TABLESPACE TSBRANCH
  IN DBBANK
  USING STOGROUP SGSAMPLE
  BUFFERPOOL BP0
  LOCKSIZE PAGE
```

The name of the tablespace is TSBRANCH and it is part of the database DBBANK. The clauses USING STOGROUP SGSAMPLE and BUFFERPOOL BP0 are optional because the DBBANK database is already associated with storage group SGSAMPLE and bufferpool BP0. We have included them for illustration. These clauses would be required, however, if you wanted to associate the tablespace with a storage group other than SGSAMPLE or a bufferpool other than BP0. The USING clause can also specify the size (primary and secondary quantity) of the VSAM ESDS to be created. By not specifying the size, we have selected DB2's default values, i.e., one track for both the primary and secondary quantity.

The LOCKSIZE clause refers to the amount of storage DB2 will protect from other users when, for instance, an update is in progress. LOCKSIZE PAGE tells DB2 to lock data in the tablespace at the page level. With LOCKSIZE TABLESPACE, DB2 locks the entire tablespace rather than individual pages. By specifying LOCKSIZE ANY, you allow DB2 to choose the appropriate unit of locking. In this case, DB2 may initially select LOCKSIZE PAGE and then subsequently escalate to LOCKSIZE TABLESPACE when the number of page locks reaches an installation-specified number.

Of all of the DDL statements possible, the CREATE TABLE statement is probably the one that an application programmer is most likely to use. It includes the name of the table and the names and attributes of its columns. You may also specify optional attributes such as primary and foreign keys which, for the time being, we will omit from our discussion:

```
CREATE TABLE BRANCH
  (BRANCH_ID      SMALLINT          NOT NULL WITH DEFAULT,
   BRANCH_CITY    CHAR     (20)     NOT NULL WITH DEFAULT,
   BRANCH_MGR     CHAR     (25)     NOT NULL WITH DEFAULT,
   BRANCH_ADDR    VARCHAR  (25)     NOT NULL WITH DEFAULT)
  IN DBBANK.TSBRANCH
```

The full name of the table will be cataloged as *authid*.BRANCH, where *authid* is the identifier of the table owner, the person creating the table. The owner of the table can refer to it later as either BRANCH or *authid*.BRANCH; all other users must use the fully qualified name and refer to it as *authid*.BRANCH.

Data type	Default value
Numeric	0
Fixed length character string	Blanks
Variable length character string	A string of length 0
Date	Current date
Time	Current time
Timestamp	Current timestamp

Figure 14.2   Default values for data types.

The BRANCH table created by this DDL will have four columns: BRANCH_ID, BRANCH_CITY, BRANCH_MGR, and BRANCH_ADDR. The column names are followed by their data types, the length of each column for character and decimal data types, and whether null values are allowed in the column. The list of the column names in the CREATE TABLE statement must be enclosed within parentheses.

The NOT NULL WITH DEFAULT clause prevents the column from having null values and specifies a default value to be used if data for the specific column is missing. The default values DB2 uses depend on the data type of the column and are listed in Fig. 14.2. Another option is the NOT NULL clause, which prevents the column from having null values but does not specify a default. With this option, all of the rows of the table must have valid data in every column. If you do not use either the NOT NULL or NOT NULL WITH DEFAULT clause, the column may contain null values and the default value will be null.

The clause IN DBBANK.TSBRANCH names the tablespace in which the table will be created. Notice that when referring to the tablespace, we use the name of the database in which it resides as a qualifier. The rows of the BRANCH table will be stored on pages of the dataset associated with the TSBRANCH tablespace.

There are three clauses that are used to specify user-written routines which encode or decode values (FIELDPROC), edit entire rows (EDITPROC), or perform a validity check (VALIDPROC). In our own experience, we have not found them to be widely used, so we won't discuss them here.

14.1.4 Index

Indexes are used for efficient access to data. An index, IXBRANCH, on table BRANCH is created by the following:

```
CREATE UNIQUE INDEX IXBRANCH
   ON BRANCH
      (BRANCHID DESC)
   USING STOGROUP SGSAMP2
   SUBPAGES 8
   CLUSTER
```

Let's break this down. The ON clause specifies the name of the table and the column(s) on which the index is based. The index, IXBRANCH, will contain the values of the BRANCH table's BRANCH_ID column in descending order. The keyword UNIQUE, which is optional, specifies that each entry in the index must be unique. In our example, the value in BRANCH_ID may not occur more than once in the index and, therefore, in the table. This ensures that the BRANCH table will not contain duplicate rows. One criteria of the relational model is that the rows in a table must be unique. Therefore, although it is not required, each table should have at least one UNIQUE index.

The linkage between an index and a database is established implicitly through the name of the table. The table BRANCH was associated with the tablespace TSBRANCH in its CREATE TABLE statement and, in turn, TSBRANCH was associated with the database DBBANK in its CREATE TABLESPACE statement. Therefore, all indexes defined on table BRANCH, including IXBRANCH, will be associated with the database DBBANK.

Because of the association of IXBRANCH with DBBANK, index IXBRANCH's indexspace would use SGSAMPLE as the default storage group and BP0 as the default bufferpool if we had not specified otherwise through the USING clause. The USING clause is similar to that of the CREATE TABLESPACE statement and is required here because we are using a storage group that is different from the default.

Each index page physically consists of 4K bytes. However, we can logically divide each page into a maximum of 16 subpages. The subpage is the unit of locking for indexes. Therefore, when subpages are used, smaller amounts of storage are locked for each individual update and fewer users are kept waiting. There is a performance trade-off for this increased concurrency because more locks may have to be taken and because inserts to the index may be less efficient, so the choice of SUBPAGES is a physical design issue. The number of subpages we want to use is specified through the SUBPAGES parameter.

The optional CLUSTER parameter defines IXBRANCH as the clustering index for table TSBRANCH. A clustering index tells DB2 to physically store the rows of a table in the same sequence as the entries in its index. By definition, it specifies the fastest path for sequential access. An index for a table in a partitioned tablespace differs in that a CLUSTER clause is required and that its format is extended to include the specification of index ranges for each partition. When the rows of the partitioned table are loaded, they are placed into a partition depending upon the value of the clustering index.

14.1.5 Primary and Foreign Key

The primary and foreign keys of a table specify the referential integrity rules. They are created through either the CREATE TABLE or ALTER TABLE statements.

A primary key is optional and may be established for any table. You'll remember that it consists of those columns that are required to ensure a row's uniqueness within a table. In Chap. 2 we learned that a foreign key consists of those columns in a dependent table that are the same as the primary key in the parent table. Let's see how both of these types of keys are established.

Creating a primary key is fairly straightforward. Let's expand our BRANCH table definition to illustrate the use of the PRIMARY KEY clause in the CREATE TABLE statement:

```
CREATE TABLE BRANCH
    (BRANCHID        SMALLINT              NOT NULL WITH DEFAULT,
     BRANCHCITY      CHAR     (20)         NOT NULL WITH DEFAULT,
     BRANCHMGR       CHAR     (25)         NOT NULL WITH DEFAULT,
     BRANCHADDR      VARCHAR  (25)         NOT NULL WITH DEFAULT,
     PRIMARY KEY (BRANCHID))
    IN DBBANK.TSBRANCH
```

Notice that we've added a PRIMARY KEY clause before the IN *database* clause.

Creating a foreign key is more involved because it assumes that the creation of a primary key in the parent table has already taken place. The sequence of primary and foreign key creation can be quite complicated if, for example, a table is self-referencing, in which case a table acts as both the parent and the dependent table. (An example of this is an employee table where an employee may manage an employee.) For clarity of presentation, we will describe the simplest scenario of creating two tables. The parent table is BRANCH as defined above, and the dependent table is CUSTOMER.

The CREATE TABLE statement for the dependent CUSTOMER table is:

```
CREATE TABLE CUSTOMER
    (CUST_SOC_SEC          INTEGER      NOT NULL WITH DEFAULT,
    CUST_FIRST_NAME        CHAR(10),
    CUST_LAST_NAME         CHAR(15),
    CUST_DATE_OF_BIRTH     CHAR(10)     NOT NULL WITH DEFAULT,
    CUST_BRANCH            SMALLINT     NOT NULL WITH DEFAULT,
    CUST_RATING            SMALLINT     NOT NULL WITH DEFAULT,
    PRIMARY KEY (CUST_SOC_SEC),
    FOREIGN KEY RC1BR (CUST_BRANCH) REFERENCES BRANCH
        ON DELETE RESTRICT)
    IN DBBANK.TSCUST
```

You should be familiar with everything down to the FOREIGN KEY clause. The CUSTOMER table has a primary key, CUST_SOC_SEC, and a foreign key, CUST_BRANCH. The FOREIGN KEY clause establishes that the customer table has a dependent relationship with the BRANCH table, called a referential constraint (*it is "constrained" from certain operations because of its dependent relationship*). A table may have any number of referential constraints and associated FOREIGN KEY clauses.

A referential constraint may be given a name; we've called it RC1BR. If a name is not specified explicitly, DB2 generates one automatically using the first eight characters of the name of the first column in the foreign key. By definition, a foreign key in a dependent table always references the primary key of its parent table. Therefore, DB2 automatically knows that the referential constraint RC1BR links CUST_BRANCH in the CUSTOMER table with the BRANCH table's primary key, BRANCH_ID.

Remember that the foreign key of a dependent table must have properties similar to the primary key of its parent table. It must have the same number and description of columns, but column names, default values, and null attributes may be different. In addition, the columns may be stored in a different sort sequence, i.e., ascending or descending.

A referential constraint may be associated with a specific delete rule through the ON DELETE clause. The choices are RESTRICT, CASCADE, and SET NULL. ON DELETE specifies the action to be taken if a DELETE statement is executed on a row in a parent table. If RESTRICT, the default, is specified and that row has an associated row in a dependent table, the DELETE operation will fail. If CASCADE is specified, associated rows in dependent tables are also DELETED. This can be dangerous and can magnify the consequences of programming errors. If SET NULL is specified, the foreign key columns of associated rows in dependent tables are set to null. With this option, a foreign key column must have been defined to permit nulls.

14.1.6 View and Synonym

Views, you may remember, are virtual tables that are derived from one or more base tables or views. Synonyms, which we have not discussed previously, are alternate names for tables or views. Both views and synonyms are "logical objects" whose definitions are stored in the DB2 Catalog. When a view or a synonym is referenced, these definitions are used to translate the queries into queries against the underlying base tables.

A view is defined through a SQL SELECT statement embedded within a CREATE:

```
CREATE VIEW CUSTNAME
    (SOC_SEC,FIRST_AND_LAST)
    AS SELECT CUST_SOC_SEC,  CUST_NAME
        FROM CUSTOMER
        WHERE CUST_SOC_SEC < 700000000
WITH CHECK OPTION
```

We're creating a view called CUSTNAME which consists of two columns from the CUSTOMER table. If the column names of the view are not specified, DB2 will use the column names from the underlying base table. The columns in our view have been renamed to SOC_SEC and FIRST_AND_LAST. The SELECT statement used to define the view may be any valid SQL statement. It may not, however, contain an ORDER BY clause or a UNION. It can refer to any previously defined table or view and may also include a join.

The WITH CHECK OPTION, which is not required, specifies that DB2 will verify all updates against the view definition before attempting the update. This will prevent legal but illogical operations against the view. For instance, in the CUSTNAME view defined above, if we performed an update to change all social security numbers to 750000000, we would have a view with no rows, since the view definition specifies that the social security number be less than 700000000. The WITH CHECK OPTION would prevent this update.

Synonyms are created as follows:

```
CREATE SYNONYM CUST
        FOR USER1.CUSTOMER
```

USER1.CUSTOMER is the fully qualified name of the CUSTOMER table. Here we've specified that we want to call the table CUST for short. The synonym CUST can now be used in place of the fully qualified name as follows:

```
SELECT *
    FROM CUST
```

The synonym CUST is valid only for the user who owns it. Remember, you can use a table's unqualified name in a program and then use synonyms to associate it with different high-level qualifiers, e.g., TEST or PROD.

14.2 ALTERING DB2 OBJECTS

The ALTER SQL statement provides you with a limited ability to modify the attributes of the objects which comprise the physical layer of DB2's data definition architecture—storage group, index, tablespace, and table. The remaining DB2 objects can only be modified by deleting and redefining them.

14.2.1 Altering Storage Group, Index, Tablespace

Alteration of storage groups, indexes, and tablespaces affects their physical attributes. For example, you can add or remove DASD volumes from storage groups or change the bufferpool names and the space allocations of the VSAM ESDSs associated with indexspaces and tablespaces. The ALTER INDEX statement names an index but is actually used to modify attributes of the indexspace that contain the index. The most commonly used ALTER statement is ALTER TABLE.

14.2.2 ALTER TABLE

Prior to DB2 version 2.1, the ALTER TABLE statement was primarily used to add columns to existing tables. Now, its scope has been expanded significantly and it is the main implementation vehicle for referential integrity. The ALTER TABLE statement can be used to create and drop primary and foreign keys. It may seem a little odd that the ALTER statement should be used to create and drop keys, but this is semantically accurate because primary and foreign keys are not DB2 objects. The only DB2 object involved in the operation, the table, is indeed being altered.

The CREATE TABLE statement defines primary and foreign keys, but ALTER TABLE is more flexible and is sometimes required. For example, an employee table might be a parent table and a dependent table (employees manage employees) at the same time. This is called a self-referencing table. The CREATE TABLE statement cannot be used to define foreign keys for self-referencing tables, but ALTER TABLE can be used to add the foreign keys after the table is created with its primary key.

14.3   DROPPING DB2 OBJECTS

The SQL DROP statement is used to delete a specific DB2 object such as a particular table or index. It accomplishes the deletion by removing the target object from the DB2 Catalog and automatically dropping all other objects that are below the target in the object hierarchy. This is a cascading delete. So, if we drop the DBBANK database, all tablespaces, tables, indexes, views, and synonyms in our sample database will also be dropped. Incidentally, this is a good example of how DB2 maintains referential integrity within its own system tables in the DB2 Catalog.

The syntax of the DROP statement is:

DROP *objecttype objectname*

where *objecttype* is a valid DB2 object such as a table, tablespace, etc., and *objectname* is its name. The only exception to the cascading delete rule in DB2 objects is the DROP STOGROUP statement. DB2 does not permit the execution of this statement as long as there is a tablespace or indexspace residing within the target storage group.

14.4   DATA CONTROL LANGUAGE

Data Control Language (DCL) is the third and final component of DB2's SQL language. Before we describe the syntax of DCL, let's review the terminology and concepts of DB2's security and authorization mechanism, of which DCL is one part.

Security in the DB2 environment consists of many different layers. At the highest level, when you use DB2, you don't log on to DB2 directly but to one of the three main DB2 attachments (TSO, CICS, IMS) instead. Software products like ACF2, RACF, TOP SECRET, etc., control access to DB2 attachments, verify the user, authenticate the connection between the attachment and DB2, and prevent unauthorized access to the VSAM ESDSs. Views may also be used as part of a security plan.

DB2 internal security requires that all users have the authority to perform each of the tasks required to complete their jobs. For example, to create the database DBBANK, a user must be authorized to create databases; to read data from the BRANCH table, a user must be authorized to SELECT data from BRANCH; to use tablespace TSBRANCH, a user must be authorized to use that tablespace. The authorization(s) can be either explicit or implicit. All authorizations are enabled through the GRANT statement and withdrawn by the REVOKE statement. Both GRANT and REVOKE are part of DCL.

14.4.1 Resources and Privileges

Security in DB2 is based on resources to be protected and privileges assigned to a user. Users are assigned privileges that entitle them to access specific DB2 resource(s). There are five major categories of privileges: table, database, plan, use, and system. Each privilege permits only authorized users to access the resource in question. The following is a summary of the types of privileges that may be granted and what they include:

1. Table privileges control the execution of the SELECT, DELETE, UPDATE, INSERT, ALTER, and CREATE INDEX SQL statements on specific tables or views.

2. Database privileges control the execution of CREATETAB, CREATETS, and DROP statements, as well as the execution of DB2 commands and DB2 utilities on specific databases.

3. Plan privileges control the execution of the DSN subcommands BIND (creation), REBIND (replacement), FREE (deletion), and EXECUTE (invocation) against specific plans. These are described in Chap. 12.

4. Use privileges provide authorization to use specific bufferpools, storage groups, or tablespaces.

5. System privileges apply to operations (e.g., -STOP DB2, -START TRACE) on the DB2 subsystem.

14.4.2 Grouped Privileges

For operational convenience, DB2 combines individual privileges into units called grouped privileges or administrative privileges. A user who is given a grouped privilege, such as DBADM (database administrator), is granted all of the individual privileges that the group includes. For DBADM, this would include LOAD, CREATETAB, etc. Grouped privileges are typically assigned to special users like the DBA and system operators.

The individual components of each grouped privilege are shown in Fig. 14.3. Note the hierarchical relationship between SYSADM (system administrator) and SYSOPR (system operator) and between SYSADM, DBADM, DBCTRL (database control), and DBMAINT (database maintenance). DBMAINT includes only the authorities needed to maintain a database, i.e., to create a table or tablespace, run utilities that do not update the database, etc. DBCTRL has all of the privileges of DBMAINT and also has the ability to DROP objects and run other utilities that update the database. DBADM has all of the privi-

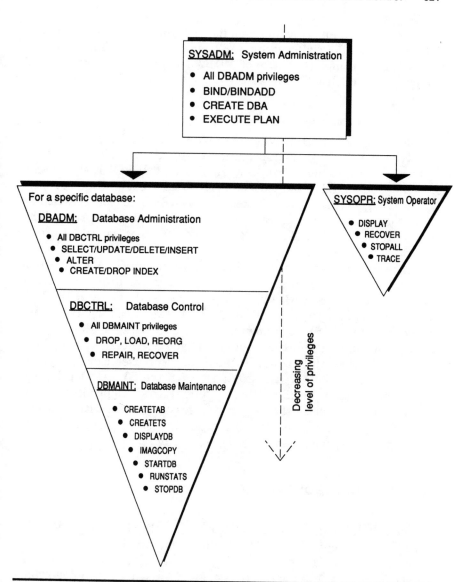

Figure 14.3 DB2's grouped privileges.

leges of DBCTRL and also has complete control over a particular DB2 database and all privileges on DB2 objects within that database. SYSADM has complete control of a DB2 subsystem. It includes all of the privileges of DBADM as well as some unique to itself.

14.4.3   Explicit and Implicit Authorization

Now let's look at how a privilege is given and withdrawn, either explicitly or implicitly. This information is stored in DB2's Catalog.

With explicit authorization, the GRANT and REVOKE statements of DCL tell the DB2 authorization mechanism to give a user the specified privilege (GRANT) or to take it away (REVOKE) for a particular DB2 resource. If the resource is an object, it must exist prior to the execution of the GRANT. The REVOKE statement cancels a previously granted privilege.

With implicit authorization, DB2 issues internal GRANT and REVOKE statements when a new object is created or dropped. USER1 has been granted the CREATETAB privilege on database DBBANK. Based on this privilege, USER1 creates the table BRANCH and inserts data into it. USER1 is now implicitly authorized to alter or drop the table, create an index or view for it, and execute, select, update, insert, and delete statements. In addition, this user can also grant these privileges to other users. A user with the SYSADM privilege who attempts to revoke any of these implicitly granted privileges from USER1, will be unsuccessful. The privileges can only be withdrawn by dropping the table BRANCH. This example also illustrates the fact that implicit privileges can never be explicitly revoked.

14.5   DATA CONTROL LANGUAGE STATEMENTS

The data control component of SQL consists of the GRANT, REVOKE, and SET statements. The GRANT statement explicitly gives a user the privilege(s) to access a specific resource or resources. The REVOKE statement takes the privilege(s) away. Only a privilege that has been explicitly granted can be revoked. The SET statement is a version 2.1 extension. It sets the current SQLID to a particular user. The basic format of these statements is discussed in the following sections.

14.5.1   GRANT

The GRANT statement authorizes user(s) to either single or grouped privileges on a DB2 resource or a set of DB2 resources. If the resource is a DB2 object, it must exist before the GRANT statement is executed.

You can grant privileges to one or several auth IDs in the same GRANT statement. You can also grant privileges to PUBLIC, which means that all DB2 users are granted those privileges. PUBLIC is a reserved word and should not be assigned to any user as an auth ID. The general form of the GRANT statement is:

GRANT *privilege* ON *resource* TO *authid*

Examples of how it is used are:

1. The SELECT and UPDATE privileges on resource BRANCH are granted to all users (PUBLIC):

   GRANT SELECT, UPDATE ON TABLE BRANCH TO PUBLIC

2. Here, USER1 and USER2 are granted the SYSADM privilege. Since SYSADM by definition has access to all resources of DB2, we did not have to include a specific resource in the GRANT statement itself:

   GRANT SYSADM TO USER1, USER2

3. Here, USER3 can use the DB2 LOAD utility to load data into any table or index in database DBBANK and can also pass this privilege on to another user. WITH GRANT OPTION entitles the user(s) named in the GRANT statement to provide the same privileges they have to other users. In contrast to the second example, we have to specify a specific resource in this example because the LOAD utility is not a systemwide privilege:

   GRANT LOAD ON DATABASE DBBANK TO USER3 WITH GRANT OPTION

4. In this example, use of the BP0 resource is granted to all users.

   GRANT USE OF BUFFERPOOL BP0 TO PUBLIC

14.5.2 REVOKE

The REVOKE statement cancels a privilege previously given explicitly through a GRANT statement. The format is similar to that of GRANT:

REVOKE *privilege* ON *resource* BY *authid*

Examples of this follow:

1. REVOKE SELECT ON TABLE BRANCH FROM PUBLIC

When a privilege is revoked from PUBLIC, auth IDs that were specifically granted that privilege will still have it. You can think of it as the privilege being revoked from the general public, but all private citizens (users) who were specifically granted SELECT on table BRANCH will continue to possess it. Those who were granted it implicitly will also retain the authority.

2. REVOKE CREATETAB FROM USER1 BY ALL

In this example, the statement revokes the CREATETAB privilege from USER1, no matter who granted it. BY ALL means "granted by anyone." You must be the SYSADM to have the authority to revoke a privilege granted by someone else.

The REVOKE statement has a cascading effect. If a higher-level privilege is revoked, all privileges derived from it will also be deleted. This is especially important to remember for the grouped privileges. For example, suppose you are the creator of the BRANCH table, and you grant all privileges on it to USER1 with the GRANT option. USER1 in turn grants SELECT on BRANCH to USER2 with the grant option. USER2 grants SELECT on BRANCH to USER3. Now, suppose USER1 quits and you revoke his or her privileges on BRANCH. USER2 and USER3 will now be unable to access BRANCH table.

14.6 PRIMARY AND SECONDARY AUTH IDs

DB2 identifies each user with an authorization ID. Prior to version 2.1, DB2 used individual user identifiers. One user was associated with only one auth ID, which was synonymous with his or her user ID, typically the log-on ID in TSO. This approach caused operational problems, especially when a user was reassigned or left a job.

With version 2.1, DB2 has overcome these problems by adding support for function-oriented identifiers. Simply put, one user (person) can now have multiple identifiers. Besides a primary auth ID, a user can also have a secondary auth ID which is identified with a department or project team, for example. Differentiating primary and secondary auth ID's for a user ID is done through special DB2 assembly language exit routines. If no exit routine is specified, the default will make the user ID equal to the primary auth ID.

One additional concept is that of the current SQLID. The current SQLID is the auth ID that is associated with a user ID at any particular time. The default is the primary auth ID. You can change the current SQLID via the SET SQL statement or an exit routine.

Another new feature of DB2 security is the differentiation between creator and owner. A user may create an object with a secondary auth ID as its owner (e.g., APPL1). This makes the owner of the object the project or team, so that if the user leaves the company, the objects he or she created will not be affected when his or her user ID is dropped. A new programmer can be given the secondary auth ID APPL1, entitling him or her to all of the privileges required for the application.

14.6.1 SET

The SET statement is used to establish a current SQLID. It may be embedded in an application program or issued interactively. Its format is:

```
SET CURRENT SQLID = USER or string constant or host variable
```

The USER option sets the current SQLID to the primary auth ID of the person issuing the SET statement. A string constant or host variable allows you to set the CURRENT SQLID to an auth ID supplied as a literal or in a host variable.

14.7 DB2 CATALOG TABLES FOR SECURITY

DB2 privileges are grouped into five categories—table, database, plan, use, and system. DB2 maintains a table for each category in its Catalog to track user privileges. DB2 uses another table to track privileges on specific columns of a table. These six tables are collectively called the authorization tables. The suffix of the name of each table is AUTH. These tables, along with a brief description, are listed in Fig. 14.4. The authorization tables are used by the authorization mechanism of DB2 to verify a user's privileges against DB2 resources. They

TABLE NAME	DESCRIPTION
	Records privileges held by auth-id's over:
SYSIBM.SYSCOLAUTH	specific columns in tables and views
SYSIBM.SYSTABAUTH	tables and views
SYSIBM.SYSDBAUTH	databases
SYSIBM.SYSPLANAUTH	application plans
SYSIBM.SYSUSERAUTH	the DB2 subsystem
SYSIBM.SYSRESAUTH	tablespaces, storage groups and bufferpools

Figure 14.4 DB2 catalog tables used for security.

can be queried by SQL statements and are periodically used by security personnel (in conjunction with the audit log) to monitor access to the DB2 subsystem.

This chapter has covered many topics. Within DDL you learned the syntax for the CREATE, ALTER, and DROP, statements. For DCL, we first broke down privileges into five categories (e.g., table privileges, database privileges, etc.) and then looked at the difference between implicit and explicit privileges. For the latter, we covered the syntax for GRANT and REVOKE. While DDL and DCL are most often used by DBAs, application programmers often find the statements useful for setting up test tables and performing routine tasks during application development.

Miscellaneous Topics

DB2 Performance

In this chapter we look at performance issues, focusing on those that are most relevant to you as an application programmer. Part of this discussion will focus on what DB2 does internally at execution time to process SQL data manipulation statements. Aspects of DB2 relevant to performance, like indexes, access paths, and sorts, will be described with performance guidelines given where appropriate.

15.1 WHEN A REQUEST IS MADE FOR DATA

Let's begin by looking at what happens when a request is made for data. We'll use our sample program, PROGRAM1 for the examples.

15.1.1 Initial Procedures

You may remember from Chap. 12 that executing a program which accesses DB2 involves running the TSO Terminal Monitor Program (TMP) and invoking DSN. When PROGRAM1 is run, the TMP invokes DSN, which makes the necessary connection to DB2 and then passes control to the application. The execution of the first SQL statement in PROGRAM1 triggers several events. A thread is created connecting DB2 to this program. The user ID is passed to DB2. It is used to verify whether the user is authorized to execute the specified plan. Needed resources including the database descriptor (DBD) and segments of the plan are copied by DB2 into the Data Base Services address space. (Remember, the plan includes information about the tables and indexes required to access the data.) At this time, DB2 also compares the timestamps on the load module and plan to verify that they match.

15.1.2 SQL Processing

DB2 is now ready to process the first SQL statement. All SQL statements are processed by the Data Base Services component of DB2. It uses the application plan and the access paths defined in it to decide what data and index rows are needed from the database and then it uses the information in the DBD to locate these rows. The required locking is done and the rows are then retrieved if they are not already in buffers. DB2 then processes the retrieved data to produce the requested result table. If an update is requested, a before and after image of the changed data is written in the DB2 log before the change is committed to the database. As the program progresses, each SQL statement is processed similarly. As you may remember, your program doesn't actually contain SQL statements. It contains the calls to DB2 which were inserted in place of the SQL statement at precompile time.

15.1.3 COMMIT and Thread Termination

At the end of the program, the thread is terminated, all DB2 resources are released by removing the locks, and a COMMIT is issued by DB2. You'll remember from our previous discussions that at the time of COMMIT, all updated DB2 log records are written to DASD. If the RELEASE option of the BIND command is specified as COMMIT (as it is in PROGRAM1), all DB2 resources will be released when the COMMIT takes place. COMMITs may also be explicitly coded in a program (e.g., EXEC SQL COMMIT END-EXEC for a batch COBOL program). In PROGRAM1, the RELEASE option of the BIND command makes no difference because no explicit COMMIT statements are coded within the program. The only COMMIT statement executed is that issued by DB2 at program termination.

15.2 DATA BASE SERVICES

We mentioned earlier that SQL statements are processed by the Data Base Services component of DB2. Let's take a look at how the subcomponents of Data Base Services—Relational Data System (RDS), Data Manager (DM), and Buffer Manager (BM)—work together to process SQL statements. These subcomponents are illustrated in Fig. 15.1.

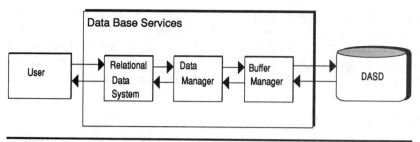

Figure 15.1   Components of Data Base Services.

15.2.1   Relational Data System

It is the RDS subcomponent of Data Base Services which controls the execution of SQL statements and is the interface to your application program or your interactive query. The RDS, in fact, provides the relational capability to DB2. At BIND time, it is the RDS that generates an application plan which describes the access path and processing required to satisfy each SQL request and then, at execution time, invokes the Data Manager component to access the data. If the condition upon which rows are to be selected is simple, the Data Manager can perform the selection. With more complicated selection criteria, the Data Manager must pass every row that it retrieves to the RDS for further processing. A statement which must be processed by the RDS as well as the Data Manager will automatically be less efficient.

15.2.2   Data Manager

The Data Manager can be viewed as a high-level access mechanism which manages the data stored in DB2 databases. The Data Manager, as per the RDS's instructions, performs either a sequential read of the tablespace or uses an index to randomly access table data. As you know, data in DB2 databases is written on DASD in 4K blocks called pages. The Data Manager retrieves data from DASD by identifying the desired page within a tablespace or an indexspace and then passing this information to the Buffer Manager—the component which is responsible for the actual reading from and writing to DASD.

15.2.3   Buffer Manager

The Buffer Manager invokes the VSAM media manager to transfer the 4K pages from DASD into virtual storage. In DB2, as in most modern DBMSs, virtual storage is used to minimize the time a request has to wait for data. In DB2, this virtual storage is called a bufferpool. The

Buffer Manager is responsible for managing the bufferpools. In fact, from a performance standpoint, the Buffer Manager is clearly the heart of DB2. The Buffer Manager uses a very efficient algorithm to manage large bufferpools to satisfy the twin goals of performance: reduced DASD I/O and fast recovery from system errors.

15.3   INDEXES IN DB2

Let's look now at indexes, which figure prominently in any discussion of performance. For each table in DB2, you can create one or more indexes. Indexes are used by DB2 to implement the primary key and referential integrity concepts of the relational model, ensure uniqueness of rows within a table, and improve performance. In this chapter, we will concentrate on the performance aspect of indexes.

15.3.1   Structure of Indexes

DB2 uses the balanced tree (B-tree) structure to implement indexes. As illustrated in Fig. 15.2, the B-tree looks like an inverted tree with its root (root page) at the top and its leaves (leaf pages) at the bottom. Index entries are distributed across the entire tree and contain index values and pointers. The index values are drawn from the column(s)

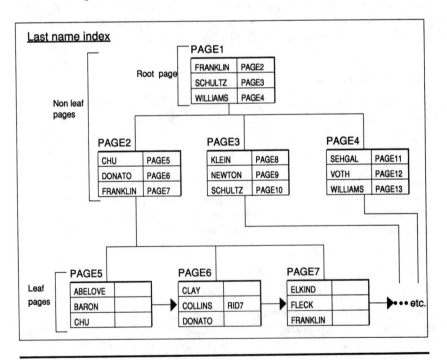

Figure 15.2   The B-tree index.

specified in the CREATE INDEX statements. The pointers on the leaf pages are row identifiers (RIDs) that point the way to the table row(s) that contain that value. If the index is unique, only one row is associated with each indexed value on a leaf page; if the index is nonunique, multiple rows are associated with each indexed value.

The B-tree always has one root page. If the index size is only one page, the root page will also be a leaf page. Otherwise it will be a nonleaf page (any page whose entries do not point to table data is considered a nonleaf page), as in Fig. 15.2. When the number of leaf pages is so large that the space on the root page is not large enough to contain the index entries which point to them, an additional intermediate level is required (PAGE2, PAGE3, and PAGE4 in the figure). A large index may need more than one intermediate level. A B-tree index may consist of only the root page or the root page and leaf pages or the root page, the leaf pages, and a number of intermediate levels.

The index in Fig. 15.2 is created from the last name column of a CUSTOMER table. To obtain the page and row address for the name COLLINS, the search begins with the root page. The root has three entries, each of which indicates the last entry on a page on the next level. Names greater than A and less than or equal to FRANKLIN are on PAGE2. Names greater than FRANKLIN and less than or equal to SCHULTZ are on PAGE3, etc. In this way the search reads a page per level until it gets to the leaf page. The leaf page points to the specific page and row on which that value, COLLINS, can be found.

As Fig. 15.2 illustrates, all leaf pages are equidistant from the root page and three I/Os, one for each level, are required to randomly access a specific leaf page. In fact, in a B-tree, the number of I/Os required to randomly access a value in the index is always equal to the number of levels in the index. This ensures consistent performance because the I/O required to access a particular index entry is independent of its value.

In addition to the pointers that lead the way down the tree, there are also pointers that connect each leaf page to the next one. We have illustrated this with arrows going from leaf page across to leaf page. We could find the name FRANKLIN by beginning with the first leaf page, PAGE5, and continuing to scan on PAGE6, etc. This feature provides the ability to efficiently scan the index sequentially. This is an important feature of DB2's index structure because it provides a second path through an index. Index access can either go down the tree structure or across the leaf pages.

15.3.2 Clustered Index

Indexes can be clustered or nonclustered. The difference has to do with how they affect the DB2 tables they are associated with, not

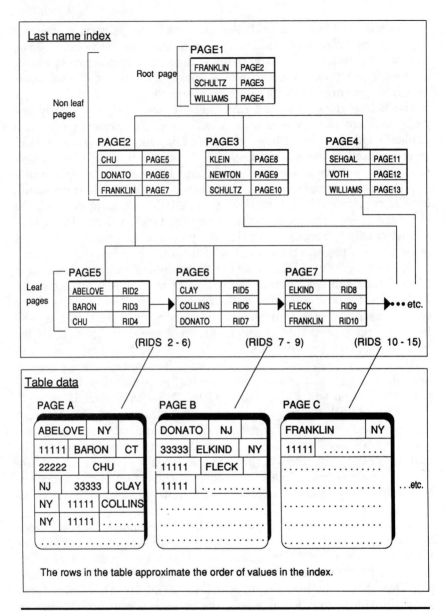

Figure 15.3   A clustered index requires less I/O.

how they themselves are stored. A clustering index causes the rows
of the table to be stored in a physical order that approximates the
order of the index entries. A table can have only one clustering index because rows can have only one physical order. If 95 percent of
the table rows are in clustering order and an index is created with

the CLUSTER parameter, DB2 marks the index as clustered in the Catalog. A clustered index may become unclustered if a large number of rows are inserted into the table later. A DBA usually monitors a database to ensure that all clustering indexes are actually clustered and uses the REORG utility (described in Chap. 17) to restore clustering when needed. Clustering indexes are important because they provide efficient access to the table data and can have a major impact on I/O and thereby on DB2's performance. In fact, given a choice, DB2's Optimizer will always select an access path that is based on the clustering index.

Figures 15.3 and 15.4 show how clustering indexes provide efficient access. These diagrams assume a unique index on the name column of the CUSTOMER table. In each illustration, the index I/O is the same for a given name. Let's look at how the index would be used to find the names ABELOVE, BARON, and CHU. Starting at the root page, PAGE1, in both figures, we are pointed to PAGE2 and then to PAGE5. The index I/O is the same for the clustered and nonclustered index. However, the table I/O is different. With the clustered index (Fig. 15.3), the data for all three rows can be found on one page, PAGEA, which means one I/O. With the nonclustered index (Fig. 15.4), first PAGEB is read for the name ABELOVE, and then there is a second I/O for the name BARON, which is on PAGEA. There is no additional I/O for the name CHU because DB2 finds that page already in its buffer. You can see how the difference in I/O can be substantial for a large table. For example, if a table contains 50 rows on a page and a specific index value can be found on 5000 rows, then 100 I/Os are required to access the 5000 rows if the index is clustered, compared with a maximum of 5000 I/Os if the index is not clustered.

15.3.3 Benefits and Costs of Index

In general, indexes improve performance because they provide a more efficient access path to data in a table. Clustered indexes are preferable to nonclustered indexes.

While indexes can improve performance, they are also expensive. Even in this age of cheap DASD, users may balk when they get their DASD utilization bill. In addition, indexes increase operational costs. For example, every index requires an indexspace and a dataset, which means more maintenance time. Also, there is a higher probability of locking problems on indexspaces than on tablespaces because a lock on an indexspace page will lock many more index entries than a corresponding lock on a tablespace page. On top of these costs, also remember that if a column that is part of

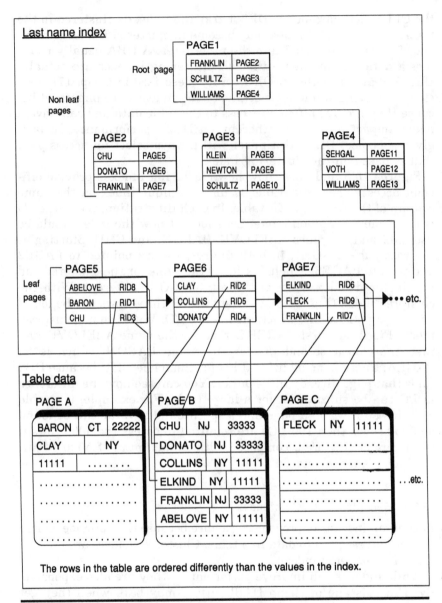

Figure 15.4.   A nonclustered index requires more I/O.

an index is updated, performance degrades because both the index and the table data have to be updated. Therefore, before deciding to use indexes in a production environment, a DBA should ensure that the benefits outweigh the costs for each index within the particular application.

15.4 ACCESS PATHS

Data may be accessed through either a sequential tablespace scan or through an index. We saw that the B-tree index structure provides two routes to data. These two types of index access are matching index scan and nonmatching index scan.

15.4.1 Tablespace Scans

Reading a tablespace sequentially is called a tablespace scan, which means that every row in the table is read. Tablespace scans differ for segmented and nonsegmented tablespaces. When the tablespace is nonsegmented, all of the rows in all of the pages in the tablespace are read. If the tablespace is segmented, only the rows in pages that belong to the table specified in the SQL statement are read.

15.4.2 Matching and Nonmatching Index Scans

A matching index scan is executed by the Data Manager, which reads the index tree to access leaf pages that contain the required index entries. This is the access used in the example where we searched for the name COLLINS. In a nonmatching index scan, the RDS (not the Data Manager) bypasses the index tree and sequentially scans the index leaf pages to find the required index entries.

Consider the following query:

```
SELECT * FROM BRANCH WHERE BRANCH_NO = 300
```

The BRANCH table has an index on the column BRANCH_NO, and a matching index scan can use the tree to access the rows which satisfy the condition BRANCH_NO = 300. If, instead, the index was composed of the concatenation of two columns, BRANCH_NO and BRANCH_MGR, the values in the index entries would each begin with branch number and end with manager, e.g., 300HOFFMAN. The Data Manager could still use a matching index to find entries in the index which begin with 300. Now, suppose that your index was composed of these same two columns but your query was:

```
SELECT * FROM BRANCH WHERE BRANCH_MGR = 'HOFFMAN'
```

The Data Manager would not be able to use a matching index scan. The index's high-order value, BRANCH_NO, is the basis for the tree structure, so the tree cannot be used to find a particular value of manager. The leaf pages do, however, contain each value in the index. The pointers on the leaf pages that contain the identifier for the next leaf page can be used to read across the leaf pages to find those entries which contain the value HOFFMAN within them. This is called a nonmatching index scan. If the query had asked for branches whose branch number is greater than 300, the access path chosen by the Optimizer might combine a matching index scan to find the leaf page entry for the value 300 with a nonmatching index scan to read across the leaf pages to find all of the branch numbers greater than 300.

The tree of an index will usually have no more than three levels, but it may have thousands of leaf pages. Since far fewer pages are read in a matching index scan than in a nonmatching index scan, the matching index scan is always more efficient.

15.4.3 Index Only

A variation of the index scan access path occurs if the Data Manager can retrieve all of the required information from the index alone, without reading the data in the tablespace. This is called index only access. Consider the following example:

```
SELECT BRANCH_MGR
    FROM BRANCH
    WHERE BRANCH_NO = 300
```

If the BRANCH table is indexed by BRANCH_NO plus BRANCH_MGR, the Data Manager can use a matching index scan to find the index leaf entry for the value 300. In addition, for this query, the Data Manager can get all of the information required by the SELECT clause from the entries on the index pages themselves without retrieving the rows from the base tables. Therefore, this access is considered index only. If the index fields were reversed, BRANCH_MGR plus BRANCH_NO, the Data Manager would have to use a nonmatching index scan, but it would still be an index only scan since BRANCH_MGR is on the leaf pages.

From the above, you can see that DB2's two basic access methods (tablespace scan and index scan) have five variations. These are tablespace scans, matching index scan with table access, nonmatching index scan with table access, matching index scan with index only access, and nonmatching index scan with index only access. In terms of I/O cost, the most efficient access path is a matching index scan without table access.

15.4.4 Sequential Prefetch

When DB2 knows it will have to retrieve a large number of pages sequentially, as when performing a tablespace scan, it uses Sequential Prefetch. It retrieves many pages with one I/O request in advance of those pages being required and stores them in the bufferpool. This way, the wait for I/O will be reduced since DB2 can process already-retrieved rows while more rows are being fetched.

15.4.5 List Prefetch

If DB2 uses a nonclustered index, it may sort the RIDs so that they are in clustering order. Then it can fetch the data rows more efficiently; it will have to fetch each data page only once, as if the index were clustered. But, even when the RIDs are sorted, they may not point to each consecutive page of the data. In such a situation, DB2 can use the List Prefetch technique. This is similar to Sequential Prefetch, but instead of prefetching consecutive pages in a tablespace, it prefetches the pages contained in a list of pages.

15.5 OPTIMIZATION

It is the user who creates indexes, but it is the Optimizer that decides whether or not to use them. *For any optimizable SQL statement, the Optimizer considers the alternative ways to satisfy the request, estimates the cost of each alternative, and then chooses the alternative with the lowest processing and I/O cost.* When considering indexes, the Optimizer must question the comparable worth of satisfying the request with or without an index. If the table has very few rows, the Optimizer will probably decide that a tablespace scan is less costly. Similarly, you would probably not use a book's index if the book was only three pages long. The Optimizer will also bypass an index if it is composed of too few values. A good example of this is a table that holds orders for a brokerage house for a given day. If the index is on ORDER DATE, there will probably be only one value in the index at any one time. The Optimizer would not find any use in such an index.

The Optimizer learns about the nature of the table, its data, and its indexes through the Catalog. For example, the SYSIBM.SYSINDEXES catalog table includes the CLUSTERING column, which indicates whether the data is actually clustered, and FIRSTKEYCARD and FULLKEYCARD, which provide information about the number of distinct values. It is only when you execute the RUNSTATS utility that this information gets into the Catalog. Thus, if you create an index for a table but do not run RUNSTATS, there is no way that the Optimizer can evaluate the nature of the index, so it doesn't use it.

How you formulate your SQL query affects the way the Optimizer evaluates its options. The results will be the same but the performance may be quite different. Since each query can be expressed in more than one way, it's important to understand how the query itself affects performance. The next sections in this chapter explain some of the factors at play here.

15.6 EFFECT OF PREDICATES ON PERFORMANCE

The Optimizer's choice of access paths is affected by the definition of the indexes and the nature of the query. Let's look at our last example again:

```
SELECT *
    FROM BRANCH
    WHERE BRANCH_NO = 300
```

BRANCH_NO = 300 is called a predicate because it compares two values. Several predicates may be combined in one statement's WHERE clause. The predicate is what Data Base Services uses as the basis for selecting or rejecting rows. It is the most important way for an application programmer to influence performance.

15.6.1 Sargable and Nonsargable Predicates

Within the Data Base Services component, simple predicates are processed by the Data Manager alone while more complicated predicates require both the Data Manager and RDS. Predicates that fall into the first category are sargable, while those of the second category are nonsargable. In some IBM publications, these predicates are referred to as stage 1 and stage 2, respectively. The word "sargable" is derived by combining the s of search with the arg of argument. Sargable means that the search argument of the query, that is, the predicate, is able to be processed by the Data Manager alone. Nonsargable predicates will always be less efficient than sargable predicates because there is the added overhead of RDS processing. The list of sargable predicates increases from release to release of DB2.

The RDS performs all data conversions, so all queries that require data conversions are nonsargable. For instance, look at the following query:

```
SELECT *
    FROM BRANCH
    WHERE BRANCH_NO > 300.5
```

BRANCH_NO is defined as small integer and this predicate asks that it be compared to a decimal number, 300.5. Since the comparison requires conversion from one format to the other, this is a nonsargable predicate. Another example of a predicate requiring data conversion and processing by the RDS is one in which a column defined as character is compared to a literal or host variable of a longer length. An example is:

```
SELECT *
   FROM ACCOUNT
   WHERE ACCT_NO = 'AE11
```

ACCT_NO is defined as CHAR(4) and is being compared to a 5-byte character string. The RDS will process this nonsargable predicate, converting the 4-byte value in ACCT_NO into a temporary 5-byte field for comparison purposes.

Another type of nonsargable predicate contains an arithmetic expression. An example is:

```
SELECT *
   FROM ACCOUNT
   WHERE ACCT_CREDIT_BALANCE > ACCT_BALANCE * 100
```

All such predicates must be processed by the RDS; the Data Manager is not equipped to handle arithmetic.

In Chap. 5, you learned about scalar and column functions. If scalar or column functions are used in the predicate of a query, the predicate is always nonsargable. However, if column functions are used, you can improve performance by avoiding predicates with column functions with more than one column in their argument, predicates with column functions on the outer table of a join, and column functions with GROUP BYs which require a sort.

Other types of predicates that are nonsargable include those in correlated subselects and those in a subselect which uses IN, SOME, EXISTS, or NOT EXISTS.

15.6.2 Indexable Predicates

Indexable predicates are those that can make use of a matching index if a suitable index exists. A matching index scan can greatly improve performance, so it is important to understand the kinds of queries that may prevent or discourage the Optimizer from choosing a matching index scan as an access path.

If your predicate includes a negation, it will usually not be indexable, for example:

```
SELECT *
   FROM BRANCH
   WHERE NOT BRANCH_NO = 111
```

The predicate specifies the retrieval of rows whose branch number is not equal to 111. An index is efficient only when there is a value that it is trying to match. Similarly, a book's index is not very helpful at finding all of the pages that do not contain information on a given sub-ject. An exception to this rule is a predicate in which an inequality operator is negated:

```
SELECT *
   FROM BRANCH
   WHERE NOT BRANCH_NO > 111
```

The Optimizer is smart enough to reinterpret this to the following positive statement, which it can then use to scan an index:

```
SELECT *
   FROM BRANCH
   WHERE BRANCH_NO < = 111
```

A predicate with a LIKE clause in it will not use a matching index scan when the leading character of the character string is a wild card:

```
SELECT *
   FROM BRANCH
   WHERE BRANCH_MGR LIKE '%MAN'
```

The structure of an index tree lends itself to finding values; therefore, it cannot be used when the initial character(s) of that value are unknown. Again, this would be like using a book's index to find entries on all subjects ending with MAN.

A predicate in an UPDATE statement will not be indexable if it references a column that is also the object of the statement's SET clause, for example:

```
UPDATE BRANCH
   SET BRANCH_ID = 800
   WHERE BRANCH_ID = 200
```

This is also true for a predicate in an embedded SQL SELECT when a column in the predicate is also in the FOR UPDATE OF clause. When you change a data value, the corresponding values in the index are also changed. DB2 recognizes that using an index to change a value that is in the index can cause a number of inconsistencies, so it doesn't use an index.

Appendix D lists those predicates that are indexable and those that are sargable, as of version 2.2. Note that a predicate that cannot make use of a matching index scan may be able to use a nonmatching index scan. This is not usually referred to as indexable, however, even though an index is used. Note also that a nonsargable predicate will not be able to use a matching index scan. This is because a nonsargable predicate requires processing by the RDS, and all matching index scans are done by the Data Manager.

15.7   ACCESS PATHS OF QUERIES WITH MULTIPLE TABLES

An SQL statement can retrieve data from multiple tables through a subquery, a correlated subquery, or a join. In many cases, more than one method can be used to return the same data. Knowing the performance differences among the choices therefore becomes important.

The noncorrelated subquery is fairly efficient and if suitable indexes exist, they will be used to retrieve data from the tables specified. This will be true only when predicates for both the inner and the outer subqueries are indexable. Look at this example of a noncorrelated subquery:

```
SELECT *
  FROM BRANCH
  WHERE BRANCH_ID =
    (SELECT CUST_BRANCH
     FROM CUSTOMER
     WHERE CUST_ID = 555555555)
```

If there is an index on CUST_ID in the CUSTOMER table, it will be used to find the row where CUST_ID equals 555555555. If there is an index on BRANCH_ID in the BRANCH table, it will then be used to find the rows where BRANCH_ID equals the branch on the record with CUST_ID 555555555.

Most joins can be expressed as correlated subqueries and visa versa. *In general, the access path for a join is more efficient than the access path for a correlated subquery.* Correlated subqueries are not sargable, so matching index scans will not be used to process them. Joins may be sargable and able to use a matching index scan. In addition, the join's WHERE condition may reduce the number of rows that are processed. DB2 has two processing options for joins—the nested loop and the merge-scan method. For any query, DB2 will use the method it considers most efficient.

15.7.1   Nested-Loop Join

In a nested-loop join, a row is retrieved from one table (the outer table) and then the second table (the inner table) is scanned for row(s) that should be joined to this row. The next row is then retrieved from the outer table and the entire inner table is scanned again for joinable rows. DB2 determines which table to consider to be the outer and the inner one based on its comparison of the efficiency of the alternatives for the particular query. Let's see how this works:

```
SELECT CUSTOMER.*
  FROM CUSTOMER, BRANCH
  WHERE BRANCH_CITY = 'ALBANY'
  AND BRANCH_ID = CUST_BRANCH
```

Assume that the BRANCH table is the outer table and the CUS-TOMER table is the inner table. DB2 will retrieve rows from the BRANCH table one by one and apply the predicate BRANCH_CITY = 'Albany' to eliminate branches that are not in Albany. For every branch in Albany, DB2 will then scan the CUSTOMER table to retrieve all of the rows whose branch number matches the branch number of the row from the BRANCH table. A tablespace scan or index scan can be used on either the outer or inner table.

In the nested-loop method, the outer table is scanned only once and the inner table is scanned many times. Therefore, this type of access is most efficient if the inner table has a very efficient access path or very few rows. Also, the smaller the number of qualified rows in the outer table, the more efficient the nested-loop join will be.

15.7.2 Merge-Scan Join

In this join method, both the inner and the outer tables must be in the same order based on the column on which the tables are being joined. Typically, this requires that both the inner and the outer tables first be sorted according to the join column. After the sort, this access method is similar to the nested-loop access method. However, since both tables are sorted, the inner table does not have to be scanned from the beginning for every qualified row in the outer table but can be scanned from the point it left off. If suitable indexes exist, DB2 may use the indexes to access the tables in sorted order instead of actually doing a sort. Let's look at our previous SELECT to see how it would be done by a merge-scan join:

```
SELECT CUSTOMER.*
  FROM CUSTOMER, BRANCH
  WHERE BRANCH_CITY = 'ALBANY'
  AND BRANCH_ID = CUST_BRANCH
```

The CUSTOMER table is sorted into CUST_BRANCH order. The BRANCH table is condensed (only the branch ID column for branches in Albany is used) and sorted by BRANCH_ID. Finally, both the CUS-TOMER table and the condensed version of the BRANCH table are accessed in branch number order to retrieve data about customers in Albany.

In earlier versions of DB2, the performance cost of sorting was prohibitive and DB2's Optimizer frequently chose not to use the merge-scan join method. Because the performance of DB2's internal sort has been improved significantly, DB2 now makes greater use of the merge-scan method in joins.

15.8 SORTS

DB2 has an internal sort that may be invoked by a join or by SQL statements that specify that data be retrieved in a certain order, as with the ORDER BY, GROUP BY, and SELECT DISTINCT clauses. Even though the DB2 internal sort has been enhanced consistently with every new DB2 release, sorts are still expensive in terms of CPU costs because the table rows must first be passed from the Data Manager to the RDS and then sorted.

A preferred alternative to the DB2 internal sort is the use of indexes which can also access table data in a specific order. Remember, the choice of an index or an internal sort is made by the Optimizer, not you, the user. However, you can influence this with the indexes you choose to create on a table and your query formulation. Note that DB2's internal sort is more flexible than an index. While an index can retrieve rows in the order of the index only, DB2's internal sort can order data over any of the column(s) in the result table.

When either indexes are not available or DB2 will not use them, you should consider using an external sort to sort the result table outside of DB2 if the number of rows is large. DB2's internal sort is optimized for 1 million 40-byte records. It's been our experience that where DB2 may take 2 CPU minutes to sort 500,000 250-byte records, a system sort may take only 23 CPU seconds for the same task.

15.9 LOCKING

A DBMS's locking strategy will affect the performance of the overall subsystem and any application running within it. Locking affects CPU usage and concurrency, which in turn affect performance. DB2 uses locks to ensure that no other user accesses data that has been changed by another user but not yet committed or has been earmarked for change. Although we will focus on table locks, locks are also taken on indexes.

The characteristics of DB2 locks are target, size, duration, and type. Target is the table being locked; size refers to whether a part of the table or the whole table is being locked; duration is the time interval for which the lock is maintained; and type refers to whether the target table is being accessed to read data or to change data. DB2 uses share (S) locks for reading data and exclusive (X) locks for changing data.

For a specific SQL request, the target and type are fixed; the only characteristics that can be influenced by either you or the DBA are the size and the duration of the lock. For maximum concurrency, the size and duration of locks must be kept to a minimum. This does, however, increase locking activity, which in turn increases CPU and virtual storage utilization. The trade-off is between concurrency and CPU and virtual storage usage. Since the performance cost of DB2 locks is quite substantial, the choice must be made judiciously. Now let's examine the size and duration characteristics of DB2 locks in detail.

15.9.1 Lock Size

The size of a DB2 lock is either a page, table, or tablespace. Note that DB2 does not provide facilities for a row-level lock. Also note that a table lock is a new feature of DB2 and applies only to segmented tablespaces, which were introduced in version 2. If the tablespace is nonsegmented, DB2 will acquire a lock on the whole tablespace when the LOCK TABLE statement is issued.

When a tablespace is created, it can be defined with LOCKSIZE PAGE, LOCKSIZE TABLE (for a segmented tablespace), LOCKSIZE TABLESPACE, or LOCKSIZE ANY. LOCKSIZE ANY leaves it up to DB2 whether to select the page or tablespace locks. Usually it will take page locks. If it is taking page locks and the number of page locks on a tablespace exceeds an installation-defined value, the lock size will be increased from page to tablespace. This is lock escalation. Indexes can be created with each 4K page further subdivided into 1 to 16 subpages. A subpage is a unit of index locking. Increasing the number of subpages increases concurrency but has a CPU overhead.

15.9.2 Lock Duration

The duration, or the time for which a lock is held, is affected by the ACQUIRE, RELEASE, and ISOLATION LEVEL clauses of the BIND/REBIND command. For a tablespace lock, the duration is determined by the ACQUIRE and RELEASE clauses. Tablespace locks are acquired either when the plan is allocated to the thread (ACQUIRE(ALLOCATE)) or when the SQL statement is executed (ACQUIRE(USE)). These locks are released either at the time of a commit (RELEASE(COMMIT)) or when the SQL processing for the thread is completed and the plan is deallocated (RELEASE(DEALLOCATE)). The ISOLATION LEVEL clause affects lock duration for read-only processing. Recall from Chap. 12 that if ISOLATION LEVEL is CURSOR STABILITY, DB2 holds a page lock only if the cursor is positioned on the page. However, if ISOLATION

LEVEL is REPEATABLE READ, DB2 will hold all page locks until the next commit point.

15.9.3 Lock Type

There are a number of different types of locks that can be imposed at the page and tablespace level. The easiest to understand are SHARE and EXCLUSIVE. SHARE means that anyone can read the page or tablespace but no one can change it. EXCLUSIVE locks out all other users. There is also an UPDATE lock at the page level only, which prevents other UPDATE or EXCLUSIVE locks but allows SHARE locks. The difference between SHARE and UPDATE is that many SHARE locks can be held on one page but only one UPDATE lock can be held. The UPDATE lock is promoted to an EXCLUSIVE lock when an update is actually about to be done.

In addition to these, there are a set of intent locks. Intent locks are at the tablespace level and are used in conjunction with page locks. Their purpose is to improve concurrency and performance. They flag a tablespace in a variety of ways to indicate at the tablespace level the types of locks that are currently held at the page level. Let's look at one example. When share locks are taken at the page level, an intent share lock is taken at the tablespace level. The intent share lock is used to simplify the checking that must be done when a transaction needs an exclusive lock. The intent share lock communicates at the tablespace level that an exclusive tablespace lock is not possible. Otherwise, each page lock needs to be checked to find this out.

It is important to write SQL queries that perform well, both for the success of your application and for the welfare of your whole installation, since a poorly performing query can use thousands of times the resources of a good performer. The most important factors in determining performance are the use of an index and the construction of queries that DB2 can process efficiently. Use of NOT should be considered carefully. Inequalities are always more costly than equalities in WHERE clauses. Careful programming practices, such as making sure that host variables match their corresponding columns in size, data type, and scale and ensuring WHERE clauses contain no arithmetic operations, have a big payoff. Small differences in query construction can have huge effects on performance. In the next chapter, where we discuss EXPLAIN, you will learn how to find out how DB2 plans to access your data and, therefore, whether your query will work efficiently as written.

Performance Considerations and EXPLAIN

The EXPLAIN function lets you look at the access and processing choices actually made by DB2. Armed with this information, you can fine tune your SQL code to improve performance.

16.1 THE EXPLAIN FUNCTION

The EXPLAIN function can be used with the SQL statements SELECT, INSERT, UPDATE, and DELETE. The BIND process parses (analyzes) these SQL statements, invokes the Optimizer function, which identifies the possible access paths, computes the access cost for each, selects the lowest-cost access path, and then produces executable code.

The output of the EXPLAIN function is stored in a table called *userid*.PLAN_TABLE, where *userid* is your DB2 authorization ID. The PLAN_TABLE contains at least one row for every table referenced in an EXPLAINed SQL statement. A PLAN_TABLE must exist for your userid before you can invoke the EXPLAIN function because DB2 will not create one for you.

16.1.1 Creating the Plan Table

You can find the DDL to create your PLAN_TABLE in the sample library provided with DB2 by IBM. The sample library is typically called *prefix* DSNSAMP, where *prefix* is specified by your data center. Member DSNTESC contains the DDL.

Here is sample DDL to create a PLAN_TABLE. You may choose any names for the columns in the PLAN_TABLE, but the order of the columns and the data types cannot change. The column names listed are those typically used in most IBM manuals:

```
CREATE TABLE PLAN_TABLE
       (QUERYNO           INTEGER         NOT NULL,
        QBLOCKNO          SMALLINT        NOT NULL,
        APPLNAME          CHAR(8)         NOT NULL,
        PROGNAME          CHAR(8)         NOT NULL,
        PLANNO            SMALLINT        NOT NULL,
        METHOD            SMALLINT        NOT NULL,
        CREATOR           CHAR(8)         NOT NULL,
        TNAME             CHAR(18)        NOT NULL,
        TABNO             SMALLINT        NOT NULL,
        ACCESSTYPE        CHAR(2)         NOT NULL,
        MATCHCOLS         SMALLINT        NOT NULL,
        ACCESSCREATOR     CHAR(8)         NOT NULL,
        ACCESSNAME        CHAR(18)        NOT NULL,
        INDEXONLY         CHAR(1)         NOT NULL,
        SORTN_UNIQ        CHAR(1)         NOT NULL,
        SORTN_JOIN        CHAR(1)         NOT NULL,
        SORTN_ORDERBY     CHAR(1)         NOT NULL,
        SORTN_GROUPBY     CHAR(1)         NOT NULL,
        SORTC_UNIQ        CHAR(1)         NOT NULL,
        SORTC_JOIN        CHAR(1)         NOT NULL,
        SORTC_ORDERBY     CHAR(1)         NOT NULL,
        SORTC_GROUPBY     CHAR(1)         NOT NULL,
        TSLOCKMODE        CHAR(3)         NOT NULL,
        TIMESTAMP         CHAR(16)        NOT NULL,
        REMARKS           VARCHAR(254)    NOT NULL)
```

You can execute this sample DDL through either SPUFI or QMF. Since we have not specified a database or tablespace for the PLAN_TABLE, DB2 will use the default database for it. If you were able to create the sample tables of Chap. 3 in the default database, you will not require any additional authorization to execute the above DDL.

If you have DB2 version 2.2, there are three optional columns that you can add to your PLAN_TABLE. These columns come after the REMARKS column, so you can execute an ALTER TABLE statement on an already-existing table to add them. These columns are:

```
PREFETCH          CHAR(1)         NOT NULL WITH DEFAULT,
COLUMN_FN_EVAL    CHAR(1)         NOT NULL WITH DEFAULT,
MIXOPSEQ          SMALLINT        NOT NULL WITH DEFAULT
```

We will describe the functions of all PLAN_TABLE columns later in this chapter.

16.1.2 Querying the Plan Table

The PLAN_TABLE is like any other user table in DB2, and you can query it with the SELECT statement or delete unneeded rows from it with a DELETE statement. The PLAN_TABLE is quite large and it is difficult to fit its output on an 80-character screen. IBM recommends using QMF to reformat the output and, from our own practical experience, we second this recommendation. Here is a sample QMF format that we've found to be useful.

NUM	COLUMN HEADING	USAGE	INDENT	WIDTH	EDIT
1	QUERY_NO.		1	5	L
2	Q_B_#		1	2	L
3	APPLNAME	OMIT	2	8	C
4	PROGNAME	OMIT	2	8	C
5	PLAN_NO.		1	4	L
6	METH		1	4	L
7	CREATOR	OMIT	2	8	C
8	TNAME		1	13	C
9	TB_NO		1	2	L
10	AC		1	2	C
11	M_COL		1	3	L
12	ACCESSCREATOR	OMIT	2	13	C
13	INDEX		1	8	C
14	IDX_ONLY		1	4	C
15	S_U		1	1	C
16	O_J		0	1	C
17	R_O		0	1	C
18	T_G		0	1	C
19	I_U		1	1	C
20	N_J		0	1	C
21	D_O		0	1	C
22	._G		0	1	C
23	TS_LOCK_MODE		1	4	C
24	TIMESTAMP	OMIT	2	16	C
25	REMARKS	OMIT	2	254	C

Figure 16.1 shows the QMF-formatted output that this produces. As you can see, the somewhat cryptic column headings of columns 15 through 22 spell out SORT IND. on the top of the sort columns. This also renames some columns, e.g., ACCESSNAME is called INDEX in the heading.

```
              E X P L A I N    O U T P U T


       Q                                                          TS
QUERY  B  PLAN                      TB    M            IDX  SORT IND. LOCK
 NO.   #  NO.  METH TNAME           NO AC COL  INDEX   ONLY UJOG UJOG MODE
-----  -- ---- ---- --------------  -- -- ---  -------- ---- ---- ---- ----
```

Figure 16.1   QMF can be used to format the output of EXPLAIN.

16.2   INVOKING EXPLAIN

The EXPLAIN function can be invoked by the SQL EXPLAIN statement or by the EXPLAIN options of the BIND and REBIND commands. The SQL EXPLAIN statement is used to "explain" a single SQL statement while the EXPLAIN options of BIND/REBIND explain every SELECT, INSERT, UPDATE, and DELETE statement in an application plan. SQL EXPLAIN is most commonly submitted through SPUFI or QMF, while the EXPLAIN option is specified through the EXPLAIN PATH SELECTION option on the BIND panel (Fig. 16.2), or EXPLAIN(YES) on a BIND control card.

The general format of the SQL EXPLAIN statement is:

```
EXPLAIN PLAN SET QUERYNO = n FOR
statement
```

Here n is any integer and *statement* is any SELECT, INSERT, UPDATE, or DELETE SQL statement. The SET QUERYNO = n clause is optional but recommended. The integer that you specify will appear in the PLAN_TABLE in the QUERYNO column, which otherwise defaults to a 1. Any one EXPLAIN will generate one or more rows in your PLAN_TABLE. Without the SET QUERYNO = n clause, it will be difficult to identify which rows to associate with which SQL statements. If the EXPLAIN function is invoked through the BIND or REBIND command, the QUERYNO column will contain the pre-

```
                              BIND
===>

Enter DBRM data set name(s):
  1   LIBRARY(s)   ===> 'USER1.DBRM'
  2   MEMBER(s)    ===> PROGRAM1
  3   PASSWORD(s) ===>

  4   MORE DBRMS? ===> NO                      (YES to list more DBRMs)

Enter options as desired:
  5   PLAN NAME ............... ===> PROGRAM1   (Required to create a plan)
  6   ACTION ON PLAN .......... ===> REPLACE    (REPLACE or ADD)
  7   RETAIN EXECUTION AUTHORITY ===> YES       (YES to retain user list)
  8   ISOLATION LEVEL ......... ===> CS         (RR or CS)
  9   PLAN VALIDATION TIME ..... ===> BIND      (RUN or BIND)
 10   RESOURCE ACQUISITION TIME  ===> USE       (USE or ALLOCATE)
 11   RESOURCE RELEASE TIME .... ===> COMMIT    (COMMIT or DEALLOCATE)
 12   EXPLAIN PATH SELECTION ... ===> YES       (NO or YES)
 13   OWNER OF PLAN (AUTHID) ... ===>           (Leave blank for your primary ID
```

Figure 16.2   EXPLAIN may be invoked on the BIND panel.

compilation statement number which is produced by DB2 when an application program is precompiled.

Two columns in the PLAN_TABLE are meaningful only when the EXPLAIN function is invoked through the BIND/REBIND command. They are APPLNAME and PROGNAME. APPLNAME holds the name of the application plan being bound or rebound; PROGNAME holds the name of the DBRM within the plan which contains the explained statement. If you look at the QMF format, you will see that these columns are omitted. They are not needed as often as the other columns in the table since you usually know the plan and program names.

16.3 INFORMATION PROVIDED BY EXPLAIN

EXPLAIN provides information that can be used to understand the access cost of the path selected by the Optimizer. This cost is a combination of the I/O cost and the CPU cost. The I/O cost is a function of the access path selected and, if tables are being joined, the order in which tables are joined and the join method selected. The CPU cost is a function of the locking strategy, calls to the Relational Data System by the Data Manager, and any internal sorts performed by DB2. The EXPLAIN function provides most of this information in the PLAN_TABLE. First we'll look at the purpose of each column.

Information relevant to the I/O cost is provided in the ACCESSTYPE, MATCHCOLS, ACCESSCREATOR, ACCESSNAME, and INDEXONLY columns. The ACCESSTYPE column contains the value I, indicating that an index is used to access the data, or R to indicate that a tablespace scan is used. If an index is used, the ACCESSNAME and ACCESSCREATOR columns show the fully qualified name of the index.

With DB2 version 2.2, additional information is available in the ACCESSTYPE column. I and R are still used, and their meanings are unchanged. In addition, I1 means a one-fetch index scan; this is used by DB2 to get the first record of an index when a MAX or MIN column function is used and there is a descending (for MAX) or ascending (for MIN) index available. The first record of the index will, in these cases, contain the value required.

N in the ACCESSTYPE column means that the index is being used for a predicate containing an IN list. M means that multiple indexes are being used on the table. Note that prior to version 2.2, DB2 used only one index per table per SQL statement. If an M appears in this column, there will be additional rows following with MX, MI, or MU in this column. MX means that the row refers to one of multiple indexes scanned; the index name is in the column ACCESSNAME. MI indicates that DB2 is performing an intersection of multiple indexes; this is done when an AND must be resolved. MU indicates that DB2 is performing a union of multiple indexes; this is done when an OR must be resolved.

MATCHCOLS indicates the type of index scan used. A nonmatching index scan, in which leaf pages are read sequentially, is indicated by the value 0 in the MATCHCOLS column. If MATCHCOLS is greater than 0, DB2 is using a matching index scan to access the data. Under these circumstances, the MATCHCOLS column indicates the number of columns used to access the index tree. This will be 1 if the index consists of one column and may be greater than 1 if the index consists of several columns and more than one column is being used for the match. The INDEXONLY column contains a Y if the request for data can be satisfied solely by reading the index pages. If both the index and table are accessed to satisfy a data request, the INDEXONLY column will show the value N. If a tablespace scan is used, INDEXONLY will contain an N, the columns ACCESSNAME and ACCESSCREATOR will be blank, and MATCHCOLS will be 0.

Let's review a few examples to clarify the concept of MATCHCOLS and INDEXONLY. The examples use the TELLER table, shown in Fig. 16.3. Refer to it as you read the examples. The table has six columns and two indexes, XDEPT on the TELLER_DEPT column and a multicolumn index XTELLER on the columns TELLER_ID, TELLER_LAST_NAME, TELLER_FIRST_NAME, and TELLER_BIRTH_DATE.

If the SQL statement is:

```
SELECT TELLER_LAST_NAME
    FROM TELLER
    WHERE TELLER_ID = 2222
```

ACCESSTYPE will be I, showing an index is used; ACCESSNAME will be XTELLER, naming the index used; MATCHCOLS will be 1 because one column, TELLER_ID, in the multicolumn index is used to match on; and INDEXONLY will be Y because all of the data required for the query, TELLER_LAST_NAME, can be found in the index.

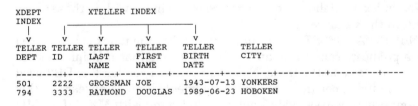

Figure 16.3   The TELLER table.

If the SQL statement is:

```
SELECT TELLER_DEPT
  FROM TELLER
 WHERE TELLER_ID = 2222
```

ACCESSTYPE will be I, ACCESSNAME will be XTELLER, MATCHCOLS will be 1, and INDEXONLY will be N. The only difference between this example and the last is that the information required by this query is TELLER_DEPT, which is not in the XTELLER index, meaning that INDEXONLY is N.

If the SQL statement is:

```
SELECT TELLER_DEPT
  FROM TELLER
 WHERE TELLER_ID = 2222
   AND TELLER_LAST_NAME > 'D'
```

ACCESSTYPE will be I, ACCESSNAME will be XTELLER, MATCHCOLS will be 2, and INDEXONLY will be N. Again, the data pages are needed for the values of TELLER_DEPT and two columns of the index were needed to satisfy the predicate, TELLER_ID and TELLER_LAST_NAME.

If the SQL statement is:

```
SELECT TELLER_DEPT
  FROM TELLER
 WHERE TELLER_LAST_NAME = 'GROSSMAN'
   AND TELLER_FIRST_NAME = 'JOE'
```

ACCESSTYPE will be I, ACCESSNAME will be XTELLER, MATCHCOLS will be 0, and INDEXONLY will be N. In this case, DB2 cannot exploit the index tree because the column TELLER_ID, the high-order column in the index, is not part of the WHERE clause. DB2 will use a nonmatching index scan to find the index entries it needs, but since the SELECT also asks for TELLER_DEPT, it will also need to access the table rows.

If the SQL statement is:

```
SELECT TELLER_DEPT
  FROM TELLER
 WHERE TELLER_CITY = 'YONKERS'
```

DB2 cannot use either XDEPT or XTELLER indexes, so ACCESSTYPE will be R, tablespace scan. ACCESSNAME will be blank, MATCHCOLS will be 0, and INDEXONLY will be N.

If the SQL statement involves more than one table, the columns of the PLAN_TABLE of interest are QBLOCKNO, PLANNO, and

METHOD. QBLOCKNO (query block number) is a number used to identify an SQL statement. Typically, there is one query block associated with each SQL SELECT, UPDATE, INSERT, and DELETE statement. However, if a query consists of nested selects, each SELECT will have a separate query block with the highest level SELECT being given a QBLOCKNO of 1.

The PLANNO column shows the order of steps within a query block, which translates to the order in which tables are accessed if there is more than one table. The METHOD column indicates access strategy. A 0 means that the table is the first table accessed. A 1 shows that a nested loop join is used, while a 2 indicates a merge scan join. A 3 means a DB2 internal sort is invoked. Any one join will have several rows in the PLAN_TABLE, each with the appropriate METHOD.

Consider the following example.

```
EXPLAIN PLAN SET QUERYNO = 1 FOR
  SELECT BRANCH_ID,BRANCH_CITY, CUST_NAME
    FROM BRANCH, CUSTOMER
    WHERE BRANCH_ID = CUST_BRANCH
```

The SELECT is looking for the customers in each branch. Let's assume that the Optimizer determines that BRANCH is the outer table and CUSTOMER is the inner table. Figure 16.4 shows a subset of the PLAN_TABLE that might result from the EXPLAIN on this statement. There are two rows in the PLAN_TABLE. In both, QUERYNO = 1 because we have set this number to 1 with SET QUERYNO = 1. The first row shows the BRANCH table in the TABNAME column, 1 in the PLANNO column and a 0 in the METHOD column. This means that this is the first step and BRANCH is the first table accessed. The second row has CUSTOMER in the TABNAME column, 2 in the PLANNO column, and 1 in the METHOD column, meaning that this is the second step and the second table accessed and that the join method will be a nested loop.

Now let's examine the PLAN_TABLE columns that provide information about CPU cost. This cost is a function of the locking strategy, calls to the Relational Data System by the Data Manager, and any internal sorts performed by DB2.

```
      Q
QUERY B PLAN
NO.   # NO.  METH TNAME
----- -- ---- ---- -------------
  1   1   1     0  BRANCH
  1   1   2     1  CUSTOMER
```

Figure 16.4 Output from a join.

The TSLOCKMODE column provides information about the locking strategy. If it contains values IX, IS, or SIX, intent locking is being used in the tablespace and page locks or table locks for segmented tablespaces only will be used. If it has values of S (share) or X (exclusive), the lock mode is tablespace. Page locking increases concurrency but also increases CPU cycle consumption because many more locks are required to be maintained in comparison to table or tablespace locking mode. If access is read only, TSLOCKMODE will show a value of either IS or S. Any other values indicate that the table specified in the TABNAME column may be updated.

The PLAN_TABLE does not directly indicate the number of calls to the Relational Data System by the Data Manager, but you can infer something about this indirectly. Recall from Chap. 15 that all matching index scans are processed by the Data Manager alone. If ACCESSTYPE contains the value I and MATCHCOLS > 0, the predicate is indexable. You know from this that additional calls to the RDS are not required and that CPU usage will therefore be minimized. Calls to the RDS increase CPU usage.

CPU use is also increased by the data sorting performed by the RDS. All DB2 data sorts are performed by the RDS. The eight PLAN_TABLE columns prefixed by 'SORT' are sort indicators, each having a value of Y or N, indicating the reason for invoking DB2's internal sort. Note that these eight indicators can be categorized into two groups. Look back at the DDL to create the PLAN_TABLE in Sec. 16.1. The column names of the first four sort columns are prefixed by SORTN and those of the second four are prefixed by SORTC. The SORTN and SORTC indicators are mutually exclusive. A Y in any of the columns that begin with SORTN indicates that the table being sorted is a permanent table. If there is a Y in any of the SORTC indicators, the table being sorted is an intermediate table which is produced by DB2 as a result of joining two tables. If SORTN_UNIQ = Y (sort unique), the sort is performed to eliminate duplicate rows. If SORTN_JOIN = Y, the table identified in the TABNAME column is sorted in the order of the join column(s) prior to DB2 performing a merge-scan join. If SORTN_ORDERBY = Y, the sort is performed to order the rows of the result table. If SORTN_GROUPBY = Y, the sort is performed to group the rows in the result table. The SORTC indicator definitions are identical. Remember that the difference between the SORTC and SORTN indicators is the type of table being processed.

Let's look at the optional PLAN_TABLE columns. The first, PREFETCH, contains an S if pure sequential prefetch was used, an L if prefetch through a page list was used, or a blank if no prefetch was used.

The second optional column, COLUMN_FN_EVAL, indicates when DB2 was able to evaluate a column function. R means that this was at data retrieval time, which is the earliest possible and implies the best performance. S means during the sort, which is the next best, while blank means the function couldn't be evaluated until after the sort was completed.

The third optional column, MIXOPSEQ, indicates the sequence of steps in a multiple index scan. Values of 1 or more are found with ACCESSTYPE column values of MX, MI, or MU. For any other ACCESSTYPE, which means this column is not applicable, MIXOPSEQ will contain 0.

16.4   EXAMPLES

We've constructed three hypothetical queries, Queries 10, 20, and 30, to see what the output of EXPLAIN looks like in practice. The queries go against Catalog tables but are meant purely for illustration.

16.4.1   Query 10

Query 10 (Fig. 16.5) selects those rows in SYSIBM.SYSCOLUMNS that are in tables located in the catalog tablespace named SYSDBASE.   The   outer   select   retrieves   from SYSIBM.SYSCOLUMNS;   the   inner   select,   from SYSIBM.SYSTABLES.

The EXPLAIN output consists of the three rows in our PLAN_TABLE (Fig. 16.6) that are identified by a 10 in the QUERY_NO column. The first row has a METHOD of 0, showing that SYSCOLUMNS is the first table accessed. The ACCESSTYPE of R indicates a tablespace scan. This means that the query will do a   tablespace   scan   on   the   SYSCOLUMNS   table.   The TS_LOCK_MODE is IS, meaning that there is no page-level locking and that the query is read only. The second row in Query 10 is a separate SELECT (the subselect), so it also has a method of 0 but

```
EXPLAIN PLAN SET QUERYNO = 10 FOR
SELECT *
   FROM SYSIBM.SYSCOLUMNS
   WHERE TBCREATOR = 'SYSIBM' AND
   TBNAME IN
      (SELECT NAME FROM SYSIBM.SYSTABLES
      WHERE CREATOR = 'SYSIBM' AND
      TSNAME = 'SYSDBASE')
```

Figure 16.5 Query 10.

E X P L A I N   O U T P U T

QUERY NO.	Q B #	PLAN NO.	METH	TNAME	TB NO	AC	M COL	INDEX	IDX ONLY	SORT UJOG	IND. UJOG	TS LOCK MODE
10	1	1	0	SYSCOLUMNS	1	R	0		N	NNNN	NNNN	IS
10	2	1	0	SYSTABLES	2	I	1	DSNDTX01	N	NNNN	NNNN	IS
10	2	2	3		0		0		N	NNNN	YNYN	
20	1	1	0	SYSTABLESPACE	1	I	1	DSNDSX01	Y	NNNN	NNNN	IS
30	1	1	0	SYSTABLES	1	I	0	DSNDTX01	Y	NNNN	NNNN	IS
30	1	2	1	SYSCOLUMNS	2	I	2	DSNDCX01	Y	NNNN	NNNN	IS
30	1	3	3		0		0		N	NNNN	NNYN	

Figure 16.6   The plan table for Queries 10, 20, and 30.

a QBLOCKNO of 2, indicating that it is the second select. It accesses SYSTABLES. ACCESSTYPE indicates an I for index and it uses one matching column. The index used on this table is DSNDTX01. The first column in this index is CREATOR, which is part of the predicate of the SELECT. The other column named in the predicate, TSNAME, is not in the index, so MATCHCOLS is 1, not 2, because one column, rather than two, in the predicate is matched in the index lookup.

The third row has a METHOD of 3, indicating that a sort took place. The two Y's in the second set of SORT_IND columns indicate that the sort was done on the intermediate result table produced by the inner select. PLANNO is 2; it is the second step within QBLOCKNO 2.

Notice that for this example and the two that follow we tell you the columns that belong to each index. You could also get this information by querying the catalog table SYSIBM.SYSKEYS.

16.4.2   Query 20

Query 20 is a plain SELECT from one table, SYSIBM.SYSTABLESPACE (Fig. 16.7). It creates one row in the PLAN_TABLE (Fig. 16.6). The I in ACCESSTYPE shows that an index named DSNDSX01 is used. The 1 in MATCHCOLS shows that it is a matching index scan, matching on the one column named in the predicate, DBNAME. The scan is index only, because DBNAME and NAME are two columns in the DSNDSX01 index. The SELECT asks

```
EXPLAIN PLAN SET QUERYNO = 20 FOR
SELECT DBNAME, NAME
   FROM SYSIBM.SYSTABLESPACE
   WHERE DBNAME = 'SYSDBASE'
```

Figure 16.7   Query 20.

for these two columns only, so the table itself does not have to be accessed.

16.4.3 Query 30

Query 30 is a join of SYSIBM.SYSTABLES and SYSIBM.SYSCOLUMNS with an ORDER BY clause (Fig. 16.8). Its EXPLAIN output consists of three rows. The first shows that SYSTABLES is the first table accessed (METHOD = 0) and that an index is used (ACCESSTYPE = I). The index, as in Query 10, is DSNDTX01. MATCH_COLS is 0, so we know it isn't a matching index scan. However, DB2 finds the information it needs without accessing the table (INDEX_ONLY = Y). The query needs the columns CREATOR and NAME and these are both in that index.

The second row for Query 30 shows that the second table, SYSCOLUMNS, will be joined to the first with METHOD 1, a nested loop join. It will be accessed with an index (ACCESSTYPE = I), which will match on two columns (MATCH_COLS = 2) and will not need the actual table (INDEX_ONLY = Y). This is because the index used is DSNDCX01 and it contains three columns, TBCREATOR, TBNAME, and NAME. The join is doing a match on the first two columns, TBCREATOR and TBNAME, and the query itself is SELECTing NAME, the third column. No other data is needed to satisfy the query.

The third row, with METHOD = 3 and a Y in the second group of SORT INDICATORS, shows that the query's ORDER BY clause will require the sorting of an intermediate results table.

A familiarity with EXPLAIN, and a willingness to use it, can help you greatly in tuning your queries. Once you've gotten used to looking at PLAN_TABLE rows, you will find that you can spot possible performance problems before they happen and can make yourself very useful to your team. Any time you notice an R in ACCESSTYPE for a large table, you should investigate. Is a new index needed? Was RUNSTATS run before instead of after the table was loaded? Should programs be rebound? Anytime there are lots of Y's in the SORT indicators, a look at the query is also called for. Are more indexes needed? Are ORDER BY or GROUP BY or SELECT DISTINCT being used unnecessarily? EXPLAIN can help with decisions about which

```
EXPLAIN PLAN SET QUERYNO = 30 FOR
SELECT A.CREATOR, A.NAME, B.NAME
   FROM SYSIBM.SYSTABLES A,
   SYSIBM.SYSCOLUMNS B
   WHERE A.CREATOR = B.TBCREATOR AND
   A.NAME = B.TBNAME
   ORDER BY 1,2,3
```

Figure 16.8 Query 30.

columns should be included in indexes and can also indicate which indexes aren't being used and can be dropped.

As new DB2 releases appear, the Optimizer gets more sophisticated and DB2 performance improves. At the same time, more information is provided in PLAN_TABLE. The result may be temporary confusion as you learn to deal with the added complexity, but you will find the effort worthwhile.

The EXPLAIN function is an important tool for application programmers. We recommend using it whenever you BIND or REBIND your programs. It's an effective way to monitor and diagnose the performance of programs in test and production.

DB2 Commands and Utilities

In this chapter we will discuss the DB2 commands that are used to interact with the DB2 subsystem and its components. They may be used to start or stop access to the entire DB2 subsystem or to individual tablespaces, to see who is using DB2, to see what is going on inside DB2, and to some extent to dynamically modify what DB2 does.

DB2 also has a set of utilities, which we will describe in this chapter. Most are used by DBAs and systems programmers, but some are of use to application programmers.

17.1 DB2 COMMANDS

We will not discuss all of the DB2 commands here, only the ones that are most likely to be of use to the application programmer. In order to execute them, you must be granted the appropriate level of authority by your DBA. The full list of commands and a description of what they do are in the *DB2 Command and Utility Reference* manual. DB2 syntax rules require that the command name be preceded by the MVS subsystem recognition character for DB2. Most installations use a hyphen as a subsystem recognition character.

Let's look first at the -DISPLAY command. It is used to look at the status of tablespaces, indexes, databases, threads, and utilities in progress. The -DISPLAY DATABASE command allows you to look at the status of one or more databases. If the name of your database is DB1, you would type:

```
-DISPLAY DATABASE(DB1)
```

This gives you a list of the tablespaces and indexspaces associated with the database and the status of each. The output of the command is shown below:

```
DSNT360I - ************************************************
DSNT361I - *  DISPLAY DATABASE SUMMARY
           *     GLOBAL
DSNT360I - ************************************************
DSNT362I -       DATABASE = DB1        STATUS = RW
                 DBD LENGTH = 4028
DSNT397I -
NAME      TYPE PART STATUS  PHYERRLO PHYERRHI CATALOG  PIECE
--------  ---- ---- ------  -------- -------- -------- -----
DB1CUSTS  TS        RW
DB1BRNTS  TS        RO
DB1ACCTS  TS        UTRO
XCUSTUX1  IX        RW
XBRANUX1  IX        RW
XACCTUX1  IX        RW
******* DISPLAY OF DATABASE DB1 ENDED ******************
DSN9022I - DSNTDDIS 'DISPLAY DATABASE' NORMAL COMPLETION
***
```

The NAME column provides you with the names of the tablespaces and indexspaces, the TYPE column indicates if they are tablespaces or indexspaces, and the STATUS column indicates the type of processing that can be done. RW means that the tablespace is available for reading and writing, RO means read only, and UTRO means that a utility is currently executing against the object and it is therefore read only. A status of COPY means that a COPY PENDING flag is on and the tablespace can't be updated but can be read.

You are most likely to do a DISPLAY DATABASE when an SQL query doesn't work, and you want to make sure the data it refers to is accessible. Type:

```
-DISPLAY DATABASE(DB1) RESTRICT
```

This command lists only those objects in that particular database that are not accessible for read or write. If you find a tablespace or indexspace used by your query on this list, you'll know why your SQL didn't work. The DISPLAY DATABASE command provides more information than the SQLCODE you will get if a resource your query needs is unavailable. DISPLAY indicates exactly which resource is unavailable and provides some information as to why.

DISPLAY can also be used to look at the status of a specific tablespace or indexspace. The command format for looking at the status of tablespace DB1CUSTS, for example, is:

```
-DISPLAY DATABASE(DB1) SPACENAM(DB1CUSTS)
```

SPACENAM can be followed by a tablespace or indexspace.

Many DB2 commands recognize an asterisk as a wild card. For example, you could type -DISPLAY DATABASE(*) to see all of the databases for which you have DISPLAY authorization. Likewise, if you want to see all of the tablespaces in database DB1 that begin with DB1C, type:

```
-DISPLAY DATABASE(DB1) SPACENAM(DB1C*)
```

The -DISPLAY THREAD command identifies which users are connected to DB2. To display all of the active users, type:

```
-DISPLAY THREAD(*)
```

The output of this command includes the user ID and the plan in use by the user. This command is useful if you're having a problem—such as getting hung up or timed out trying to do something—and you want to figure out who might be in contention with you for the same DB2 objects. When you find out who else is using the objects, you can know how long you might have to wait (for example, if a utility is running) or you might be able to ask someone to get out of QMF briefly while you run a needed job.

The -STOP DATABASE and -START DATABASE commands stop databases or tablespaces in them from being accessed and start them again. Ordinarily, when DB2 comes up, all of the databases are started automatically; you will only need the -START command if a -STOP command was issued previously. We will see how -START and -STOP can be used in conjunction with DB2 utilities and the commands associated with utilities in upcoming sections.

17.1.1 DB2 Command Execution

DB2 commands can be issued from the MVS console (an unlikely spot for an application programmer), from CICS with the DSNC command, from TSO with DB2I or DSN, and from batch with DSN. If you wanted to enter the DISPLAY THREAD command from TSO and you had the authority necessary, you have several choices.

Option 7 on the DB2I Menu (Fig. 17.1) brings you to the DB2 Command Panel (Fig. 17.2). Enter the command on the panel and then hit Enter. Alternatively, you can invoke the DSN command from TSO. DSN is a command processor that submits commands from TSO to DB2. We've seen it used with batch JCL for BIND and RUN commands. DSN can also be used interactively. To enter the DISPLAY THREAD command from the TSO READY prompt or from Option 6 of ISPF, you would type:

```
DSN SYSTEM(DB2A)
```

and then hit Enter. This command invokes the DSN command processor for the DB2 subsystem named DB2A. DSN comes back with the prompt,

```
                                                     DB2I PRIMARY OPTION MENU
===>

Select one of the following DB2 functions and press ENTER.

   1  SPUFI                   (Process SQL statements)
   2  DCLGEN                  (Generate SQL and source language declarations)
   3  PROGRAM PREPARATION     (Prepare a DB2 application program to run)
   4  PRECOMPILE              (Invoke DB2 precompiler)
   5  BIND/REBIND/FREE        (BIND, REBIND, or FREE application plans)
   6  RUN                     (RUN an SQL program)
   7  DB2 COMMANDS            (Issue DB2 commands)
   8  UTILITIES               (Invoke DB2 utilities)
   D  DB2I DEFAULTS           (Set global parameters)
   X  EXIT                    (Leave DB2I)




   PRESS:  END to exit        HELP for more information
```

Figure 17.1   DB2I primary option menu can be used to execute commands and utilities.

```
                            DB2 COMMANDS
===>

Enter a single DB2 command on up to 4 lines below:

   1  ===> -display thread(*)
   2  ===>
   3  ===>
   4  ===>









   PRESS:  ENTER to process       END to exit     HELP for more information
```

Figure 17.2   DB2I Command Panel.

DSN

You would then enter

-DISPLAY THREAD(*)

DSN displays the output of the command on your screen. When you hit Enter after the display is finished, the system will return you to the DSN prompt again. You can enter another command or terminate DSN by entering:

· END

If you wanted to enter the DISPLAY THREAD command from CICS and you had the authority necessary, you would enter:

DSNC -DISPLAY THREAD(*)

In CICS, the DSNC transaction functions like the DSN command in TSO; that is, it is a command processor that passes commands to DB2. Since a CICS region is connected to only one DB2 subsystem at a time, you don't have to specify the subsystem. DSNC is more limited in its capabilities than is DSN, but it can execute most DB2 commands.

Of the other DISPLAY commands, DISPLAY UTILITY is also commonly used and we will discuss it in the next section.

17.2   UTILITIES

DB2 has an extensive set of utilities. While it is helpful to be familiar with their names and functions, as application programmers you will not need to use most of them. Those that you are most likely to use, LOAD, RUNSTATS, and COPY, we'll describe in detail later in the chapter.

CHECK has two functions. It can check indexes to make sure that they are consistent with the data by checking that the pointers in the index point to valid rows and that all rows are pointed to by an index pointer. The utility issues warning messages if it finds inconsistencies. Secondly, it checks data to make sure that it meets referential constraints by making sure that rows in dependent tables have corresponding rows in parent tables. It issues warning messages when it finds inconsistencies and can, if desired, delete rows in violation of referential constraints and write them to an exception table.

COPY creates an image copy of a tablespace or dataset within a tablespace. An image copy is a page-for-page copy of a dataset; in other words, if an image copy is used to recover data, the data is not reorganized in the process. In addition to a full image copy, COPY can create an incremental image copy consisting only of pages changed since the last COPY was run. Note that image copies cannot be made of indexes; indexes are recovered from the underlying tables.

DIAGNOSE is a special utility used to diagnose internal DB2 problems; it's only meant to be used under the direction of IBM support personnel.

LOAD adds data into one or more tables in a tablespace or replaces data already there. It is normally more efficient to load data into a table rather than doing inserts with an application program or with SPUFI.

MERGECOPY consolidates several incremental image copies or consolidates several incremental copies with the last full image copy to create a new full image copy.

DB2 keeps information about image copies in SYSIBM.SYSCOPY Catalog table. MODIFY is used to delete this information when the image copies are no longer needed. DB2 keeps this information so it can call for them when needed for recovery. This utility does not affect the image copies themselves.

QUIESCE establishes the current log relative byte address (RBA) for a tablespace and places it in the SYSIBM.SYSCOPY Catalog table. Called a quiesce point, it is a point of consistency, that is, a point at which there are no pending updates to the tablespace. To recover a tablespace to a quiesce point means that the data in it is internally consistent and that no recovery procedures are needed to deal with in doubt or in flight transactions. In effect, this utility records log RBAs that can be used as checkpoints.

RECOVER can be used to recover or restore data from image copies and the DB2 log to either the current state, a particular image copy, or a specific log RBA. (The specified log RBA might be one produced by the QUIESCE utility.)

REORG does an unload and a load to reorganize a tablespace and its indexes. The unload phase copies the rows in clustering index sequence, as opposed to an image copy, which copies entire pages regardless of the sequence of rows in the page. REORG can be used separately on indexes to reorganize them.

REPAIR can be used to change any DB2 data, including internal pointers, etc. It can damage data if used incorrectly and is not normally used by application programmers.

REPORT extracts Catalog and Directory information needed to recover a tablespace.

RUNSTATS updates the DB2 Catalog with information obtained by reading tablespaces and indexes. The data is used by the Optimizer to determine access paths and is useful in deciding when tablespaces and indexes need to be reorganized.

STOSPACE updates the DB2 Catalog with information about the space allocated to storage groups.

Note that all of these utilities run as regular MVS batch jobs. They have their own attach facilities and DB2 must be up for them to run.

17.2.1 Utility Execution

DB2 utilities always run as MVS batch jobs and there are several ways to generate the required JCL. We recommend that you get JCL models for each utility from your DBA, although we will describe JCL generation from DB2I.

Option 8 on the DB2I Menu (Fig. 17.1) brings you to the DB2 Utilities Panel (Fig. 17.3). Field 1, FUNCTION, provides four choices; SUBMIT, DISPLAY, EDITJCL, and TERMINATE. SUBMIT creates the JCL and submits it. DISPLAY invokes the -DISPLAY UTILITY command, which shows you the status of a utility. EDITJCL lets you edit the JCL it creates. TERMINATE invokes the -TERM UTILITY command to terminate the selected utility. There will be more on DISPLAY UTILITY and TERMINATE UTILITY later.

In some installations, a job card is automatically created for you when JCL is submitted. If this is not true in your installation, you must make sure that you go into the DB2I Defaults Panel and set up

```
                        DB2 UTILITIES
 ===>

 Select from the following:

   1 FUNCTION ===>                 (SUBMIT job, EDITJCL, DISPLAY, TERMINATE)
   2 JOB ID   ===>                 (A unique job identifier string)
   3 UTILITY  ===>                 (CHECK, COPY, LOAD, MERGECOPY, MODIFY,
                                    RECOVER INDEX, RECOVER TABLESPACE,
                                    REORG INDEX, REORG TABLESPACE,
                                    REPAIR, RUNSTATS, STOSPACE)

   4 CONTROL CARDS DATA SET    ===>
   5 RECDSN  (LOAD,
              REORG TABLESPACE)===>
   6 DISCDSN (LOAD)            ===>
   7 COPYDSN (COPY, MERGECOPY) ===>

 To RESTART a utility, specify starting point, otherwise enter NO.
   8 RESTART   ===>              (NO, At CURRENT position, or beginning of PHASE)


 PRESS:  ENTER to process     END to exit    HELP for more information
```

Figure 17.3 DB2I Utilities Panel.

a job card that can be used by DB2I in creating all subsequent JCLs. Alternatively, you may use EDITJCL to add a job card.

Field 2, JOB ID, is where you enter a unique utility identifier. Although this panel calls the field JOB ID, in other parts of DB2 the same field is called UTILID or UTILITY ID. This is a value of up to 18 characters that identifies this particular execution of a utility. For instance, if you are loading a table called CUSTOMER, you might choose a utility ID of LOADCUST. At any given time, a utility ID must be unique within a DB2 subsystem.

Field 3, UTILITY, is where you put the name of the utility you want to run, such as LOAD.

Field 4, CONTROL CARDS DATA SET, allows you to enter the name of a dataset that contains the control statements needed to execute the utility. The dataset must exist prior to entering this screen. DB2I does not generate utility control statements for you, but it does provide HELP panels that are meant to give you some guidance. If you need help, either contact someone at your installation or refer to the *DB2 Command and Utility Reference.*

Field 5, RECDSN, is where you enter the dataset name of the input file. This is a required field for LOAD and REORG. In REORG, this dataset receives the output of the unload phase and is the input to the load phase.

Field 6, DISCDSN (discard dataset name) is only used when loading a table and is only needed then if you want to capture the records rejected by the LOAD utility. If you do not provide a discard dataset and the load utility encounters a bad record, the job will abend.

Field 7, COPYDSN, is needed only for the COPY and MERGECOPY utilities and points to the output dataset name.

Field 8, RESTART, is set to NO unless you are restarting the selected utility. NO is the default on the panel. Although some utilities may be restarted, we will not discuss them here; it is infrequent that utilities made available to application programmers are those that should be restarted.

17.2.2 Utility Monitoring and Control

The status of a utility that is running or one that has failed before completion can be viewed with the -DISPLAY UTILITY command. The command can be invoked from the Utilities Panel of DB2I, from the Command Panel, or from TSO as described in the discussion of DB2 commands. The command syntax is -DISPLAY UTILITY(*), if you want to see all of the utility jobs currently known to DB2 that you are authorized to see, or -DISPLAY UTILITY(*utilid*) to look at the status of a specific job. *Utilid* is the JOBID you created on the Utility Panel. -DISPLAY UTILITY(*aaa**) will provide the status of all of the utility jobs whose *utilid* begins with *aaa* and ends with any other character(s).

Suppose your user ID is USER1 and you have run a RUNSTATS utility job with a utility ID of RUNSTX. Let's say your job had been running but it was cancelled by Operations. If you executed the command

```
-DISP UTIL(RUNSTX)
```

you would get the following output:

```
DSNU100I - DSNUGDIS - USERID = USER1
              UTILID = RUNSTX
              PROCESSING UTILITY STATEMENT 1
              UTILITY = RUNSTATS
              PHASE = RUNSTATS COUNT = 0
              STATUS = STOPPED
DSN9022I - DSNUGCC '-DISP UTIL' NORMAL COMPLETION
```

In this message, the words prefixed by DSN in the display are IBM DB2 message identifiers. The first line indicates the requestor's user ID. The second line indicates the utility ID of the utility job being displayed. The third line is relevant if the job contains more than one utility control statement.

The fourth line indicates the name of the utility you are running, RUNSTATS here. And the fifth line indicates a PHASE and a COUNT. Different utilities have different phases or steps in their processing. All have an initialization and setup phase, UTILINIT, and a clean-up, UTILTERM, phase. Most, like the RUNSTATS example, have one processing phase which carries the same name as the utility. COUNT is the number of rows processed so far by the phase currently executing. In the reload phase of a LOAD job, for instance, this will give the number of rows loaded into the table.

The next line, STATUS, will identify the job as either ACTIVE, meaning that it is running, or STOPPED, meaning that it has to be restarted or terminated. A new job with the same utility ID can't be submitted until the existing job is terminated.

A utility is terminated with the -TERM UTILITY(*utilid*) command. If you use an asterisk (*) instead of a specific utility ID, all utilities for which you have authorization will be terminated, so be careful! You can also terminate a related group of jobs by using a partial ID and an asterisk (*aa**).

The terminate command can be issued wherever a DB2 command can be issued. In some shops, each utility job step is followed by a -TERM UTILITY command job step to be executed when the utility step fails. Operations can then resubmit the job without manually terminating the utility.

When running utilities, you may need to use the -START DATABASE and -STOP DATABASE commands discussed earlier in this chapter. Suppose, for example, that you want to run the COPY utility on tablespace TS1 in database DB1 and you don't want any updates taking place while the COPY is running. You could -STOP the tablespace by typing:

```
-STOP DATABASE(DB1) SPACENAM(TS1)
```

Then you could restart the database with restricted access by typing:

```
-START DATABASE(DB1) SPACENAM(TS1) ACCESS(RO)
```

This would mean the tablespace could be read but not updated. If you wanted to restrict access to your utility only, you could type:

```
-START DATABASE(DB1) SPACENAM(TS1) ACCESS(UT)
```

The ACCESS(UT) parameter permits access to utilities only. When the utility is finished and you're ready to allow normal access to the tablespace, you can execute:

```
-START DATABASE(DB1) SPACENAME(TS1)
```

If you don't specify a specific ACCESS type, the default is RW (read/write).

17.3   THE LOAD UTILITY

The LOAD utility is probably the one most used by application programmers because it places data from a flat file into a table. If the table contains more than a few rows, LOAD is more efficient to use than SQL INSERT statements in QMF or SPUFI and is often more convenient.

LOAD requires an input dataset that should be sorted in the sequence of the table's clustering index, if there is one. It should not contain duplicate values in columns that must be unique.

Now let's look at the LOAD syntax. Consider a simple case first, the LOAD control statement for loading a table called TABLE1:

```
LOAD INTO TABLE TABLE1
```

This statement tells the utility to load the input data into the empty

table TABLE1. If the table already has rows in it, code LOAD RE-
SUME YES if you want the new rows added to the end of the table. If
you want to replace the current data with new input data, you have to
add the REPLACE parameter and code:

```
LOAD REPLACE INTO TABLE TABLE1
```

This statement tells the utility to REPLACE the rows already in the
table, if any, with these newer rows.

LOAD control statements have dozens of options and can be quite
complicated, but in practice it's not necessary to use most of them. One
option which is important is LOG YES or LOG NO. The LOG parameter determines whether log records are written for the inserted rows.
LOG YES, the default, means that log records are written; LOG NO
means that they're not. LOG NO is much more efficient than LOG
YES but will cause a COPY PENDING flag to be turned on and will
set the tablespace's status to COPY. This is because DB2 wants you to
make an image copy of the table since you didn't record the loaded
rows in the log. Running the COPY utility will turn off the COPY
PENDING flag and will set the status to RW. This is part of DB2's
mechanism to ensure that your new table will be recoverable. The
COPY utility will be described shortly.

If you have used LOG NO and want to avoid the COPY step, you can
use the -START DATABASE command to turn off the COPY PEND-
ING flag. For tablespace TS1 in database DB1 you would code:

```
-START DATABASE(DB1) SPACENAM(TS1) ACCESS(FORCE)
```

This command with the FORCE parameter will start the tablespace
in the status of RW, changing its former status of COPY. The
tablespace will not, however, be recoverable until the COPY utility
is run. (It is possible to turn off the COPY PENDING flag with the
REPAIR utility, but we do not recommend its use for this purpose
since the -START DATABASE command can do the same thing
with less risk.)

The other option you need to know about is field specifications.
There are three conditions under which field specifications are
required on the LOAD statement. One is that the data in the input
record is not in the same order as it will be in the table row. Another is if data is in a different representation than DB2 expects
(e.g., the column is DECIMAL, but the input is DISPLAY). The last
condition is that the input record does not contain data for every
column in the row. If one field specification is needed, DB2 expects
a field specification for every field for which there is data in the input record.

Let's look at an example using field specifications. The table we are loading, TABLE1, has 3 columns defined as follows:

```
ID_NO         CHAR(5)
BALANCE       DECIMAL(7, 2)
DESCRIPTION   CHAR(15) NOT NULL WITH DEFAULT
```

Our test data is in 13-byte records. The first 5 bytes are the ID_NO, the next 7 bytes are the BALANCE column (note that DB2 LOAD can convert a DISPLAY number to packed), and the thirteenth byte is a code we will use to indicate when the balance field should be set to null. If the thirteenth byte is A, the column should be nulled. We need this because LOAD, unlike INSERT, cannot recognize the word "null" on an input record. We tell LOAD what to look for to decide whether a column should contain nulls with the NULLIF parameter. An input file might look like:

```
AAAAA0020025B
BBBBB0050000B
CCCCC0000000A
```

You may have noted that we are not providing data for the DESCRIPTION column; it will be loaded with its default, spaces. We do not use a field specification for this field in our LOAD control statement because there is no data for it on the input record. When specifying fields on the LOAD control statement, you must specify the starting position of each field on the input record; ending positions are optional if the columns are fixed length and the data in the input record does not need conversion, but we will use them for clarity. To load the above table, the following control statements are used:

```
LOAD REPLACE LOG NO INTO TABLE TABLE1
  (ID_NO     POSITION (1:5)  CHAR(5),
   BALANCE   POSITION (6:12) DECIMAL EXTERNAL(7,2)
             NULLIF  (13:13) = 'A')
```

When the utility is run, the first five characters of the input record will be put into the ID_NO column. LOAD's NULLIF parameter specifies that if the thirteenth byte of the input record contains A, BALANCE should be set to null; otherwise, the characters in bytes 6 through 12 will be assumed to be numeric and will be packed into the BALANCE column. In our sample input file, the third record will set balance to null because there is an A in the thirteenth byte.

For DECIMAL columns, fields can be specified as DECIMAL if they already contain packed numbers. If the numbers are in display format, you use DECIMAL EXTERNAL with a length and scale number, as in our example.

For INTEGER columns, fields can be specified as INTEGER if the data is already in binary format or as INTEGER EXTERNAL (length) if the data is in display format; the length refers to the actual number of bytes in the input field.

Putting negative numbers into EXTERNAL format presents special problems that won't be dealt with here; let's just say that you'll probably want to use a program or a utility to put them into internal format (packed for DECIMAL, comp for INT).

Other data types that can be used as field specifications on LOAD control statements include VARCHAR for VARCHAR data, TIME EXTERNAL for character representation of TIME data, and DATE EXTERNAL for character representation of DATE data. If you have VARCHAR columns in the table to be loaded, each VARCHAR field in the input record must be preceded by a 2-byte binary field giving the length of the input data for the VARCHAR column. POSITION on the LOAD control statement must point to this 2-byte binary number.

If you have DATE and TIME data to load, it should be in character format.

You may want to run the LOAD utility with a discard dataset to capture records with bad data. If there is any bad data and you have not specified a discard dataset, the job will abend.

The LOAD utility has several phases. It starts, as all utilities do, with UTILINIT, a setup phase. The next phase, RELOAD, is where the input data is read, rows are inserted into the table, and the index and foreign keys are written to temporary datasets. The next phase, SORT, sorts the index and foreign keys extracted in the RELOAD phase. The fourth phase, BUILD, creates the indexes and detects duplicates. The next step, INDEXVAL, deletes rows that would cause unique index violations, then the ENFORCE step checks referential constraints if requested by a control statement. Next, DISCARD copies any records that are causing errors to the DISCARD dataset. Finally, REPORT generates a summary report and UTILTERM cleans up.

While we recommend getting a model JCL for the LOAD utility from your DBA, take a look at the following sample for LOAD JCL; it will load our table TABLE1:

```
//LOADJOB   JOB   JOBCARD
//* The PARM includes the DB2 subsystem name and the
//* utilid.
//LOADSTEP  EXEC  PGM=DSNUTILB,
//     PARM='DB2A,LOAD1'
//* The following 2 statements are required for all
//* utilities.
//SYSPRINT  DD    SYSOUT=A
//UTPRINT   DD    SYSOUT=A
//SYSUDUMP  DD    SYSOUT=A
//* SORTWK DD statements are required if there are any
//* indexes or foreign keys
//SORTWK01  DD    UNIT=SYSDA,SPACE=(CYL,(10,10))
//SORTWK02  DD    UNIT=SYSDA,SPACE=(CYL,(10,10))
//SORTWK03  DD    UNIT=SYSDA,SPACE=(CYL,(10,10))
//* SYSUT1 is a temporary dataset used for keys to be
//* sorted. SORTOUT is for the sorted keys.
//SYSUT1    DD    UNIT=SYSDA,SPACE=(CYL,(10,10))
//SORTOUT   DD    UNIT=SYSDA,SPACE=(CYL,(10,10))
//* SYSREC is the data to be loaded.
//SYSREC    DD    DSN=TABLE1.LOAD.DATA,DISP=SHR
//SYSIN     DD *
   LOAD DATA REPLACE LOG NO
     INTO TABLE TABLE1
     (ID_NO POSITION (1:5) CHAR (5),
     BALANCE  POSITION (6:12) DECIMAL EXTERNAL (7, 2)
     NULLIF (13:13) = 'A')
```

Note that utility control statements do not require any special continuation characters to be continued on the next line. They must be
placed in columns 1 through 72 of 80-byte records.

17.4   THE RUNSTATS UTILITY

The RUNSTATS utility reads DB2 tablespaces and associated indexes
to gather statistical information with which it then updates the DB2
Catalog. This is the information that the Optimizer uses to select an
access path to the data. Catalog tables that RUNSTATS updates are
also used by DBAs to decide when to reorganize tables and indexes,
etc.   RUNSTATS   updates   the   following   Catalog   tables:
SYSCOLUMNS, SYSINDEXES, SYSTABLES, SYSTABLESPACE,
SYSTABLEPART, and SYSINDEXPART. These tables are described
in App. B.

Remember that until RUNSTATS is run on a tablespace with data
in it, the Optimizer may not use any of its indexes. Therefore,
RUNSTATS must be run at least once for every tablespace that has
associated indexes. RUNSTATS should be run after the data is loaded
or inserted into tables and after any reorganizations that are to be
done have completed. Application plans must be bound or rebound after running RUNSTATS for the Optimizer to take advantage of the
information gained.

RUNSTATS requires the minimum set of DD statements for utilities, SYSIN, SYSPRINT, and UTPRINT; it uses no input files except SYSIN for control statements. Typically, it can be run with several control statements, one for each tablespace and its associated indexes to be scanned by RUNSTATS. The syntax of a control statement is

RUNSTATS TABLESPACE *dbname.tspacename* INDEX (ALL)

This statement will cause RUNSTATS to collect statistics for the named tablespace in the named database. The INDEX(ALL) parameter causes RUNSTATS to collect statistics for all of the tablespace's associated indexes. This statement uses the recommended default of SHRLEVEL REFERENCE, which means that the tablespace can be read but not updated while RUNSTATS is scanning it. The alternative is SHRLEVEL CHANGE, which permits updates. To use the SHRLEVEL CHANGE option, just add it to the end of the control statement:

RUNSTATS TABLESPACE *dbname.tspacename* INDEX (ALL)
    SHRLEVEL CHANGE

RUNSTATS puts out informational messages as it updates Catalog tables. It finishes with a condition code 0 if there are no errors or warnings; a condition code 4 means that a tablespace is in COPY PENDING status.

17.5 THE COPY UTILITY

The COPY utility makes an image copy of a tablespace that can be used for recovery. An image copy also resets the COPY PENDING flag. Using the LOAD utility with the LOG NO option turns the COPY PENDING flag on, preventing updates to the table. The COPY utility is used to reset this flag.

An image copy is a page for page copy of a tablespace; no reorganization takes place. In addition to full image copies, the utility can make an incremental image copy which copies only those pages that have been changed since the last image copy. Aside from the minimum set of utility *ddnames*, the COPY utility uses the SYSCOPY *ddname* for the output of the image copy. The control statement for COPY utility to make a full image copy is:

COPY TABLESPACE *dbname.tspacename* DEVT SYSDA

DEVT, for device type, must contain the same name as the UNIT parameter on the SYSCOPY DD statement; the above example says that we are writing the copy to disk. The default of SHRLEVEL REF-

ERENCE means that the table can be read but not updated while the copy is taking place; this is recommended.

You may specify a BLKSIZE parameter on the output DD statement, but there are only three permissible values. The default (and maximum) is 16,384. This is fine for tape, but for a 3380 disk the most efficient in terms of bytes stored per track is 8192; 4096 is the other permissible value.

We think you will find the above discussion of DB2 commands and utilities helpful in your work. While in some shops they are more often the province of the DBA, it is not uncommon for application programmers to use them for test applications, and your familiarity with the DB2 commands and utilities will be considered an asset.

18

Distributed Database Facility

With the availability of version 2 release 2, DB2 now supports data distribution. Using this facility, a user connected to one DB2 subsystem can read and update data stored at another (Fig. 18.1). Contrast this with the earlier releases of DB2 where you could access data from only a single, local DB2 subsystem.

Distributed Data Facility (DDF) is a significant enhancement to DB2 and it merits extended coverage. At the same time, it is important to note that there are many levels of data distribution and DB2 currently does not support all of them. For example, in the completely distributed data environment, a single SQL statement should be able to access relational data at any location. In DB2 2.2, an SQL statement can access data from only one DB2 subsystem. Therefore, you cannot join two tables from different DB2 subsystems. You can, however, include multiple SQL statements in an application program and thereby access data at multiple DB2 subsystems.

In the following discussion, we will present an overview of DB2's current implementation of data distribution and its implications for an application programmer. To gain a broader perspective of the subject, we will also present some key concepts of data distribution.

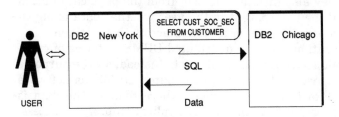

Figure 18.1 Overview of data distribution.

18.1 CONCEPTS OF DISTRIBUTED DATABASES

You are already aware that a database can be thought of as a collection of interrelated data, able to serve multiple applications. The data requirements for related applications are integrated, creating a data pool that can then be shared by multiple applications. In a distributed database, the common data pool, instead of being stored at a central location, is broken up into several pieces that are physically stored at multiple sites. But why distribute data? Some of the reasons are organization structure, capacity, risk management, and economics.

For example, a bank may have branches located in different places. Each branch may have its own database, and there may be a need to access information about customer accounts at other branches. Since data is spread across multiple branches, the storage capacity required at each branch is a small fraction of the whole. In addition, if the database sytem is not operational at say the Chicago branch, the branch in New York could still operate and access data at all other locations except Chicago. This approach also minimizes the risk of a complete system outage in which all branches become nonoperational. Furthermore, instead of building the complete system at all branch locations in one shot, the bank may adopt a pay-as-you-go philosophy and stage the implementation of database systems across the branch network. It will certainly be easier to secure funding for a database system at one branch than for database systems for all branches.

18.1.1 What is a Distributed DBMS?

In simplistic terms, a distributed DBMS manages data stored at multiple sites. It has all the features of a traditional centralized DBMS and also some new ones. For example, centralized DBMSs like IMS, IDMS, ADABAS, and DB2 (prior to version 2 release 2) provide facilities for security, recovery, concurrency, and integrity and generally insulate the user from the actual physical storage medium. Distributed DBMSs, like DB2 2.2, support all the above features and also go a step further. They also insulate the user from the physical location of the data. It will be transparent to the user whether data is physically stored at the local system or a system across the continent.

The formal definition of a true distributed DBMS in terms of criteria and rules is outside the scope of this book. Instead, for the purposes of this discussion, we will define a distributed DBMS as software which manages data in an environment where some of the data is stored at another computer, or the user or application program accessing the data is on another computer, or both. Note that the ultimate goal of a distributed DBMS is to manage distributed data and still make it appear to the user as a single centralized DBMS.

18.1.2 Local and Remote

The DB2 subsystem to which an interactive user or application system is connected is called the local DB2 subsystem. All other DB2 subsystems that you can access from your local subsystem are called remote DB2 subsystems (Fig. 18.2). This same terminology also applies to DB2 objects and the DB2 Catalog. For example, the DB2 Catalog on the local subsystem is called the local Catalog and the Catalog on the remote subsystem is called the remote Catalog.

Note that the terms local and remote are not used in the context of distance. In fact, two or more DB2 subsystems may be running under one MVS operating system on one computer, and in this case, both the local and remote DB2 subsystems will be at the same physical site. Figure 18.2 shows an example of this. The user is connected to the DB2A subsystem and therefore, DB2A is the local subsystem. DB2B and DB2C are the remote subsystems. DB2C is installed in Chicago;

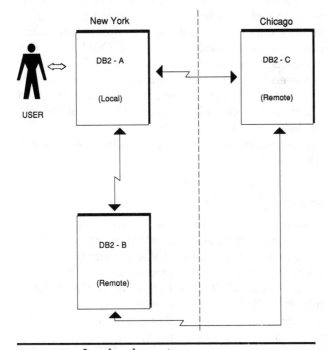

Figure 18.2 Local and remote.

both DB2A and DB2B are installed in New York. The remote subsystem DB2B may be installed on the same MVS system running DB2A or it may be installed on a second computer across the hall.

18.1.3 Commit Scope and Logical Unit of Work

The commit scope defines the boundary of a logical unit of work. It is identified by the SQL COMMIT statement (or the equivalent SYNCPOINT in a CICS environment). In the SQL language, all database updates are provisional until committed. A COMMIT permanently updates the database, frees locks on DB2 resources (tables, application plans, etc.), and essentially enables data sharing. Now let's examine it in more detail.

A logical unit of work is a set of changes to data that must all complete successfully to be valid. If only part of the logical unit succeeds, the changes should be backed out and the data restored to its original condition before the updates began. COMMIT is the process of making a change permanent, while ROLLBACK is the process of undoing changes that have been made but are not yet permanent.

In a batch or TSO program, DB2 treats the entire execution of the program as one logical unit of work unless the programmer specifies otherwise. A programmer may break up an application program into multiple logical units of work by explicitly issuing COMMITs (Fig. 18.3). If you do not explicitly issue a COMMIT, DB2 will automatically issue one upon successful completion of a program. Therefore, we can also define the scope of a commit as the duration between the start of a program or the last explicit commit point and the end of the program, or the next explicit commit point.

We will use the terms commit scope and logical unit of work interchangeably in this discussion.

18.1.4 Location Transparency

One goal of a distributed DBMS is to insulate the user from the location of a specific piece of data. This feature is called location transparency. It allows the user to access data from any site without having to specify the location. The DBMS itself automatically locates the remote data. For example, distributed DB2 uses tables in its Catalog and Communication Database (CDB) to determine whether the required data is local or remote and, if it is remote, its actual location.

One key advantage of location transparency is that it simplifies application programming. Application and data portability is another

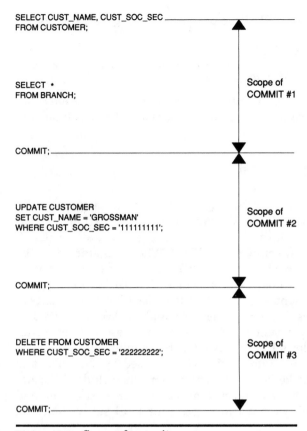

```
SELECT CUST_NAME, CUST_SOC_SEC
FROM CUSTOMER;


SELECT *                                    Scope of
FROM BRANCH;                                COMMIT #1



COMMIT;


UPDATE CUSTOMER
SET CUST_NAME = 'GROSSMAN'                   Scope of
WHERE CUST_SOC_SEC = '111111111';           COMMIT #2



COMMIT;


DELETE FROM CUSTOMER                         Scope of
WHERE CUST_SOC_SEC = '222222222';           COMMIT #3



COMMIT;
```

Figure 18.3   Scope of commit.

benefit. For example, both the data and the application can be moved from one DB2 subsystem to another without changing any application programs.

18.1.5 Local Autonomy

Each individual site participating in a distributed database is an autonomous, self-sufficient database that is independent of any central control. The DBMSs at each site are peers. This approach improves data availability. Even if one or more sites are disabled, the rest of the network can continue to operate in the local mode and communicate with other working sites.

Every DB2 site has complete control over the data it manages. For example, users can access remote data only if they are explicitly authorized by the remote site. In addition, the DB2 Governor can be used to control the amount of CPU time permitted for the execution of remote SQL statements.

18.2   DATA DISTRIBUTION IN DB2 2.2

DB2 2.2 is IBM's first implementation of a distributed relational database. The key features of this release are described in the following subsections.

18.2.1   Communicating With Other Subsystems

To communicate with other DB2 subsystems, you need the Distributed Data Facility (DDF), a Virtual Telecommunications Access Method (VTAM) network, and a Communications Database (CDB) (Fig. 18.4). DDF is a new component of DB2. When it is started by the operator, a user connected to one DB2 subsystem can access data stored at another DB2 subsystem on which the DDF is also active. DDF is a major component of DB2. Like the three other components of DB2 (Systems Services, Data Base Services, and IRLM), it has its own address space. VTAM provides the underlying access method in an SNA network that allows DB2 subsystems to communicate with each other. The CDB contains information that is used by the DDF and VTAM to transfer data between DB2 subsystems. It includes information about which remote DB2 subsystems can be accessed by you and which remote DB2 subsystems can access your local subsystem. The

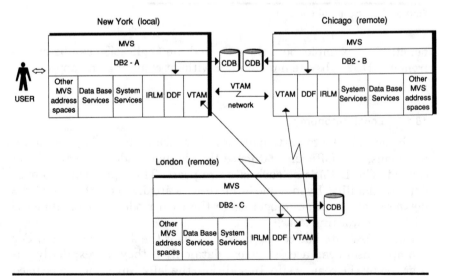

Figure 18.4   Communicating with other subsystems.

tables in the CDB are not part of DB2's Catalog. They have to be created separately after DB2 is installed.

18.2.2 Three-Part Names for Tables and Views

In the earlier releases, DB2 used a two-part name for tables and views such as *authid.objectname*. In this naming scheme, *authid* identifies the owner of the table or view and *objectname* is the name of the table or view. Starting with version 2 release 2, DB2 uses a three-part naming scheme: *location.authid.objectname*. The three-part name is actually a two-part name with an added 16 character location qualifier which uniquely identifies the DB2 subsystem where the data is stored. The location qualifier must match a valid location name in the CDB. If you do not use the location qualifier, DB2 assumes that you are accessing data from the local database. To access data from remote objects, you must use the fully qualified three-part name.

For example, a user in New York can select data from the local BRANCH table by using either the name NEWYORK.*authid*.BRANCH or the name *authid*.BRANCH in a query. Furthermore, if that user is also the owner of the BRANCH table, he or she can refer to it simply by the name BRANCH. However, if he or she is accessing the BRANCH table in Chicago, it must be referred to using the fully qualified name, which could be CHICAGO.DBA1.BRANCH.

The three-part naming scheme also makes applications portable. For example, using three-part names, you can run a query developed and currently being executed in Chicago, without any change, on any DB2 subsystem in the network. The only modification you would need would be an update of relevant tables in the CDB.

Note that three-part names can be used for tables and views in all instances except in the CREATE SYNONYM statement and the LOAD utility. A synonym uses a one-part name and always refers to a local object; the LOAD utility loads data only into local tables.

In the next subsection, we will show you yet another way of accessing remote data using aliases.

18.2.3 Using Aliases

Aliases are alternate names for tables and views. They are similar to synonyms in the sense that both allow you to use simple names to represent tables and views. Both of them are also "logical objects" whose definitions are stored in DB2's Catalog. But this is where the similarity ends. The main difference between the two is that while a synonym can represent only local tables and views, an alias can represent both local and remote tables and views. In addition, a synonym can only be used by its creator. An alias, on the other hand, can be used by anyone and is therefore also called a "public name."

Alias names are similar to table and view names. You can use either a one-, two-, or three-part name for local aliases, i.e., aliases that were created on your local DB2 subsystem and whose definitions exist in the local DB2 Catalog. Three-part alias names must be used for remote aliases, i.e., aliases that were created on a remote DB2 subsystem and whose definitions reside on a remote DB2 Catalog. The location qualifier in the three-part alias name is used to identify the DB2 subsystem where the alias definition is stored. Aliases are important because they provide the location transparency feature in DB2. Once they have been created, a user is oblivious to where the data is stored. For example, assume that the DBA in New York creates an alias   USER1.BRANCH   for   the   BRANCH   table   called CHICAGO.DBA1.BRANCH in Chicago. The true location of the data is transparent to a user in New York referencing the alias USER1.BRANCH.

An alias can be created for a local table or view, a remote table or view, or a nonexistent object. It is up to the alias creator to ensure that at execution time, aliases reference the correct tables and views. Aliases are created as follows:

```
CREATE ALIAS USER1.BRANCH
    FOR CHICAGO.DBA1.BRANCH
```

CHICAGO.DBA1.BRANCH is the fully qualified name of the BRANCH table in Chicago. Assuming that the alias was created in New York, all local users may use the alias as follows:

```
SELECT * FROM USER1.BRANCH
```

All users remote to New York may use the alias as follows:

```
SELECT * FROM NEWYORK.USER1.BRANCH
```

You can create an alias if you have either the CREATEALIAS or the SYSADM privilege.

The SQL DROP ALIAS statement is used to delete aliases. You can delete an alias if you are either the owner or have the SYSADM privilege.

18.2.4   Date, Time, and Other Special Registers

DB2 has a set of six storage areas called special registers that may be referenced by SQL. They are CURRENT DATE, CURRENT TIME,

CURRENT TIMESTAMP, CURRENT TIMEZONE, CURRENT SQLID, and USER. Except for a few differences, these special registers return similar values for both locally and remotely executed SQL statements. We will define a locally executable SQL statement as one that accesses local tables and views and a remotely executable SQL statement as one that accesses remote tables and views. Since each SQL statement can access data from only one DB2 subsystem (local or remote), an SQL statement can either be locally or remotely executable, but never both.

Four of these registers (CURRENT DATE, CURRENT TIME, CURRENT TIMESTAMP, CURRENT TIMEZONE) maintain date and time data. The values in these registers reflect the current date, time, timestamp, and time zone at the DB2 subsystem (local or remote) where the SQL statement executes.

The CURRENT SQLID and USER registers return the value of the user's current SQLID and the user's primary auth ID, respectively, for a locally executed statement. The USER register returns a translated version of the primary auth ID (translation rules are defined in the CDB) for a remotely executed SQL statement. This translated primary auth ID is the one that is used for checking the authorization of a dynamic SQL statement executing at a remote site. The CURRENT SQLID register cannot be used for a remotely executable statement.

18.2.5 Referential Integrity Limitations

Distributed DB2 does not support referential integrity (RI) across multiple DB2 subsystems. RI maintains the consistency of relationships between tables by requiring that every foreign key value in a table have a matching primary key value in a corresponding table or else be labeled null. DB2's implementation of RI is accomplished through the definition of referential constraints. These constraints are defined in DB2's Catalog and enable DB2 to enforce referential integrity automatically.

However, DB2 does not automatically enforce referential constraints across multiple DB2 subsystems. Since they cannot be defined across multiple DB2 subsystems, each referential structure must reside on a single DB2 subsystem. A referential structure can be thought of as a related set of tables in which all data references from one table to another are valid.

18.3 ACCESSING REMOTE DATA

DB2 provides access, using SQL, to remote data either interactively (through SPUFI and QMF) or from user-written application programs.

The following sections describe what remote data you can access, how to do it, and what you cannot do.

18.3.1 Remote Table Name Translation

From your local DB2 subsystem, you can use either a table name, view name, or alias name to specify the source of remote data. Recall that synonyms cannot be used to reference remote tables and views.

Figure 18.5 illustrates the object name translation process for remote objects. First DB2 uses the local Catalog to convert any alias name references to the three-part names they represent. Then, it determines the name and location of the remote subsystem from the location qualifier in the three-part name. Now DB2 uses the CDB and the DDF to transmit the SQL statement to the target remote subsystem. At this point, the location qualifier is stripped from the three-part name. If the remaining two-part names represent a view, or an alias, DB2 uses the remote Catalog to translate it into table names.

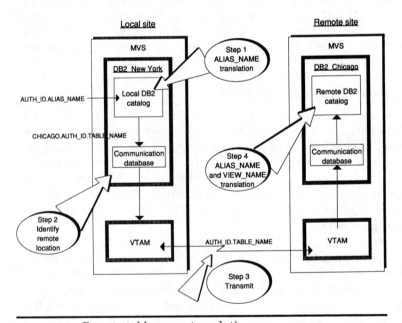

Figure 18.5 Remote table name translation.

18.3.2   Query and BLOCK FETCH

You can use SELECT statements to retrieve data from multiple DB2 subsystems. However, each SELECT statement must access tables and views from only one DB2 site. Therefore, you cannot do a join between a local table and a remote table. Within the scope of a commit (i.e., logical unit of work), you can issue multiple SELECTs to retrieve data from more than one location (Fig. 18.6). The SELECT statement can be issued from any of the environments that are used to access DB2: TSO, batch, IMS, and CICS.

Let's review what happens whan a request is made for remote data. The process is similar to what happens in the nondistributed scenario. For any SQL statement, the tasks performed by DB2 are thread creation, SQL processing, and COMMIT and thread termination. In the distributed scenario a couple of extra steps occur. Both the local and remote subsystems perform the tasks of thread creation, SQL processing, and COMMIT and thread termination. In addition, data is transmitted between the local and remote DB2 subsystems. Therefore, the total cost of the query is the sum of the processor cost, I/O cost, and communication cost. The communication cost may, at times, be excessive and therefore attempts should be made to minimize the flow of data between the local and remote DB2 subsystems. This data flow can be reduced by using the BLOCK FETCH facility for queries.

BLOCK FETCH is initiated when the remote DB2 subsystem is assured that the local DB2 subsystem will not update the result rows

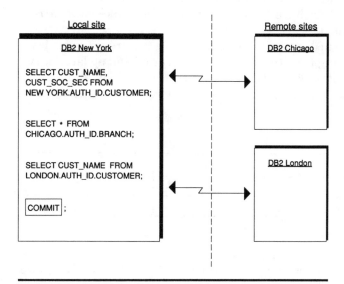

Figure 18.6   Multiple site read within a commit scope.

and send them back. In the BLOCK FETCH, instead of sending the query results one row at a time, DB2 blocks the result rows (for example, in blocks of 1000 rows) and transmits them a block at a time. Each transmitted block is stored in the local DDF component. The local DB2 subsystem retrieves the result, one row at a time, by executing the FETCH SQL statement. Blocking (sending multiple rows in one transmission) significantly reduces the communication overhead and improves response time for the local subsystem.

The SQL SELECT statement has been extended to include the FOR FETCH ONLY clause. You should include this clause in all of your read only remotely executable SELECTs to initiate the BLOCK FETCH facility. Even if you do not specify the FOR FETCH ONLY clause, DB2 is sometimes smart enough to figure out when the query is read only and it will then initiate the BLOCK FETCH automatically.

18.3.3 Update

You can use the INSERT, SELECT, and UPDATE SQL statements to update remote data. This feature is provided only for users accessing DB2 through TSO and Batch. IMS/DC and CICS users can update local data only. Figure 18.7 summarizes the access limitations for the various host environments through which you can access DB2. In addition, within the scope of a commit (i.e., a logical unit of recovery), although you can read data from multiple sites, you may update data at only one site (Fig. 18.8). To update data at any other site, local or remote, you will first have to issue a commit and make your current changes permanent.

The single-site update within a commit scope feature is a significant limitation resulting from the problem of synchronizing updates at two DB2 sites without affecting DB2's performance seriously. In fact, this is the reason why DB2 cannot support referential integrity across multiple sites.

Host environment	Read remote data	Update remote data
TSO	✔	✔
Batch	✔	✔
IMS/DC	✔	
CICS	✔	

You can both read and update remote data from TSO or Batch; IMS/DC and CICS can only be used to read remote data.

Figure 18.7 Accessing remote data.

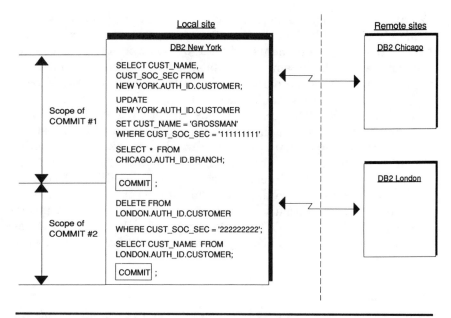

Figure 18.8   Single-site update within a commit scope.

18.3.4 Authorization in Distributed Environment

One result of local autonomy is that users can access remote data only if they have authorization at the remote site and the privileges are documented in the remote DB2 Catalog.

The authorization required at the remote site is the same as if you were accessing data from a local table or view. The auth ID to which privileges are granted at the remote site is translated from your primary ID (for SQL statements submitted through SPUFI and QMF) or the owner of the application plan (for static SQL statements embedded in an application program).

18.3.5 Program Preparation

As we already know, preparation of application programs using embedded SQL requires two additional steps—precompile and BIND. The precompile step separates the host language's procedural code from the SQL code. Each is compiled separately (the SQL compilation is called BIND) and then rejoined at execution time. Let's look at the impact of data distribution on the precompile and BIND steps.

A DB2 program may be precompiled at any DB2 site. In fact, DB2 does not even have to be active for this step. The BIND is another story. A program must be bound at the same DB2 site where it will execute, so all programs must be bound on the local DB2 subsystem. Remotely executable SQL statements are prepared at the remote site. Note that all SQL statements (whether dynamic or static) execute at the remote site as dynamic SQL statements, and all dynamic SQL statements must be prepared (equivalent of BIND for static SQL statements) before they can be executed.

In DB2 2.2, the BIND command has an option that allows you to defer until execution time the preparation of SQL statements that access remote data. This option can be invoked by coding DEFER(PREPARE) on the BIND command. The default is NODEFER(PREPARE). In most cases, the DEFER(PREPARE) option will improve the response time by reducing the communication overhead. We recommend that you use this option for all SQL statements except the SELECT INTO. The preparation of SELECT INTO statements cannot be deferred because of the way DB2 handles host variables.

18.3.6 Limitations

DB2 2.2 allows you to update data at only one location (local or remote) within a commit scope. Because of this limitation, DB2 cannot automatically enforce referential integrity constraints across multiple DB2 subsystems. In addition, you may not issue SQL statements that update a remote Catalog. For example, CREATE, ALTER, GRANT, REVOKE, and LOCK TABLE statements are not permitted against remote objects. In fact, you cannot issue any Data Definition or Data Control SQL statements against any remote object.

DB2 2.2 does not support the EXPLAIN statement when referencing remote objects. It also does not support the update of remote objects through CICS and IMS. At present, DB2 supports only homogeneous (DB2 to DB2) data distribution. You cannot access IBM's other three relational and SAA compliant DBMSs (OS/2 EE, SQL/400, and SQL/DS) from DB2, and vice versa.

The ultimate goal of IBM's data distribution strategy is to access and update data stored at any location and on any of the aforementioned SAA DBMSs from within a single SQL statement. Given where we are on the data distribution technology spectrum, you can tell that we may see it in the not-too-distant future.

Glossary

abend Abnormal end of job.

abend reason code A 4-byte number (in hex) which specifies the reason for the abend. DB2 abend reason codes are described in the *DB2 Messages and Codes Manual*.

Access Method Services (AMS) A utility program that provides various functions for catalog management and VSAM and non-VSAM files. Specifically with DB2, AMS is used to define, delete, and otherwise manage user-defined VSAM datasets for tablespaces and indexspaces.

access path Path used by DB2 (tablespace scan, index scan, or one of the other variations) to retrieve user data. The EXPLAIN feature of DB2 describes the access path for specific SQL statements.

alias An alternative name for local and remote tables and views in DB2; this is created by the CREATE ALIAS statement.

AMS See Access Method Services.

ANSII American National Standard for Information Interchange.

application plan The output produced by the BIND process; it contains information about resources (tables, indexes) required and the access path used by DB2 to satisfy an SQL request.

arithmetic operator A mathematical symbol (such as + for addition, – for subtraction, * for multiplication, and / for division) which represents an arithmetic operation.

attachment facility Services provided by DB2 to manage the interface between DB2 and host environments (TSO, CICS, IMS, and batch address spaces).

attribute The formal name for characteristics of entities; typically represented as columns in DB2 tables.

authorization ID A character string which identifies a user to DB2; represents either the primary or secondary auth ID.

AUTOCOMMIT   An option in SPUFI which automatically commits the result of successful SQL statements.

automatic bind   The process whereby DB2 automatically rebinds an invalid application plan at execution time; for example, a plan is marked invalid if it is using an index and the index is dropped.

base table   A table created with the CREATE TABLE statement; it physically exists on DASD in contrast to a view which is a logical definition in DB2's Catalog.

BIND   A process that compiles one or more DBRMs into an application plan; also see automatic bind and rebind.

Buffer Manager   The subcomponent of DB2 which controls the actual transfer of data between secondary storage (DASD) and the bufferpools.

bufferpool   An area of virtual storage reserved for tablespaces, indexspaces, and associated DB2 objects when I/O is performed; data is read from DASD into bufferpools and is written to DASD from the bufferpools.

built-in function   A scalar or column function provided in SQL to perform a common operation (e.g., AVG, MAX) on rows and columns.

CAF   See Call Attach Facility.

Call Attach Facility (CAF)   An interface between DB2 and programs running in TSO or batch; an alternative to the DSN command processor in the TSO environment.

cascade delete   The process whereby DB2 deletes all rows dependent on a deleted row in the parent table; used by DB2 to maintain referential integrity.

CDB   See Communications Database.

checkpoint   A point of consistency at which DB2 writes control information to the log; if DB2 abends, this information will be used to recover DB2.

clause   A component of an SQL statement such as SELECT clause, GROUP BY clause, etc.

clustering index   A type of index; DB2 attempts to store rows in a tablespace in the same physical order as this index.

column function   An SQL function such as AVG, MIN, or SUM which operates on one or more rows and a specific column.

commit   A statement that terminates a unit of recovery; DB2 releases all locks held by a program and actually updates tables and indexes used by the program. Data that was changed by the program is guaranteed to be consistent again.

commit point   The point at which the commit statement is executed; all previous changes are considered permanent and cannot be rolled back (undone).

Communications Database (CDB)   Contains information which is used by the DDF and VTAM to transfer data between DB2 subsystems.

comparison operator   Operators such as > (greater than), < (less than),

= (equal to), < = (less than or equal to) which are used to compare the values of two operands.

composite privileges   The combination of privileges held by the primary auth ID and its associated secondary auth IDs.

concurrency   The shared use of DB2 resources, such as tables and indexes, by several programs simultaneously; DB2 uses locks to guarantee data integrity.

connection   DB2's attachment facilities establish the connection between DB2 and host environments; once the connection is established, programs executing in the host environment address space can access DB2.

correlated subquery   A query consisting of two or more SELECT clauses where the inner SELECT operates on a set of rows retrieved from a table or view named in the outer SELECT.

correlation name   An identifier which can be used as the alternative name of a table or view; this association with the table or view name is established in the first reference to the table or view name in the SQL statement.

current SQLID   The auth ID which is associated with a dynamic SQL user at any particular point in time.

cursor   Declared in application programs for SQL statements which retrieve multiple rows from tables; conceptually, a cursor is a pointer that identifies one row as the current row. This allows an application program to retrieve rows from a set of rows and process them one at a time.

cursor stability   An isolation level which is specified in the BIND process; with this, DB2 holds locks only on the current row of each active cursor and all uncommitted changes.

cursor table   A copy which DB2 makes of the application plan at execution time.

date and time functions   A set of built-in functions which are specifically related to date and time; examples are DATE, TIME, DAYS.

Data Base Services   The component of DB2 which supports the functions of the SQL language such as definition, access control, retrieval, and update of system and user data.

Data Control Language (DCL)   SQL statements used to grant and revoke DB2 privileges, i.e., access to DB2 resources such as tables, views, and plans.

Data Definition Language (DDL)   SQL statements used to create, alter, and drop DB2 objects such as tables, views, indexes, etc.

Data Manager   The subcomponent of DB2 which supervises access to the actual data in VSAM datasets; it can be thought of as a high-level access mechanism.

Data Manipulation Language (DML)   SQL statements used to select, insert, update, and delete data.

database   In DB2, an operational unit of control consisting of tablespaces, tables, indexes, indexspaces, and views.

Data Base Request Module (DBRM)   Contains information about SQL statements in an application program and is the output of DB2's Precompiler; used as input to the BIND process.

DBA   Data Base Administration.

DBMS   Data Base Management System.

DBRM   See Data Base Request Module.

DB2 Catalog   System tables used by DB2 to manage itself; these tables contain information about DB2 objects such as tables, views, etc.

DB2 commands   These are distinct from SQL statements and DSN subcommands; examples of DB2 commands are -DISPLAY UTIL(*) and -TERM UTIL(LOADA).

DB2 Directory   Both DB2's Catalog and Directory contain system tables which DB2 uses to manage itself; the difference is that the Catalog can be accessed by both DB2 and DB2 users and the Directory can be accessed only by DB2.

DB2 Governor   A facility provided with DB2 which allows a site to limit by user ID, plan, or both the CPU time permitted for the execution of dynamic SQL statements; also called the Resource Limit Facility (RLF).

DB2I   See DB2 Interactive.

DB2 Interactive (DB2I)   A facility provided with DB2 that allows for the online execution of SQL statements, DB2 commands, and DSN subcommands and simplifies program preparation, etc.

DB2 objects   Anything that you can create or manipulate with SQL, such as databases, tables, tablespaces, indexes, indexspaces, views, and storage groups.

DCLGEN   See Declarations Generator.

DDF   See Distributed Data Facility.

deadlock   Fatal contention between two or more threads for DB2 resources such as plans, tables, etc.; to resolve this situation, one or more threads must abend.

deadly embrace   Also called a deadlock.

Declarations Generator (DCLGEN)   A subcomponent of DB2 which automatically generates host language (e.g., COBOL) declarations for SQL tables.

dependent table   Used in the context of referential integrity; it contains the foreign key(s) which reference the primary key in a parent table.

Distributed Data Facility (DDF)   The component of DB2 which allows a user connected to one DB2 subsystem to access data stored at another.

distributed DBMS   Software which manages data in an environment where some of the data is stored at another computer or the user or application program accessing the data is on another computer or both.

DSN   The name of a command processor supplied with DB2 for the TSO environment; provides a flexible and stable DB2 application development platform for the TSO environment.

DSNTEP2 A program supplied by IBM to submit SQL statements in batch that can process almost all statements which can be processed by SPUFI.

DSNTIAD A program supplied by IBM to submit SQL statements in batch that can process all statements except those SELECT statements which return more than one row of data.

DSNTIAR A program supplied by IBM to format the SQLCA; it can be invoked from a COBOL program.

DSNTIAUL A program supplied by IBM to unload data fron DB2 tables and write it as a sequential file.

dynamic SQL Set of facilities which allow the development of generalized programs; these programs, in contrast to static SQL programs, can accept actual SQL statements at execution time and prepare and execute them.

embedded SQL SQL statements are embedded within a host language program and are prepared (via the BIND process) before the program is executed.

entity Something of interest about which you want to hold information; it may be a person, place, thing, event, or concept.

foreign key The columns in a table which are the same as the columns making up the primary key in some other table; foreign keys define the relationships between entities.

form A temporary storage area used in QMF to hold formatting instructions for data retrieved by QMF queries.

governor See DB2 Governor and Resource Limit Facility.

host language A language such as COBOL in which SQL statements can be embedded.

host structures A set of host variables which are referenced as a group item by embedded SQL statements in a program.

host variable A variable referenced by embedded SQL statements in a program.

IKJTEF01 The name of the TSO Terminal Monitor Program (TMP), the program which simulates a TSO environment in batch.

IMS Resource Lock Manager Provides locking services which isolate different users of DB2 from each other and thereby provide data integrity when data is accessed concurrently by multiple users.

independent table Used in the context of referential integrity; an independent table is neither a parent nor a dependent table.

index An ordered set of pointers to the data in a DB2 table; indexes can potentially provide quicker access to data based upon the value of a key field. DB2 also uses indexes to define the primary key.

indexspace A collection of 4K pages which are used to store the index entries of exactly one index.

IRLM See IMS Resource Lock Manager.

JCL IBM's Job Control Language.

join The process of selecting data from two or more tables based on common column value(s).

key elements The primary and foreign keys of an entity; key elements define the structure of the database.

local autonomy A feature of distributed DBMS which allows every site to have complete control over the data it manages.

local DB2 subsystem The DB2 subsystem to which an interactive user or application program is connected.

location transparency A feature of distributed DBMS which allows a user to access data from any site without having to specify the location.

lock A control structure which is used to serialize data updates and thereby prevent access to inconsistent data during concurrent access by multiple users.

log DB2 maintains log datasets that contain records about various events that occur (including changes made to user and system tables); this information may subsequently be used for recovery if DB2 or a subtask of DB2 abends.

logical unit of work A set of changes to data which must all complete successfully to be valid; these changes can be made permanent by a COMMIT statement or backed out by a ROLLBACK statement. Also see scope of commit.

nested select A query consisting of two or more SELECT clauses; the inner SELECT is specified in the WHERE or HAVING clause of an outer SELECT statement. This is also called a subquery.

nonkey elements The attributes of an entity which are left after excluding the attributes which comprise the primary and foreign keys; nonkey elements define the content of the database.

normalization Describes a methodology for eliminating redundant nonkey data elements in a database.

null A special value that signifies that a value is not yet assigned, is unknown, or is not applicable.

Optimizer The subcomponent of DB2 which analyzes the SQL statement and determines the access path for retrieving the data.

outer join The process of selecting data from two or more tables based on nonmatching column value(s).

parent table Used in the context of referential integrity; parent tables contain the primary key which may be referenced by one or more foreign keys in the dependent table.

partition A collection of 4K pages; each partition corresponds to a single dataset.

partitioned indexspace A collection of 4K pages which are used to store the index entries of exactly one partition of an index.

partitioned tablespace Contains exactly one table which is divided into multiple partitions (based upon a range of values of the clustering index). Each partition can be processed independently by DB2 utilities. See also tablespace.

precompilation The process which takes a program's source code and replaces the embedded SQL statements with statements that are recognized by the host language compiler; in addition, the SQL statements are stored in a Data Base Request Module (DBRM) and used as input to the BIND process.

predicate The comparison operation component of a search condition. See also search condition.

primary auth ID Identifies a user to DB2 and has DB2 privileges associated with it; same as authorization ID prior to DB2 version 2.

privilege Authority given to a user to access DB2 resources such as bufferpool, database, index.

primary key The minimal set of attributes (data elements) which uniquely identify an instance of an entity.

Prompted Query A language interface offered with QMF; others are SQL and QBE.

Query by Example (QBE) A language interface offered with QMF; others are SQL and Prompted Query.

Query Management Facility (QMF) An IBM product which provides facilities for panels, forms, and procedures to create sophisticated query applications for data in DB2 and SQL/DS databases.

QMF See Query Management Facility.

RCT See Resource Control Table.

RDBMS Relational Data Base Management System.

REBIND Replaces an application plan and is typically performed when a new index is added to a table; the difference between BIND with the REPLACE option and a REBIND is that BIND(REPLACE) requires a precompile and a compile of the program while a REBIND does not. In addition, BIND(REPLACE) uses one or more DBRMs as input while REBIND uses rows from SYSIBM.SYSSTMT. Also see BIND and automatic bind.

referential constraint Used to specify the relationship which must be maintained between the primary and foreign keys of parent and dependent tables to satisfy referential integrity; these constraints are enforced during operations (e.g., DELETE, LOAD) which update the database.

referential integrity   Maintains the consistency of relationships between tables by requiring that every foreign key value in a table have a matching primary key value in a corresponding table or else be null.

remote DB2 subsystem   Any other DB2 subsystem which you access from your local DB2 subsystem.

repeatable read   An isolation level which is input to the BIND process; with this, DB2 holds locks on all rows referenced by a program until a commit point is reached.

Resource Control Table (RCT)   Defines the connection between DB2 and CICS; contains information about DB2 privileges for every transaction.

Resource Limit Facility (RLF)   A facility provided with DB2 which allows a site to limit by user ID, plan, or both the CPU time permitted for the execution of dynamic SQL statements; also called the Governor.

ROLLBACK   Used to restore data to the previous commit point; all updates since the execution of the last COMMIT statement are backed out.

SAA   See Systems Application Architecture.

scope of commit   Duration between the start of a program, or the last explicit commit point and the end of the program, or the next explicit commit point; also see logical unit of work.

search condition   Selection criteria specified in the WHERE and HAVING clauses of SQL statements to select row(s) from a table; it consists of one or more predicates.

secondary auth ID   An authorization ID which is linked to the primary auth ID; whereas the primary auth ID typically represents an individual user, the secondary auth ID typically represents a function.

segment   A collection of 4K pages with the restriction that all segments of a tablespace have an identical number of pages and a segment must contain rows from only one table. See also segmented tablespace.

segmented tablespace   Contains multiple tables with the restriction that a segment must contain rows from only one table. See also tablespace.

simple subquery   In contrast to a correlated subquery, in a simple query the inner SELECT clause does not reference any rows from an outer SELECT clause.

simple tablespace   May contain one or more tables. It has exactly one segment and one partition. See also tablespace.

SNA   Systems Network Architecture.

SPUFI   SQL Processor Using File Input, a facility provided with DB2I which allows a user to execute SQL statements without embedding them in a program.

SQL   See Structured Query Language.

SQLCA   See SQL Communication Area.

SQL Communication Area (SQLCA)   A data structure used by DB2 to return the status of the execution of an SQL statement to a program.

SQLDA   See SQL Descriptor Area.

SQL Descriptor Area (SQLDA)   A data structure used to pass data from or to DB2; used by dynamic SQL programs.

SQL/DS   SQL Data System, IBM's RDBMS for the VM operating system.

SQL ID   See current SQL ID.

static SQL   See embedded SQL.

storage group   A set of one or more DASD volumes on which DB2 data can be stored.

subpage   Each 4K index page can be logically divided into subpages; a subpage is the unit of locking for indexes.

subquery   A query consisting of two or more SELECT clauses; the inner SELECT is specified in the WHERE or HAVING clause of an outer SELECT statement; also called a nested select.

sync point   See commit point.

synonym   An alternative name for a local table or view in DB2; created by the CREATE SYNONYM SQL statement.

Systems Application Architecture (SAA)   An application development architecture (consisting of common user access, common programming interface, and common communications support) across all the application development platforms in the IBM environment, i.e., OS/2 EE, OS/400, VM, and MVS.

System Services   Controls the overall DB2 execution environment.

table   A collection of rows and columns in which each row contains the same number of columns; in the relational model, all data is externally represented as tables.

tablespace   A collection of 4K pages which contain one or more tables; it can be simple, partitioned, or segmented.

Terminal Monitor Program   Simulates the TSO environment in batch; the actual name of the program is IKJTEF01.

timeout   A situation in which a program (or a thread) exceeds a time limit (specified at DB2 installation time) while waiting for a DB2 resource (tables, indexes, etc.) to become available.

thread   A unit of work for DB2; a thread is started with the execution of the first SQL statement of a program. In addition, threads are the DB2 mechanism that track each occurrence of a DB2 connection.

TMP   See Terminal Monitor Program.

TSO   IBM's Time Sharing Option.

UNION   Used to merge the results of two SQL SELECT statements.

unique index   An index which enforces uniqueness of key values in a table.

unit of recovery   A set of changes to data which must all complete successfully to be valid; these changes can be made permanent by a COMMIT statement or backed out by a ROLLBACK statement.

user ID   Identifies a user to a DB2 attachment; typically it's the log-on ID for TSO.

view   A logical representation of data from one or more base tables and/or views; the view definition is stored in DB2's Catalog.

Virtual Telecommunications Access Method (VTAM)   Provides the underlying access method in an SNA network that allows DB2 subsystems to communicate with each other.

VTAM   See Virtual Telecommunications Access Method.

B

DB2's System/CATALOG Tables

Table name	Description
SYSIBM.SYSCOLAUTH	Records users and plans who can issue the SQL UPDATE statement on individual columns of a table or view
SYSIBM.SYSCOLUMNS	Describes the columns of tables and views; contains one row for every column of each table and view
SYSIBM.SYSCOPY	Contains information for recovery of tablespaces; also details the actual operation (e.g., LOAD, IMAGE COPY) which inserted the row
SYSIBM.SYSDATABASE	Describes the databases; contains one row for each database, except the DB2 Directory (DSNDB01)
SYSIBM.SYSDBAUTH	Records the privileges held by users and plans over databases
SYSIBM.SYSDBRM	Describes the DBRM; contains one row for each DBRM of each plan
SYSIBM.SYSFIELDS	Describes the field procedures which are used for encoding and compressing columns; contains one row for every column that has a field procedure
SYSIBM.SYSFOREIGNKEYS	Describes the foreign keys; contains one row for every column of every foreign key
SYSIBM.SYSINDEXES	Describes the indexes; contains one row for every index
SYSIBM.SYSINDEXPART	Describes the index partitions; contains one row for each unpartitioned index and one for each partition of a partitioned index

Table name	Description
SYSIBM.SYSKEYS	Describes the columns in the indexes; contains one row for each column of an index
SYSIBM.SYSLINKS	Describes the links in the DB2 Catalog; contains one row for every link
SYSIBM.SYSPLAN	Describes the plans; contains one row for each application plan
SYSIBM.SYSPLANAUTH	Records the privileges (BIND or EXECUTE) held by users over plans
SYSIBM.SYSPLANDEP	Records the dependencies of plans on DB2 objects, which are tables, views, aliases, synonyms, tablespaces, and indexes
SYSIBM.SYSRELS	Describes the referential integrity constraints; contains one row for every relationship
SYSIBM.SYSRESAUTH	Records the privileges held by users and plans over bufferpools, tablespaces, and storage groups
SYSIBM.SYSSTMT	Describes the SQL statements; contains one or more rows for each SQL statement of each DBRM
SYSIBM.SYSSTOGROUP	Describes storage groups; contains one row for each storage group
SYSIBM.SYSSYNONYMS	Describes synonyms; contains one row for each synonym of a table or view
SYSIBM.SYSTABAUTH	Records the privileges held by users and plans on tables and views
SYSIBM.SYSTABLEPART	Describes the tablespace partitions; contains one row for each partition of a partitioned tablespace
SYSIBM.SYSTABLES	Describes aliases, tables, and views; contains one row for each alias, table, and view
SYSIBM.SYSTABLESPACE	Describes tablespaces; contains one row for each tablespace
SYSIBM.SYSUSERAUTH	Records system privileges held by users and plans
SYSIBM.SYSVIEWDEP	Records the dependencies of views or tables and other views
SYSIBM.SYSVIEWS	Describes the CREATE VIEW statements used to define the views; contains one or more rows for each view

Table name	Description
SYSIBM.SYSVLTREE	Contains the overflow from SYSIBM.SYSVTREE if any (the remaining part of the parse tree representation)
SYSIBM.SYSVOLUMES	Describes the volumes (serial numbers) which are associated with storage groups; contains one row for each volume of each storage group
SYSIBM.SYSVTREE	Contains one row for each view; if the parse tree is longer than 4000 bytes, the remaining portion of the parse tree is stored in the table SYSIBM.SYSVLTREE

C

Syntax

SCOPE

The syntax of all SQL statements, except those which are used exclusively in dynamic SQL application programs, is described in the following pages. Specifically, we have omitted the following SQL statements: EXECUTE, EXECUTE IMMEDIATE, DESCRIBE, DECLARE STATEMENT, and PREPARE.

The complete syntax for SQL is quite complicated and, in fact, intimidating for an inexperienced user. Therefore, in this appendix, we have emphasized readability over complete accuracy. For precisely this reason we have skipped storage allocation details, such as VCATs, ERASE options, and PRIMARY space allocations. The complete syntax for SQL is available in IBM's *SQL Reference Guide*.

HOW TO READ THE SYNTAX

We have adopted the following convention for presentation of SQL syntax.

1. All items within < > are required. Choice between multiple items is indicated by the word "or."

2. Optional items appear within [ ].

3. Keywords are written in uppercase and must be entered exactly as shown.

4. Variables are written in lowercase.

5. Default parameters are underscored.

6. Usage indicates whether the SQL statement can be issued interactively from SPUFI/QMF and/or through application programs

written in languages such as COBOL, PL/I, and CSP. Interactive usage is indicated by the letter I and application program usage is indicated by the letter A.

7. A (*) next to the SQL statement (under the USAGE clause) indicates that we have omitted the storage allocation details. For example, in the ALTER INDEX statement, we have omitted the CLOSE, DSETPASS, FREEPAGE, PCTFREE, USING, PRIQTY, SECQTY, and ERASE clauses.

8. The word "list" is used to represent a single item or multiple items separated by a comma. For example, for [column-name list], you may use either a single column name such as BRANCH_ID or multiple column names, such as BRANCH_ID, BRANCH_CITY, etc.

9. The phrase "column definition" indicates those columns needed to define a column. This is defined only in the CREATE TABLE syntax.

10. All SQL statements used in application programs must start with EXEC SQL. If the host language is COBOL, they must end with END-EXEC.

11. Aliases and synonyms are alternate names for tables and views. Even though we do not explicitly show it, you can use alias names and synonym names in lieu of table names and view names in the following syntax. The only two exceptions are the CREATE ALIAS and CREATE SYNONYM statements.

You cannot use an alias name in lieu of a table name or view name in the CREATE ALIAS statement, and you cannot use a synonym name in lieu of a table name or view name in the CREATE SYNONYM statement.

SYNTAX

- ALTER INDEX   USAGE: A, I
                                                                      (*)

```
ALTER INDEX <index-name>
  <PART <integer>> or
  <BUFFERPOOL <BP0 or BP1 or BP2>>
```

Any of the above blocks may be repeated.

- ALTER STOGROUP   USAGE: A, I
                                                                      (*)

```
ALTER STOGROUP <stogroup-name>
```

```
<ADD VOLUMES <list of vol-ids>>
<REMOVE VOLUMES <list of vol-ids>>
```

Any of the above blocks may be repeated.

- ALTER TABLE   USAGE: A, I
                                                                  (*)

```
ALTER TABLE <table-name>
   <ADD <column definition list>> or
   <AUDIT <NONE or CHANGES or ALL>> or
   <PRIMARY KEY <list of column-names>> or
   <referential constraint> or
   <DROP PRIMARY KEY> or
   <DROP FOREIGN KEY <referential-constraint-name>>
```

Any of the above blocks may be repeated.

- ALTER TABLESPACE   USAGE: A, I
                                                                  (*)

```
ALTER TABLESPACE [database-name.]<tablespace-name>
   <PART <integer>> or
   <BUFFERPOOL <BP0 or BP1 or BP2>> or
   <LOCKSIZE <ANY or PAGE or TABLESPACE or TABLE>>
```

Any of the above blocks may be repeated.

- BEGIN DECLARE SECTION   USAGE: A

```
BEGIN DECLARE SECTION
```

Note: The BEGIN DECLARE SECTION is used to specify host-variable declarations for application programs written in C. However, it may be used in any host language if you want to conform to the SAA definition of SQL. See END DECLARE SECTION.

- CLOSE   USAGE: A

```
CLOSE <cursor-name>
```

- COMMENT ON   USAGE: A, I

```
COMMENT ON
   <TABLE <table-name or view-name> IS
                       <comment-string>> or
   <ALIAS <alias-name> IS <comment-string>> or
   <COLUMN <table-name.column-name or
           view-name.column-name> IS
                       <comment-string>>
```

- COMMIT   USAGE: A, I

```
COMMIT [WORK]
```

- **CREATE ALIAS**   USAGE: A, I

```
CREATE ALIAS <alias-name> FOR
                <table-name or view-name>
```

- **CREATE DATABASE**   USAGE: A, I

```
CREATE DATABASE <database-name>
  [STOGROUP <stogroup-name>]
  [BUFFERPOOL <BP0 or BP1 or BP2 or BP32K>]
```

- **CREATE INDEX**   USAGE: A, I
                                                                        (*)

```
CREATE [UNIQUE] INDEX <index-name> ON <table-name>
  <index-column list>
  [CLUSTER [(PART integer VALUES <(constant or range)>)]]
  [SUBPAGES <1 or 2 or 4 or 8 or 16> ]
  [BUFFERPOOL <BP0 or BP1 or BP2> ]
```

where index-column is:

```
column-name [ASC or DESC]
```

- **CREATE STOGROUP**   USAGE: A, I
                                                                        (*)

```
CREATE STOGROUP <stogroup-name> VOLUMES <vol-id list>
```

- **CREATE SYNONYM**   USAGE: A, I

```
CREATE SYNONYM <synonym> FOR
                <table-name or view-name>
```

- **CREATE TABLE**   USAGE: A, I
                                                                        (*)

```
CREATE TABLE <table-name>
  <LIKE <table-name or view-name>> or
  <<column definition list>
    [PRIMARY KEY <(column-name list)>]
    [referential constraint]>
  [IN <database-name.tablespace-name or
      tablespace-name or
      DATABASE <database-name>> ]
  [AUDIT <NONE or CHANGES or ALL> ]
```

where column definition is:

```
column-name data-type [Length] [FOR BIT DATA] [NOT NULL
                            or NOT NULL WITH DEFAULT] [,]
```

where referential constraint is:

```
FOREIGN KEY [constraint-name] <(column-name list)>
```

```
REFERENCES <table-name>
[ON DELETE <RESTRICT or CASCADE or SET NULL>]
```

▪ CREATE TABLESPACE   USAGE: A, I
                                          (*)

```
CREATE TABLESPACE <tablespace-name>
               [IN <database-name> ]
[USING <VCAT <catalog-name>> or <STOGROUP>
                    <stogroup-name> ]
[NUMPARTS <integer>]
[BUFFERPOOL <BP0 or BP1 or BP2 or BP32K> ]
[LOCKSIZE <ANY or PAGE or TABLESPACE or TABLE>> ]
[SEGSIZE <integer> ]
```

▪ CREATE VIEW   USAGE: A, I

```
CREATE VIEW <view-name> [(column-name list)]
AS <subselect statement> [WITH CHECK OPTION]
```

▪ DECLARE CURSOR   USAGE: A

```
DECLARE <cursor-name> CURSOR FOR <select statement>
```

▪ DECLARE TABLE   USAGE: A

```
DECLARE <table-name or view-name> TABLE
<(column definition list)>
```

where column definition is:

```
column-name data-type [NOT NULL or
NOT NULL WITH DEFAULT]
```

Note: In lieu of this statement, you can use the DSN subcommand DCLGEN to generate table declarations of those tables and views which have already been created.

▪ DELETE   USAGE: A, I

If cursors are not used:

```
DELETE FROM <table-name or view-name>
[WHERE <search condition> ]
```

If cursors are used:

```
DELETE FROM <table-name or view-name>
WHERE CURRENT OF <cursor-name>
```

▪ DROP   USAGE: A, I

```
DROP <ALIAS <alias-name>> or
<DATABASE <database-name>> or
<INDEX <index-name>> or
```

```
<STOGROUP <stogroup-name>> or
<SYNONYM <synonym>> or
<TABLE <table-name>> or
<TABLESPACE [database-name.]<tablespace-name>> or
<VIEW <view-name>>
```

- ## END DECLARE SECTION   USAGE: A

  END DECLARE SECTION

- ## EXPLAIN   USAGE: A, I

  ```
  EXPLAIN <PLAN or ALL> [SET QUERYNO = integer] FOR
    <explainable statement>
  ```

  where explainable statement is any SQL statements that starts with SELECT, INSERT, UPDATE, or DELETE.

- ## FETCH   USAGE: A, I

  ```
  FETCH cursor-name INTO <host-variable list>
  ```

- ## GRANT—database privileges   USAGE: A, I

  ```
  GRANT <database-privilege list>
    ON DATABASE <database-name list>
    TO <PUBLIC or auth-id list> [WITH GRANT OPTION]
  ```

  where database privilege is:

  ```
  DBADM, DBCTRL, DBMAINT, CREATETAB, CREATETS, DISPLAYDB, IMAGCOPY,
  LOAD, RECOVERDB, REORG, REPAIR, STARTDB, STATS, STOPDB
  ```

- ## GRANT—plan privilege   USAGE: A, I

  ```
  GRANT <plan-privilege list> ON PLAN <plan-name list>
    TO <PUBLIC or auth-id list> [WITH GRANT OPTION]
  ```

  where plan privilege is:

  ```
  BIND, EXECUTE
  ```

- ## GRANT—system privilege   USAGE: A, I

  ```
  GRANT <system-privilege list>
    TO <PUBLIC or auth-id list> [WITH GRANT OPTION]
  ```

  where system privilege is:

  ```
  SYSADM, SYSOPR, BINDADD, BSDS, CREATEDBA, CREATEDBC, CREATESG,
  DISPLAY, RECOVER, STOPALL, STOSPACE, TRACE, MONITOR1, MONITOR2
  ```

- ## GRANT—table privileges   USAGE: A, I

  ```
  GRANT <ALL or ALL PRIVILEGES or table-privilege list>
    ON [TABLE] <table-name or view-name list>
  ```

```
  TO <PUBLIC or PUBLIC AT ALL LOCATIONS or
                        auth-id list>
  [WITH GRANT OPTION]
```

where table privilege is:

```
ALTER, DELETE, INDEX, INSERT, SELECT, UPDATE, UPDATE <(column-name
list)>
```

- GRANT—use privileges   USAGE: A, I

```
GRANT USE OF <BUFFERPOOL <buffer-pool list> or
             STOGROUP <stogroup-name list> or
             TABLESPACE
                <[database-name.]tablespace-name list>>
  TO <PUBLIC or auth-id list> [WITH GRANT OPTION]
```

- INCLUDE   USAGE: A

```
INCLUDE <SQLCA or SQLDA or member-name>
```

where member-name is a member of a partitioned dataset.

- INSERT   USAGE: A, I

```
INSERT INTO <table-name or view-name>
  [column-name list] <subselect statement or
                      VALUES <constant or
                              host-variable or NULL
                              or special-register >>
```

- LABEL   USAGE: A, I

```
LABEL ON
  <ALIAS <alias-name> IS <string>> or
  <TABLE <table-name or view-name> IS <string>> or
  <COLUMN <table-name.column-name> IS <string>> or
  <COLUMN <view-name.column-name> IS <string>> or
  <<table-name or view-name> <(column-string list)>>
```

where column-string is:

```
column-name IS string
```

- LOCK TABLE   USAGE: A, I

```
LOCK TABLE <table-name>IN <SHARE or EXCLUSIVE> MODE
```

- OPEN   USAGE: A

```
OPEN <cursor-name>
[USING <host-variable list>]
```

- REVOKE—database privileges   USAGE: A, I

```
REVOKE <database-privilege list>
```

```
ON DATABASE <database-name list>
FROM <PUBLIC or auth-id list>
[BY <ALL or auth-id list>]
```

where database privilege is:

```
DBADM, DBCTRL, DBMAINT, CREATETAB, CREATETS, DISPLAYDB, IMAGCOPY,
LOAD, RECOVERDB, REORG, REPAIR, STARTDB, STATS, STOPDB
```

- **REVOKE—plan privilege**   USAGE: A, I

```
REVOKE <plan-privilege list> ON PLAN <plan-name list>
FROM <PUBLIC or auth-id list>
[BY <ALL or auth-id list>]
```

where plan privilege is:

```
BIND, EXECUTE
```

- **REVOKE—system privilege**   USAGE: A, I

```
REVOKE <system-privilege list>
FROM <PUBLIC or auth-id list>
[BY <ALL or auth-id list>]
```

where system privilege is:

```
SYSADM, SYSOPR, BINDADD, BSDS, CREATEDBA,CREATEDBC, CREATESG,
DISPLAY, RECOVER, STOPALL, STOSPACE, TRACE, MONITOR1, MONITOR2
```

- **REVOKE—table privileges**   USAGE: A, I

```
REVOKE <ALL or ALL PRIVILEGES or
       table-privilege list>
ON [TABLE] <table-name or view-name list>
FROM <PUBLIC or PUBLIC AT ALL LOCATIONS
                       or auth-id list>
[BY <ALL or auth-id list>]
```

where table privilege is:

```
ALTER, DELETE, INDEX, INSERT, SELECT, UPDATE,
```

- **REVOKE—use privileges**   USAGE: A, I

```
REVOKE USE OF <BUFFERPOOL <buffer-pool list> or
         STOGROUP <stogroup-name list> or
         TABLESPACE          *
             <[database-name.]tablespace-name list>>
FROM <PUBLIC or auth-id list>
[BY <ALL or auth-id list>]
```

- **ROLLBACK**   USAGE: A, I

```
ROLLBACK [WORK]
```

- select   USAGE: A, I

```
<subselect> [<ORDER BY <column-order list>
                  [FOR FETCH ONLY]> or
              <FOR UPDATE OF <column-name list>> or
              <FOR FETCH ONLY >]
```

or

```
<fullselect> [<ORDER BY <column-order list>
                  [FOR FETCH ONLY]> or
              <FOR UPDATE OF <column-name list>> or
              <FOR FETCH ONLY >]
```

where column-order is:

```
<column-name or integer> <ASC or DESC>
```

Note: FOR UPDATE OF clause can only be used in application programs.

- subselect   USAGE: A, I

```
SELECT [ALL or DISTINCT] <* or column-name list>
  FROM <table-name list or view-name list>
  [WHERE <search condition> ]
  [GROUP BY <column-name list> ]
  [HAVING <search condition> ]
```

- fullselect   USAGE: A, I

```
<subselect or fullselect> <UNION or UNION ALL>
```

- SELECT INTO   USAGE: A

```
SELECT [ALL or DISTINCT] <* or column-name list>
  INTO <host-variable list>
  FROM <table-name list or view-name list>
  [WHERE <search condition> ]
```

Note: GROUP BY and HAVING clauses are not used because this statement should only be used when one row will be returned in the result table.

- SET CURRENT SQLID   USAGE: A, I

```
SET CURRENT SQLID = <USER or string or host-variable>
```

- UPDATE   USAGE: A, I

If cursors are not used:

```
UPDATE <table_name or view_name> [correlation_name]
  SET <column-update list>
  [WHERE <search condition>]
```

If cursors are used:

```
UPDATE <table_name or view_name >
  SET <column-update list>
  WHERE CURRENT OF <cursor-name>
```

column-update is:

```
column-name = <expression or NULL>
```

■ WHENEVER   USAGE: A

```
WHENEVER <NOT FOUND or SQLERROR or SQLWARNING>
  <CONTINUE or GO TO host-label or GOTO host-label>
```

Predicate Types and Processing

This appendix shows the different types of predicates and whether or not these predicate types can be indexed and applied at stage 1. Appendix D uses these conventions:

- Op is any of the operators $>$, $>=$, $<$, $<=$, $\neg>$, $\neg> =$, $\neg<$, $\neg<=$.
- Value is a literal, a host variable, or a value returned by a noncorrelated subquery.
- Char is any character string that does not include the special characters for percent (%) or underscore (_).
- Expression is any expression involving arithmetic operators, scalar functions, or column functions.
- Predicate is a predicate of any type.
- For a list with only one item, COL IN (list) is treated like COL = VALUE.

Stage 1 is the same as sargable.

Predicate type	Indexing possible?	Stage 1?	Notes
COL = value	Yes	Yes	
COL IS NUL	Yes	Yes	
COL op value	Yes	Yes	
COL BETWEEN value1 AND value2	Yes	Yes	
COL LIKE 'char%'	Yes	Yes	
COL IN (list)	Yes	Yes	1
COL $\neg$ = value	No	Yes	1
COL IS NOT NULL	No	Yes	1
COL NOT BETWEEN (value1, value2)	No	Yes	1
COL NOT IN (list)	No	Yes	1

Predicate type	Indexing possible?	Stage 1?	Notes
COL NOT LIKE '%char'	No	Yes	1
COL LIKE '_CHAR'	No	Yes	1
COL LIKE host variable	No	Yes	1
T1.COL = T2.COL (different tables)	Yes	Yes	2
T1.COL op T2.COL	Yes	Yes	2
T1.COL¬ = T2.COL	No	Yes	2
T1.COL1 = T1.COL2 (same table)	No	No	3
T1.COL1 op T1.COL2	No	No	3
T1.COL1¬ = T1.COL2	No	No	3
COL op ANY (noncorrelated subquery)	Yes	Yes	
COL op ALL (noncorrelated subquery)	Yes	Yes	
COL IN (nocorrelated subquery)	No	No	4
COL NOT IN (noncorrelated subquery)	No	No	
COL = ANY (noncorrelated subquery)	No	No	
COL¬ = ALL (noncorrelated subquery)	No	No	
COL = (correlated subquery)	No	No	5
COL op (correlated subquery)	No	No	5
COL¬ = (correlated subquery)	No	No	5
COL = expression	No	No	
expression = value	No	No	
expression = value	No	No	
expression op value	No	No	
predicate1 AND predicate2	Yes	Yes	
predicate1 OR predicate2	Yes	Yes	

[1]The processing for WHERE NOT COL = value is like that for WHERE COL¬ = value, and so on.

[2]Within each statement, the columns are of the same type. Examples of different column types include:

- Different data types, such as INTEGER and DECIMAL
- Different column lengths, such as DECIMAL(7,2) and DECIMAL(6,2)
- Different precisions, such as DECIMAL(7,3) and DECIMAL(7,4)

[3]If both COL1 and COL2 are from the same table, access through an index on either one is not considered for these predicates. However, the following query is an exception:

```
SELECT * FROM T1 A, T1 B
WHERE A.C1 = B.C2;
```

By using correlation names, the query treats one table as if it were two separate tables. Therefore, indexes on columns C1 and C2 are considered for access.

[4]For predicates whose left side is a single column.

[5]For correlated subqueries returning a single value. If the subquery has already been evaluated for a given correlation value, then the subquery may not have to be reevaluated.

E

Acronyms

ANSI	American National Standards Institute
BSDS	Boot Strap Data Set
CICS	Customer Information Control System
CLIST	Command list—TSO
CS	Cursor Stability
DBA	Database Administrator
DBMS	Database Management System
DBRM	Data Base Request Module
DB2	IBM Database 2
DB2I	DB2 Interactive
DCLGEN	Declarations Generator
DM	Data Manager
I/O	Input-Output
IMS	Information Management System
IRLM	IMS Resource Lock Manager
ISO	International Standards Organization
ISPF	Interactive System Productivity Facility
MVS	Multiple Virtual Storage
MVS/ESA	Multiple Virtual Storage/Enterprise Systems Architecture
MVS/XA	Multiple Virtual Storage/Extended Architecture
QBE	Query By Example
QMF	Query Management Facility
RDS	Relational Data System
RID	Record ID
RR	Repeatable Read

SPUFI	SQL Processor Using File Input
SQL	Structured Query Language
SQLCA	SQL Communications Area
TSO	Time Sharing Option
VSAM	Virtual Storage Access Method
VTAM	Virtual Telecommunications Access Method

Index